Australian Pows

The Untold Stories Of WWI

David Coombes

16pt

Copyright Page from the Original Book

Copyright © David Coombes 2021

First published 2011 (Title: Crossing the Wire)
This edition 2021

Copyright remains the property of the author and apart from any fair dealing for the purposes of private study, research, criticism or review, as permitted under the Copyright Act, no part may be reproduced by any process without written permission.

All inquiries should be made to the publishers..

Big Sky Publishing Pty Ltd
PO Box 303, Newport, NSW 2106, Australia
Phone: (61 2) 9918 2168
Email: info@bigskypublishing.com.au
Web: www.bigskypublishing.com.au

Cover design and typesetting: Think Productions

National Library of Australia Cataloguing-in-Publication entry
Author: Coombes, David.
Title: Australian POWs: The Untold Stories of WWI

A catalogue record for this book is available from the National Library of Australia

TABLE OF CONTENTS

List of Maps	i
Acknowledgements	iii
Introduction	vi
CHAPTER ONE: PRELUDE TO WAR	2
CHAPTER TWO: GALLIPOLI	38
CHAPTER THREE: THE WESTERN FRONT	124
CHAPTER FOUR: STORMY TRENCH	191
CHAPTER FIVE: FIRST BATTLE OF BULLECOURT	227
CHAPTER SIX: CAPTIVITY	257
CHAPTER SEVEN: THE STATUS AND TREATMENT OF POWS	292
CHAPTER EIGHT: BEHIND THE LINES	304
CHAPTER NINE: GERMAN POW HOSPITALS	379
CHAPTER TEN: THE RED CROSS SOCIETY	424
CHAPTER ELEVEN: ATTEMPTING TO GET AWAY	448
CHAPTER TWELVE: IN GERMANY	503
CHAPTER THIRTEEN: PEACE	609
Postscript	645
APPENDIX 1: The Chalk Collection	648
APPENDIX 2: Notes from the interviewer	651
A note from the interviewer (Bill Bradnock)	657
A note from the interviewer (Ernest Etchell)	660
A note from the interviewer (Len Pooley)	663
A note from the interviewer (Frank Lawrie)	665
A note from the interviewer (Horatio Ganson)	667
A note from the interviewer (John Doggett)	669
A note from the interviewer (Charles Devers)	671
A note from the interviewer (John Cunliffe)	673
Endnotes	675
Bibliography	723

Back Cover Material 744
Index 747

List of Maps

Map 2   The Western Front – Area of Operations 1916-1918

Map 3   Map showing Bullecourt and the Arras Front

Map 4   The situation at Bullecourt at about 9.30a.m., 11 April 1917, after the capture of portion of the Hindenburg Line by the 4th Australian Division

To Veronika, Peta and Tally for their love and encouragement.

Acknowledgements

I am grateful for the excellent support I received from the School of History and Classics at the University of Tasmania. In particular, I would like to single out Professor Michael Bennett and Associate Professor Stefan Petrow who read the first draft of the manuscript and offered valuable advice. I am also indebted to Professor Bennett for helping to secure funding for the project from the Tasmanian government and the Commonwealth Department of Veterans' Affairs. I wish to thank research assistant Elisabeth Wilson who retyped, checked and catalogued the Chalk transcripts and Associate Professor Peter Chapman for his help. My thanks extend also to Lyn Richards, Cheryl Hughes and Julie Hill from the school's administrative staff who offered valuable secretarial assistance whenever needed.

As usual, the staff at the Research Centre, Australian War Memorial, were extremely helpful during my visits there. I also wish to thank the staff at the Mitchell Library, Sydney; the Mortlock Library, Adelaide; Battye Library of WA History, Perth; and the Liddell Hart Centre for Military Archives, King's College, London, for the help offered. Patricia Boxhall, Curator of the Pioneer

Village Museum in Burnie, provided valuable assistance, particularly in relation to David Chalk's wonderful collection of World War I books and memorabilia which are exhibited at the museum.

I thank Sharon Evans and Denny Neave at Big Sky Publishing for the help they provided, particularly in organising the photographs and maps. I also thank Cathy McCullagh for her painstaking editing and Ian Faulkner for drawing the maps. I express my appreciation to the Australian Army History Unit—in particular to Mr Roger Lee and Dr Andrew Richardson—for helping to fund the project and providing money for additional research at the Australian War Memorial, Canberra. I also thank the Tasmanian Government, through the Department of Arts, and the Commonwealth Department of Veterans' Affairs for other funding.

Last, but by no means least, I would like to record my gratitude to Ian and Jenny Chalk of Wynyard, Tasmania, for entrusting me with completing the research and the task of writing this book following the unfortunate death of their nephew, David Chalk. David left a valuable collection of interviews, personal papers, photographs and unpublished manuscripts—all now deposited with the School of History and Classics at the Hobart campus of the University of Tasmania. In writing this book, I have barely tapped into the collection—there is still much on offer for the enthusiastic researcher or postgraduate student.

Ian and Jenny Chalk always offered me encouragement and cheerfully answered all my questions, also making me welcome in their home. I can only hope that this book serves, in some small way, to honour the memory of their nephew, David Chalk, and that of his grandfather, ex-POW Ernie Chalk.

Introduction

I am a Kriegsgefangener
I wish that I were dead
It's all through drinking sauerkraut
And eating mouldy bread.

My bed is in the corner,
I sleep upon the floor
My back is nearly broken
My ribs are very sore.

And when the war is over
And I settle down to rest,
If ever I meet a squarehead,
I'll smash his bloody chest.[1]

This stark verse, written by an Australian prisoner of war (POW) in World War I, was circulated around the camps in Germany during the latter stages of the war. Representing probably the greatest hardship suffered by those being held captive—privation—the doggerel quickly came to signify the plight of Australian POWs. While figures vary, at least 4,000 Australian soldiers who fought in France and Flanders were captured by the Germans.[2] By far the greatest number—almost 1,200—were taken at the First Battle of Bullecourt on 11 April 1917.

Drawing on research and interviews conducted by the late David Chalk during the 1980s and early 1990s, *Australian POWs* describes the wartime travails of Australian soldiers through the Gallipoli campaign, the Western Front, and their internment as POWs in France and Germany. The book's narrative portrays the experiences of almost three dozen veterans of the 4th Australian Infantry Brigade, their accounts supported by the letters, diaries and narratives of others in the brigade.

David Chalk became interested in the plight of Australian POWs after reading the diaries, letters and recollections of his grandfather, Ernest Chalk, who was captured at Bullecourt. Over the years this interest blossomed—so much so that, at considerable personal expense, David travelled the length and breadth of Australia, documenting other 4th Brigade veterans' stories of their period in captivity, interviewing them, collecting photos, images and unpublished manuscripts—in fact anything of any relevance that he could find. At the same time, he amassed a large collection of memorabilia, most of it connected to the men he had interviewed.[3] David intended to write a book documenting the experiences of these men under the title 'Among the Angels: the road to Bullecourt'. Unfortunately, he fell ill before he could commence writing his book and passed away soon after. To me has fallen the task of completing David's cherished work and I have attempted to follow his outline and chapter plans as closely as possible. *Australian POWs* is a tribute to David Chalk's determination to relate an extraordinary story that, but for him, would have died with the men of the 4th Brigade.

As its central theme, *Australian POWs* takes the history of the 4th Brigade (4th Australian Division) from its formation in Australia to the First Battle of Bullecourt. Drawing on interviews and memoirs, I have endeavoured to remain faithful to David's wish, and have largely used the men's own words to tell the story by editing the transcripts of interviews and/or their diaries and unpublished memoirs. While some of those recollections may appear a little fanciful at times, they generally convey an accurate firsthand description of the men's suffering and deprivation. The men David Chalk interviewed are introduced in the first chapter and the perceptive comments he compiled on some of their personalities are included in Appendix 2.

The 4th Brigade presents an excellent vehicle for this story because it was one of the original brigades formed, and its experiences on Gallipoli and in France were, in many ways, similar to those of other Australian brigades. However, unlike many brigades which comprised men from the more populous states, the 4th boasted men from *all* the Australian states—in particular, smaller states such as Tasmania and Western Australia. Its experience is thus more representative of the nation as a whole. The 4th is also noteworthy because it was initially commanded by John Monash and played a significant role in the fighting on Gallipoli. While the Gallipoli campaign itself has been thoroughly examined, the First Battle of Bullecourt—which has little prominence in the national consciousness—continues to suffer a lack of any real analysis from the Australian perspective. First Bullecourt is a natural starting point for any description of the POW experience because of the large number of Australians captured in that battle on 11 April 1917.

***

A great deal has been written about the brutal treatment of Australian POWs under the Japanese in World War II. The suffering of Australian soldiers captured at the fall of Singapore and forced to work on the Burma-Thailand 'Death' Railway for example, has, over time, become linked to the Australian national consciousness. The tremendous skill, compassion and courage of Dr Edward 'Weary' Dunlop who, for three years, cared for seriously ill POWs, has come to represent the true meaning of the term 'hero' in the Australian psyche.[4] While visiting Thailand recently, I was moved by the sight of the cemetery, not far from the River Kwai, where hundreds of Australian POWs are buried—as are similar numbers of British and Dutch prisoners. Comments such as 'Forever In My Heart', and the tender age of most of the young men who died gave me particular cause for reflection on the enduring scars of the POW experience—both for those in captivity and their anxious families.

Since the first edition of *Crossing the Wire* was published, in 2011, there have been another two books outlining the Australian POW experience in the First World War. In 2018 Kate Ariotti wrote her ground-breaking account of the 198 Australian soldiers who became prisoners of the Ottomans.[5] These men's experience in captivity was quite dissimilar to those captured by the Germans. They not only questioned their role as soldiers but, moreover, needed to adjust to a 'culturally, religiously and linguistically different enemy.' In 2020 Aaron Pegram's *Surviving The Great War* was published.[6] Pegram's book goes into greater detail about how the POWs experience was at odds with the so called ANZAC legend of wonderful, natural fighting men where victory, not defeat, was taken for granted. Yet, as Pegram points out, while Australian POWs 'endured a broad range of experiences in German captivity, [they] all regarded survival as a personal triumph.'

This book principally looks into soldiers from the 4th Australian Division taken POW during the first battle of Bullecourt. After their capture, during almost unimaginable bloody fighting, these men suffered a trauma unique to war and one that almost always left a lasting imprint long after the end of the conflict. These were men who suffered not only the horrors of trench warfare, but endured also the particular anguish of being deprived of their liberty with no idea when they might expect to be freed. These were men who carried more than just the scars of battle and yet whose voices have seldom been heard. This, then, is their story – the men who crossed the wire now have their chance to speak.

David Chalk

CHAPTER ONE
Prelude to War
'We Marched Out to Meet the Supposed Enemy'

CHAPTER ONE

PRELUDE TO WAR

'We Marched Out to Meet the Supposed Enemy'

In the British Empire's far-flung Australian dominion, the first decade of the twentieth century was marked by three major developments, all of which were to shape the character of the young nation. First, the Australian economy showed strong signs of recovery from the depression of the 1890s and many sectors of society enjoyed a new-found prosperity. Second, the soldiers of the Australian colonies—soon to be states of the new Commonwealth—ventured forth to join British forces fighting in the Boer War. Third, and perhaps most significantly, Federation in 1901 heralded the union of those six separate colonies into the Commonwealth of Australia. But the creation of a federal seat of government came at a price. While, in theory, Australia could develop and pursue its own foreign policy, in practice, the government usually conformed to the policy adopted by the British government in Westminster. Although a form of nationalism was emerging in Australia—'characterised by a general belief that the new nation could do things afresh'—that 'new nation' was still part of the British Empire. Of a population of approximately 3.7 million, 85% could claim to be of British descent.[1]

In the years just prior to Federation, the Australian colonies became embroiled in a conflict not of their own making. Hundreds of young men enthusiastically took up arms for Britain and departed in a number of contingents for South Africa to fight the Boers. In what became known as the Second Boer War (or South African War), troops from the Australian Mounted Infantry performed their often hazardous duties in the veldt country, sometimes suffering huge casualties in what had essentially devolved into guerrilla warfare. When Boer opposition was finally crushed in mid-1901, Australian soldiers—despite their occasional bouts of ill discipline—had won a name for audacity and bravery. These men unwittingly gave birth to Australia's military reputation—'one renowned for dash and courage ... relying more on natural skills developed in the Australian bush than those instilled on the parade ground.' The same troops were forerunners of what became known as the 1st AIF (Australian Imperial Force), having 'left a bitter-sweet and lasting legacy for the new Federation: the tradition of the citizen soldier in action.'[2]

***

On 2 August 1914, the German army invaded neutral Belgium. Left with little option, Britain declared war on Germany two days later, at 11.00p.m. on 4 August 1914. Britain was neatly caught between the 'moral issue' of the London Treaty of 1839 (in which the more powerful European nations had guaranteed Belgium's neutrality) and her own national security issues. Only the English Channel separated Belgium from London, and the capture of ports along the Belgian coast eventually would have given the Germans a strategic stranglehold over Britain.[3] Australia—still theoretically aligned to British foreign policy and without any real discretion over its external affairs—was obliged to follow Britain's lead. The Australian Prime Minister, Joseph Cook, fully supported by the Leader of the Federal Opposition, Andrew Fisher, had previously pledged to place the small number of Royal Australian Navy ships at the discretion of the British Admiralty and offered a force of 20,000 troops, adding that 'the cost of despatch and maintenance will be borne by this Government.'[4] And, while there may have been an election campaign in Australia at the same time as the crisis in Europe, Cook vowed that 'all our resources in Australia are in the Empire and for the Empire, and for the preservation and security of Empire.' For his part, Fisher announced that 'Australians will stand beside our own to help and defend her [Britain] to our last man and our last shilling.' Not long afterwards, the Australian Governor-General informed the British government that 'there is indescribable enthusiasm and entire unanimity throughout Australia in support of all that tends to provide for the security of the empire in war.'[5]

***

    The multicultural Australia that its citizens now take for granted bears no resemblance to the Australia of the first decades of the twentieth century. At the time of Federation, 'Queen [Victoria] was still sovereign and the old rules applied.'[6] By 1901, Australian cultural identity could be broadly defined as the expansion of English ideals. British historian J.G. Fuller describes Australian schools in the early part of the century as emphasising the indebtedness of Australians to Britain and reinforcing the loyalty they owed the mother country.[7] Certainly Australian private schools intentionally followed the pattern set by their British counterparts and stressed 'the values of honour, duty, sacrifice and patriotism, obligation to Britain and pride of race.'[8] Meaney's explanation that Australians had 'not turned their backs on Britain nor rejected their British cultural heritage ... and took inordinate pride in being of British stock' serves to reinforce the notion that the majority of Australians felt that they had obligations of obedience to Britain. As the response to the South African conflict illustrates so clearly, war endowed them with an even greater sense of belonging to Britain. Adds Meaney, 'this patently [demonstrated that] ... at the time of the Boer War they were for the empire "right or wrong". The imperial cause was all.'[9] By 1914 not much had changed—those of British stock had little difficulty committing themselves to the sentiment of being British-Australian and adhering to the British Empire in both a constitutional and an emotional sense.

While there appeared to be popular support and enthusiasm for the war—particularly among those of English descent—only 52,561 from an eligible male population of approximately 820,000 (or only 6.4%) had enlisted by the end of 1914. The historian Eric Andrews has suggested that those 'who make much of the "rush to enlist" might therefore do better to ask why 93.6 per cent of eligibles did not enlist.'[10] Others, including Bill Gammage, have claimed that thousands of young Australian men 'were called to defend England. What had begun chiefly as a concern for their [English] security was to take them to the uttermost ends of the earth, to die in tens of thousands, in a war in no way of their making.'[11] While to some degree rational, this view fails to consider Australia's self-interest. Should Britain be defeated, Australia—indeed the entire empire—would have lost the protection of the 'mother country'. Australia would have been increasingly vulnerable to the threats of militaristic Asian nations, particularly Japan. On 6 August 1914, *The Sydney Morning Herald* echoed the enthusiasm spreading throughout the nation when it declared, 'It is our baptism of fire ... Australia knows something of the flames of war, but its realities have never been brought so close as they will be in the near future.'[12]

The defeat of the once-powerful Russian army by Japan in 1904—05 altered dramatically the hierarchy of military dominance in the Pacific sphere. The possibility of a Japanese attack on Australia could no longer be ignored. More than ever, Australia needed to rely on the Royal Navy and the British army for protection. Yet, as Britain became more deeply engrossed in European affairs, Australia began to consider that her need for defence preparedness might best be met by a citizen army based on universal military service. In 1909, Field Marshal Lord Kitchener visited Australia at the instigation of the Prime Minister, Alfred Deakin, to report on the nation's defence capabilities. One of his recommendations was implemented in the *Australian Defence Bill* which endorsed 'the principle that every citizen should be trained to defend his county.'[13] The Act was not enforced until 1 January 1911, when the recently elected Labor government of Andrew Fisher settled on a peacetime army of 80,000 men, recruited through three levels of universal compulsory service. Boys as young as twelve were conscripted into the junior cadets, while fourteen to eighteen-year-olds were required to enrol in the senior cadets. Young men between eighteen and twenty-six were enlisted in the Citizen Military Force (CMF). Senior cabinet ministers expressed their satisfaction that these changes had prepared the country for war. Moreover, by 1914, the provisions of the Act meant, in theory, 'that the men [enlisting] could be organised, equipped and ready for departure within six weeks.'[14]

When war was declared, Australia found herself not quite as unprepared as initially feared by some federal government ministers. However, while 'wise precautions' and early planning had created the necessary framework for an expeditionary force, the legislation did not permit the government to send the CMF outside Australia. Its role was clearly defined: the CMF was to defend the nation against invasion. Rather than amend the Act, cabinet decided to implement the recommendation of the acting chief of staff, Major Cyril Brudenell White. White proposed that a force of 20,000 volunteers be trained and equipped for overseas service within a period of six weeks. The AIF—Australia's contribution to imperial defence—was a volunteer army, divorced from the CMF.[15] The newly promoted inspector-general, Brigadier General William Bridges, was appointed to command and organise the force, while Brudenell White was confirmed as his chief of staff.

Raising, training and equipping an expeditionary force of such a considerable size was always going to present problems for Bridges and Brudenell White. Unlike Britain—the last of the main belligerents to mobilise—which had a blueprint to put four divisions in the field within days of the declaration of war, Australia lacked any mobilisation framework at all. While Brudenell White preferred the enlistment of 'volunteer detachments from the existing home service battalions, and other units ... [and] linking the home service army with the contingent for overseas,' Bridges recognised the problems that this could engender. His primary grievance related to the way those units could be disbanded and scattered 'separately among British divisions'. Bridges advocated a more practical solution: the establishment of 'a special force by enlistment from the whole population'.[16] The Commander of the New Zealand Expeditionary Force, Major General Alexander Godley (a regular British officer), was among the senior officers and politicians who praised Bridges for his orderly organisation of the AIF. 'They have not been stinted at all,' Godley enthused, 'and expect to spend £12 million on their Expeditionary Force. They consequently have everything that they could want in the way of motor transport etc.' However, Godley failed to take into account 'the AIF's degree of preparedness and potential effectiveness. On Gallipoli it was short of such basic requirements as howitzers for the artillery. Ammunition shortages were also common and other deficiencies had been apparent from the outset.'[17]

Although the AIF was an army comprised completely of volunteers, what is sometimes overlooked is that many of those first eager young recruits had recently completed basic military training in the CMF. For several weeks each year they had taken part in 'military and physical training and [understanding] the ... value of ... discipline.'[18] Once the men enlisted, experienced officers and non-commissioned officers (NCOs) further developed that discipline and extended their training. Bridges chose mid-ranking staff officers from the small regular staff that administered and trained the CMF. Others were selected from British regular officers who were on loan to the Australian army. For battalion and brigade commanders, he looked for suitable officers from the CMF.[19] However, Bridges' plan to draw half the volunteers from those with CMF experience and the other half from those without any military background remained unrealised.

***

The 'digger tradition' is also a factor worthy of consideration. The AIF, in common with all armies, was exclusively made up of men—apart from a few female nurses. But, as Graham Seal points out, in the ranks of the AIF

> masculinity was imbued with especially powerful associations derived from prevailing notions of the Australian 'character'. These notions involved the stereotypical representation of the ideal Australian as a tall, tough, laconic, hard-drinking, hard-swearing, hard-gambling, independent,

resourceful, anti-authoritarian, manual labouring, itinerant, white male.[20]

The 1st AIF was generally regarded as egalitarian and this was reinforced by the appointment of junior officers initially chosen from within the ranks of the CMF. However, by January 1915, the only way to gain a commission was by enlisting first as a private soldier and demonstrating the qualities of leadership necessary to become an officer. Of course there were exceptions, such as newly graduated subalterns from Duntroon, although their numbers were too few to impact on the AIF's ethos.

***

Recruitment commenced on 10 August 1914. Men and boys of all ages—some as young as thirteen, others in their early seventies—from all occupations and diverse socio-economic backgrounds rushed eagerly to makeshift recruiting centres, first in Sydney and then in other capital cities. At first many of the men failed to meet the strict standards imposed by the army. They had to be at least 5 feet 6 inches (1.6 metres) tall, 34 inches (86 centimetres) around the chest, and between nineteen and thirty-eight years of age. Due to the enormous number of volunteers, men were rejected for seemingly minor reasons, including lack of military experience, poor teeth, corns or bunions and even flat feet.[21] According to one of the early volunteers, 'Many of those who were rejected were so disgusted that they "went and got married" while some committed suicide.'[22]

Many reasons motivated men to volunteer. Charles Bean's certainty—expressed in his official history—that 'the qualities of independence and initiative' displayed by Australian bushmen were the characteristics of the 1st AIF's recruits which 'makes superb soldiers,' has since been dismissed as overly jingoistic. Lloyd Robson, for example, argues that Bean's belief in the mythology of the bushman caused him to stereotype the reasons men (and boys) enlisted. Certainly, in the early stages, recruitment focused on men with military experience who, in the majority of cases, came from cities or larger provincial towns.[23]

Richard White asserts that middle-class recruits were likely to have enlisted because of abstract motives such as duty and honour, interwoven with self-interest. Men from the working class were driven to enlist, adds White, for reasons of 'judicious self-interest'.[24] While John McQuilton's research is based exclusively on Yackandandah, in north-eastern Victoria, the motivations that drove the local men to volunteer often represent the larger canvas in microcosm. Expanding White's conclusion,

McQuilton argues that economic and social considerations were more important than sectarian factors.[25] Gammage suggests that some men considered they had an obligation to volunteer. These were men who had been educated in the ideal that 'readiness to die for one's country equated with sexual maturity and now their manhood took up the gauntlet'. Still others volunteered out of 'hatred of Germany'.[26]

Patriotism, duty—even propaganda—contributed to the rush, as did the lure of foreign travel and adventure. One volunteer remembered that

> those idealistic views of youth were built chiefly upon the spirit of chivalry and romance that permeated my history books and such poems as Macaulay's 'Lays Of Ancient Rome' and his ballad of 'How well Horatio kept the bridge in the brave days of old'. War presented itself chiefly under the mantle of brilliant uniforms, marching soldiers, music, drums and glory.[27]

Undeniably, the majority of volunteers—whether from the bush or city—never fully understood the Australian government's reasons for sending them away to fight and die in distant foreign fields.

***

Like many others, John Cunliffe was impatient to volunteer. On 9 September 1914, Cunliffe (aged eighteen years, eight months) walked from his home to Liverpool camp on the outskirts of Sydney. In an interview conducted shortly before his death, Cunliffe described his service in the school cadets:

> When the first compulsory training started ... I had a commission ... I didn't go into the militia ... But they wouldn't take anybody with a commission ... so when the war started I went away as a sergeant ... I was in charge of the company and there was four sections making up the company. I was in charge of the lot in their training, and rifle shooting and all the rest of it.[28]

John Doggett was seven years older when he enlisted at Anglesea Barracks in Hobart, on 30 January 1915, although his reasons for seeking adventure were more ambivalent. 'I wanted to tell this young lady,' he recalled, 'that I ... didn't want to get engaged then go straight away. We had a little serious talk and I said to her that I was going away and if I came back we [would get] married.'[29] Bill Bradnock was almost twenty-two years of age on 22 September 1914 when he volunteered at Enoggera in Queensland. He commented that he and his friends 'were nothing more ... than schoolboys' in their attitude to life and the only memory they had retrospectively 'would be what sort of a good time' they had at school.[30]

Frank McGinty, who enlisted at the age of sixteen not long after war was declared, remembered that it was one of the most exciting moments of his life. Having secured his parents' consent, Frank went

> through Victoria Barracks. It was very crude in those days ... everyone—they're all in their 'nuddy' and—this doctor is looking at your teeth, and this fellow is weighing you, and this fellow is doing your chest. And there was a big bunch of young fellows going through from Newcastle. Young miners. And more or less, I was under everything, I remember, bar the chest measurement. I always had a good chest. Anyhow they put me through.[31]

Victor Groutsch, who hailed from Tocumwal in country Victoria, travelled to Melbourne:

> You enlisted in your local area of course. And all the people from Tocumwal, all the young blokes, were going to Melbourne because that was our centre. I enlisted at Cobram and I went to Melbourne, and was rejected promptly by the 'medicos' there for having a weak heart ... So then I had to enlist again in

Tocumwal. It was early in April 1915. It was just a bit before the Landing. I'd been reading about the doings of all the boys in and around Cairo ... and it sounded very attractive, of course at that time.[32]

Reginald Colmer's motivation was simple. 'I suppose the army wanted assistance,' he said.[33] By contrast, R.A. Goldrick volunteered because 'I was ... proud, romantic and reserved but ever ready to accept responsibility.' He subsequently wrote:

> There appeared to be an insistent something in the innate make-up of many of us which kept biologically alight the flame of chivalry, ardour and idealism. Most of us were filled with an ever surging patriotism; with admiration for the capacity, courage and camaraderie of our Australian companions in arms. We had unbounded confidence in our Empire and found fortitude in a most intense belief in the moral right of our cause.[34]

Whatever their reason for volunteering, all men needed to pass another medical examination, then take the oath of enlistment before undergoing further military training in camps scattered throughout Australia. Only then would they embark on their great adventure.

***

By September 1914, early training was under way, often in harsh surrounds. Victor Groutsch recalled that, when he and the other recruits were 'marched off to Liverpool camp, they thought of themselves as brave soldiers', although a 'bloody rag-tag mob too'. The camp proved very basic:

> It was very rugged. When we came in the first thing they had to do was put up tents of course. And then they had to prepare a kitchen with a trench dug in the ground with iron bars over it. That's where the cooks prepared the meals. We were issued with tin mugs and tin plates and all that sort of stuff. And our washing up place was a heap of sand down near the latrines.

Somewhat prosaically, he added, 'that wasn't very hygienic' before concluding that 'the training was quite proficient we thought. It was something we had never been subjected to before ... The staff sar'majors who did our training called us warriors, so we really were warriors.'[35]

Following his enlistment at Victoria Barracks in Sydney, Donald Fraser was required to 'fall in' and march 'out to Liverpool camp' where he took 'the oath for king and country.' But Fraser

> never had any drill [and] didn't know anything about forming fours or anything. The sergeant-major soon showed us how

it was done. Fall in line and number off, and how to form fours. Then march down from Victoria Barracks, down to the railway station on to the train out to Liverpool. We got issued with a waterproof sheet and two blankets and lay on the floor ... Then we went into extensive training. We were marmalades [sic] first ... They give us dungarees. They shifted us then into tents, after about a week, in the bell tents. It was better laying on the ground than it was on those hard floors ... you had to clean the dixies, and you had no hot water to clean them, take them down and scrub them with sand.

For breakfast you got porridge if you wanted it, Bully beef and so on and bread. [For] dinner you would get some ... [b]oiled potatoes and bully beef or something ... At tea time all you got was bread and jam. Oh ... you got the tea in a Dixie ... A tin with a lid on it ... We went to [the rifle range at] Long Bay ... One time there I was a marker. They tailed me as a marker. And the bloke who was firing at it, he never even hit the target. And they said, 'What's wrong with the target, so and so?' 'Well,' I said, 'there are no bullet holes in it.' Nothing hitting it. I don't know what was wrong with the bloke who was shooting. He couldn't hit it anyway.

Not long afterwards, the troops were required to perform 'a mock landing at Middle Head ... [for] a film on the landing at Gallipoli', which Fraser saw at a picture theatre shortly before his departure for the war zone.[36]

Frank Massey's memories of training at Holsworthy Camp, in New South Wales, were somewhat more laconic. 'We were there for a few months,' he recalled, describing the training of recruits in forming

> 'fours' discipline and bayonet fighting. But we hadn't got bayonets anyhow. It was just sticks ... we had a rifle range ... we had to shoot, and had to pass at target practice. That was ... near Coogee ... [W]e went to Liverpool Camp for the final—about a month.[37]

Percy Toft summarised his view of army life: 'There is nothing romantic in soldiering at first,' he wrote. 'Ill-fitting dungarees, dirty tent floors, irksome and strange drill, oily rifles, unpalatable roughly served food, unknown tent mates. Ignorant fault-finding nco's, experimental troop manoeuvring, all made a complete uncertainty in effort and human relationship.'[38] Roy Kyle was even more disapproving. 'I found army life demoralising,' he noted. 'The plunge from a life of reasonable privacy to one completely devoid of it was shattering. I, of course, accepted it eventually but was never happy being herded like a mob of cattle.'[39]

At a training camp at Randwick racecourse, recruits took part in early morning parades. After a short break, they practised tactical manoeuvres before performing the more demanding tasks set by the battalion's commanding officer (CO). Because officers were required to train alongside their men, a more uniform approach was adopted.[40] Training was also conducted in specialist skills such as artillery, although, initially at least, there were few sufficiently accomplished officers and NCOs capable of instructing.[41] Despite locating suitable men, other problems—usually associated with archaic British military doctrine—persisted. All training was dogged by a constant shortage of ammunition. In some artillery batteries, the troops were unable to fire a live round during training.[42]

Archibald Barwick wrote that, by early October, 'we all had our kakhi [sic] & how proud we were to get it. [While] they worked us pretty hard ... there was ... the keenest rivalry between the different companies ... [and] we had plenty of route marches & a fair bit of musketry.'[43] Even the so-called 'advanced' training was rudimentary and usually involved the tactics of attack and defence. This training would prove totally unsuited to the type of warfare that lay ahead. Recruits soon became bored with the monotony of the daily routine, leading to drunkenness and lack of discipline. More intense musketry training came later, as did exercises involving combat with an imaginary enemy. Further medical examinations were conducted in an endeavour to weed out those men unsuited to military duties. Only then were the remainder inoculated against typhoid and smallpox.

***

In the 15th Battalion, men from different states were brought together to form a single unit. Recruitment began in Brisbane on 14 September 1914 and, because no officers had been allocated, recruits were instructed initially by NCOs from the instructional staff. On 30 September, the 653 men who had enlisted from all over Queensland were assembled at Enoggera. There they were divided into six companies, based initially on the area from which they had enlisted:

A Company comprised men from around the Townsville district.

B Company consisted of recruits from around Rockhampton.

C Company included all men from the district around Wide Bay and Maryborough.

D Company claimed all the men from the city of Brisbane.

E Company was based on men from the Darling Downs, including Toowoomba.

F Company comprised all the recruits from the Northern Rivers of New South Wales.

On 22 November, having completed basic training, the six companies left by rail for Broadmeadows camp near Melbourne, where they joined G and H companies from Tasmania. The battalion was assigned to the 4th Brigade under the command of Colonel (later General) John Monash. Lieutenant Colonel J.H. Cannan was the battalion's first CO, with Major H.R. Carter as his deputy.[44]

Ernest Etchell had been training at Claremont camp in Tasmania for only five days when he heard the call for volunteers for the 15th Battalion. 'They were some short,' he recalled,

> Some had fallen out sick, and they called for volunteers. I wanted to get away ... There were 36 of us [who] went from Tasmania, to join D Company ... We was all mates ... We used to knock about together ... We came over in the *Loongana* from Launceston ... Burnie had no safe port.

We was kept on our own. We had reserved tables, and the passengers didn't mix with us at all. Lieutenant Frank Lane was in charge of us. He was a good joker. He was one of the troops really.[45]

New Recruits photographed during a break in training at Claremont Camp on the outskirts of Hobart, Tasmania, September 1914.

***

Troop convoys began leaving Australian ports on 18 October, less than two months after the commencement of training. Most of the men, while possessing a basic understanding of military discipline, remained seriously undertrained. The convoy's destination was kept secret, although most of the troops believed that they were going to Britain to undertake further training before moving on to the Western Front. On 2 November 1914, however, Turkey joined the Central Powers, taking up arms against Britain. Shortly afterwards, 'speculation was renewed that the troops would be disembarked before reaching England. Aboard the transports the men half-expected that they would now be called upon to defend Egypt.'[46]

By the time the first ships began arriving in Alexandria on 3 December, plans had been formulated for the second convoy, which included Monash's 4th Australian Brigade, now comprising the 13th, 14th, 15th and 16th Battalions. Troops from those units were, if anything, slightly better trained than the men from the earlier convoy. Sergeant A.L. Guppy wrote on 22 December, 'We left ... Broadmeadows, where we had been in camp since the middle of September ... the 13th and 14th Battalions and [4th] Brigade Headquarters are aboard our Boat [*Ulysses*].' Troops from the 15th and 16th Battalions were assigned to the *Ceramic*. On board his ship, Percy Toft was glad to be finally leaving for the front, although his preference was to fight 'the Hun' rather than 'the Turk'.

On 28 December, the ships of the second convoy began assembling in the Western Australian port of Albany. On 29 December, Guppy wrote that 'the New Zealand Transports steamed in to the pier ... Physical exercise at 8.30am and ... lecture to NCOs on map reading at 8.30pm.' Parades and training in military skills continued, although a few men became involved in wild brawls, mostly as a result of drunkenness. On 31 December, the convoy finally departed. The troops 'said goodbye to the last part of Aussie that we shall see for some time,' wrote Guppy. 'There are 17 transports in the convoy travelling in three lines, and half a mile from the other, with the Ulysses as flagship. The Berrima is towing the Australian submarine A.E. 2 which is our only escort.'[47]

According to Gammage, the majority of volunteers believed that 'active service began on the day they left Australia. They embarked with the stamp of the soldier noticeably upon them, but they were still largely civilians.' One day out from Albany, Sergeant C.F. Laseron wrote: 'This is the start of perhaps the most adventurous period of my life, and it is even very likely the last period ... for the first time we ... have really began the game in deadly earnest.'[48] Percy Toft's memories echoed this solemn sentiment:

> Our hearts and minds were full, as, in a calm sea, we moved forward to the Great Unknown, and 'left our country, former days, and youth ...' Our food was poor. Bread, jam and rabbit stew arrived invariably

at each meal ... The voyage to Egypt was made rather tedious by the lectures. Some were interesting, particularly those that touched on subjects as 'How we were to behave to the enemy women folk' and 'What regular soldiers were like.' However, to attend school again, and in the blazing tropics, was irksome.[49]

Private Robert Henry described conditions on board:

> We were supposed to have hammocks ... They were always given out after they got through The [Sydney] Heads ... and I got that sick I didn't get one. I just laid down on the floor, and I can still hear that propeller grinding away. I suffered from extreme biliousness. You wished you were dead. The eating arrangements—they had tables to eat off, of course. You were crammed pretty tight when you sat down. Anyhow there seemed to be any amount. It kept us going. I lost a bit of weight going across The Bight. We had physical exercises.[50]

The men found various ways to celebrate the New Year at sea. Guppy recalled that most on the *Ulysses* had fun

> with chorus singing and much cheering. Our Brigadier Colonel [sic] Monash at

midnight wished us all a Happy New Year. We trust it will be so and will bring to the Allied forces victory in the great cause. A Queensland soldier died aboard the Bordea and was buried at 10.55am. The whole convoy stopped for a few minutes during service. Another troopship from Perth joined us today making now 18.[51]

In fact, life on board the troopships was little different to the men's experience in the camps, Brudenell White having ordered that exercises and training were to continue as the convoys crossed the ocean.

Following a relatively incident free voyage marred only by illness—particularly sea-sickness—and minor lapses of discipline, the convoy reached the Suez Canal on 29 January 1915, soon 'after the Turks had made a disorganised and fruitless attack on the Canal.' Percy Toft and his battalion mates saw their first seaplanes, noted the 'trenches on [the canal's] banks, held by our own countrymen, real soldiers now—men of the 1st Division.'[52] On 1 February the convoy reached Alexandria. That same day, the men departed by train for Cairo and, afterwards, took the sixteen-kilometre trip to Mena camp, not far from the famous pyramids. There they were given the opportunity to purchase Charles Bean's booklet 'A Guide for

Australasian Soldiers, What to Know in Egypt', which listed 'protocol for contact with the natives, camp rules and sights to see'. Considering what lay ahead, possibly the most important 'rule' related to women. 'Men must be careful to avoid any attempts at familiarity with native women,' Bean wrote, 'because if they are respectable they will get into trouble, and if they are not, venereal disease will probably be contracted.'[53]

Some troops enjoyed their initial encounter with Egypt, particularly Cairo with its 'many interesting places'.[54] Others, however, were not so pleased with what they saw and experienced. Roy Kyle believed that:

> Egypt proved to be an unfortunate environment for Australians. They were young men in search of adventure and they had no special interest in old tombs, no matter how imposing. They climbed the pyramids in order to scratch their names into the stone at their peaks, had their pictures taken mounted on the back of a camel and then looked around for something else to do ... [and] attempted to get pissed on what the Egyptians had the temerity to pass for beer.
>
> Egypt was in every way a disappointment, after all, they [the Australians] had volunteered to fight the

Hun, someone they thought of as a worthy opponent. Now they were stuck in a godforsaken land of shifting sand and wily wogs. They'd come to test their manhood and they'd not been taken seriously by Britain who, in giving them the Turk, had allocated a second-rate enemy in an insignificant location well away from the real action of the war.[55]

Percy Toft noted with some chagrin that 'the more desirable part of Cairo was reserved for officers. Other ranks had the native area to amuse themselves in.'[56]

John Cunliffe enjoyed visiting the eye-catching buildings in Cairo, 'especially the museum'. The darker side, such as the grubby bordellos in the Wazzir district, held little fascination for him. 'The place was chock-a-block full of nothing else but brothels.' He described an incident which would later gain notoriety as 'The Battle of Wazzir':

> Some of the men were not quite satisfied with the service that they were getting. So they started throwing furniture out of the window into the street and setting it alight. That's what they call the Battle of the Wazzir. They called in the English military police, but they had no effect. They didn't take any notice of them.

When the military police came to try and stop the riot there was a fight. They brought out horses to put the fires out, and the troops cut the horses ... The only thing that stopped the riot was the Light Horse. They called the Light Horse in, and that stopped them.

I was in charge of a guard and I had to go back to the Wazzir and pick up all these Australians who were still lying around. If you told them in the morning where you found them they wouldn't believe you. The local drink is nothing like ordinary drink. They were just frightful concoctions that would send the men off their nut immediately ... Drunkenness was fairly prolific. These chaps would come from decent homes with a decent education, and they'd get this muck into their insides and they were not responsible for their actions. They had a camp there called the Gonorrhea Guards. It was filled up with all these chaps who had taken the risk and gone into the Wazzir and got gonorrhea.[57]

A large number of those men—and a few perennial troublemakers—were sent home to Australia, their fate an example to their fellows.[58]

The Australians continued their training in the tactics of modern warfare. Due to the senior officers' insistence on 'thoroughness', it was not 'till February that the troops were exercised as brigades'.[59] While some training was to prove useful in the conflict ahead, other exercises, such as lengthy desert marches, were completely impractical. Many of the troops questioned the necessity for extended marches while others, such as Private C.W. Avery, become disheartened. Avery confided to his diary that he was experiencing 'great disappointment of utter disgust,' adding philosophically, 'but one soon becomes used to practically anything.'[60]

The training was not uniform across every battalion. Moreover, little of it related 'to the actual fighting'. 'There was no training in the use of bombs', for example, or even in the tactics of 'trench warfare'.[61] Brudenell White was to admit later that the exercises 'had been based on obsolete tactical theory and aimed chiefly at wearing out the men so that they would be less of a nuisance in Cairo in the evenings.'[62] By mid-January, exercises involved never-ending parades, route marches and musketry practice. The training also involved a 'bonding process', which attempted to further bind the men to their battalions—in military parlance, their 'home'.[63] Yet, probably due to conflicting personalities and the fact that juvenile 'men had been abruptly removed from the constraints of neighbourhood and occupation', maintaining discipline had become an even more serious problem, as had the spread of venereal disease.

As training progressed in Egypt, more men continued to enlist in the AIF in Australia. Jock Williamson, a native Scot, had arrived in Fremantle in January 1910, aged seventeen. When war broke out he was working near Kalgoorlie laying the tracks for the Trans-Australia railway line. On 18 February 1915, Williamson enlisted and, following some basic training at Blackboy Hill camp, sailed for Egypt on the troopship HMAT *Hororata*. In Egypt, Williamson underwent further training before being assigned to the 16th Battalion as a reinforcement.[64]

***

By late February, training in Egypt had intensified. Route marches were longer, mock attacks more frequent, and the constant digging of trenches exhausted the men. Guppy recalled that, on 25 February, the troops went 'out on manouvre [sic] this morning, taking our lunch with us and did a big day's work over sand and ridges. We arrived back in camp at about 4pm.' The following day he wrote:

Reveille [was] at 5.30am ... and after breakfast blank ammunition and lunch were issued. We were ordered to stand by ready to defend the camp against a sham attack. However at 2pm we marched out to meet the supposed enemy and drove him off.

The historical significance of the region was not lost on Guppy who noticed when the troops 'passed over an old battlefield where Napoleon with the French defeated a large force of Orientals.'[65]

By mid-March, expectation of combat was rife. Bayonet drill and musketry practice had assumed a monotonous regularity. Percy Toft noted that 'all phases of training were run through from section to division work. Our brigade commanders were keen to know the exact limit of endurance in their men.' He added:

> We were kept at work from early morning to late in the evening. On field days we left the parade ground at 6.30am and arrived back in camp at 8.30pm. On the hardest day 35 miles were covered. Over the desert troops marched. Sometimes on hard sand, when men ricked their ankles through rolling on pebbles. Sometimes men trudged through loose sand which covered their boots. Up and down hills ... formations were kept, whilst the sun scorched, the

glare hurt the eyes, and dust, stirred by men's feet, hung like a pall.[66]

By late February, rumours were spreading throughout the AIF of an amphibious assault on the 'battered forts of the neighbouring Dardanelles'.[67] On 29 March, the Commander-in-Chief of the Mediterranean Expeditionary Force (MEF), General Sir Ian Hamilton, stopped over in Cairo to review ANZAC troops. The men were familiar with the British habit of senior officers looking over divisions before being sent into battle and Gunner Ray Brownell commented that 'this inspection by the Big Chiefs could mean nothing surer than a move to some war theatre.'[68] On 1 April, all leave was cancelled. Three days later, the first convoy carrying Australians departed Alexandria, bound for Mudros Island in the Aegean Sea. The 4th Brigade waited until 12 April for its order to embark. Percy Toft recalled that, 'as the vessels headed north, we guessed we were going to Turkey ... [and became] very interested when we neared Lemnos Island, which, the "Egyptian Times" had told us, was the base for operations.'[69] As the troopships sailed into port, Guppy noticed 'a great number of other transports loaded with troops. There are about 27 allied battleships, cruisers, destroyers etc anchored here.'[70]

By the time the 4th Brigade arrived on Lemnos, plans were well advanced for the Allied amphibious assault on the Dardanelles. However, the training which the AIF had pursued so vigorously in Egypt was to prove totally inappropriate for what lay ahead. Certainly, as Grey contends, 'very few of the developments in warfare imposed rapidly by action in France and Belgium had permeated through to the forces in Egypt, nor had any of the advances in the materials of war—bombs, periscopes, and the heightened use of the machine gun.'[71]

Australian Sergeant-Major G.S. Feist cursorily summarised his training as 'long marches and climbing hills, etc., [and] getting fit.' Added Feist, when 'at last the word came—we were going to have a fly at the Turks. Well, you can bet it was like putting a bit of roast meat to a starving man—we sprung on it.'[72] Little did he realise the horrors that lay ahead.

CHAPTER TWO
Gallipoli
'The Eyes of the World Are On Us'

CHAPTER TWO

GALLIPOLI

'The Eyes of the World Are On Us'

By early 1915, fighting in France and Flanders had deteriorated into a stalemate and the belligerents faced one another in a muddy stand-off. On the Eastern Front, the Russian army suffered a string of costly defeats and its soldiers wallowed in despondency. Following a request from the Russian government, the British decided that the best way to assist their ally—and help crush Germany—was to knock Turkey out of the war. Winston Churchill (then First Lord of the Admiralty) argued that Royal Navy ships could destroy Turkish forts guarding the narrow entrance to the Dardanelles, sail on up the channel, and capture Constantinople. Churchill believed that the reopened ice-free sea passage would allow Russia to obtain essential military hardware and food supplies. Reinvigorated Russian troops could then resume their attacks and force the Germans to transfer divisions from the Western to the Eastern Front. The prospect of securing the Suez Canal and British oilfields in

Persia further strengthened Churchill's argument and sealed the War Council's decision.[1]

Despite the imposing and heavily defended fortifications that guarded the straits leading to the Dardanelles, Churchill informed the War Council in London in no uncertain terms that a naval operation would be successful. On 19 February 1915, bombardment of the outer forts began and, during the next few days, some initial successes were recorded. However, when Admiral Carden's flotilla reached the inner forts, Turkish mobile howitzers prevented his minesweepers from clearing well-laid minefields, while fire from the British battleships' huge 12 and 15-inch guns did little damage to the forts. Noting the futility of continuing, Carden advocated an amphibious assault using ground troops to destroy the inner fortifications. But London had made its decision: infantry would only be used as a last resort, and the Navy was ordered to resume its shelling of the forts.[2] Churchill was unhappy with Carden's apparent lack of resolve and replaced him with a more resolute commander. On 18 March, Admiral John de Robeck's fleet, comprising sixteen British and French battleships—including the modern super dreadnought *Queen Elizabeth* as well as a number of smaller ships—attempted to force The Narrows.[3] The attack ended in failure as one third of the battleships were either sunk or badly damaged. What de Robeck could not have known, however, was that the apparently resolute Turkish defence had all but crumbled in the face of the mighty British onslaught.

Faced with the failure of the naval operation, the War Council reverted to its back-up strategy—a bold, ambitious assault on the peninsula. The 62-year-old soldier and poet, General Sir Ian Hamilton, was chosen as commander of the MEF. Hamilton retained his faith in a naval victory despite the earlier setbacks. A little over three weeks before the planned military landing, Hamilton informed Admiral de Robeck that the 'wisest procedure' was to resume the naval campaign, adding that 'it is always possible that opposition may suddenly crumble. If you should succeed be sure to leave me cruisers enough to see me through my military attack in the event of that being necessary.'[4] The Admiralty did not agree with Hamilton's assessment and finally halted the naval attack—at least until after a military landing which, they argued, would silence the Turkish guns and allow the fleet safe passage. Naval vessels would, however, be used to support Hamilton's amphibious assault.

Although the two-month advance warning provided to the Turks by the naval assault had deprived Hamilton of any element of strategic surprise, he could still hope for some tactical success. Early planning called for three amphibious assaults supported by naval gunfire. The main landing at Cape Helles would be complemented by two feints—one by the Australian and New Zealand Army Corps (ANZAC) force—and the other a naval demonstration at Bulair (eighty kilometres north-east of Helles) designed to divert Turkish attention from the major attack. History would prove that this task was well beyond the capabilities of the courageous but indecisive Hamilton and his optimistic co-planners. Hamilton was far too compliant with the demands of senior officers and too weak with subordinates, a fact not lost on the Secretary to the British War Council, Sir Morris Hankey. Disappointed by Hamilton's appointment and what he regarded as the feeble effort devoted to planning the campaign, Hankey noted prophetically, 'it is conceivable that a serious disaster may occur.'[5] The War Council would also bear partial responsibility for any such disaster given the lack of advance planning for such a large amphibious attack and the questionable British attitude towards the fighting qualities of the Turks. Indeed, it is uncertain whether a more energetic and resourceful general could have achieved better results given the prevailing mindset in London.

Probably more culpable for the approaching 'serious disaster' was the man who originally appointed Hamilton, Field Marshal Lord Kitchener of Khartoum, the British Secretary of State for War. Kitchener and the War Council, inexplicably, had no definite plan of operation in place for the MEF. Moreover, Hamilton's five divisions (approximately 70,000 men) amounted to only half the number which could, realistically, seize and hold the peninsula. Hamilton should have been aware of this, but deferred to the judgement of senior officers and politicians. Without a murmur of complaint he accepted his limited force, knowing full well that its numbers were considerably inferior to those of the Turks. Probably more significantly, this 'left him without a strategic reserve necessary for his hazardous operation.'[6]

***

On Lemnos, the Australians continued their strict training regime. On 15 April, the transport A31 *Seang Choon* arrived in Mudros harbour carrying the last contingent of troops from the 4th Australian Brigade. Despite their limited knowledge of amphibious assaults, junior officers attempted to train their men in the execution of such attacks. Hamilton's optimistic plan failed to take into account many apparent difficulties including the lack of preparation, the men's inexperience and the logistical problems of a seaborne operation. With the lack of adequate preparation at General Headquarters (GHQ), 'ANZAC staffs ... laboured and improvised like blacksmiths.'[7] Captain Leslie Morshead noted that, at first, his men 'looked very much at sea,' although, after some additional training, he rather optimistically considered that they were 'much more successful both from the Navy and the Army points of view.' Morshead added that he was becoming increasingly concerned about the unsatisfactory planning, especially after 'the Brigadier & B[attalio]n Commanders went to the Dardanelles on board the Queen Elizabeth. Our CO gave us a graphic description of what he saw of the peninsula of Gallipoli. They were fired on four times.'[8]

Not all the men's time was taken up with training. Concerts were held in what Percy Toft referred to as a 'natural amphitheatre'. According to Toft, there were two 'main artists'—a well-known baritone from New Zealand, and the other, their brigade commander, John Monash, who addressed the men 'for five minutes on any current topic and his oratory held us spellbound.'

Considering Monash's achievements later in the war, Toft's appraisal is worthy of note:

> We did not come into much personal contact with ... [Monash]. He was an intellectual, a spirit which kept him aloof from his men. He had no spare moments and was well employed, but he was like the unseen head of some huge business organisation which he controlled thoroughly but had no discernible personal friendship for the men ... who were not machines. His men should mean more than a mass of individuals ... He was an engineer by profession and his work only mattered. The members of his brigade were only thought of for their usefulness to him and his work. Of course he succeeded ... He had a single mind with a single aim—achievement ... General Monash's aloofness made him interesting to all.[9]

***

By 19 April, the training exercises focused almost exclusively on troops disembarking from transports into the rowing boats which were to take them ashore. Guppy recalled practising 'disembarking with full kit up ... there is no doubt our equipment is heavy now, with 200 rounds of ammunition added, especially when one comes to climbing down and up rope ladders to the boats alongside.'[10] Toft remembered that his

vessel was tied alongside another transport ship, making it possible for our neighbour, Victorian companies of the 8th Battalion and our companies to visit each other and make pleasant acquaintances. Day by day warships would come and go. In the far distant north we could hear the booming of the guns.

In this beautiful and large harbour we remained ten days practicing running up and down rope ladders thrown over the ship's side. We were fully equipped, carrying rifles and extra ammunition and a faggot, required for firewood, strapped to our packs. We would then climb into one of the ship's boats, and taking an oar, pull to the shore a mile away. We were drilled to take the same boatplace to avoid confusion. It was said that there was no wood on Gallipoli, and as none could be supplied for some time, it was necessary to carry some...

Every soldier could not negotiate the ladders. Some fell into the water to be unceremoniously hauled to the boat by a man supplied with a boat hook. We were permitted to swim, but the water was cold and few enjoyed more than a brief dip.[11]

On 23 April, junior officers and their troops were given two days' notice that they were to prepare for an amphibious landing on a beach near Gaba Tepe. The 3rd Australian Brigade would form the first wave, while the 4th Brigade would follow in the second landing. Some troops would come ashore on the afternoon of 25 April, while others would follow the next day.[12]

***

Senior British staff officers had already planned the landing of the 3rd Infantry Brigade at first light to secure the beachhead. The remainder of the force was to follow and take the important heights around Mal Tepe, five kilometres inland. Overlooking Maidos and the entrance to the Dardanelles, Mal Tepe allowed Turkish observers to keep their commanders on the southern tip of the peninsula abreast of the developing situation. British planners also believed that this action would cut off the Turkish forts, isolating them from supplies and reinforcements. Enemy troops around Cape Helles would likewise be starved of food and ammunition. British troops could then simply move north and mop up any remaining pockets of Turkish resistance. It seemed a simple matter to the British staff. Unsurprisingly, the reality was to prove entirely different.

On 24 April, Australian soldiers noted the unsettling sight of five hospital ships, capable of treating 2,500 wounded, heading for the landing site.[13] Later the same day, the convoy of almost 200 transports, escorted by Royal Navy warships, began leaving Mudros. Bill Bradnock recalled, 'About three o'clock in the afternoon we were all grouped together on the deck of the ship.' His ship, he explained,

> we called "The Hungry Goose." It had a goose painted on the funnel and because we got very poor tucker on that boat, we called it "The Hungry Goose". I think its number was A40. Just before four o'clock, Dr Luther rounded us up. Luther was a very fine fellow. He was a senior captain ... a medical doctor ... He said, "Well boys, the man you're going to fight, he knows no mercy—and he'll give no mercy. Get that in your brainbox!" Before the landing we were given a little hand-book with Kipling's poems nicely printed in it. "There's one thing that I want you to remember, boys," he said, referring to the book, "and you've got to try and visualise it, and live up to it. It goes back to Afghanistan. Kipling wrote this poem:
> *When you're wounded and lying on*
> *Afghanistan's plains*

And the women come out to cut off what remains
Just roll to your rifle, and blow out your brains
And go to your God like a soldier!

"These troops that we are going to be opposed to are mostly Mohammedan, and they'll show no mercy. They don't mind being killed. That's the funny part about it, if there is anything funny about it, because the minute they're killed they go straight to Paradise. When you're killed, you'll go straight to Hell. That's the difference."[14]

Archie Barwick conveyed the general feeling amongst Australian troops who had grown 'heartily sick of the place [Lemnos].'[15] Others who were to come ashore later as reinforcements were required to stay a little longer. Percy Toft described the frenzy of movement:

On Sunday morning, 25th April, 1915, we woke early to find many transports had left during the night. The Fleet, too, was gone. A continuous boom sounded from 50 miles away. We realized the big day had come. What were the other men's feelings? I cannot describe my own. Transport after transport left. Early in the forenoon our ship moved off.

Barwick recalled that, earlier:

> General Birdwood spoke to us, among other things he warned us to be careful with our water, food & ammunition & told us that the eyes of the world would be on us, to see how we fought ... That night everyone was as happy as they could possibly be ... [N]obody thought of what was going to happen on the morrow ... At about 4 o'clock reveille sounded ... & while we were munching [breakfast] ... we heard a tremendous roar, up we all rushed to get a look at what was going on.[16]

Archie Barwick was witnessing the dawn landing of Australian troops. At around 3.30a.m. on 25 April, the convoy anchored three kilometres off the coastline. A little later, the twelve tows began casting off and headed for the beach. At 4.30a.m. the troops waded ashore.

The unsuspecting Australians, however, had been landed at the wrong place. Instead of 'Z' Beach, strong currents had forced the tows two kilometres north to Ari Burnu (subsequently known as Anzac Cove), a tiny bay beneath the menacing 260-metre summit of Chunuk Bair. The area was described as 'a narrow beach and steep cliffs and a hinterland of tangled hills and gullies instead of the open plain or gentle slopes they had expected.'[17] Paradoxically, had the men landed at the correct beach, there is every chance that they would have suffered greater casualties, as the Turkish defences there were far better prepared. Casualties were high in any case, with some men killed before they could land. Charles Kelly recalled, with a touch of black humour, seeing 'the first casualty ... before we got on shore. The bullet came in and hit this fellow ... in the forehead. Now, it was nearly spent. It was the funniest thing you ever saw. It went along his forehead, and his two eyes fell out. He pushed them in again.'[18] A Turkish officer, Major Mahmut Bey, saw firsthand the courage of his own troops and that of the Australians. He later recounted: 'the enemy approached the shore in lifeboats. When they came into range, our men opened fire. Here, for years, the colour of the sea had always been the same, but now it turned red with the blood of our enemies.'[19]

Bill Bradnock (15th Battalion) took part in the second landing and recalled vividly the rampant confusion at the beachhead:

> The second lot would go in, and the idea would be that the men that had been just loaded on the first boat would, after they'd towed them along ... load them on to smaller boats and tie them together with a rope, and they would try and tow in as

far as they could inshore, so that they could hop out ... Make the landing. That was what happened to the first lot. I wasn't in that lot. I was in the next lot. All I can remember was the yelling and shouting ... I would say there was about 450 men. The din was terrific ... There were no bloomin' hills to go up in. It was just like landing here [flat]. If you go across the country, there's no hills there, until you got three or four miles in, then you got some hills.

Well you see, we couldn't get any reinforcements, we couldn't get any ammo, we couldn't get any tucker, and when we landed we took our own iron rations with us and that's what we had—little weeny hard biscuits. Oh cripes the bully beef. There was no means of opening the tins. It was terrible ... The whole stunt was badly organised.[20]

Reginald Colmer (13th Battalion) also came ashore in the second wave:

We all got christened when we were in the boat that took us right to the beach—the little boat. We got christened before we landed. There were two wounded badly. Apparently one was killed and another wounded ... [by] snipers shooting them ... We had to go straight up [the rugged cliffs].

You see these hills up in front of you ... It was a case of slaughter before you got anywhere near the hills. You had to fight your way all the way to get up there to where we built our positions, that remained our positions for the rest of our career there ... We were in the front-line trenches, the 15th [Battalion] was just back down the hill behind us, in reserve.[21]

The movement of troops already ashore devolved into chaos in the difficult terrain and under the witheringly accurate enemy rifle and machine-gun fire. Instead of advancing as a unit, the men had been instructed to form small groups. In the heat of battle, they were forced to make decisions on the spot 'and fight their own battles.'[22] Despite this, the Australians were able to take the first ridge and push inland for over a kilometre. However, they failed to capture Gun Ridge, their primary objective.

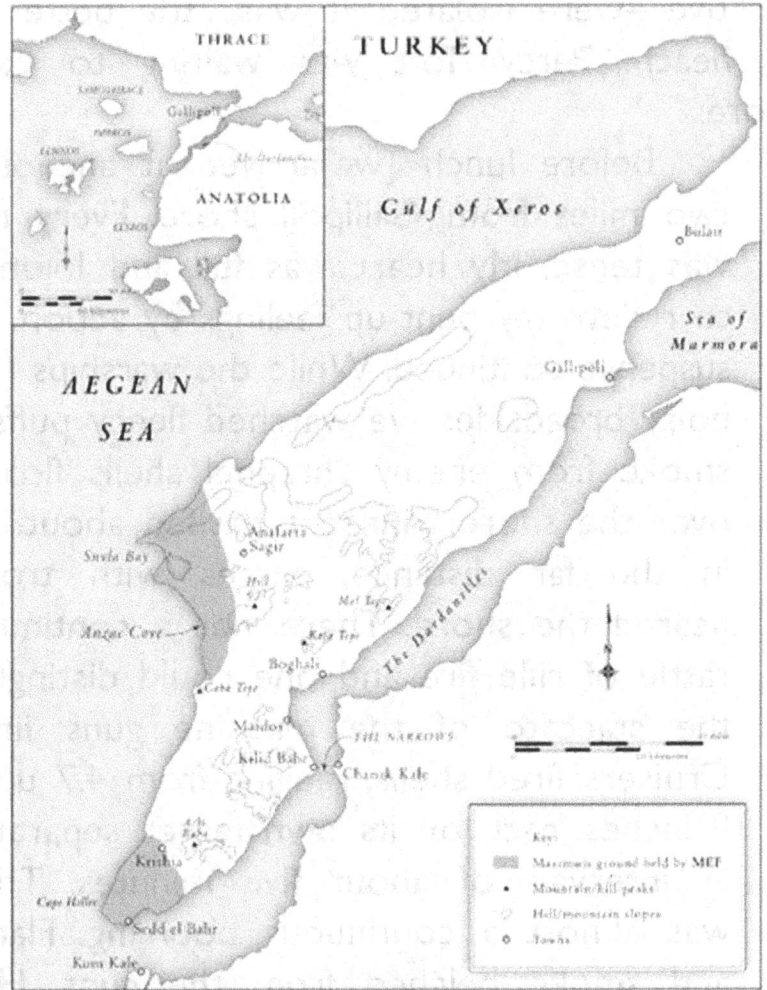

Map 1: The Gallipoli Peninsula showing the landing site At ANZAC Cove, 25 April 1915 and the area captured (shaded) by the ANZACS and British (at Cape Helles). Inset: Position of Gallipoli Peninsula and Lemnos.

Obsolete and worthless maps, coupled with the unfamiliar terrain and lack of artillery support, meant that those few groups that penetrated to the second ridge—and fewer still to the main objective—were isolated. It was little better on the beach. Percy Toft was waiting to come ashore:

> Before lunch [we] arrived at anchorage two miles from Gallipoli shore. Every man was tense. My heart was full and I longed to relieve my pent-up feelings by action. But suspense continued. While the warships fired noisy broadsides we watched fleecy puffs of smoke from enemy shrapnel shells floating over the shore. Pinnaces dashed about, and in the far distance, barges with troops neared the shore. There was a continuous rattle of rifle fire and one could distinguish the staccato of the machine guns firing. Cruisers fired shells, ranging from 4.7 up to 9 inches, each on its own target, separately, at intervals of about five minutes. There was almost a continuous booming. Flames and smoke belched from the guns. Here was noise at its greatest.[23]

John Cunliffe (13th Battalion) also came ashore in a subsequent landing. 'The strongest impression I have of the landing was to see these English midshipmen standing to attention with a cane under their arm and their caps on,' he recounted later. They were

> giving instructions to British soldiers about where to go. Shells were coming over

hell for leather, and there was not a wink from them. You'd think they were just on the parade ground. That was the first impression I got. I saw them as we landed, and we then went straight ahead. We were right alongside the *Queen Elizabeth*, and that was putting its fifteen-inch shells right over the beach ... We went into open boats from the troopship, and we were all exposed, just sitting ducks ... We were under fire all the time coming in. There was shrapnel coming all over where we were ... There were quite a number of casualties on the pontoons before we got ashore. When we got close in to the shore we hopped into the water, but a lot of us were hit ... before we got ashore. The water was up to our waists, but we soon got out of it. Then we went straight on.

It was almost dusk when we landed. It was practically dark, and everybody got lost. As far as I was concerned it was just everyone for themselves once you landed there. I don't remember seeing any others from our company, or platoon, or section. I don't remember any of my platoon at all being with me at the time. It was just everyone for themselves. No-one was giving instructions. You just went on, on your own initiative.

It was just on dark when we got up to Quinn's, and we couldn't go any further than that ... The first feeling I had was that there were two prospects of getting off, and they were nil. You had no idea you'd ever get out of it, because there was nowhere to go. There was only the sea behind you. It was no good retreating because there was nowhere to retreat to.[24]

Ernest Guest (13th Battalion) and his mates got ashore and we went in towards the high rise. They were calling out ... just ahead of us, "Come on fellows, anywhere, get in, we are short handed," and all this sort of stuff. We went up to them and dug in. And it was stupid the way they did things. Instead of resting the men as much as possible, we were all up listening to lectures and talking, all through from Mudros on. We were all bagged before ever we got out of the boats.[25]

By dusk on the 25th, the Australians' early confidence had waned. 'Our infantry getting an awful time on the open ridges from enemy shrapnel,' wrote the Australian artillery commander, Colonel Talbot Hobbs, before adding,

'Great confusion.'[26] By the end of the day, ANZAC troops had taken approximately three square kilometres of enemy ground. The 1st Division was holding terrain near Gaba Tepe through to what subsequently became known as 'Steele's Post'. The 4th Australian Brigade and the New Zealand Division were sited on the left flank running down to 'Fisherman's Hut.'

Overall, the plan was a dismal failure. Reinforcements allowed Turkish troops to hold most of the high ground. Evacuation was discussed on board *Queen Elizabeth*, which served as Hamilton's headquarters. Discounting this option, Hamilton believed that his best chance of success lay further south, around Helles, where British forces were engaged. The ANZACs needed only to hold their position and undertake small-scale offensives while British troops attempted an all-out attack. The Commander of the ANZAC Corps, General Sir William Birdwood, was informed that his men 'have got through the difficult business. Now you have only to dig, dig, dig, until you are safe.'[27]

The 26th of April was similar to the previous day. Numerous command bungles impeded whatever chance the Australians may have had of moving their beachhead forward. Shortly after 8.00a.m., Monash, his staff, and the remainder of the 14th Battalion landed. On board the troopships, men were becoming edgy. 'At 10.45am we climbed through doors that had been built in the side of the ship,' Toft recalled, but

> it was too dangerous for the destroyer to approach close to the shore and remain stationary, so we were trans-shipped to an open barge which held us all, the iron sides giving us a certain amount of protection from shrapnel. The shrapnel being aimed at us was flying in narrow strips across the water. The barge was towed by a small steam boat ... We came to the shore and saw the water was deep, which allowed the barge to almost touch the land.

Unlike the previous day, there was little or no Turkish resistance. 'Wading through a foot of water we waited until the company had landed.' Toft continued,

> then we sat down in groups on the beach and immediately started on our midday meal. Crowds of men were carrying supplies ashore. The naval arrangements were orderly and free from fuss. The enemy shelled the ships and barges, but no shellfire was directed at the beach.
>
> About 2pm we moved off. We were guided to the head of Monash's Gully, there we dumped our packs, including our overcoats and all personal belongings. We

were handed another bandolier of cartridges, which altogether made 350 rounds in our equipment pouches and bandoliers. In file we moved off to fight.[28]

And fight they did. The 4th Australian Brigade settled in, holding key positions at the head of Monash Valley, on the centre-left of the ANZAC perimeter.

***

In the hours following the landing, that part of Monash Valley—commonly called Quinn's Post—in front of the Turks, was 'fringed with several strong posts'. Situated 'between Russell's Top on its left or western side, and the steep and much-indented ridge on the right,' Monash Valley was a key component of the ANZAC defence network. Its tactical significance was not lost on either side. In the words of C.E.W. Bean, the 'branch to the left runs for another half-mile between steep-sides, gradually becoming gentler till it ends in a spoon-shaped depression at The Nek. The branch to the right is shorter, narrower, and much steeper, and ends abruptly on a part of the inland slope of Baby 700, which came later to be known [from the trenches which afterwards gridironed it] as the "Chessboard."'[29] Cunliffe recalled fighting from the trenches at Quinn's Post:

By the second day the trench was as deep as it ever got—about four feet deep and about three feet wide. The ground was mostly sandy. To do any firing, your shoulders and head were above the trench, and you were a target all the time. You'd be firing all the time, spraying as many as you could. That's why there were so many casualties. And then you'd dig in the dugout behind to have a spell.[30]

Anticipating a Turkish attack, the members of Percy Toft's company dug themselves in:

Sometime during the afternoon [of the 26th], Captain Moran from A Company came across and took command of the sector we occupied. Our right flank was about 400 yards from the sea and about 100 yards in front of Shrapnel Gully. We were on a plain with a distinct gully running across our front five chains ahead. In between the dugouts and around us, particularly to the rear, were clumps of scrubby undergrowth about three feet tall, which gave cover from view. A small cleared patch of a quarter acre, evidently a cultivation area, was forty yards to our left front. Another height commenced about a quarter-mile ahead and was Turk's country.

Our position was not exactly known, but "Johnny Turk" made a good guess. For a couple of hours on Tuesday [27 April] afternoon we crouched at the bottom of our holes. The shrapnel shell fire half enfilading from the right generally went a little to our rear. At 5pm Turks could be seen gathering in a gully and considerable movement was seen on tracks skirting the hills in front of us. Just on sunset, an hour later, the country ahead seemed to be swarming with Turks. They were hurrying to and fro.

Our skipper, Frank Moran, said to us "Those Turks are gathering to attack. We'll wait for them. Men! Don't fire until they are five yards away, then let them have it! We'll give them a surprise!"

We waited patiently for them to come on. About 8 o'clock we heard them approach and soon afterwards saw figures in the poor light carrying long gleaming bayonets. They came in mass formation, blowing bugles and calling on Allah. The attack extended on both sides of our front.

We waited until the first man stood on our parapet ... "FIRE!" Moran ordered. Next morning this Turk was found pierced by nineteen bullet wounds. Rifles were fired until they almost blazed with heat. This rapid fire, together with the surprise the Turks received effectively stopped the advance. Our machine guns were pouring lead across our front. There was shouting but the enemy did not reform to charge us.

The Fleet had been advised that an attack was forming, and when our fire rang out, one of the warships, HMS *Orion* .. had taken up a position near the shore, in direct enfilade of the gully in front. At point blank range, she opened up shellfire with shrapnel. The enemy attack was completely broken.[31]

Similar scenarios were reported along other parts of the Australian front.

Earlier, the Turkish Commander, Mustafa Kemal, had received another two regiments of reinforcements. Settling on a large-scale attack, Kemal effectively underestimated the resolve of the Australians and the defensive network that they had already established—and, crucially, the firepower of the British naval ships stationed offshore. The resultant massacre drastically altered Kemal's thinking. In future, he would wait until more divisions were available before attacking 'down slopes exposed to the warships' guns.'[32] Two companies from the 14th Battalion also suffered severe casualties. While digging a support trench, almost 200 men were caught in crossfire from a machine-gun. Amongst those killed were some promising young officers, including Captain Hoggart who, Monash recalled, 'won my shield at Williamstown two years ago', and Gordon Hanby who was 'struck through the chest while trying to drag a wounded soldier to safety.' There is some indication that the Australians may have been victims of 'friendly fire'. At the time, the men of the 14th Battalion assumed the gunfire had come from Turkish trenches. Others, however, sensed that it had come from around 75 metres away in the direction of Courtney's Post which, at the time, was held by the 15th Battalion.[33]

Over the next few days, death from a sniper's bullet became the main fear for most Australian soldiers. 'The snipers were excellent shots and extremely cunning,' remembered Eric Hanman (15th Battalion), remarking on one sniper in particular:

> Several were captured, most of them having short shrift [killed], but one was taken prisoner and photographed as a curiosity. His hands and face were painted green, his rifle was also the same colour. He was entirely covered by a bush, which was fastened to his person. The disguise

was wonderful. When still, he looked like a common or garden bush. It would take a very keen pair of eyes to detect anything human about it.[34]

Bill Bradnock recalled, 'You had to keep as low as you could, to cut down any silhouette that you might make, and that became a habit ... Many of the troops who were ashore after the landing died from sniper fire ... Many went during the first week. They were too innocent and too ignorant. They hadn't any experience, or knew how to gain it.'[35] Sergeant John Kidd wrote that a man close to him 'very cautiously raised his head about six inches [above the parapet] and was killed instantly. I noticed dust about six feet in front of me so I watched. The sniper was so close I could have touched him, so I just had to wait, and when the next man of ours dropped, I pop-shot the sniper on the top of his head. He wore a tight khaki skull cap. He was a very brave man.'[36]

Percy Toft described his platoon's attack on an enemy sniper post under cover of darkness:

> We moved along the gully and came to a very high and steep hill—Pope's Hill named after the 16th Battalion Commander. We pulled ourselves up in the dark and jumped across a narrow ravine, on our way to Russell's Top. In one place a rope had

been spiked down to give us a hold to clamber up. Hands helped us across the gullies. It was so black in the shade of the hill that we touched the man in front to prevent ourselves being lost.

Enemy snipers made posts ... [in No Man's Ridge, opposite Pope's Hill and Quinn's Post] which permitted them by day to snipe men moving past certain spots in Monash Gully and the bottom of Quinn's Post ... To capture No Man's Ridge, an attack would have to succeed from Russell's Top and Pope's Hill to first capture the opposing positions ... In the early light I saw the enemy trench parallel to our own trench about five chains away ... I heard a plop. Looking up I saw my mate crumpling and sliding to the bottom of the trench. One look and I saw that his head had been cut off in a straight line above the ears, from the eyebrows. A sniper's bullet must have hit a pebble on the parapet of the trench and the bullet ricocheting made the ghastly severance ... In the afternoon a big Turkish attack launched in front of Quinn's and Courtney's was defeated.[37]

Despite continuous attempts to eliminate enemy snipers, they continued to take a toll on Australian soldiers. Their principal target was officers. Donald Fraser commented that the Turks had 'noiseless sniper rifles. There was one fellow behind our lines ... for a good while ... And he ... shot a lot of people. He only had to shoot in the daylight. You couldn't see of a night. But one of the mule drivers [an Indian Ghurka] ... went out in the night and got him. Cut his head off.'[38] Hanman added that the 'Indians excelled in finding and despatching snipers. They knew the art of concealment and stealth, and could meet the Turk with his own weapon.'[39]

***

By this time, the surviving Australians were thoroughly exhausted. Despite this, and for their own safety, they were ordered to dig deeper. Toft noted that his company members

> were in position below Courtney's Post. All day we watched men coming and going and were struck with the fact that they appeared old. The men slouched along ... Nothing now appeared new. There were still the wounded—who if not being carried walked. Working parties moved up and down. The mountain guns still blazed at their targets [usually Turkish machine-gun positions].

According to Toft, when the company was due to go into action, this was usually signalled by 'obtaining water, receiving a supply of ammunition, replacing our emergency rations and obtaining the next day's ration.'

By early May, the AIF's advance had completely bogged down. Any Australian attack was halted, usually with heavy casualties. The assault on 'Bloody Angle' trench exemplified the difficulties faced. 'This trench had been giving us considerable trouble owing to its position,' wrote Signaller Ellis Silas:

> It overlooked the road along which our supplies were brought. Eventually it became quite impossible to get further stores through. This naturally caused great anxiety. So at dawn [on] 2-3 May, we were ordered to storm the heights. It is difficult to describe the almost impossibility of the task. It was a sheer slope of sandy soil, which made it extremely difficult to obtain a foothold. Up we went, and, despite the murderous fire that was poured into us, we sang "Tipperary". The cries of the wounded, the tremendous fusillade of rifles and screaming of shells, were indescribable. Quite impossible to hear orders, it was each man for himself. We knew what we had come to do, and we did it—at a price! It was on this occasion that the 16th Battalion was practically wiped. One fellow whom I

came across, frightfully wounded said: "My! But they're willing." Another poor man came tearing along, his right hand blown off, waving the bleeding stump, and calling out: "My God! But I've done my duty! Hallo, that you, Silas, old chap. I've done my duty haven't I?" ... We gained the trenches, but at a frightful loss. The hill was swept by an enfilading fire from the enemy. Then came the cry: "We're short of ammunition!" All night long we were getting supplies of it up the lead-swept slope, and as dawn broke our position became more exposed to the enemy's fire. We could hang on no longer, and had to retire; but despite the retirement, we had saved a very critical situation, having driven off a force far superior in strength. [At] dawn I shall never forget the indescribable scene in the gully; it was choked with dead and wounded. These poor lumps of clay had once been my comrades—men I had smoked and worked and laughed and joked with. Oh God! The pity of it. It rained lead in this gully.[40]

Turkish artillery also pounded Australian positions constantly, causing some infantry officers to question why their own artillery appeared conspicuous in its absence.[41] As Hobbs wrote, the truth was that there were simply too few Australian guns on the peninsula to respond.[42] While naval barrages were supposed to compensate for this shortfall, the shells—fired on a flat trajectory—were unable to destroy enemy trenches and earthen defences. John Cunliffe recalled the severity of the shellfire:

> I can remember how many casualties there were all around where we were. The shells were screaming in from every direction, and there was a terrific noise from all the rifle fire. It wasn't much longer after that [3 May] that I got hit myself. I had my shoulders and head above the parapet firing the rifle. The Turks were coming in flat out. It looked as if they'd be successful. A shell landed directly in front of me. It spreads out in a "V" shape. We got the full force of it forward, and then it spread out on either side of us. The two men on either side of me were killed. It shows how lucky you can be. I lost my right arm and had shrapnel through my left arm. As soon as I got hit somebody must have pulled me out, and I was lying out in the open ... I was told afterwards that a stretcher-bearer going pass saw just a movement of me kicking. He thought I was

dead meat. But he ... picked me up and took me down to B Company.[43]

Cunliffe remained unconscious for three days. He woke in a marquee erected to take extra casualties next to the military hospital at Heliopolis in Egypt. His arm had been amputated. After only eight days of fighting, his war was over. He remained in hospitals in Egypt for another two months before he was sent to a convalescent home in Sexton, Manchester. On 8 October 1915 he sailed for Australia.

The Australians continued to mount small-scale attacks along Quinn's Post. Lieutenant Burford Sampson (15th Battalion) wrote of one 'undertaking' on 9 May. Despite 'strong objections' from Lieutenant A.G. Hinman on the grounds that 'in the morning following the assault the Australians would certainly be driven out of any captured trenches by the Turkish machine-guns, which would enfilade them from both flanks', Lieutenant-Colonel J.H. Cannan (the battalion CO) ordered the attack to proceed. According to Sampson, the initial 'assault was successful ... Hinman died most gallantly leading his men, [his] body not recovered.' But Hinman's prediction came to fruition. 'Up-hill retirement,' Sampson added, 'our casualties ... during retirement very heavy, principally [due to] machine-guns and bombs. Many picks & shovels lost and I fear much ammunition. Never thought to come out alive and marvel at narrow escapes. Jacket & shirt torn by bullets, haversack and water bottle riddled. Shoulder very painful, but still fit to do my duty. Thank God for all his mercies.' Having been relieved by the 16th Battalion the following morning, Sampson confided to his diary the thoughts of most men: 'Notwithstanding severe mauling & punishment the morale of our Regiment is good and the men heroes.'[44]

***

By mid-May the Turks and Australians had constructed a labyrinth of trenches along the ragged cliffs in close proximity to each other—sometimes only ten metres separated friend from foe. Australians continued to be killed or wounded on a daily basis. Eugene Fathers suffered minor shrapnel wounds from one encounter, remembering only that he had received 'a good whack ... Then I had to walk down ... from Beck's Bluff ... to Anzac Cove, to the jetty ... they had a casualty clearing station—a big marquee tent.' Medical treatment was primitive and medical staff were in short supply. 'My head was bleeding,' Fathers added, 'I remember laying down on the ground, and ... some chappie next to me hitting me on the head with his mess tin. He didn't know what he was doing. He just whacked me on the head. The next thing I know, I'm in hospital in Egypt, in Heliopolis.'[45]

The stench from grotesquely swollen bodies lying unburied in no man's land in the heat of the day was putrid. 'The strongest memory I have of Gallipoli is the smell of the dead,' declared Bill Bradnock. 'They were left lying there, and the crows would come around. It's one of the cruellest things I remember.'[46] The prospect of dysentery also loomed large over the peninsula. The worse cases were sent to hospital in Egypt before they became delirious. Some of the more unfortunate soldiers died before they could be treated properly.

On 19 May the Turks took the initiative in an effort to force the Australians back to the beachhead. Four and a half Turkish divisions—almost 42,000 men—launched an attack, meeting fierce opposition from the 17,000 ANZACs facing them. Constant shelling from British warships anchored offshore ripped through wave after wave of advancing Turkish soldiers. Those lucky enough to escape the ships' firepower were cut down by ANZAC riflemen and machine-gunners. Private Ranford remembered the Turkish 'dead ... close around our section of the trenches ... were thick enough to satisfy the most martial, but further along on our right they were in thousands, acres and acres simply covered with them ... when they charged so bravely [they] were simply mowed down like hay before the mower.'[47]

In some places, however, Turkish infantry fought their way into trenches occupied by the 14th Battalion. Guppy wrote:

> Early this morning a strong party of Turks managed to force their way up close to a sector of our trench and with the aid of bombs killed and wounded every man in it and took possession of the sector. One of our boys, Sgt. Sadler though badly wounded, managed to get out and reported what had happened to Lieut. Hamilton who immediately called on some men around him to follow him in. At the entrance to the sector Hamilton was shot also the next man behind him, then L/Cpl. Jacka leaped over their bodies and got in among the Turks. He quickly shot three and bayoneted four more and cleared the sector.
>
> Eighteen Turkish rifles were this morning found in the trench. Jacka has been recommended for the VC. Our two Companies had a heavy loss 10 killed including Lieut Hamilton and 30 wounded including Lieuts Boyle and Smith ... The New

Zealanders and Light Horse on our left did well. They counter attacked and took some trenches, and when the Turks attempted this afternoon to retake them they were repulsed with very severe losses.[48]

William Howard recalled being wounded early in the attack. 'I got hit ... chasing the Turks out,' he wrote, 'I was dressed then I lay in a dugout ... [At night] I was then taken to the beach. Arrived at Malta on 24th May, [and] taken to Military Hospital Valetta.'[49] Enemy infantry made another three attempts to force the Australian line. All were in vain. At the end of the day, when the attack was finally called off, 10,000 Turkish soldiers lay dead or wounded. The ANZACs lost 160 men killed and another 468 wounded.[50]

On 29 May a depleted 4th Brigade was finally relieved and allowed some respite in Reserve Gully. The rest coincided with the closure of the campaign's first phase. That phase ended in tactical and strategic failure for the ANZACs, and both sides—for the moment at least—reassessed the pointlessness of attempting large-scale attacks against a well-entrenched enemy, protected by effective artillery and machine-gun fire.

New methods of attack were also being tested. Tunnelling, while highly dangerous to the miners themselves, was tried with some success by both Turks and ANZACs, and mines became a constant threat to infantry in their front-line trenches. By mid-June, fighting had become more akin to that on the Western Front. Patrols and raids—to ascertain the strength of the enemy and take prisoners—were now more common.

***

Turkish soldiers taken prisoner by the Australians usually suffered a far worse fate than ANZACs captured by the Turks. Given the lack of suitable areas for a POW cage, Turkish prisoners were occasionally shot rather than detained. By contrast, most of the almost seventy Australians taken prisoner were housed in POW camps—once they had endured the anguish of forced marches and uncomfortable railway journeys. Many suffered the effects of improper diet, disease and poor medical services and around twenty died while working as forced labour building railways in the Taurus Mountains. However, there was only one reported case of an officer dying. This was most likely due to the provisions of international law which specified that officers did not have to endure the same hardships, including performing manual work, as the men they commanded.

***

For ten weeks—from the end of May until mid-August—there were no large-scale attacks by either side. However, the conditions in which the troops had to live and fight gradually deteriorated and, by late July, the number of men lost through sickness rivalled the toll of casualties on the first day. Periodic landing of reinforcements could only slow the drain of troops which continued unrelentingly. Charles Devers was attached to one group (part of the 15th Battalion) which came ashore on 13 July:

> We landed in the middle of the night, there were about a hundred of us ... We went into Anzac Cove, and then onto Walker's Ridge. There were dugouts there, and we had to dig our own ... Don Buchanan and I ... had a rather good dugout because we stole some stuff from the other dugouts. There was nobody using them so we took enough boards to make a bed to lie on, with the old palliasses ... Every two or three days we would go down to the beach for a swim. We were in Rest Gully ... The Turks from right back could see us on the beach ... There'd be a splash of water here and there [from Turkish fire]. You used to run quicker than a bullet travelled.[51]

Jock Williamson (16th Battalion) also arrived in July, just as plans were being formulated for an attack on the heights of Sari Bair with the intention of capturing Hill 971 and pushing on to Chunuk Bair.

***

To try to break the impasse, Hamilton had decided to implement a plan which had been brewing since late May. Australian troops were given an almost suicidal task—an uphill attack from Anzac Cove—supported by a diversionary strike by the British at Helles, and another amphibious landing (by three fresh British divisions) further north at Suvla Bay.[52] Control of the heights would mean control of the peninsula.

While the Suvla landing was virtually unopposed, poorly led British soldiers moved inland far too slowly. 'Suvla Bay was the biggest shemozzle,' Charles Devers recalled, 'the British all went ashore. From where we were in the morning you could see smoke from camp fires everywhere. They bivouacked there for the night, instead of moving up the same as us. [If they had] things might have been altogether different.'[53] The Turks quickly moved reinforcements into the area and stalled the British attack. With the British unable to take the heights and offer the Australians any assistance, the attack on Lone Pine seemed destined to fail. Over the three days leading up to 6 August, ANZAC artillery constantly pounded Turkish strongpoints. At 4.30p.m. on 6 August, the gunfire escalated. One hour later, troops left their trenches and made a dash for the enemy line. But they were unable to beat the Turkish machine-gunners who returned to their posts within seconds of the lifting of the barrage. In an incredible feat of arms, by 6.00p.m.—and despite countless casualties on both sides—Lone Pine had been captured. The Turks, however, refused to yield, and made the first of numerous counter-attacks. From dusk on 6 August, wrote Bean, 'until the night of the 9th the bomb fight went on almost continuously, flaring up four times into many hours of desperate fighting when successive Turkish reinforcements were thrown in.'[54]

Left: George Jamieson on the right, with his close friend from Gympie, Leo Thomas. George and Leo attempted to enlist together in August 1914, but Leo Thomas was refused because he was too 'hairy.' Leo later joined the 49th Battalion, and met George Jamieson again in Egypt. Right: George Jamieson, 1985.

The 4th Brigade did not join the fight until the night of 6/7 August. The task of assaulting Hill 971—the highest point on the Sari Bair Range—was allocated to Monash's brigade, assisted by some elite Gurkhas from the 29th Indian Brigade. The day before, noted Guppy, 'General Monash told us something of what our next job is going to be ... The boys are all in great spirits in the expectation of another move after the inactivity of the last weeks. It is strange the feeling that possesses men on the eve of an action.' John Doggett recalled that the '15th

Battalion['s] role was to march out along the ANZAC coast in the night.. We got to the outposts and then turned in to the right and go up through the bush with the object of capturing [Hill] 971. Needless to say, they all got bushed kilos away from the top of 971.'[55]

The 16th Battalion also moved off in darkness towards the tangle of hills and ravines that was the Sari Bair Range. In the difficult terrain and the enshrouding gloom, the men of the 16th entered the wrong valley. By dawn, the troops were confronted by gullies, deep narrow gorges and precipices that made further progress almost impossible. Lethal fire from well-positioned enemy machine-guns and riflemen further hampered their efforts. Panic and confusion led to many casualties. According to Guppy, the early part of the climb

> was entirely successful. Our Brigade (The Northern attacking column) moved from Reserve Gully at 9pm and made its way along the beach to the extreme left of our lines ... We struck out in a Northerly direction for a time and then turned inland, forcing our way over the ridges and valley by the aid of map and compass. No man was allowed to load a rifle and all work had to be done as silently as possible, only bayonet and rifle butt being used. A

regiment of Ghurkas, a Tommy Brigade and some New Zealanders were on our right ... By dawn we had forced our way about a mile and a half inland, and reached our appointed position, where we at once commenced to dig in. The Turks evidently did not know what to make of our silent advance, and did not stop long to resist us on the various positions. We did not have a great number of casualties. The troops on our right met with more opposition but succeeded in gaining their objectives.

The Australians worked 'all day digging and consolidating our position, sustaining many casualties in so doing, and tonight are nearly worn out, but still work must go on.' Guppy added, 'at 3am we were relieved on our position by a Regiment of Kings Own.' A couple of hours later, at daybreak, the survivors

started an attack on a ridge about a mile in front of our position. We succeeded ... but suffered very heavy casualties from rifle, machine gun and shrapnel fire. At about noon we were told that we should have to retire to our original position ... because the English troops that were to fight their way up on our left [from Suvla Bay] had failed to do so, thereby leaving our left flank exposed. Parties of men were detailed to take back all wounded and then some more of us had to remain and fight a rearguard action. We slowly withdrew and reached our late line a sad and sorry few. A little later in the day we had a roll call and found that from our three Battalions there were over 1000 men killed and missing for the day. Only one of my Company officers remain. Tonight we are allowed to have a well earned rest, being almost too tired to walk. The Tommies on our right, succeeded today, in reaching the crest of the highest ridge and looked down on the waters of the Straits, only to be forced off again a few minutes later.[56]

William Fitzpatrick (14th Battalion) commented that the battalion was 'short of men. And the 6th Reinforcements reinforced them ... there were over 100 killed in the 14th in that attack [on Hill 971]. And most of them were the 6th Reinforcements, all with their new uniforms on ... It was awful.'[57] Despite the ever-increasing casualty bill, the 4th Brigade was not finally relieved until around midday on 11 August. Subsequent Turkish counter-attacks forced the Australians from the few points on the heights they had won. Hamilton recognised that any further attempt would be too costly and would most likely result in similar failure. For the remainder of the campaign, enemy troops and artillery would continue to hold the heights around ANZAC.

One of only 98 of its kind, this medallion showing the shoulder patch colours of the 9th Battalion was presented – and worn proudly – to George Jamieson for serving continuously on the Gallipoli Peninsula from 25 April to 25 October 1915.

Memorabilia belonging to George Jamieson, photographed by David Chalk. Shown are his lieutenant 'pips,' 'rising sun' badges, the 'Australia' badge worn on the epaulettes, his whistle and lanyard and the crossed machine-gun badge of the 3rd M.G. Company. The lanyard is still stained with blood from Jamieson's wound at Passchendaele. The trench map shows a section of trenches held by the Australians near Ploegsteert Wood in Flanders in May 1917.

In the aftermath of Lone Pine, an air of gloom settled on the Australians along the Gallipoli peninsula. The atmosphere of jocularity and optimism had been supplanted by despondent realism. Gone was any chance of a rapid and illustrious victory. Gone, too, were the profound delusions of military glory. Instead the men had now become acquainted with the hideousness of the modern technological battlefield. They had also become more aware of the callous disregard for Australian lives that appeared to characterise their unconcerned and egocentric officers, perhaps best illustrated by the infamous attack at The Nek. While the 4th Brigade was not directly involved, news quickly spread throughout the three battalions.[58]

In the early morning of 7 August, Brigadier General Hughes's 3rd Australian Light Horse Brigade, fighting as infantry, assaulted enemy lines 'not a stone's throw away.'[59] While the precise reasons for the attack remain unclear, the assault was probably designed as nothing more than a feint for the main operation against Chunuk Bair by the New Zealand Division. The New Zealanders, however, took heavy casualties and their attack faltered. Magnifying the setback, the Australian preliminary artillery bombardment inexplicably ended seven minutes before the troops were to leave their trenches. Despite this, the attack was ordered to proceed by an Australian staff officer, Colonel J.M. Antill. In the resultant slaughter, 234 'dead light horsemen lay in an area a little larger than a tennis court.'[60] For the ANZACs on Gallipoli, Lone Pine and The Nek symbolised the heartlessness of senior officers—both British and Australian. While for some (notably contemporary politicians), the struggles have become 'epics in Australian military history and will always be remembered with pride', for those who survived the slaughter, the attacks were ill-conceived and unwarranted.[61]

From mid-August the ANZACs and Turks spent much of their time strengthening their trenches. By now, medicines and food were in short supply and, as Gammage writes, the poor condition of the troops 'was a certain indication of shaken morale.'[62] Elsewhere, the disastrous offensive had greater repercussions. In London, the Dardanelles Committee began considering the evacuation of the entire peninsula. In Australia, the persuasive journalist, Keith Murdoch, described the exposed Australian position at ANZAC to the Prime Minister, adding that 'our holdings are so small and narrow that we cannot hide from the Turks the positions of our guns and repeatedly damage [from enemy artillery] is done to them.' Advocating the evacuation of the Australian troops, Murdoch also told the Prime Minister that the poorly performing Hamilton should be sacked.[63] On 14 October, Hamilton was duly replaced by General Charles Monro. Two weeks later, Monro arrived on the peninsula to assume command. After three days of consultations, he sent a memo to the British government recommending the withdrawal of all troops, to be effected as soon as practicable. On 4 November, Birdwood was ordered to draft plans for the ANZACs' departure.[64]

***

In mid-August, the 4th Australian Brigade was ordered to prepare for another mission of questionable tactical worth—an attack on Hill 60. On 20 August, Monash was issued final orders for an assault by 250 men from the 13th and 14th Battalions, to be launched the following day. The 15th Battalion was to act as a covering force, and attack only after other troops had passed through enemy lines. However, 'the state of the brigade did not augur well for success'—for the 14th Battalion, in particular, finding 250 'fit' men proved almost impossible, while the 13th was operating only 'by sheer force of will.' Monash's poor planning led to imprecise artillery and machine-gun 'covering fire' on Turkish positions, coupled with confusion in the 'issue of orders at lower level' which resulted in heavy casualties. Monash subsequently laid the blame squarely on inadequate artillery cooperation and a last-minute change of orders. More significantly, he also acknowledged that 'commanders were still learning the methods of trench warfare and making the same mistakes as their contemporaries on the Western Front.'[65] Bean, however, blamed the failure solely on Monash, writing: '[He] certainly knows less of the situation than any other Brigadier I have seen.'[66] Guppy was temporarily attached to the headquarters staff of the 163rd British Brigade, and commented that 'we could see the attack by the aid of field glasses. It was on Hill 60 and Chocolate Hills. Just where the English troops and Aussies join.'[67] But it was Percy Toft who, possibly best of all, summed up the mood of pessimism: '[the Turks] had defended strongly and were determined their flank would not be turned. Our great chance had gone.'[68]

On 25 August—a mere two days later—plans were made for yet another assault on Hill 60. Despite the condition of the 4th Brigade—described as 'deplorable' (its complement now under 1,450)—Monash's request for a reduction in his attack front fell on deaf ears. Ignoring the earlier setback, he persisted with similar plans. The 13th and 14th Battalions would each provide

100 men, while another fifty were to be provided by the 15th. Again, an ineffective preparatory artillery barrage slowed down the troops, who were caught in an intensive crossfire, described by Lieutenant A.N. Brierley 'as if bracing oneself against a strong headwind.' Of the 300 men who crossed no man's land, only 100 were not listed as casualties.[69] While Monash must again share at least partial responsibility, he once more attempted to divert the blame elsewhere: 'The whole was a rotten, badly organised show,' he wrote, 'and those who planned it are responsible for heavy loss to this brigade.'[70]

Postcard of Cairo and the Pyramids, Egypt. Australian soldiers had different opinions of Cairo, yet a good few were delighted to send this and similar postcards, depicting Egyptian scenes, to their loved ones back in Australia.

After the setback, smaller engagements continued almost daily. In October and November, fighting on the Gallipoli peninsula could best be described as static warfare. The weather had also turned nasty. On 29 November, Private A.A. Fletcher (14th Battalion) wrote, 'our first snow storm ... had just started ... but we could easily have done without it.'[71] Alec Campbell (who arrived with the 8th Reinforcements in October) remembered that

> there was always ... constant rifle fire on Gallipoli. Always. Day and night there was a fire kept up ... Then back in Hay Gully ... was a pretty safe place to be... there wasn't very much doing. You were sneaking around in the bushes, being sent out on patrol work at night. There were no heavy casualties—a few people were hit in Hay Gully. In the Turk's artillery they had a battery of like French 75s ... whizzbangs. They used to come over the valley, and that was terrifying. But there was no bayonet charge or anything like that. Your worst enemies were the flies and the lice, and then the blizzards came.
>
> I got darned cold, and the saps were half filled with snow ... You still had to bring ... the only water supply ... from the beach. They used to land it and put it in a

great steel tank on the beach. We'd have water fatigues carrying the water up. You were always likely to get hit doing that because there were still a few Turkish snipers around who would have pot shots at you; or, if there were not snipers, there was always a constant rifle fire there.

There was always a chance, until you got back ... And then [came]the evacuation ... none of us really wanted to leave, strange to say. We always felt we'd be leaving a job unfinished.[72]

Others felt that, by leaving, they were dishonouring the memory of mates left behind. 'It was a sad day for us,' recalled Private A.L. Smith,

when the order for the evacuation was issued. Every man ... has someone whom he honoured and respected, lying in one of those graves at ANZAC, the thought of having to leave these sacred spots to the mercy of the enemy made the spirit of the men revolt and cry out in anguish at the thought of it. It has even been said that some of the men broke down and cried ... when they heard the order ... It drives me almost to despair.[73]

Another soldier, gesturing towards the cemetery where his friends lay buried, remarked to Birdwood, 'I hope they won't hear us marching down the deres.'[74]

Whatever the men's feelings, evacuation commenced in mid-December. On the 15th, Guppy noted:

> Still steady and certain preparations for what appears like a complete evacuation are being made. We have been for some days living on our reserve stores and we hear that they are now nearly used up. All reserve men have been withdrawn and embarked and the line considerably weakened. Everything we are told depends on absolute secrecy, and demonstrations are being made frequently to divert suspicion and make Jacko [enemy troops] think we intend to shortly make a big attack. A very heavy bombardment has been going on, night and day at Atchi Baba and Cape Helles. It is just a continuous roar, and even at this distance the earth trembles with the violence of the explosions. Our ordinance on the beach has been thrown open and men are allowed to go and take what they require in the way of clothing. Stacks of spare rifles, picks, shovels etc are being smashed up and cast into the sea. Stacks of foodstuffs and mule fodder are being got ready for burning at the last moment.[75]

By 20 December 1915, the withdrawal had been effectively completed. Brudenell White, as chief planner, deserves most of the accolades for what has been described as 'the best-executed operation of the campaign ... a masterpiece of planning.' However, the eight months on Gallipoli had left 8,141 Australians and 2,431 New Zealanders dead.

On Gallipoli, the 4th Australian Brigade had acquired a degree of fame as one of the finest led brigades in the AIF. Despite his questionable tactics at Hill 60, Monash had proven himself an accomplished brigade commander. Others, including Albert Jacka (who was awarded the AIF's first Victoria Cross), Harry Murray and Percy Black, had all made a name for themselves as company commanders. All three, through their initiative and courage, had risen from the ranks. Indeed, the 14th Battalion went on to acquire the sobriquet 'Jacka's Mob'. Most of the 4th Brigade's survivors were satisfied that now, at last, they would have the opportunity to fight the real enemy—the Hun—'for he had caused the war.'[76]

***

Before the evacuation was complete, a decision had been made to send the AIF back to Egypt for retraining, and to absorb reinforcements to rebuild the severely depleted battalions. The British government also considered that Australian troops would be required to defend Egypt from a probable Turkish invasion. Some troops, however, simply returned to Mudros where Percy Toft recalled spending a week doing 'practically nothing' except having 'the tents erected for the [rest of] the battalion in time.'[77] Keith Tamblyn commented that 'the men had a good time being fed on beer and stout and all the best goodies that the Army did not get regularly.'[78]

Most Australians went directly to Egypt, while those on Mudros commenced their embarkation on 23 December, bound for Alexandria. Toft reflected, 'We sailed through the beautiful islands disillusioned men.' Troops remaining behind had a 'strange' Christmas Day. Soon afterwards they received orders to be 'ready packed up for moving.'[79] By the end of the month, all the remnants of the 4th Brigade were in Egypt, based at Tel-el-Kebir. Tamblyn remembered that base fondly, 'She was some camp-and-a-half, a good gambling school.'

Arriving at Alexandria on 26 December, Percy Toft took time to reflect on the eight-month campaign. He noted: 'We now knew that men's lives were held cheaply, that war was not a glorious thing but a mad business. About

2000 men had so far been enrolled in our unit, and probably 1500 actually reached the front, of whom eleven hundred were casualties.' He added, however, that 'in Egypt we found an accumulation of reinforcements,' due to another rush to enlist in the AIF during the early part of 'Gallipoli, and the sudden, first, terrible casualty lists.'[80] Among those who arrived at the end of January 1916 was Private Ernest Chalk, a farmer from Burnie in Tasmania.

Chalk's enlistment, in mid-1915, followed the usual pattern of the time. As Australians began to realise that the war was going to last longer than anticipated and would cost the lives of many more men, Chalk was among the many thousands who visited recruiting centres in provincial towns such as Burnie:

> The whole of the country was galvanised in mid-1915 with the Gallipoli campaign. The recruiting drive at that time was by far the most successful of the war ... Ernie Chalk wakes up. It is nearly four o'clock in the morning. It is raining again ... Today he is going to Hobart to enlist. It is Monday. The Hobart train leaves Burnie Station at seven o'clock, three hours from now. He has to catch that train. It all happened so quickly. This time last week his thoughts were of the farm, of the winter

repairs with the machinery in the barn, of the cropping and harvesting program, of potato prices in Sydney. The war was something the family had discussed and read about in *The North West Advocate and Emu Bay Times,* but not something they felt involved them. They read about the landing in Gallipoli, they talked about it at night, and in the last few weeks the meaning of it all had started to come home. None of the Burnie boys had been lost yet, but there were casualties.

Then last Friday his father, George Chalk, had come home from the Council meeting saying something like, 'Major ... was with us today, and everybody is needed. Ernie has to go. There's a big recruiting drive. Ernie has to go down to Hobart and into camp.'

He was English, George Chalk, and although he had been in Australia for twenty-seven years, and was a settled family man with five children, the Hampshire countryside was home. There was clearly a need for Ernie to join up, and as a Councillor, his family had to set an example. So Ernie found himself committed, with little more than a weekend to organise himself.

It had all happened so quickly. So it was that simple. He was needed, that's why he was going. But it was a surprise all the same.

'The Call of Empire' epitomised not only Chalk's desire to enlist, but became the theme of a successful recruiting campaign in Tasmania. The local *North-Western Advocate and Emu Bay Times* newspaper reported that, in mid-1915, a number of civic leaders and politicians toured the state, 'holding campaign meetings in most towns'. On 27 July, the group reached Burnie 'with scenes of intense enthusiasm'. The half-page article described the scene in which 'the Burnie Band ... rendered stirring patriotic music prior to the speeches and the vast assemblage was warmed to a pitch of high enthusiasm.' Then it was the turn of the 'Rev Father O'Donnell' who

> urged young men to be done with cricket and football and show they were soldiers. J.T.H. Whitsitt, MHA, appealed to womanhood to make manhood go to the front. The motto should be, 'March on, ye brave to liberty and death.' What did it matter if the blood flowed away on the battlefield? It was the blood of worthy sons of worthy sires!
>
> (Applause).

At the conclusion of the meeting 'amidst scenes of great enthusiasm, 25 volunteers mounted the platform.' Burnie councillor George Chalk returned to his home and told his son Ernest that he should enlist immediately.[81]

Edward Pinnell, a letter carrier from Perth in Western Australia, enlisted a few months later—not long after the evacuation from Gallipoli. Pinnell's reason was unsophisticated. He simply felt that it was his duty. 'I reckoned I should, I suppose. I didn't have to,' he said, 'I thought as soon as I'm twenty-one I'll enlist. And that didn't put any obligation on my mother and father. Otherwise I'd had to have got their permission to.' Still, there were strict guidelines for recruits. 'I had two goes before I enlisted.' Pinnell, a small man, added, 'the first time they knocked me back. I couldn't quite do the expansion of the chest.' But the AIF needed more men for the new divisions being assembled in Egypt. 'The chest [expansion] ... they wiped that off, after a while,' Pinnell remembered, 'we all went in [to camp] within a day or two of passing the medical.' He recalled training at Blackboy Hill: 'Up in the morning, and I think we used to have physical training before we had breakfast. Of course, we'd have the procedure of having our wash and getting warmed up for the day's drill,' including a route march 'right from Blackboy Hill to Subiaco.'[82]

In early 1916, with the huge casualty bill from Gallipoli and a reduction in the number of recruits, the AIF's stringent medical conditions were relaxed. Len Pooley was 'only sixteen' in 1914, but still wanted to enlist. 'Mum wouldn't let me go,' he recalled, 'she said I was too young. They told me to go home when I went into Perth to enlist.' But, in April 1916, Pooley

> went down to Fremantle to enlist ... and mum came down with me. It was at the drill hall in Fremantle, and mum said, "Well, I'll wait out here while you go in and get tested." And I went through without any problem. They didn't ask to see mum at all, so when I came out she said, "Well, where do I come in?" And I said, "You don't, I'm in!" She was a bit worried anyway ... I don't think she liked it, all the same.[83]

***

By the time Ernie Chalk arrived in Egypt as part of the 10th Reinforcements for the 15th Battalion, the training regime followed guidelines prepared mostly by Brudenell White. Monash had made a few changes for the 4th Brigade, with 'musketry, bayonet fighting and marching with gradually heavier loads,' playing a major part. His own preference for signals training 'was stressed'. Perhaps, more significantly, 'every sub-unit was to be instructed by its commander, thus developing teamwork and mutual confidence.' In brigade exercises, Monash 'simulated as closely as possible the physical demands of operations by ensuring that his men wore field marching order and carried all their equipment, including machine-guns and ammunition packs.'[84] All battalions—especially those in the two new divisions being assembled from the raw recruits constantly arriving from Australia—were deliberately designed to comprise a mix: half veterans from the Gallipoli campaign, and half untried troops.

Left: Ernest Chalk c1916. Right: Ernest Chalk c1948.

Another new arrival, Lance Corporal Percy Mansfield (13th Reinforcements, 7th Battalion, 2nd Australian Infantry Brigade), was excited to finally arrive in Egypt on 30 January 1916. In his letters to his family, Percy described the countryside, the history of old Cairo, and his camp which, he added,

> is almost in Heliopolis and about four miles from Cairo ... Yes we are in a bonza camp as far as soldiering is concerned but we are a long way from home. Don't think I am home sick but we have been away from home over six weeks now and [I] have not heard a word at all, but I know you are all well. I have never felt better in all my life and we are getting grand food ... The work is pretty tough but we are fit enough now ... We left Suez about 2.30pm on the 31-1-1916 and detrained at Zeitoun at 9pm and marched to our camp ... The [railway] line followed the canal pretty well the whole way ... there were many small farms and I can tell you everything was lovely and green. The natives irrigate them from springs. Each farmer has about a dozen sheep, a couple of cows, a donkey to do the farm work and a camel to cart their produce with. It was really like a lovely big garden, while on the other side of the line there was nothing but a sea of sand as far as the eye could see with not a shrub to be seen The native houses are built with four mud walls about three feet high and

about three or four feet of earth taken out from inside the walls so that the floor is really a few feet below the surface. This is done for coolness ... Heliopolis is a most beautiful city and far cleaner than Cairo ... We went to Cairo one night last week and had a walk round but its dirty people sickened me ... Old Cairo itself is nothing more than a mass of crumbled buildings, but there are still some buildings left which are over 1,300 years old. The first place we visited was a tomb of some great man [Amru] ... One of its pillars is supposed to have come from Mecca...

We are very lucky. A new brigade is being formed and I am certain that we are to form part of it. We will be sent to France in a month or two that will do me alright. Fancy having the honour of being the first Australian troops to land in France. What a reception we will get ... We are having a great time and all are well.[85]

Will Peach's thoughts on Cairo echoed those of Percy Mansfield. Young Will was particularly fascinated by

Aeroplanes [which] are very common things with us already. We don't take much notice of them when we see them flying about. Our hours for drill here are longer than we have been used to, but of course we must expect that. We drill from 7am to 9am, 10am to 12.30 noon; 2pm to 4.30pm. When we arrived here we were under the impression that we would be in the firing line in a week or a fortnight, but I'm afraid now we will be a couple of months before we get there.

Peach added that 'the natives here are very funny. Everywhere one goes he finds a half a dozen wanting to clean his boots or sell him something or other. We carry a good strong walking stick with us to keep them off. They have a great opinion of the Australian boys, I don't think they care too much for the English tommies.'[86]

Three Australian 'tourists under the Sphinx,' Egypt, c 1916.

Donald Fraser recalled his time spent in Cairo, particularly the 'Gyppos down praying ... to Allah, looking towards Mecca, or supposed to be.' The pyramids also seemed to attract many young Australians. The Great Pyramid, revealed Fraser, 'covers thirteen acres at ground level ... And it's also a clock as well. A sundial ... It is a marvellous thing, and ... I think it was just about 4,000 [sic] years BC. It's a long time ago ... [and] there's the other one laying alongside it, Rameses II. And then there's a little one, I don't know who he is. There is also the Sphinx there too. It's a big lion with a man's head on it. Napoleon shot the nose off him.'[87] Not all of the men were interested in historical sights. A large number wanted nothing more than to visit the brothels of Cairo. Robert Henry's recollections focused on their bawdy behaviour. 'I got into Cairo once,' he remembered, 'a lot of the troops got into trouble in Cairo. They got into the brothels there, and a lot of them got VD.'[88] Henry also described the Australians' lack of regard for the local Egyptians: 'We didn't have much to do with them, they would walk in selling oranges and so forth, which we weren't supposed to buy. We were on a train one time, and the fellows bought the oranges off them, and the officers came along and made them throw them [oranges] away. I suppose they thought there might have been some disease on them.'[89] Roy Kyle commented that, 'as a rule, the Australian troops did not like Arabs.'[90]

***

More intensive exercises were conducted throughout February and into early March. Manoeuvres involving attacks and counter-attacks against an imaginary enemy occupied a great deal of the men's time. According to John Doggett, the 15th Battalion 'had one field day at Serapeum ... The attacking party went out into the desert, and then turned back towards the [Suez] Canal and pretended they were attacking the Canal.' Soon afterwards, all the troops 'had to [be] fully equipped and just so, ready for the order to go to France.'[91] But the order never came. Instead, the 14th Brigade resumed their training on the finer points of trench warfare. Reinforcements from Australia continued to arrive, resulting in more men being transferred from the 15th Battalion to form a new unit, the 47th Battalion.

Further restructuring and expansion continued. While valuable experience was spread more consistently throughout the AIF, the restructure also drained existing battalions of their best officers and NCOs. The reorganised 4th Brigade finally left the New Zealand and Australian Division on 1/2 March and, along with the 12th and 13th Brigades, formed the 4th Australian Division under the command of an Indian army officer, Major General Vaughan Cox. But not all proceeded smoothly. Transfers were never popular; the 14th Battalion was reportedly 'a seething mass of discontent for a few days,' while, in the 15th, some officers and NCOs, when told they were being transferred to the 47th, at first 'refused to leave.'

"C" Company Football Team, Egypt, c 1916. Sporting competitions were important in each Australian battalion, helping build up morale as well as giving the troops an interest.

Percy Toft (a senior acting NCO himself) remarked that, not long afterwards, other senior acting NCOs discovered that there were insufficient places in the 15th, and the

> old hands disgustedly learnt that a class of instruction was to be held over a period of three weeks, and then a competitive examination would be held for all vacant positions. Some had permanent appointments and the examination would not concern us, but I thought I was in honour bound to take the part of the acting non-commissioned officers. They had proved themselves in war which is the real test for

leadership. They had no chance in competition with the reinforcements who had attended schools of instruction, and were almost word perfect in drill movements and arms drill.

The Gallipoli NCOs in our company sent in their resignations, and asked to be reverted to the ranks. I was considered ringleader, and my commission was cancelled. The permanent NCOs resignations were not accepted. A soldier has no right to take direct action, and therein we were in the wrong. The course of instruction was abandoned, and many sighs of relief were heaved. Few of our acting NCOs [from the Gallipoli campaign] received appointments. All of the reinforcement NCOs received permanent appointments.[92]

Still, as Grey argues, the AIF's growth produced new chances for promotion. COs, with the Gallipoli experience behind them, were elevated to lead brigades. Company commanders—some in their early twenties—were appointed to command battalions. Likewise, junior officers and NCOs were promoted to more senior positions. New divisional commanders were also required.[93]

***

An expected attack from the Turks—who were reported to be massing at Beersheba (about 200 kilometres away) in late March—saw the brigade forced to march sixty-five kilometres through sand and endure the relentless desert heat until they reached the Suez Canal. Frank Lawrie remembered the march well:

> The ... battalion did the forced march across the desert from Tel-el-Kebir to Serapeum. I'd only just come out of the hospital. I had otitis in the right ear. The first day I thought well, I'll manage it. I did the first day alright. The next morning we were getting ready to move off again when they found out everyone was out of water ... Someone was going to have to get water. There were eight camels attached to the Battalion, but no handlers. The Indian handlers had not turned up. So they came round and called for volunteers, anyone experienced with camels, to ride into Moascar with the water bottles. I was the first to put my hand up, and when they said, 'What experience have you had?' I said, 'The Murchison Goldfields.' That was OK. That carried. But I didn't know how to handle a camel from a mountain goat, although I had been watching the different Egyptian handlers ... I didn't know what to

do, so I just let him [the camel] go, let him have his head. He seemed to know where the water tanks were. It was about 114 degrees in the shade, and ... we got to Moascar about one o'clock in the afternoon. There was an English colonel and an English major there with four Egyptian off-siders ... I got the camel down, and as fast as the Egyptians carried the bottles to the tanks, the officers filled them. We just sat and watched them. It only took a quarter of an hour ... It was just getting on dusk when we run into the battalion. I could see the mob coming over the sand hill, with their tongues hanging out a foot long. They spotted the camels coming, and they made one bloody beeline rush for me. I was about a quarter of a mile in front of the other camels, and I was worried the camels might scatter and get lost.

After we got back with the water, everybody sat down and had a half hour rest. Then we got orders to move off ... But we only got about five miles, I suppose, when men started falling out, and they tied all the bloody packs and rifles onto each camel. You couldn't see me for packs and rifles! I was sitting on this hard saddle on top of these big rope nets, and when I got into Serapeum my backside was red raw.[94]

***

The stifling heat at Serapeum, compounded by biting insects 'and the barrenness of the desert', led to widespread disillusionment, and even Monash experienced bouts of depression.[95] By mid-April the men were becoming tired of the daily grind of kit inspections and digging trenches in the sand—which usually collapsed—as well as tedious and tiring route marches. Further training involved mock battles, field operations and musketry practice. There were endless incursions into the Sinai Desert where more trenches were dug—usually with the same result. Roy Kyle noted that the troops quickly learned to place 'trusses made of bamboo and plaited rushes, trussed them top and bottom, and shovelled back the sand we had dug out. Then we lined the top with sandbags and fixed other trusses on top with openings to fire through at intervals, shovelled more sand on that as camouflage, and had very good trenches.' Foot patrols into the desert were loathed. Five men, usually in diamond formation with an NCO leading from the centre, would leave the Australian line before dawn. The patrol was expected to cover around eight kilometres and return not long after first light. While Turkish soldiers were seldom encountered, Kyle recounted that the 'going was slow, except in the early stages where the sand was damp with the nightly heavy dew. Once the sun's rays appeared over the horizon, it would only take a short time for the sand to dry out, after which we'd sink ankle-deep with every step. The never ending lines of sand dunes made things more difficult.'[96]

Australian soldiers resting during a break in their desert training near Cairo, Egypt, c 1916.

Percy Toft recalled that 'we soon got to hate the grind of peace soldiering and longingly looked forward to the time when we could obtain a break, even if it meant going to fight.

The monotony of futile work made us feel desperate.' Somewhat ironically, he added that they all

> loved the Suez Canal. Often twice a day we could swim if we desired ... After Gallipoli it was a God-send ... When the swim was over there was the inevitable search through the clothes for lice ... Of course there was a canteen, but the men were soberly inclined ... The canteen was not opened on the Sabbath ... There were letters to write and time must be found for one swim at least ... Some men preferred to engage in another pleasure. Should one take a stroll through the lines on a Sunday afternoon, very few would be found in camp, but ... the mess huts ... contain[ed] many men. The fact that men gambled was known to the 'Heads' but unless 'two up' or some form of gambling was played too conspicuously, it was never noticed ... Officers played bridge for cash, and it was decided to allow the men to play Nap, to give them an outlet.
>
> It was considered the easiest and fairest game to play for money.

Most officers turned a blind eye to the gambling, allowing it to proceed. One over-zealous officer, however, took time to look into a mess hut, discovering

> large numbers of men gambling. 'What are you men doing?' he cried. 'Stand to attention everybody. Stand clear of the tables.' With his orderly corporal he went along each table, and picking up the money said: 'This is cash forfeited to regimental funds. Dismiss!' ... The company commander, Captain Johnson ... explained that orders permitted the game ... Never again, to my knowledge, was gambling interfered with.[97]

Robert Henry added, 'there was a lot of gambling after payday. One would get broke, and the odd ones would make a lot of money. It was dangerous to have a lot of money. You might get donged on the head by somebody.'[98]

The men found the daily routine of 'physical jerks' before breakfast, morning parades and afternoon exercises as well as nightly route marches, becoming increasingly tedious. There were also a number of unfortunate accidents. Henry related an incident that occurred as rifles were being examined and 'a fellow was shot right through the eye ... He was on the ground ... looking straight down the sights. He was killed instantly. It was an accident.' Henry himself was not the average soldier. The son of a farmer from Doolarra in Victoria, he was proud of his 'good Christian upbringing, and I kept to those principles ... while I was in the army.' He never 'joined in any gambling games ... never smoked nor drank.' Nor did he ever visit the brothels of Cairo.[99]

***

A break in the routine came not long afterwards. On Easter Sunday (23 April) 1916, Ernie Chalk wrote to his mother in Burnie, telling her that:

> This morning at seven o'clock we had a compulsory service, and then I attended a communion service at eleven. I will also be going to a service in the YMCA hut this evening if I am not called out for picquet, so you will guess I have had quite a happy day. They have a book printed on the work of the Australians on Gallipoli here now ... They are having a great day here on the 25th Anzac Day, to commemorate the landing on Gallipoli. We are having Divine Service at six o'clock, and then a whole holiday. They are having aquatic sports and they promise to be a great success.[100]

On 25 April, all the men were awake early. At 5.00a.m. the military band marched 'around the camp and [their] playing aroused the camp.' Proudly wearing their decorations received the previous day, those men who had taken part in the Gallipoli campaign attended mass 'given in commemoration of our fallen comrades, and to commemorate the landing at Anzac.' 'I wore a red and a blue ribbon,' Tom Carroll recalled proudly, 'those who had no ribbons was not an Anzac, those who wore a red ribbon landed the first week after the 25th, those who wore a blue ribbon was fighting at Anzac.' Young Tom was also interested in the many water activities on the canal:

> During all this last week a few soldiers had been busy making crafts for the carnival. Some of them made canoes, some rafts, some battle ships, and others house boats ... We seen a grand sight when we got down to the place where the carnival was to take place. Sitting on the banks of the canal and on a high embankment a little further back, were thousands of soldiers ... Anchored close to the opposite bank was a minesweeper, and she was decorated up with so many flags. She had been brought there for the purpose of taking the bands on board, so that they could play some music while the sports were going on. On our side of the canal, a high stage had been built. It stood about 20 feet high. This was built for the high diving competition.

The next item of interest was a Steam launch coming up the canal. All eyes were turned on to it. There was a lady on board her, and when the soldiers seen her they yelled out—'Smother Up!' This is a warning to those who are naked to put their clothes on, or hide until it passed. There was a scatter everywhere for their clothes. Instead of the launch passing it stopped near the minesweeper, and it stayed there all the afternoon ... [A] gun boat was coming full speed down the canal. She pull[ed] up near the minesweeper, and as she was stopping, the band started to play 'God Save the King.' The Prince of Wales was on board. He came down to see the carnival.

Also present was Bill Bradnock, now a corporal, who apparently knew why the occasion had royal patronage:

The Prince of Wales was stationed on the Suez Canal at a place called Zeitoun. I think the house he was in had been built especially for the foremen of the construction workers when the canal was being built. It was a well guarded position and from his house the Prince could get an eyeful of the Suez towards Port Said, and back again to Alexandria way. He used to come out from his digs there dressed in almost white coloured trousers with top boots, and the red band of Headquarters around his cap...

I used to go for a swim in there every morning. I'd swim across the canal and come up to the bank. It was out of bounds to troops, or out of bounds to anybody really. You daren't go any further. And I'd see the poor beggar there morning after morning, thoroughly fed up with himself. I used to feel sorry for him. He was a bit of a gay spark, that was the trouble, I suppose.[101]

Robert Henry was ecstatic when he glimpsed the future king. He recalled that 'several thousand troops ... lined up, and I remember him coming up on horseback. They cantered up. You could see him shaking hands with the officers.'[102]

The 1st and 2nd Australian Divisions—the 4th Division had taken over their sector of the front at Suez—now began moving to Alexandria. When their troopships left Egypt bound for the Western Front, the men of the 4th Brigade knew that their turn would come soon enough. On 4 April, Charles Devers informed his sister, Chrissie, in Australia, that 'we will be leaving Egypt in a month's time for England, I think.'[103] While Devers was right about the time, he was wrong about the destination—he was bound for the Western Front. William Barry noted that, when the men

> were ordered on parade and our Lieutenant-Colonel came and addressed us and said that we were ready to leave Egypt and embark for France. Up went a cheer. 'But,' he continued, 'Owing to certain information, it is better to remain in Egypt a little longer, or else we would be floating in the Mediterranean a corpse. It turned out afterwards that a wireless plant had been found in one of the leading hotels at Cairo and had been in communication with the enemy's submarines and when the Lieu-Col had finished, the boys gave a groan of disgust for we were all fed up with the heat, sand and flies of Egypt. Any rate, our officer told us that we would put in our time by resting and would not do very much drill as the men were badly in want of a rest.[104]

The entire 4th Australian Division went back into camp at Tel el Kebir.

***

In late May, the division finally received orders to prepare for a move and, on 1 June, the convoy left Alexandria. Keith Tamblyn recalled that the troopships were 'sent across to France in convoy. The whole Division went, including artillery and everything that went with it. There was quite a fleet of us and we were under escort of British Destroyers all the way across and never ran into any submarines or anything like that.' On 7 June the men began arriving in Marseilles where, according to Tamblyn, 'there were not enough trains. The French had run out of trains, so we had to stay at Marseilles overnight which we did and caught trains next day.'[105]

'To be in a European country again,' Percy Toft recalled, 'and away from Asiatics, was splendid.' He added that the 'short stay' in Marseilles

> showed us that the French were really foreigners. In all ways, type, and otherwise, they were different from us—whether better class, officers, soldiers or peasants. Their speech and gestures interested us, and we antipodeans realised for the first time how much races of people differ from one another. We regarded them favourably, for were they not our Allies ... It was a delight to see and speak to Europeans again after our long isolation from civilisation. The children and the young women were beautiful ... From Paris we journeyed through Amiens [to] Hazebrouck, ... [where

we] detrained at midnight on 10th June, happy with the recollections of the beautiful females.[106]

From the railway junction of Hazebrouck the troops marched along main roads fringed by trees, hearing birds singing, until they reached muddy tracks that would take them to their billets, about twenty kilometres behind the front. The singing of birds was now replaced by the sporadic sound of artillery fire.

***

While the men of the 4th Brigade were eager to reach the front, they were still hopelessly undertrained in the intricacies of trench warfare. Even the veterans of Gallipoli were to discover that their experience provided little preparation for what awaited in France and Flanders. While Gallipoli was anything but a picnic, life in the trenches on the Western Front would prove a great deal worse than the darkest days on the peninsula. The Australians were now to become acquainted with the horrors of gas, flame-throwers, huge defensive belts of barbed wire, mass machine-gun nests, and the relentless thump of the artillery barrages. There were recent innovations that bespoke modern technological warfare—the aircraft and tank—and the Australians were also to meet their German adversary—a cleverer and more lethal foe than the Turk. The Australians arrived in blissful ignorance, as Private Barry noted, 'we were enjoying lovely weather and everybody was in the best of health.'[107] For Barry and the other Australian soldiers, their good health would last only until their introduction to the horrors of the Somme.

> To the dear ones at Home, I'm sending this as a souviener from France, and hope it will find you all in the best of health, as it leaves us at present. We are having lovely weather now. Have done some night work lately and expect to be in the trenches in a very short time. I'm sending you a few more cards later.

Fabrication française — R. R. Paris.

CHAPTER THREE
The Western Front
'A Hot Shop'

> love and best wishes to all from both your loving son and bro.

CHAPTER THREE

THE WESTERN FRONT

'A Hot Shop'

By mid-1916 large numbers of Australians had arrived in France where they would fight as a small component of the British Expeditionary Force (BEF). The Western Front, where the main Allied effort was concentrated, extended almost 400 kilometres from the English Channel to neutral Switzerland. Despite numerous attacks and counter-attacks by both sides throughout 1915 and early 1916, the front remained an almost static line, with slight bulges where a local offensive may have been successful for either side. Artillery, machine-guns and barbed wire dominated the so-called modern technological battlefield. The cratered terrain ensured that, if enemy forward trenches were captured and the enemy artillery to the rear eliminated (which rarely happened), it was almost impossible to pursue retreating troops and prevent the construction of fresh defensive positions. In June 1916, when the British Commander-in-Chief, General Sir Douglas Haig, had planned to launch the British army's main summer operation around the River Somme, the Australians had been assigned to assist a British advance near Amiens, close to the point at which the French and British sectors met.

***

The 4th Australian Brigade's first experience of the front line was in a relatively quiet sector known as a 'nursery' where inexperienced troops were given an early taste of conditions on the front. The nursery sector near Armentieres was ideal for training as it lacked any worthwhile tactical objective for either the British or the Germans. The area was marred, however, by an inadequate drainage system and perennial ankle-deep mud, while the local road network was almost impassable in bad weather. Despite the difficult conditions, training in the finer points of trench warfare such as trench raids and working alongside machine-guns now intensified.

Ernest Etchell arrived in France and was immediately transferred to one of the more important elements of a battalion—the machine-gun section. 'The training was very rigid,' he recounted,

> I was a big strong fellow. I could carry plenty of magazines and ammunition. I forget how many panniers of ammunition we had to carry, but it was a lot. It takes a lot of

men to keep ammunition up to them. And the gun was 26 pounds. Well, you had to be pretty strong if you were going to handle that without wanting it on its legs all the time. We invented our own way from the hip. I had a strap arranged on mine to go around the radiator, around my shoulder, and back onto the butt of the gun. I rigged it up myself ... And I could run at the double like that, and fire it accurately ... We had 36 guns in the finish. When the Lewis Gun Section was formed there was only four guns, each with a crew of six. It took six men to work them, two on the gun, like one controlling it and the other loading it. And the other four were loading panniers and getting them up to the gun. They were placed 90 feet apart ... yet they sounded together. They were very fast. You had no hope of counting how many rounds you were firing. They had a terrific firepower those things. But if you was good at it you could fire them singly ... To begin with they worked one gun to each company. But they could change them about as they saw fit. Where the fighting was toughest, they went. We were the first to get there, and the last to leave ... I was a top gunner. I always said I wasn't frightened of a thousand men if I had a Lewis gun on my hip. We were feared by the Germans very much.[1]

A group of Australian officers taking part in one of the Australian soldiers' favourite pastimes – a game of two-up, France c 1916.

Private Raymond Embrey was one of many reinforcements sent to France. Having completed his basic training in Australia, he attended an infantry school in Britain before receiving his 'advanced training' at the infamous 'Bull Ring' at Etaples camp in France. 'It was brutal and it was meant to be,' he remembered,

> I do not know why others enlisted but on my part it was for King and Country and adventure. We were all volunteers and at this final session we sacrificed our integrity as individuals, bludgeoned into

submission by our sergeants. We lost all our names and assumed new and insulting ones; we were subjected to verbal abuse couched in foul terms and made to believe our only value was as killers with a collective blind allegiance to our battalion. Humiliation, not encouragement was used to drag us all into line and many of the older men fell behind and were weeded out.

At the end of his training, Embrey joined his battalion close to the front-line trenches.

'Three lads!' Two officers of the 3rd Machine Gun Company, Lieutenant George Harrington (left) and Captain Mulholland (centre) – and Lieutenant O'Neil of the Trench Mortars – taken in France in 1916. Harrington was killed by a 'Daisy Cutter' at Strazelle in early 1917.

***

Whatever the discomforts, conditions were initially better than those on Gallipoli. The men were billeted only a few kilometres from the front by the local population of stoic French villagers. According to Bean, the troops could purchase 'eggs, or champagne at five francs a bottle ... to visit ... the comfortably furnished reading or writing huts of the Church Army or YMCA ... to buy at the army canteens any quantity of groceries, tobacco, or even clothing at prices below those of peace time; to find a French newsboy calling the Paris *Daily Mail* (with special items for Anzac troops) down a country lane within sight of the communication trenches; to be ordered occasionally, as a military fatigue, to help the French people with the work of their farms; to be able, after work, to walk up the road and buy champagne at the nearest estaminet—all this meant a wide removal from the joyless conditions of Anzac.'[2]

Monash's first impressions of the Western Front echoed Bean's. 'It hasn't taken us many hours to tumble into the regular routine of trench life,' he wrote, 'but oh dear! compared to Anzac, the people here don't know what war is.'[3] Artillery officer Captain F.L. Biddle (4th Battery) also reflected Monash's sentiments: 'We are still having a picnic as far as fighting goes. We have been a month in action but have done very little shooting. We are now going into a rest. Some war this one! It's a bit of a change from Gallipoli isn't it?'[4] Despite Biddle's so-called 'picnic,' and the 'nursery' tag of their sector, the Australians quickly discovered that the distribution of gas respirators and steel helmets, the constant menace of aircraft, and the effectiveness of German gunners and infantry who 'fought stubbornly for control of no man's land were signs that this theatre would really be far tougher.'[5]

Training continued, although not as intensively as in Egypt. Discipline, too, was an early problem. 'When we got to France,' Robert Henry remembered, 'the boys started drinking wine like beer. And we had a route march the next day, and they were falling out thick and fast ... We got a dressing down next morning on parade. When we were in Egypt, you didn't have much chance to get good strong drink. [In France] it would be sold at the canteens.'[6] Roy Easton (14th Battalion) considered conditions in France infinitely preferable to those he experienced while training in Egypt. 'We are enjoying our little selves immensely,' he wrote, 'and manage to get a good scrub down regularly in hot water so we are absolutely well off and keeping as clean as new pins.'[7] Easton's joy was short-lived. He was wounded while acting as a battalion 'runner' in a raid near La Houssoi on the night of 2 July 1916 and died two days later.

***

Three young Australian officers photographed with their mascot 'Whiskey, France c 1916. It was not unusual for officers – and other ranks – to have a mascot, usually a dog, near the front.

For others, the first few days behind the lines were incident free, albeit exhausting. Ernest Etchell recalled:

> We were billeted at farmhouses. The people really fed us. You wouldn't all be at one farm. You'd be off in sections, a section at one farmhouse, and a section at another.

They used to chase the pigs out to put us in. They'd cram us all into sheds and barns. You slept alright, for you were tired. You were knocked out [due to the training] and could do with all the sleep you could get—which wasn't much.[8]

As well as enjoying the company of their French hosts, the men appreciated their daily swims, although the water was much colder than the balmy canal waters of Egypt.

Clarence James (13th Battalion) described the 4th Brigade camp at Jesus Farm in June. 'It was a dilapidated old place,' he said, 'we were camped in cowsheds ... [on] the straw where they used to bed the cow down, and [full of] cow piss. It was crook ... But we went to sleep on the straw ... We went from there into Bois Grenier. That was supposed to be the quietest sector in the whole of France at the time.'[9]

> France
> 22-6-16.
>
> To the dear ones at Home,
> Am sending this as a souviener from France, and hope it will find you all in the best of health, as it leaves us at present. We are having lovely weather now. Have done some night work lately and expect to be in the trenches in a very short time. Am sending you a few more cards later. Have not heard from you now for about 2 months. I must close now, with fond love and best wishes to all from both your loving son and bro

An example of a letter written by an Australian soldier to his family back home, not long after arriving in France (22 June 1916).

At the end of June, the 13th and 16th Battalions occupied a system of reserve trenches.

Percy Toft wrote that 'at night we formed digging parties. We would leave our trenches at midnight, and go forward to dig reserve trenches, and returned at dawn to rest.... The front line positions were just in front of Bois Grenier.'[10]

Troops who had survived Gallipoli understood that death visited the trenches in a random, sporadic way. Those new to this form of warfare soon learned. Lieutenant Norman Meagher, fresh from training, noted how 'one quickly becomes a fatalist here. If you are hit, that is your bad luck; if somebody else is hit, that is your good luck. Such is life! Trench life has been described as "awful boredom, punctuated by moments of intense fear." I can vouch for the "boredom," but not as yet for the "intense fear." That may come when we are holding a 500 yards front with 50 men whose nerves are as jumpy as one's own.'[11]

Monash spent countless hours planning 'a raid, for identification purposes'—the raid in which Roy Easton was killed.[12] Preparations included the construction of a replica of the German trenches (based on intelligence reports) at La Rolanderie Farm, where the men readied themselves for the foray, having spent four days in the trenches to familiarise themselves with that part of no man's land. Monash also requested a preparatory box barrage of almost

3,700 rounds to cover the men as they moved towards the enemy line. Follow-up fire would then be provided by the trench-mortar crews. However, scouts sent out in advance of the main raiding party (eighty-three men and six officers) noticed enemy soldiers laying more wire in front of the trenches and tried unsuccessfully to contact Lieutenant A.T. Harvey, the raid's commander. The raiding party reached the enemy line only to discover four belts of uncut barbed wire. German troops poured machine-gun and shrapnel fire onto the hapless Australians and a large number were killed or wounded, while 'others found themselves scrambling forward over the bodies of the wounded.'[13]

Led by Captain H.B. Wanliss, one group managed to fight its way into the enemy trench. Cut off from their own line, and with only a few minutes before their artillery was to shorten its range onto the German parapet, the men 'rushed in, "upper cut" everyone about, and then came back.' The retreat proved more difficult than the raid itself. 'In recrossing the wire,' Bean wrote, 'on which the Germans were still firing with machine-guns from both flanks, many more of the party were hit; others struggled free with the greatest difficulty, partly, as before, over the bodies of their dead or wounded comrades.' Fifty German soldiers were reportedly killed (based on 'slight evidence'—the figure appears 'much exaggerated'), while the raid cost thirty-eight Australian casualties. Regardless of Monash's hype, it was another unnecessary disaster. Bean was terse in his condemnation: 'like most other hurriedly organised attacks with inexperienced troops, this operation, in spite of much gallantry, did more harm to the raiders than to the enemy.'[14]

The following night, German troops conducted two raids of their own against Australian trenches—one in the sector occupied by the 14th Battalion. At 10.23p.m., enemy artillery commenced pounding Australian positions, smashing breastwork and dugouts and burying a large number of men. Despite the despatch of an urgent signal to 4th Division Headquarters, Australian gunners took what seemed an eternity to reply. The subsequent attack by enemy infantry came as no shock. Numerous heroic deeds followed as German troops infiltrated parts of the Australian trenches. The Germans finally withdrew, but took one prisoner—Private A.A. Stephens, who later lost his left eye. Roll calls revealed that forty Australians from the 14th were listed as killed, wounded or missing.[15]

The 4th Brigade was finally relieved by the 8th Australian Brigade (5th Division) on 12 July, leaving Bailleul by train early the next day, and reaching Fienvillers, in the Somme sector, at 1.00p.m. After marching almost twenty-five kilometres loaded with full packs, the men arrived at St Ouen, where they stayed another two nights. Their next stop was Naours, where Brigadier General Charles Brand took over command of the brigade, Monash having been promoted to major general and assumed command of the 3rd Australian Division. Ernest Etchell recalled Brand 'taking over ... on a cold Sunday morning Church parade ... And he tells us off good and proper ... We thought he was going to be a bugger of a man ... But he turned out to be a champion joker.'[16]

Lieutenant Tom Chataway was also appreciative of Brand's qualities, although he was stinging in his appraisal of Monash:

> The change of commanders was by us most appreciated, for General Monash had always been a very distant man, and many of us rarely if ever saw him except upon some extra important parade. But General Brand mixed more with the men, and his lean frame became as well known to us as our own colonel's. He placed the men's comfort before that of vigorous discipline, and there is no doubt the brigade did not suffer because of this extra care.[17]

Map 2: The Western Front – Area of Operations 1916-1918..

Percy Toft remembered Brand's first brigade parade, on 17 July:

> I was astonished to see this lean, active soldier, of whom we had heard glowing reports, looking tired, old and furious. He

took us severely to task for our remissness in saluting ... We remained at Naours until the 25th, by which time we had played the 13th Battalion (NSW) Rugby Union football team. We also made a route march of a dozen miles to Wagnieres and Haverness in brilliant weather, through pretty and peaceful countryside, and we were all of the opinion that France was worth fighting for ... Then we moved through Toutencourt, Harponville and on to Warloy Baillon, and here our holiday ended.[18]

The entire 4th Division set up camp west of the Amiens—Doullens road near Picardy, within reach of the front at Pozières.

***

As early as February 1916, Marshal Joseph Joffre (the French Commander-in-Chief) and Haig had settled on a joint attack at the Somme. While the British wanted to postpone the offensive until 5 August, Joffre demanded that it be launched in late June, although without the promised number of French divisions (cut from thirty-nine to twenty-two) due to the massive German attacks at Verdun. On the morning of 1 July 1916, Haig's Somme offensive swung into action with a number of strikes against the German line around the Bapaume Plateau before the assault force turned north. Again, due to inadequate preliminary artillery barrages—which failed to do much damage to the machine-gun posts, field artillery or, indeed, cut the barbed wire—enemy lines opposite the British trenches remained virtually intact. When the British infantry advanced, they were massacred. By the end of the first day, of the approximately 120,000 British soldiers who went forward, almost 57,000 lay dead, dying or wounded in no man's land and subsequent battalion roll calls revealed that over 19,000 had been killed. While the French took most of their first day objectives, the British made few if any gains. Little wonder that 1 July 1916 has long been remembered as the worst day in the history of the British army.[19]

Australian troops—already committed to the offensive—would also suffer enormous casualties over the next few weeks. The 5th Division was the first to go into battle on 17 July. North of the Somme battlefield lay the tiny French village of Fromelles. The attack on Fromelles was intended as a 'feint' to prevent German reinforcements being sent to the Somme. However, poor planning by both British and Australian staff officers ensured that the attack was another disaster. In its first experience of battle, the division counted 5,533 casualties—including around 400 Australians taken prisoner—in one night of bitter fighting against German troops on the well-defended 'Sugar Loaf' salient. Brudenell White summarised the outcome: 'We wanted to make the Germans think we were attacking there so he would hold his troops there. As a matter of fact, we proved to him that we intended nothing serious. He was in doubt until we attacked. We have now given him the information. He can withdraw half the men who are on that front [to the Somme] and we have put out of action a fine division.'[20]

Not long afterwards, it was the turn of the 1st and 2nd Australian Divisions. On 22 July, the 1st Division attacked enemy positions around the tiny village of Pozières. While elsewhere in the British sector the advance had stalled, by 23 July, the Australians had succeeded in capturing the village. But the Germans were not content to yield control of such a tactically significant position—particularly as it controlled the heights behind, with dominating views over the entire battlefield. Subjected to intense artillery barrages, the division suffered 5,286 casualties before it was relieved by Major General J.G. Legge's 2nd Division. Another attack on 29 July, hurriedly planned by Legge, was a debacle, claiming a further 3,500 casualties. Bean described the horrors of the battlefield in the aftermath of the action:

The dead lay sometimes in batches of ten or twelve together ... There was not a soul in sight; only the powdered grey earth. No sign of any trenches of ours. All as still and dead and deserted as an ash heap ... I turned back and followed a goat-track path. There were only blackened dead and occasionally bits of men and torn bits of limbs unrecognisably along it. I wandered on for five minutes without seeing a sign of anybody till I came to a gradually improving trench, quite deserted, peopled only by dead men, half buried, some sitting upright with bandaged heads, apparently little hurt except for the bandaged wound; others lying half covered in little holes they had scratched in the trench side ... I didn't want to go through Pozières again. I have seen it once now.[21]

Legge ordered another attack on 4 August. Having taken some of their objectives, the 2nd was relieved by the 4th Division. The 1st and 2nd Divisions had advanced the line north, some small distance past Pozières. Now the 4th was to press forward against another main objective of Haig's plan—Thiepval.

Considering Australian soldiers' well-documented irreverence towards British officers, a comment by Bill Bradnock is worthy of mention. 'I remember hearing Birdwood give a talk at Pozieres,' he said, 'you could hear what he was saying ... [and] you'd think, oh, that's a nice thing to say ... I think of all the officers we had in the war, British or otherwise, there was no-one better than "Birdie". He was human, whereas the others weren't.'[22]

***

Before going into battle on 24 July, Corporal John Doggett scribbled a few letters to his sister, Edith, in Burnie, Tasmania—the contents far removed from the reality of what he was about to encounter:

> I am quite well and am having some good times in this country as well as the rough spells. At present we are in Billets far enough back to be out of range of shell fire. The weather is splendid and we are in a beautiful locality. You can guess we are making most of this good time, though we get quite enough chores and plenty of marching. I live in a hay loft, and considering am on active service am very fortunate in getting so comfortable a place. We are seeing quite a lot of France. What a difference between this pleasant countryside and the awful desert we were so glad to leave. Dare say you have seen in the papers

how our chaps are getting plenty of excitement in this great advance and also in the trench raids. We are waiting our turn. Hope we may have the whole bunch of Kaiser Bill's Huns chased well over the German border before winter comes.

Two days later, he wrote what he thought might be his last letter. Trying his best not to show signs of fear, he wrote:

We have been out marching and skirmishing all day. We feel like a lot of two-legged camels with our full packs up and all the varied articles which comprises our full equipment. What sights we look in our Steel Helmets, or "Tin Hats", as the boys generally call them. They are fine things all the same when one is under shrapnel fire. What we take most care of is our gas helmet and I wish I could tell you of our experiences already with this truly terrible idea [poison gas] of Fritzy.[23]

On 30 July, Lieutenant Len Wadsley (15th Battalion) wrote to his 'Home Folk' in a similar vein, telling them, 'we are moving up for another big stunt & when we get into it I know not, but will be pleased when it is over ... The Padre is conducting an evening service in the open ... some others are playing cards ... The country here is very similar to "Tassy" [Tasmania] & the evenings are just the same.'[24]

Percy Toft was also concerned about his immediate future. He noted that, as the 4th Brigade was preparing to move towards the front near Warloy Baillon,

> wounded of the 1st and 2nd Australian Divisions were brought to a casualty clearing station ... How the doctors and nurses kept sane after years of attention to wounded cases brought in uncleaned, and covered in filth, and shattered badly beats me. We settled down in earnest to practice bomb throwing, bayonet fighting and trench wiring. Every man was in deadly earnest. Should a hand-to-hand encounter take place, the best man wins, and to win would not be easy, and to apologise for being useless would be useless. So we worked with a will because we were going now to tackle the Germans, whom as an adversary we held in respect. On the 4th August we left for the Brickfields, near Albert, and camped out in trenches. Next day we prepared everything, even to a sharp edge on our bayonets. On the 5th August I met my brother, who informed me we were going into hell.[25]

***

British planners had already decided that Australian troops would isolate the village of Thiepval, creating a salient. As the 4th Division was preparing to launch its attack, the Australians discovered even more hideous evidence of previous battles. During the night of 5/6 August, Hamilton Warrell was among those taking over a sector which included the trench lines 'OG1' and 'OG2'. Warrell wrote: 'The country was one mass of dead humans, there were English and Germans with crossed bayonets in the same shell holes.'[26]

On the same night, the Germans responded with a massive artillery pounding—a barrage that John Doggett remembered clearly:

The bombardment was frightful. We ... had to take our turn in lining what was the captured German OG 1. We were going up the assembly trenches. We had to go up one behind the other. I can remember one fellow coming the other way, coming back from the front line, and he had absolutely gone mad with fright. He'd seen something that was so horrible it had upset his balance, and he just had a mad idea to run back to get away from it. He was not responsible for his actions, this poor, demented chap coming back.[27]

Frank Massey recalled, 'in the 13th Battalion's sector we were 72 hours under bombardment. Nobody could move backwards or forwards ... And there were quite a few casualties we couldn't get out from the front line ... I took about six of my mates, and helped them down to the RAP [Regimental Aid Post]. And they were strong fine men ... They were suffering from shell shock ... a wound more serious than a flesh wound. They'd become blithering idiots ... Crying and weeping and—absolutely useless as a fighting man.'[28]

At 'K Trench', the 15th Battalion was subjected to what Major Terence McSharry considered 'the heaviest barrage the battalion ever saw.' Ernest Etchell agreed: 'the shell fire was the worst that we had to get through ... I think it was worse than Bullecourt ... We lost a lot of men there.'[29] Troops in other parts of the Australian line came under similarly heavy shelling. Lieutenant Colonel Ray Leane, CO of the 48th Battalion (12th Brigade), declared that night 'the worst in his whole experience of the war.' In Leane's sector, 'dead and wounded lay everywhere, some killed on their stretchers, with the stretcher bearers lying dead beside them.'[30]

Lieutenant Tom Chataway (a Lewis machine-gun officer with the 15th Battalion) described the scene in more detail:

We entered the Somme salient a separate entity, leading the Battalion into that unholy sector "The Devil's Playground". We left the Brickfields beside Amiens at six o'clock on the evening of the 6th August 1916. We had at the most five miles to go to the front line. From the front line to the commencement of the communications saps at Wire Trench and Chalk Pit, close by Sausage Gully, where 18-pounders were locked wheel to wheel belching forth return hate to the Huns, the enemy laid down an intense barrage, and through this barrage we had to march. The short distance of about one mile took us from seven o'clock until three next morning, the 7th, to negotiate. The Lewis gunners and two platoons of our leading company were the only men to get in. The rest were blocked over and over again by the shell fire, one company losing seventy men or more. The [machine-]gun crews were extremely lucky losing about fifteen men only. And they had learnt their ... first lesson—not to put all their eggs into the one basket. Never again did the gunners go into the line as a separate section. They were distributed throughout the four companies so as to minimize the chance of total annihilation.

To the infantrymen who followed us in the day following [7 August], credit is due ... They salvaged for us the [ammunition] panniers lost by out killed and wounded the night before and brought them into the line for us. Already ... the spirit of confidence had begun to work, so much so, that men fatigued after twelve hours of heavy shellfire, and in the daylight still being shelled by an enemy who could see every movement made, added to their burdens extra panniers of Lewis gun ammunition.[31]

Frank Lawrie (a pioneer with the 16th Battalion), who followed the Lewis gun crews in, recalled the awful experience and the occasion that he saw his first dead German soldier. 'We were crawling along the line in day time and there's a German in a shell hole with his rifle. One of our snipers got him. He'd got a bullet right through the centre of the head, and the maggots were crawling in and out of his nose. I thought his nose was bleeding at first. It looked just like he was alive.'[32]

The Military Cross awarded to Second Lieutenant George Jamieson in France. 'I had a wonderful lot of fellows, as game as could be, and of course, without their courage and loyalty you are no good on your own. Any honours that I got I put down to the men. They earned it, they were good.'

Continual enemy shelling wrought a massive psychological effect on the Australians. Clarence James, from the 13th Battalion, recalled:

> We had enfilade fire from both the back and the front ... we had to scoot out of it for our lives at daybreak, and get back into the hop-out trenches again. We lost a lot of men ... Lost a lot of our officers [too] ... We were damned lucky to get out,

any of us ... We got trapped. We were in a shell hole, and we could see the Germans coming over. It was lucky ... We were flat out down in this shell hole and they were walking past us ... It only wanted one of them to spot us and we were gone ... It was about 3am in the morning, flares were going up all the time, everywhere. Because we were trying to make an advance, and they were counter-attacking.[33]

Percy Toft described the 15th Battalion's part in the attack:

[The] enemy's larger guns were fired and at a greater height, we heard flights of shells droning, going back, to our gun positions. Our guns reciprocated in full, and in a like manner, and all carrying parties and other bodies of men moving on both sides, as well as the men of the artillery, had an anxious night, at least ... Our part of the trench was missed, the shells going just over and throwing up earth from five to twenty five yards behind us. But to our right, in our eleven platoon sector, every shell either hit or shook the walls of the trench. In a very short space of time most of the men were casualties, or were brought into our trench which was a deep one ... I was never again in such a bombardment. The noise was deafening ... It was just breaking day and sure enough the Boche attack was starting. The Germans expected a walk over for they must have thought nothing could live in such a terrific bombardment. They were surprised when our cheerful machine gunners (the survivors—ours and the 14th's), and our remaining riflemen came into the picture. Our artillery, waiting for the SOS rocket that burst high above, crashed shells on to the attacker's and the enemy's first line of troops surrendered. In our first engagement in France, one German Major and over a hundred prisoners were captured, between us and the 14th Battalion. Lieutenants Jacka VC (14th) and Lieutenant Dunworth (15th) the respective platoon commanders received Military Crosses for their joint share in the enemy repulse, and the gain of so many prisoners ... It gave us immense satisfaction. I walked across to the right flank of the Company and found that for fifty yards no trench existed. It was completely destroyed and No 11 platoon were almost all casualties.[34]

Jacka's action is worthy of mention, if for no other reason than many observers thought that he deserved a second Victoria Cross (or bar), rather than the Military Cross (MC). Earlier, enemy troops had captured around fifty Australians from the 48th Battalion. Leading from the front, Jacka charged the Germans, forcing them to flee, releasing a number of prisoners and restoring the Australian line. Wounded seven times, Jacka's achievement 'stands as the most dramatic and effective act of individual audacity in the history of the AIF.'[35]

The Australians had little time to rest. During the night of 8 August, the exhausted troops commenced another attack. 'We charged from our trenches,' Chataway wrote,

> to secure the enemy line at the point of the salient we were occupying ... When our barrage opened and before our men moved forward the enemy's barrage fell, and their barrage line was our trench except upon the extreme right. Shell after shell fell in among us and when I finally got clear of the trench I had with me but one man, until reinforced by a stray infantryman whom we commandeered to carry a few panniers of ammunition ... The charge was made in four waves—the first on the tape some twenty yards in front of our position, and the other three waves within the trench ready to move after the first wave got in motion. The LGs [Lewis machine-guns] were

distributed throughout the companies, though still controlled from Battalion Headquarters. That such control was impracticable is shown by the fact that my gun-team like many others did not see the officer commanding throughout the whole term in the line ... Four Lewis Guns, out of the eight we then possessed actually got into the German line.[36]

'It was hell,' wrote William Fitzpatrick.[37] Despite horrendous casualties, the 4th Brigade was given no respite.

From his hospital bed in Rouen, Captain Hubert Brettingham-Moore (15th Battalion) told his mother, in Hobart, of the aftermath:

> I had a good run for my money in the big push & got 10 of the blighters with my little gun (.45). We had a hell of a time going over the 250 yards to their trenches with shrapnel and machine guns in front & left flank. Only 25 of us got over but we dished up "Fritz" & took 30 prisoners and machine-guns, much spoil, & 600 yards of trench which the rest of the Battalion was able to occupy in the morning, & hung-on to ... It is hard writing here in bed, even if one is cracked below the belt. I got two machine-gun wounds & a lot of scratches from a bomb, besides shots (machine-gun)

through my tunic which never touched me. I managed to carry on all right during the scrap, but they stiffened up in the morning & here I am. By jove then old dear it was tip top, & I never felt cooler in my life. So it is all about one losing one's block in the hell that they dish up then ... The "Boys" (what were left) were great with not a squib among them.[38]

***

Planning for the second part of the offensive—the northern thrust which was to cut 'off Thiepval and ... [provide] observation over Courcelette and Grandcourt'—was now being finalised. General Hubert Gough's plans meant that Mouquet Farm, a little over one kilometre north of Pozières, had to be taken no later than 15 August. The offensive was 'fraught with danger ... [as the] advance they would be making would take place on an exceedingly narrow front [1.6 kilometres]. Moreover, the Australians on the right would attempt the advance along the very crest of the ridge. All their troop movements would be easily observable by German forces around Courcelette, who would be able to direct machine-gun and artillery fire against them.'[39] Following a preliminary bombardment designed to destroy enemy trenches north and north-east of the Australians' recently won positions, the exhausted 4th Division was ordered to attack Mouquet Farm.

John Doggett (47th Battalion) found unpleasant memories stirred by the move 'through Sausage Valley and up to the ... battlefield [where] there were unburied corpses and all the old battlefield smells. It brought back the memory of the terrible smells on Gallipoli. Many of the soldiers in my platoon hadn't been to Gallipoli and consequently hadn't smelt the dead before.' The front was even worse. 'When we got up to the line,' he added,

> the shelling was terrible ... I can remember this very vocal ... chap. He was swearing and cussing ... All of a sudden there was a swish—Bang! He was blown to bits. God, one minute he was cussing and the next minute he was gone ... There was a young lieutenant who had not long been appointed to our particular platoon, and the two of us were filling a sandbag. The lieutenant was holding the sandbag and I was shoveling away, when the lieutenant cried out, "Oh!" A shell had chopped his leg right off ... I suppose I became excited. I don't know of anyone who wouldn't be affected. I went back along the line to the sergeant. I said, "Let me take a message to

the Colonel. We'll all be dead!". He gave me a message, a written note, saying that it was a pretty hot place to be, and they wanted more sandbags sent up there. And I went back ... to where the colonel was, in a dugout in the support line. It was just pock-marked with shell hole after shell hole. You would tumble out of one and into another. It was an awful place. I had a respite in the Colonel's dugout. "Eccles" Snowdon was our colonel. He had been with D Company on Gallipoli. I was fortunate in taking that message to the colonel. But by that time I couldn't stop the shakes.

Not long afterwards, Doggett was wounded and 'invalided back to the casualty clearing station'. For him, the front around 'Mouquet Farm was a horrible place, a most horrible place ... It was a cruel type of fighting, among this horrible rain of shells. It was like a bushfire.'[40]

As Lewis machine-gun sections moved towards the front, Chataway experienced similar sentiments to those expressed by Doggett. He wrote of 'passing along the same saps as when we entered Pozières, only with the twelve guns distributed throughout the battalion.'[41] T.A. White (13th Battalion) described the task of taking Mouquet Farm as 'one of the hardest nuts [to crack] in the war with underground dugouts so reinforced with steel and cement as to be impervious to any of our shells and into which hundreds of Germans could retire the instant shelling started, ready to rush back the instant it ceased. There were well lit galleries with crowds of dry, fresh men and stores of munitions and food and even pulleys to haul machine-guns up and down.'[42]

Keith Tamblyn recalled the way he 'dug-in in the hopping off trench. Jerry didn't know where we were. He had no idea. We didn't exactly know the position of Mouquet Farm. We knew it was strongly fortified. We attacked it in the Monday, and we lost half the battalion or more—killed or wounded.'[43] In the 15th Battalion's sector, Percy Toft described the progress of his battalion's assault:

> After a short bombardment [we] set out on our way and got to our objective ... which was the right flank ... The left company could not make its objective. We encountered much machine gun fire, but the enemy shells, which at first dropped among us, flew over our heads as we went forward ... [W]e lost altogether by shell and machine gun and rifle fire 50 per cent casualties ... George Newton, a youngster, with a comrade, struggled along with their gun.

> Calm, steady and reliable, it gave one the greatest pleasure to notice untried men making good—the equal of veterans ... Marking out trench sites, the men were set digging. Loyal Tom Turner asked me, 'How deep shall we go?' I answered, 'Dig for water.' I liked a deep trench, with so many shells flying about. We worked very hard and the ground being chalky and easily picked, we got down to nine feet and the parapet gave us another two feet ... In the morning we found things had not gone well to our left ... [and] our flanks were exposed.[44]

Two of Chataway's machine-guns were supporting the 14th Battalion's advance:

> When that unit leapt forward to their attack, the crews were astounded to discover German machine-gunners springing up from the earth itself and pouring a deadly fire into the attacking troops. Two of our Lewis guns immediately opened fire upon the German gun teams putting one out of action and forcing the other back into the concrete shelter. The two Lewis guns that opened fire ... had a narrow escape from being wiped out of existence for a silent German machine-gun slightly to their rear suddenly opened out ... and only

the fact that ... another Lewis gun ... engaged this new gun immediately ... a disaster was avoided ... One young officer spoilt a splendid Lewis gun target just after the 14th Battalion attack had been repulsed by the enemy. Fritz, wishing to re-man his line in case of a new attack, rushed some troops up to the position. The three Lewis guns ... were watching this manoeuvre with interest and were waiting for the men to enter a certain flat piece of country, where they would prove an excellent target for congested men. To their astonishment before the first Hun reached the point ... the young officer ... opened with rifle fire at the indistinct targets ... some yards further on, with the result that Lewis guns did not fire a single shot ... This incident caused much discussion when we came out of the line and Colonel McSharry [CO 15th Battalion] ordered every officer in the Battalion to become fully acquainted with the Lewis guns.[45]

The advance along all parts of the front was similarly disastrous. Unable to secure their objectives, the Australians were forced to withdraw.

The following night they attacked yet again. Strong German artillery and machine-gun fire—from three sides of the salient—decimated the attacking units. Vicious hand-to-hand fighting ensued. Frank Lawrie recalled 'jumping down into the German trench, and I could hear our chaps throwing bombs down the dugouts underneath. Then a German jumped in the bloody trench on top of me. As soon as I got my bearings, I got up and hit him on the chin and dropped him. But the poor little bugger had a bullet right through the chest. He was only about eighteen, and he opened his shirt and showed me this bleeding wound. So—it was a silly thing to do—I gave him a drink out of my water bottle. But the water just poured out of this hole in his chest. He didn't live long. He died alongside of me.'[46] Ray Embrey was somewhat more fortunate. Badly wounded, he was captured and taken to a German first aid post.

Frank Lawrie, 1918.

Attack after attack followed over six consecutive nights. All produced similar results. Frank Massey (13th Battalion) recalled that

> the dead were unburied ... the corpses were rotting [and] the smell ... was so bad that they had to chain-smoke all the time ... Of course, the dead were churned over and over. They would just fill them in the trenches ... In the trench leading in towards the front line, "Tom's Cut," was an arm

sticking out of the trench wall ... some wag had pinned a little inscription, "Gibbit backsheesh". "Backsheesh" was Egyptian for hand-out ... [There was] a 15th Battalion man at the bottom of the German dugout. He was as dead as dead could be. He died there. Probably wounded and carried down to the dugout ... And I had to stay down with him. We were in the trench up top and when the shell exploded it got me and a few others. I had three pieces of shrapnel in me—and I went out from there ... into a line of trenches, and you pass one or two men round a machine-gun, just spread about ... Probably 100 to 150 yards to the next two or three men. Perhaps half a dozen at a time, and all the way out of the front line. It was so lightly held that way.[47]

Frederick Febey (15th Battalion) was also wounded. Numerous Australians were buried by the shelling, including Febey—although only up to his waist: 'I didn't want to be anything further, either, once you cut your wind off, you've gone.'[48]

According to Ernest Etchell, 'when the NCOs got killed, privates took charge. They done a mighty job. In fact, we wasn't looking for officers to tell us what to do, whereas the English ... wouldn't do anything without an officer.'[49] The conditions in which the men fought were, as Bean noted, almost beyond description:

> Most of the horrors of the ... fighting cannot be described ... The reader must take for granted many of the conditions—the flayed land, shell-hole bordering shell-hole, corpses of young men lying against the trench walls or in shell holes; some—except for the dust settling on them—seemed to sleep; others torn in half; others rotting, swollen, and discoloured ... the air fetid with their stench or at times pungent with the chemical reek of high explosive; the troops of both sides—always in desperate need of sleep—working or fighting by night and living by day in niches scooped in the trench sides—dangerous places perilously shaken with the crashing thump of each heavy shell whose burst might all too easily shovel them on top of their occupants.[50]

Each attack made no worthwhile gain. Yet Gough refused to halt the offensive.

Frank Lawrie, photographed with his two sisters while in England, c 1916.

As the attack frontage narrowed, the Germans were able to concentrate more artillery and machine-gun fire onto the Australian infantry. The sheer ferocity of the fighting can be gauged by an attack on what was left of the farm by the 50th (temporarily assigned to the 4th Brigade) and 13th Battalions on 13 August. Despite the objections of a British officer, Lieutenant Colonel A.M. Ross (CO 51st Battalion), who cautioned that 'It is my genuine (not depressed) opinion ... it would be a mistake to press the offensive further locally in this salient'—objections which were relayed to Gough—the attack went ahead.[51] Captain Harry Murray, soon to be Australia's most decorated soldier, took his A Company forward and captured around 180 metres of the German Fabeck Graben Trench, north-east of the farm. Enemy infantry, however, soon began to encircle the outnumbered Australians.

Concerned about the increasing number of casualties amongst his men, Murray ordered a withdrawal back to their own line. In what Bean has described as 'one of the most skillfully conducted fights in the history of the AIF,' Murray took the initial precaution of moving his wounded men out of harm's way. Supported by mortar and machine-gun fire, enemy troops moved closer to the survivors, but Murray refused to countenance defeat. Equipping each man with thirty bombs, he ordered 'two sections of the bombing platoon,' to renew the attack. Within a few minutes 'they had chased the Germans a hundred yards up the trench [before] Murray's men returned across the old No Man's Land entirely unmolested.'

Frank Lawrie, 1988.

Similar scenes were reported from other Australian units. Bean noted that

> Gough's northward advance had thus met with its first check. Faced with the strong and continuous defence line through Mouquet Farm, the I Anzac Corps, though part of its attacking troops were fresh, had not won an inch of enemy ground. The 51st

had lost some 300 officers and men, the 13th (in this and the earlier engagements) 386, the 50th 414.

All three battalions were worn out. The relief of the 4th Division by the 1st ... was therefore at once begun. Brought in on the night of August 5th, the 4th Division had in nine days not only borne the brunt of the German counter-measures against Pozières heights, but in six successive night attacks—with only one night's interval—had brought the line within striking distance of Mouquet Farm. Its losses were considerably lighter than those of its two predecessors, 4,649 in all.[52]

For the men of the 4th Brigade, the opportunity for a rest behind the front came as a welcome relief. According to Percy Toft, during that first battle for Mouquet Farm, the 4th 'probably did more pioneering in the rough stuff than any other brigade in the AIF', losing forty-nine officers and 1,714 other ranks.[53]

***

The 4th Brigade enjoyed a brief respite at Warloy following its 'terrible experience' of Pozières and Mouquet Farm. 'The bursting of shells affect many men badly, the noise shattering the nerves,' wrote Toft, 'and I have the deepest sympathy for those whose systems could not stand it, and who became shell shocked.' Reflecting on the horrendous damage artillery shells could do to the body, he added that 'wounds received in France ... were more severe. They were mostly ugly large wounds, torn by jagged pieces of shell fragments, whereas in Gallipoli they were mainly caused by bullets or shrapnel pellets which made a neater hole.'[54]

As Australian troops marched further away from the front and reached villages such as Halloy-Pernois, their spirits rose markedly. On 19 August, Toft was promoted to second lieutenant and assumed command of Number 10 Platoon, meeting the brigade commander a little while later. General Brand made quite an impression on Toft, who later recalled:

> General Brand was energy personified. He was enthusiasm and fire. A keen brain ... he jumped to conclusions quickly and correctly. He had a rare sense of intuition ... and he was absolutely fair ... He dearly loved to be hailed by the men, when in action. 'Hello, Brig!' would cause his face to beam ... [He] knew every man in his brigade who was out of the ordinary—good character or bad. What a change to General Monash, who knew the battalion men by their colours ... Before long we realised we

had the finest Brigadier in all the Armies. From close contact and personal observation, I consider him peerless. Let other Brigades have their 'Billie' Glasgow, 'Pompey' Elliott, Rosenthal, or any other, ours did us.

Percy Toft was also impressed by the CO of the 15th Battalion, Lieutenant Colonel McSharry, whom he considered 'had no superior as a Battalion Commander.'[55]

The men had little time for proper rest, however. On 26 August, once all the battalions had been reinforced and refitted, the 4th Australian Division was ordered back into the line. On the 29th, the 4th Brigade renewed its assault on Mouquet Farm. Those troops who had already suffered so grievously discovered how little the line had moved. The 1st and 2nd Australian Divisions had endured similar numbers of casualties—all for negligible gain. To make matters worse, relentless rain had turned the ground, over which the men were expected to attack, into a quagmire. 'The trenches, crumbling under the constant soaking rain,' noted T.A. White, 'were nowhere less than knee deep in "sticky mud or soup." Crashing salvos smashed them still more and their occupants too; and the bearers were wearied even before the line was reached.'[56] Moreover, the enemy front line remained 'impervious to the heaviest shelling, and the complicated trench systems around it were protected by machine-gun nests with fixed sightings to sweep away any attacking force even in the dark. Also, German artillery had long ago ranged accurately on the trenches used for jumping off purposes by the Australians, and also on to No Man's Land.'[57]

At 11.00p.m. on 29 August, the 13th and 16th Battalions attacked, and hundreds more Australians were massacred. Despite the horrendous conditions which clogged rifles and Lewis guns, and the devastatingly accurate German artillery and machine-gun fire, the men's resolve never wavered. Fierce hand-to-hand combat was again the norm. The 16th Battalion charged directly at the farm. Reaching their objective, the men managed to destroy a machine-gun nest before fighting their way into what was left of the farmhouse. Enemy infantry emerged from their underground shelters, engaging Australian troops in a bomb fight. Forced to withdraw, the 16th Battalion was unable to link up with the left flank of the 13th Battalion. The 13th had taken most of its objectives, including the Fabeck Graben Trench, and beaten off four formidable enemy counter-attacks. Lacking sufficient reinforcements and adequate machine-guns, they were unable to hold off the desperate final attack. Having endured thirty hours of shelling, hand-to-hand fighting and bomb-throwing in the mud and rain, some Australians were understandably reluctant to withdraw.

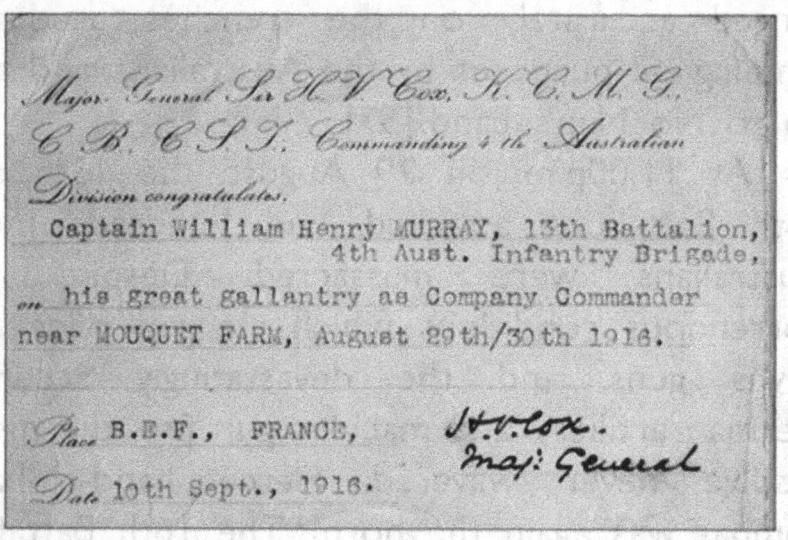

Message of congratulations from Major-General H.V. Cox, GOC 4th Australian Division, to Captain Henry William Murray for gallantry at Mouquet Farm, France 1916.

Captain Harry Murray's company was yet again caught up in the thick of battle. The 13th Battalion's historian wrote that:

> On his return [from a raid] Murray found the enemy attacking ... [with] Lt Marper now "A's" only unwounded officer, setting an example of cheerful and gallant leadership. Again an enemy repulsed. Still again came another attack ... Murray's men

were now only 16 and were consequently scattered in ones and twos, each fighting grimly in the mud and darkness without knowing what was happening five yards from him; knowing only that he was going to the last. Murray moved rapidly from man to man, fighting alongside one after another, or encouraging the lonely man. Not one but would gladly have died for such a leader.[58]

This latest attack on Mouquet Farm had far-reaching consequences for the Australians. Roll calls indicated that the 13th Battalion had ten officers and 221 other ranks (ORs) listed as casualties, while the 16th Battalion identified nine officers and 219 men as killed or wounded. Little wonder that, for the survivors, the woeful planning reinforced their belief in the British High Command's lack of concern for their lives. By now most Australian soldiers had little time for the majority of senior British—and some senior Australian—officers. In the words of Bean, 'they felt little confidence in the high tactics and strategy of it all. Indeed not a few British and oversea divisions that served there under [General] Gough dreaded ever again to experience the results of his optimistic tactical aims and his urgency when caution was needed.'[59]

The 1st, 2nd and 4th Australian Divisions were devastated. The 4th alone had made at least seven attempts to capture Mouquet Farm, all of which had ended in failure. True, some Australians may have occupied parts of the farm—others had even advanced past their objective—but, in reality, each attack was made by a force too small and too poorly supported to seize the prize. Despite this, men belonging to the 4th Australian Brigade retained their sense of humour and cherished their 'mateship'. Percy Toft believed that it was these 'acts of comradeship that kept the AIF together. No one permitted himself the thought of giving up the fight, in face of the past self sacrifice made by men for their cobbers. The trust was left to the survivors and they were required to keep the spirit going to the end of the War.'[60]

Portrait of Henry William Murray by George Bell. Regarded as a shy and modest man, Murray was described as the most distinguished fighting officer of the AIF. (AWM ART00101)

Following further training in Britain, Edward Pinnell arrived in France in September 1916. Before he joined the 16th Battalion, however, he, too, spent 'a couple of weeks,' completing 'advanced training' at Etaples:

>We went from Folkestone across to Boulogne, that's when we had to climb a sort of a pretty steep sort of a hill, and there was tents ... there. They used to call it "one blanket hill" ... in the morning we were up early to go to Etaples ... We came

to a cemetery there. And there [were] all these wooden crosses from the ... couple of fairly big hospitals around there ... it looked pretty sad with all these ... wooden crosses ... [At Etaples] we went through a sort of a little passageway that ... was doctored up in some sort of stuff that would make your eyes a bit sore ... they gave you ... these gas masks ... They were a material, and they fitted over [the] head. You just tied them around ... The other one [the box respirator] only had a couple of eyes in the material, and it was sort of gas-proofed by some chemical and ... you could breathe through that ... cloth.

The men were issued with helmets, webbing and other front-line equipment. They were also trained to throw a Mills bomb. 'I might have been able to throw them about twenty-five yards,' Pinnell recalled. Etaples' reputation for tough training justified the sobriquet 'Bull Ring' according to Pinnell, 'they were really trying you out.' Having completed his training, Pinnell left Etaples to join the battalion at Reninghelst.[61]

***

Having left the line, the 4th Australian Division was given limited time for rest at Quebec Camp near Reninghelst, in Belgium.

Training was quickly resumed. On 17 September, the 4th Brigade was back in a quiet sector of the front line at St Eloi, having relieved the Canadians. According to Toft, the Australians 'liked to take over from Colonial troops as we knew the enemy in front would have been tamed.' The brigade remained in the area for around three weeks. Somewhat strangely—and paradoxically, after what they had earlier experienced—the men became bored with the endless lack of activity. Games of cricket and football (usually Australian Rules or rugby union, though occasionally to torment the British troops nearby, 'the round ball game of soccer') were played, sometimes within range of enemy guns. Toft added that the sporadic 'rifle and *minnerwerfer* fire from the Germans, and Stokes mortar fire from our lines broke the monotony.'[62]

Regardless of the tactical insignificance of the sector, the British High Command ordered more raids and patrols. Patrols were despised by the men for the needless loss of life and the fact that they appeared to serve little purpose, except perhaps to capture enemy soldiers who usually had no useful information to divulge. Patrols were routinely sent out into no man's land between 10.00p.m. and 4.00a.m. and were a highly risky venture, as Percy Toft describes:

I was asked to take the first patrol, the next to go out at midnight, after I reported back and discussed my findings. It was thought a party of six men would not prove cumbersome and would give adequate protection if attacked by an enemy patrol. As I thought the first venture was more in the nature of a reconnaissance, I asked Sergeant George Havers to accompany me.

We set out with a revolver each fully loaded, as well as a couple of Mills bombs in our pockets. The sky was overcast, the night like ink. Sometimes it was lit up by a Verey light fired by the enemy, when we would either stand motionless or lie down, should we have time. As on each side troops had been brought to this sector to rest, not many lights were fired. Owing to the serpentine [curved] nature of the lines, one had to continually keep his sense of direction, particularly as shell holes with water in them and clumps of broken barb wire had to be negotiated. We obtained connection with our patrols on both flanks but observed no enemy patrols. However we found two enemy listening posts immediately on going out, and heard large enemy working parties.... Clambering over broken wire, we eventually came to a mound, which we thought to be the parapet of a trench. At that moment up went a Verey light a few yards away and we found we were standing on top of a crater, and below a German working party, of perhaps fifty men, were seated eating.... Unloading a bomb each, which would annoy them, off we scuttled, making a flying dive over the wire ... We remained in a shell hole until machine gunners tired of wasting ammunition.

Still unable to capture any prisoner to identify the German regiment in the trench opposite, a larger raid was ordered for two days later. Again Toft describes what transpired:

The bombing and rifle grenade section, then grouped as a bombing section of about twenty men, under an officer, sergeant and corporal, were detailed to carry out the raid ... two listening posts to be rushed. I was asked to take Lieutenant Rex Moore and Sergeant Farr out in No Man's Land to show them the best route over which to make their attack ... Rex asked that most of the section—a dozen men should be taken out. I never cared for a crowd, and it took a lot of persuasion to make me agree to take this number ... [But] as they said, once the raid started, it would be mainly an individual matter, so all should know the country. However, I pledged them all to strict silence as they were notoriously foolhardy. Rex Moore, the leader of the raid was himself hard to suppress. He seemed to believe there was joy in everything. Sergeant Farr was quiet. He would do his best to restrain the men. There was Clancy (who could hurl a bomb nearly seventy yards) ... Out we crept. My objective was a double shell hole formed by two five-nines hitting a couple of yards from each other, a big hole resulting. This was about seventy yards in front, and was about fifteen yards from the enemy posts, which were the same distance apart. The double hole formed the apex of an equilateral triangle. The shell hole formed an ideal base from which to dart across in the raid ... We reached this spot and fifteen of us crouched around the rim of the circle, on the bank of the hole, in which there was two feet of water ... We could plainly see the enemy and hear them talking. One of the men suggested that the next night had been arranged and the raid was to follow a bombardment. I did not know whether our attack was to synchronise with others along the line, or be purely an isolated raid ... We decided to act and risk the consequences of a row at home. The job looked so easy. The colonel would soon forgive us for landing home with the bacon and stealing a march on other Battalions...

We were grouped discussing the plan of operation, whispering in each other's ears, and standing in water to keep well out of sight, when we noticed that quiet Sergeant Farr was in distress ... [attempting] to prevent ... a sneeze ... It was the loudest sneeze that was ever heard in France. For a few seconds silence followed ... A few men were struck with the funny side of the incident, and began to laugh ... I am sure the Huns thought a lot of madmen were let loose. Fritz did not relish the comedy, as over came egg and stick bombs, and a moment later his machine gun barrage opened and the night's peace was shattered. Hurling our bombs, our chaps broke back, and we did not lose a man.[63]

Over the next few months, the 4th Brigade remained in the sector, allowing some men to take turns at leave in other parts of Belgium and France. Others, with wounds or illness, recovered at military hospitals scattered throughout France and Britain.

Those Australian soldiers who had escaped wounding or illness now had the opportunity to reassess their lot. Most men considered that they inhabited 'three totally different universes', the first of which was the front line with all its hazards. Second was the base area, not far behind the line where, still within 'a disciplined military environment', dangers were considerably less and some forms of entertainment were available.[64] Last came the cities (such as Paris and London), far removed from the line, where a soldier could take his mind off the horrors of industrialised slaughter. When on leave (or recovering from wounds or illness), the men usually went sightseeing, visiting places they had only ever dreamt of such as Buckingham Palace or the Champs Élysées. And, while most of the men's accounts list the sightseeing attractions, the primary appeal in visiting cities such as London or Paris was the expectation of female company. For some, such company was simply platonic; the majority, however, hoped to form a relationship that would lend them some form of intimacy or, failing that, visit the local brothel.

The recently promoted Percy Toft recalled, somewhat jokingly, that when he was due to go on leave, he still had not been issued with officer's 'pips', and 'indelible pencil markings told the world I was a 2nd lieutenant.' In November

1916, having disembarked at Southampton, Toft found a train was waiting, and shortly afterwards we steamed towards London. There were three other officers, British, in the first class carriage I occupied. They were immaculately dressed. They looked at me as if I were something a cat had brought in. To the three officers I remained a terrible specie, and a long silence continued until we reached London. I wondered how it was that intelligent men of breeding could be so small. What a contrast to see the lovely countryside even at its worst near the approaching winter? How comfortable the carriage was?

As it was Sunday, I could not buy an officer's uniform, so I bought a private's 'rig-out' ... This purchase gave me an idea: 'Why not remain a private on leave?' I would not be known. I could go where I chose without any remark and be free. I would look nicer as a private swinging along as if London were mine; I would be uncomfortable and look miserable trying to be as an officer, swanking around in flash places. There was no argument, a private I remained.[65]

For all Toft's humour, had he been caught 'masquerading in the uniform of a private soldier,' he most likely would have had the remainder of his leave cancelled, been returned to France and severely reprimanded.

Percy Toft—in common with all Australians on leave—was required to report to AIF Headquarters in Horseferry Rd, Westminster. He then needed to purchase an 'officers tunic,' from an 'outfitter's shop'. Afterwards, he was free to do what he wanted. Feeling lonely and friendless, Toft remembered:

> None of the girls, except the wrong kind, looked at me. Of course there were homes that welcomed officers on leave, but what had I in common with these people? ... So when I was not eating, and the cold climate and tempting food made one always hungry, I saw the regular sights—the Tower, the Zoo, Madame Tussaud's Waxworks, etc, the Bank in Threadneedle Street, to see if a cable for cash had been answered; look through Australia House and do everything a tourist does, or is said to do. I would ride around in a taxi or on a bus or tram, travel quickly in a tube train, buy a new pair of shoes (generally a size too small), and hobble around to see the matinee or evening's performance.[66]

Bill Bradnock's recollections are more unusual. Bradnock arrived in London at precisely the same time as German biplane bombers launched one of their infrequent raids. 'We got a train [from Plymouth] and we got out at Victoria Station—in London'

and we'd no sooner hit the bloomin' pavement than old Fritz came over. Yes, and he dropped a few too! ... It would be about four o'clock in the afternoon, and there were a few sirens went and the next thing WOOFBANG! WOOF-BANG! And most of the people on the station ... panicked a bit, and I suppose I was among them too. I wondered what the blazes was happening. And we came out of the station when the allclear went ... and the road had been pock-marked with bombs that had dropped there. The ambulances, they had enough sirens ... there were just mounted police and they were blowing their bloomin' whistles and that, and trying to get everything sorted out.[67]

***

Other Australian soldiers were sent to Britain because of sickness or wounds and were usually befriended by the local population. John Doggett recalled that, when he 'first went to

England—to the Birmingham hospital—I was suffering from dysentery in the latter stages. I had to stay in bed for some time—and eventually got better. There were some afternoons when some of the local people might take us out for the afternoon.'[68] John Cunliffe went to Sexton, Manchester, first to a convalescent home in a big mansion called Widdesley. I was the only Australian there, but there was a chap there who'd been out to Sydney, so he made it his business to come along to see me. From then on he was a constant visitor, and he wrote a five-page letter home to my people telling them all the news. The only relative I had in England was my sister, Isabel. She had married a French man from New Caledonia. He tried to enlist here in Sydney but had lost his big toe, and they didn't accept him. So he married my sister and they both went over to England. He was accepted there without any trouble at all, and he went off to the front. Right through the war my sister was doing war work making shells. But before she left Australia, if you dropped a cup or made a bang she was so nervous she would almost go into a fit. She was a bundle of nerves, but she lost all that while she was in England.[69]

While the majority of men wanted nothing more than a lengthy stay in hospital, a few were keen to get back into the thick of battle. The highly decorated Murray, who was badly wounded in the fighting at Mouquet Farm (grenade splinters had penetrated a lung), spent only four weeks in hospital and another two convalescing before demanding to return to France.[70]

Other Australians remained homesick and isolated, perhaps because they viewed London as large and solitary. The same men, nevertheless, returned at every opportunity, probably because London was far removed from the carnage of the front line. As one soldier on leave remarked: 'you have no idea of the relief it is to us to be among such beautiful and lovely sights, such a contrast to the torn and battered battlefields.' Or, quite simply, it may have been due to the plentiful supply of female company. According to Percy Toft:

> Gladys Cooper was my ideal of beautiful womanhood, but as she was unapproachable, I tried to interest a pretty fair haired ticket seller, but she seemed afraid of Australians. Later seeing she was engaged, I won a friendly look when I purchased stall tickets for her intended and herself to applaud Oscar Asche's Chu Chin Chow show. Nearing the end of my leave I decided to

ask an attractive Italian waitress at my hotel to accompany me to 'Theodore and Coy.,' which was acclaimed as being one of the brightest of the shows, but it was quite lost on me. I kept well away from my unwashed companion, and we did not speak on the homeward taxi drive. I guess she thought me queer.[71]

Frederick Febey travelled to Scotland on leave and decided that the 'Scots lassies were very good. They would take you, and show you around. They took me over and showed me the heather and all that. The girl's name was Cissy Swanny. She showed me about quite a lot.'[72]

***

The 4th Brigade's initial experience of combat on the Western Front could not have been much worse. At first, raids and patrols claimed a significant number of casualties. Although they missed the devastating first day of the Somme, what followed was equally appalling and the brigade was given little time to train to fight in conditions peculiar to the Western Front. However, at Pozières and at Mouquet Farm, the men performed heroically. Whatever hopes they cherished for a rapid end to the fighting were dashed by the reality of 'mechanical slaughter' in France and Flanders. If they thought 1916 was a bad year, worse was to follow. For the fortunate, there was some respite in the bonus of leave in Britain or Paris. For others, there was a period of rest and recreation behind the front. Away from the carnage, the men had a fleeting opportunity to forget the horrors of the front line. While some had become fatalistic, believing that they would soon be killed or, worse still, maimed, they seized the opportunity to enjoy life while they could. They had every right to be philosophical. While they were enjoying their hard-won leave, the British High Command was planning operations that guaranteed them a prominent role.

CHAPTER FOUR
Stormy Trench
'It is easy to make excuses'

CHAPTER FOUR

STORMY TRENCH

'It is easy to make excuses'

While the Australians were enduring the worst French winter for thirty-six years, the strategic position on the Western Front changed dramatically. The devastating Battle of the Somme had deprived the British army of manpower, weapons and equipment. On the German side, questionable tactics, particularly unnecessary counter-attacks, had all but exhausted the German army's supplies of men and equipment. For its part, British Fourth Army Headquarters ordered I ANZAC Corps to adopt a more offensive approach. Told that the German division (the 4th Ersatz) 'which faced it, was considered a poor one,' Birdwood planned to conduct 'a number of small operations in those sectors [around Gueudecourt] in which No Man's Land was not too wide and some German salient tempted attack.' Listed among seven possible operations was the 'capture [of] "Stormy Trench," north of Cloudy Trench (which would be seized by Operation No 1). This attack must be prepared by March 1st.'[1]

***

Once leave and any indulgence in female company was over, Australian soldiers faced the unpleasant business of returning to the front and again coming face-to-face with the revulsions of trench warfare. The winter conditions were truly appalling, as Percy Toft's description of the brigade's hardships during early January, when the 'freezing cold had set in', illustrates:

> What had been liquid froze, trenches half full of ooze became shallow when frozen. Everything external was covered by snow and ice. The days were worse. The sun rose at 8am and set at 4pm, but, as the white background made moving figures too conspicuous, and gave enemy observers an opportunity of spotting the meeting places—with shellfire a certainty afterwards—no movement by day was encouraged. However, enemy aeroplanes by air photos showed the enemy our main tracks and our principal gathering places. The black tracks were very conspicuous against the snow background. The detail of our and their front line system was given plainly on the aeroplane photos.
>
> To sit still in the cold meant an absence of circulation and cold feet. A soldier could

not carry, nor could they be issued sufficient blankets to keep the cold out. So everybody welcomed the nights during which the body could be exercised, and, for a change, everybody was keen to be in a working party ... We were provided with sheepskin coats with the wool turned inwards; also sheepskin gloves. A balaclava cap of knitted wool covered the face, and a scarf, the throat, leaving the tips of the ears, nose and mouth exposed. These had often to be rubbed warm. Shelling, five-nines mainly, was severe, owing to the enemy knowing our positions. When shells came, they burst the ice, and jagged pieces would fly in all directions. I saw one piece, at least a half ton in weight, sent yards.

The wounded had a bad time. The loss of blood caused intense chilling to the exposed man, and many limbs were lost, as also lives, through exposure in a weak condition. The men in the forward area had to pick the ice and melt it, so as to obtain water for tea making. This was a slow process ... Many men gathered around fires and suffered from chilblains. I kept warm by moving about going to the fire as little as possible.[2]

More than 65,000 sheepskin coats were despatched from Australia to help make life as comfortable as possible. Recent advances in medicine were augmented, providing men suffering from trench-foot and frostbite a greater chance of recovery.

Another infantryman, Lewis Sharp, from the 13th Battalion, remembered that the Australians

> had sheepskin coats, and we had those balaclava hats ... And while we were digging the trenches—the engineers were supposed to have done that, but we were doing it—so one of the staff officers was there and he said to me, 'Feeling the cold at all?' I said 'What do you think we have all this paraphernalia on for?' And he laughed. And we went back to work. One of our sergeants, he said, 'You remember when you were speaking to that staff officer. You were swearing and complaining. That was General Birdwood.

Sharp also recalled the darker side of war. 'The most ungodly sight,' he wrote, 'was in the front position ... There was two—a German and a New Zealander, both of them with a bayonet in each others guts.'[3]

***

Reinforcements for the AIF continued to arrive at irregular intervals. Horatio Ganson, who enlisted at Merredin, Western Australia, on 17 April 1916, was a typical reinforcement. He trained at Blackboy Hill camp until his embarkation for England in October 1916. Arriving at Plymouth in early December, Ganson went to Codford camp on Salisbury Plain to complete his training:

> We went across to France in January 1917. We went through to Folkestone, and from there they took us to Boulogne, and up to the big military depot at Etaples. That's where they dished us out with everything—blankets, rifles, billygoat skins for the winter, ammunition, tucker—everything. God knows what they didn't give us! You looked like a packhorse when you left there. We were supposed to go through the Bull Ring ... at Etaples but somehow we missed it. They split the reinforcements up there ... I went to the 16th ... The Bull Ring was a toughening up place for the boys, but the 16th Battalion had just been out of the line for a rest, and was ready to go back. So they sent us right up to them. We didn't have to wait. It was bloody cold. By Jeez, it was cold ... Everything in France was one solid mass of

frozen ground. Where there was a water tank it would be frozen stiff with icicles hanging down. If you took your boots off they'd freeze stiff in about ten minutes ... The soup came up in jerry cans, but it would be cold by the time it got into the line.[4]

For most Australians this was 'the hardest [phase] of the war'. A number of men froze to death in the seemingly never-ending rain, cold and snow. Others suffered trench-foot, which necessitated the amputation of limbs. According to Gammage, several 'shot themselves, more malingered, and one or two deserted to the enemy, an offence usually unheard of in the AIF.'[5]

Guppy wrote in mid-January 1917 that 'everything is freezing ... such cold as I have never before experienced.' A week later, he added that, although 'awfully cold things are better than when here before for, instead of about three or four feet of mud everything is frozen to a depth of several feet. Here we have to go out and break the solid ice in the shell holes with a pick to get it to melt for water for tea and washing.'[6] Edward Pinnell, a recently arrived reinforcement for the 16th Battalion, wrote, 'it was a dreadful winter ... They [his feet] were frostbitten too. That was more than just trench feet. With frostbite sometimes you could lose your foot.'[7] The nights were also generally freezing. Walter Downing mentioned that 'by day, the bitter winds cut through greatcoats and sheepskins [and] one awoke at evening with one's clothes stiff as a board with frozen sweat ... The principal haven from the storm and stress of the flame ... was England.'[8]

***

The 4th Australian Division remained close to the line. Horatio Ganson never forgot his initial taste of the front:

> From Etaples we went up into the line at Albert. That was the first time we could hear all the guns—the first time we knew there was a war on. The Germans had shelled Albert and hit the cathedral. There was a crucifix on top which had been hit, and fallen until it was horizontal. They always used to say, "When that falls off, the war will finish." Eventually it did. The Germans shelled it and brought it down ... From Albert we went up to Ribemont and joined the Battalion ... The Tommy army was camped about a mile out from Ribemont, and they had a big canteen. We used to go over there and buy stuff from them. Ribemont was only just big enough

to handle what was left of a battalion coming out of the line for a rest. The French were still living there ... right up near the front line. The village was bombed now and then, because the Jerries knew the reserves were there.[9]

The battalion remained in Ribemont for four days before moving closer to the front, at Bazentin.

By mid-January, the 4th Australian Division was holding the line. The new commander, Major General William Holmes, knew the salient from his time as a brigade commander. He was aware that the area (100 metres in front of where the 4th and 5th Divisions met) was situated 'on a nek of one of the shallow spurs leading to the valley before Bapaume. Beyond it was a depression into which the Australians could not see. It was therefore a position of some advantage, but too close to be bombarded with safety.'[10]

Holmes initially planned a dawn attack on 17 January—without artillery support. However, the commander of the adjoining division (2nd Australian), Major General Neville Smyth, highlighted the dangers of such a venture. Directly in front of the enemy trenches lay thick strands of barbed wire—in some places, on the eastern approach to the salient, up to five metres deep and a metre high—which could be cut only by artillery or trench-mortar shells. Since the Australian trenches were so close to those of the Germans, there were fears that the artillery fire might fall short, causing casualties among Holmes' own men. Moreover, because the mortar emplacements were virtually under water, it was difficult for the crews to offer assistance. Finally, after some improvement in the weather, Holmes decided that the 15th Battalion should advance along a front of around 300 metres at 7.00p.m. on 1 February following a two-minute preliminary barrage from the 2-inch mortars of X4A Battery.

Given the obstacles his troops faced in assembling from trenches that were not linked ('Grease' and 'Shine'), Brand ordered that a smaller squad attack from the right, after taking cover in a forward observation trench which had been dug earlier by Brigadier General Thomas Glasgow's adjoining 13th Brigade. On the left flank, three officers and 150 men assembled in conditions that were only slightly less dangerous. On 1 February, trench-mortars began firing at the wire. Lieutenant W. McPherson, the officer responsible for the shoot, informed Brand's headquarters that several 'plumb-pudding' bombs had failed to detonate while others had fallen perilously close to the Australian positions. A further attempt the following day met with similar results; on this occasion 'the ammunition appeared to have been affected by the weather, and the seventeenth round fell just outside the emplacement of the mortar and burst, killing or wounding the crew.'[11] Brand had little option but to request that artillery bombard the still uncut wire.

Field artillery 18-pounders, in combination with the adjacent division's heavy artillery, commenced shelling enemy positions at precisely 7.00p.m. Donald Fraser recalled that a 'tremendous artillery barrage opened up. There must have been hundreds of guns trained on Stormy Trench. The shrapnel shells were bursting over our heads.'[12] According to Percy Toft, not everything proceeded as planned:

> [There] had been faulty staff work, and a supply of bombs and ammunition, which were expected, had not been brought to the dump at Chalk Pit. Whose fault it was never laid bare. The front line men had the trench supply of ammunition and bombs, which were frozen. The ammunition would not run on the cartridge clips, and the spring on the bombs would not act in all cases ... [N]o one at Brigade [headquarters] anticipated any difficulty that the trench would be held.[13]

Major W. Mundell, commander of the attacking group on the left, ordered his men forward. They crossed the thirty or so metres of no man's land before rushing the enemy trench and taking a large number of prisoners, including two officers. Bean recorded that 'the trench had been easily captured, its garrison showing such poor spirit as to arouse some contempt among their captors. Three deep dugouts ... and many small shelters, and large quantities of bombs' were discovered.[14] Captain D. Dunworth's right section found the going tougher due to the presence of uncut wire. McSharry (the unit's CO) ordered a platoon from Mundell's company to join Dunworth. The platoon, led by Lieutenant W. Domeney (a telegraph linesman from Flowerpot, Tasmania) took part of the trench before consolidating the flank against a counter-attack.

Mundell's men now faced a fierce counter-attack from the Germans. According to Bean's account, the Australians used seven cases of 'stick-bombs' (German hand-grenades) and 200 'egg-bombs' discovered in the dugouts. Percy Toft described how they

> beat down a bombing counter-attack on their left, and the trench was consolidated. Several Lewis gunners were sent out in advance, but, partly through

danger from the shells of their own side, were afterwards withdrawn. Mundell sent back for bombs every man he could spare, and a third company of the 15th [Battalion] and forty men of the 14th assisted with the carriage of ammunition and food. The German barrage, which at 7.15 fell on No Man's Land and about the old front line, was severe, and continued so, causing heavy casualties among these parties. At 1.55 the Germans again counter-attacked, and Mundell fired the SOS signal—at that time, a rifle-grenade ... The artillery re-opened at once, and the attack was beaten off.

At about 4.05p.m., the Germans counter-attacked again. Following a preliminary barrage which destroyed both Stokes mortars, two battalions of enemy troops advanced. 'The assailants were able to come close to the trench under cover of darkness, and our men cursed as bomb after bomb thrown proved "duds"', recalled Toft. 'There had been no time to send forward supporting troops, and they would have had no useful bombs. Lewis gunners cursed trying to fire their guns, whilst the bullets jammed.'[15]

The artillery response from the 4th and 5th Australian Divisions was less than satisfactory, with barely 8,600 shells—'little more than would be used in a trench-raid'—fired.[16] Enemy troops reached the right flank of the Australian trench, forcing a withdrawal. While the remaining Lewis and Vickers machine-guns were moved to safety, a few Australians (including Lieutenant W. Murdoch) were captured. Roll calls revealed that 144 officers and men from the 15th Battalion were listed as killed or missing.

No-one, it seemed, was prepared to accept responsibility for the disaster. Holmes blamed the inadequate leadership of junior officers—particularly their failure to place Lewis machine-guns forward of the captured trench—and the infantry's lack of resolve. No mention was made of the inadequate artillery barrage (which would have placed some responsibility on his shoulders). The German account, however, provides other—perhaps more persuasive—reasons for the failure of the attack: The report of the Guard Reserve Corps, after accurately describing the attack, says that an immediate counter-attack by elements of the 362nd IR was beaten off by the Australians with Lewis gun fire. A second attempt to counter-attack was also baulked by their watchfulness. Finally the artilleries of the 4th Guard and 4th Ersatz Division were concentrated upon the salient; the 362nd IR was ordered to counter-attack from the west, and the 360th, with a detachment of 'storm troops' from the east. The Australian artillery barrage was not sufficient to prevent the counter-attack from getting through. The Australians' position was now very critical; they had run out of bombs, their signal flares were wet, their machine guns had been put out of action, their runners could not get alive through the barrage. The artillery of both sides (so the captured Australians said) was falling on their trench. A further supply of bombs came, but there was no hope of holding the position. The 362nd pressed in from the west, but the storm troops in their first onslaught suffered heavy losses, and they continued to meet with stiff resistance. Eventually, after silencing two machine guns with bombs, they began to make headway, inflicting many casualties. The Australians, driven into a short length of trench, attempted to flee across the open No Man's Land.

The Germans claimed to have captured an officer and twenty-five men. Their own losses amounted to 163, of whom two officers and forty-two men were missing.[17]

Toft expressed the thoughts of many. 'It is easy to make excuses,' he wrote, 'but another company to support with useful weapons would have made a brilliant victory. It was not thought for a moment they would be beaten back. The counter attack was so heavy ... Our men were bombed back, and our small supply of bombs soon gave out. I learnt that there were outstanding examples of bravery.'[18]

***

Holmes informed Brand that the 4th Brigade should make another attempt on the night of 4 February. 'No chances were taken in the next attack, two nights later,' noted Toft. 'The mistakes were rectified.'[19] Plans were already underway for an operation on the far right of the ANZAC line where the 5th Australian Division would attack 'Finch' and 'Orion' Trenches. Holmes decided that another battalion from the 4th Brigade should commence the offensive—to coincide with that of the 5th Division—at 10.00p.m. on 4 February. The task was not given to Durrant's 13th Battalion until 8.00p.m. on 3 February—barely twenty-six hours before the scheduled attack. At brigade level, considerably more thought was devoted to planning. Durrant was told that four companies from his battalion—plus Captain S. Hansen's company from the 14th Battalion—supported by two field artillery brigades, were to launch the attack.

To meet the anticipated counter-attack, Durrant was supplied with more than 12,000 bombs (hand grenades) which would be brought forward to the 'jumping-off' trench ('Grease'), while around 8,000 more would be kept in reserve at battalion headquarters ('Chalk Pit'), situated in a quarry not far from the front. Thirty-six men from each company were required to carry twenty or more bombs—a formidable task considering the extreme cold, the terrain and each bomb's weight—while another twenty bomb-carriers (each lugging twenty-four bombs) followed behind. All other infantry were expected to carry extra bombs in their greatcoat pockets. More significantly—considering eggbombs used by the Germans consistently out-ranged British bombs—the battalion was supplied with numerous rifle-grenades.

Despite the limited planning time, all troops participating in the attack were given a thorough briefing by Durrant and others who earlier had reconnoitered no man's land. Murray and some other officers and NCOs had crawled over the terrain, intent on checking the enemy wire. Last, but by no means least, Durrant was cautious of the problems that the artillery had encountered in the earlier attack. Artillery officers, including the artillery group commander (Lieutenant Colonel W. Waite) were instructed to operate from battalion headquarters.

The troops were confident that Durrant and Brand had done all they could to make the attack a success. Bean noted that the men 'were in magnificent spirit'.[20] Murray's biographer added that 'a mood of enthusiasm was sweeping through the battalion. Eight men due to depart on leave insisted on staying for the "stunt"'; Lieutenant R.H. Kell from Murray's company left a sickbed to take part. Murray himself participated despite a severe dose of influenza.

Captain Winn, the 14th Battalion's Medical Officer, 'came to Murray's dugout to look him over. Winn found him obviously ill with a temperature of 103, and [unsuccessfully] started arrangements to evacuate him.'[21] Shortly before the attack, Durrant made more changes: 'To avoid noise during assembly, the men's feet were muffled with sandbags, and, to keep the Lewis guns from freezing, the gunners smeared the parts with kerosene. The plans for the artillery, except as to its strength, were much the same as before.'[22] To prevent enemy observers detecting increased activity, the line was garrisoned by only two platoons from A and B Companies. The remaining two companies were to remain in reserve, only moving to their jumping-off trench after nightfall.

Six hours before the men were due to assault, Durrant held a final briefing for his company commanders. Murray's (A) company would attack from the right flank, with C, B and D Companies taking the left flank. Durrant suspected 'the heaviest weight of the inevitable counterattacks ... [would] fall on "A" Company, and stressed this to Murray.' Murray's response echoed the resolve and mindset of the men: 'If the enemy ever get my trenches back,' he told his CO, 'they will only find a cemetery.'[23]

Company commanders called together their platoon commanders and NCOs. In the short time available before the attack, junior officers had the unenviable task of explaining revised plans to their men. They were pleased to hear, however, that enemy troops had already withdrawn from 'Finch' and 'Orion' Trenches following a successful assault by the 29th British Division on 27 January and that a rum issue would be provided during the assembly—allegedly to fortify them against the cold—instead of after the offensive as was the usual custom.

***

But not all went as planned. Yet again, troops found it difficult to assemble for the attack as some trenches had been cut off. A platoon from A Company had to advance from 'Shine' Trench, almost 90 metres behind the other platoons. A full moon only added to the anxiety. 'In places men had to be trickled into the front trench in twos and threes to avoid giving warning of the operation.'[24] Other operations were also under way to divert German attention from Stormy Trench. The same morning the Royal Naval Division launched an attack on 'Puisieux' and 'River' Trenches on the left flank of I ANZAC Corps, capturing almost all of their objectives. Later that evening, the artillery of the 1st Australian Division commenced a 'feint' barrage on 'The Maze' Trenches, while the 2nd and 18th British Divisions raided German trenches opposite their part of the line.

The Australians anxiously awaited zero hour in their shallow jumping-off trenches. As the artillery opened fire—first with a whimper to heat the barrels before unleashing the full barrage—troops made one final check of their weapons and equipment, then settled themselves to wait for the whistle, their signal to move beyond the parapet. At exactly 10.00p.m., the officers blew their whistles. On the left, the advance progressed better than expected. Bean remarked that the 'men ... of the 14th [Battalion] moving into the front line as the 13th left it, were deeply impressed by the spectacle of the dark well-ordered line, grimly advancing across the snow.'[25] After crossing no man's land, one squad took out an advanced German machine-gun post. Another machinegun, which commenced firing on the Australians, was smashed by an artillery shell. The Australians had gained the trenches well before enemy troops could reach their parapet from deep underground dugouts.

On the right flank, Murray's group encountered numerous difficulties. According to one report, when the barrage lifted:

> The company springs to its feet and Murray leads his men around the broken end of the entanglement; they pour down into the deep, wide trench, the 'bombing' sections now taking the lead. The [uncut] wire has prevented the attackers from hitting all sections of the trench at once, and although many of the Germans have been caught in their dugouts by the swiftness of the Australian advance, resistance stiffens further along the position. On their own initiative, some of the attackers run in the open outside the trench to save time. The Germans who manage to emerge from the dugouts fight back with grenades, but they are quickly overcome by the Australians, and those who are not

killed or captured flee along the trench to the right ... The company reaches the lowest point, crosses a flat portion and starts to move uphill towards the point of its final objective, another 100 metres further along. Corporal Roy Withers calls into a dugout entrance for the occupants to surrender. A shot from within cuts his ear. Enraged, he hurls two grenades down the shaft. Seven of the eight men ... are killed; the eighth, a terribly injured officer, manages to stagger up the steps ... The fighting in the trench has now died down, and Murray has a moment to think ... [he] knows a grenade fight is inevitable when the counterattack comes, and he quickly decides to pull back to the bottom of the slope, leaving sixty metres of flat ground in front, and hold on there, 100 metres short of the planned objective. He orders the building of a 'bomb-stop' at this point. The Australians ... improvise a barricade from duckboards, planks, sandbags and clods of frozen earth. Sergeant 'Scotty' Thompson sites his three Lewis guns and their crews along the position, and twenty minutes after taking the trench Murray is satisfied the Australians are ready to defend it ... On the left, the other three companies have quickly taken their objectives, again following the barrage so closely that they are on top of the Germans before an effective defence can be organised. They have captured an advanced machine-gun in no man's land on the way across, and sent back many prisoners. The 13th has won a quick victory, but they are all aware that the real test is still to come.

The German counter-stroke begins with a hurricane of artillery and mortar fire all along the captured trench. More shells crash into the communication trenches and the Australian lines, disrupting the carrying parties and support troops. On the right, 'A' Company stays alert for the infantry assault which must follow. The bombardment ceases abruptly at 10.40pm; the dark figures of men are seen moving ahead of and around 'A's right flank.

Murray instructed his machine-gunners to fire on advancing enemy infantry. However, a number of Germans penetrated the deadly hail of bullets, lobbing stick-grenades into part of the trench which killed seven men and wounded another two.

As sections of his company attempted to withdraw, Murray ordered an SOS signal to be fired to call in additional artillery support while he brought up a reserve bombing squad from another part of the trench. Guns from the 4th and 5th Australian Divisions immediately answered Murray's plea. 'Murray flung himself into the most famous fight of his life,' Bean wrote, adding that he 'was a leader whose presence always raised other men to heights of valour and energy.' With Murray leading from the front—in what he himself called 'a bomb fight of the first magnitude'—the men hurled their bombs and fired their riflegrenades. The enemy refused to give in and soon beat back the Australian bombthrowers. Murray ordered his men to engage in hand-to-hand combat. 'Revolver in hand, and still shaking with fever,'

> he leads a bayonet charge over the top against one of the German posts; jumping into a group of six opponents, he shoots three in seconds, and the others throw up their hands in surrender and are sent to the rear. His party puts the remaining Germans to flight. Murray carries three wounded diggers back to the trench one by one ... On the other sides of the position, more bayonet charges—and Roy Withers running along the parapet hurling grenades despite an injured knee—have driven off the remaining group of Germans.[26]

The Australians then attempted to consolidate their gains. Victor Groutsch recalled that the Germans 'had good deep dugouts ... the old Hun did know how to build a dugout ... you could put a company in them.'[27]

***

Australian artillery continued to pound the enemy line and a barrage fell among advancing infantry and their support lines, isolating the Germans from supplies and reinforcements. Durrant and Waite decided to orchestrate another heavier barrage 'to be laid on the depression beyond Stormy Trench, and for a gun to be kept firing in enfilade down the German front trench just beyond Murray's right.'[28] Enemy guns immediately replied. The bulk of the shells lobbed onto A Company. 'The storm of shells shatters the sides of the trench into great boulders of frozen earth,' one report noted. Casualties soon mounted—'some men are blown to pieces, others killed or wounded by splinters, some buried under the frozen blocks.'[29]

At 11.50p.m., German infantry launched another counter-attack. Murray never wavered, and the Australian guns responded immediately to his SOS flares. But the Australians were outnumbered and enemy troops were now close enough to hurl stick-bombs into their trenches.

Murray replied by ordering another bayonet charge. Again the Germans were forced to withdraw. A soldier from A Company, Jack King, described the reaction when Murray

> came walking down the track, 'How are you, boys?' Nobody answers because we didn't have anybody in charge of us. It was nobody's place to answer. The second, time he says 'How are you going, boys?' Well I spoke up. It wasn't my place any more than anybody else's. Somebody had to—and I said, 'We are alright. I don't know where our corporal is ... we've got three prisoners over sitting in the corner there.' Probably they were glad to be caught ... I said, 'I think I got hit in the feet...
> And he said, 'Let's have a look.' Talk about a mess, blood pouring out of them ... But Captain Murray says, 'Can you find your way back where we came from?' I said, 'Oh, yes, it's only about half a mile.' And it was light as day, although it was midnight. Flares and Vary lights, and shells bursting everywhere, it was light as day ... He said 'Well, away you go.' I said, 'Oh, I don't think it's that bad ... You need all your men here.' He said, 'I'm well aware of that, but ... the stretcher bearers will have enough to carry without carrying you.'

... By the time I walked back I met Bob Hird who enlisted with me. He'd been already back ... And he collected some more hand grenades and he's going back up to the front again.[30]

***

Shortly afterwards, German troops attacked again—and again they were forced back. In the space of roughly fifteen minutes, five separate counterattacks were launched, all with similar results. With casualties soaring, German officers decided to regroup their men. An Australian report noted:

> 'A' Company's strength has dwindled further, but there is no thought of abandoning the fight. After another pause, which the remaining Australians use to rebuild their barricades and clear some of the rubble from the trench, the German artillery starts up again.
>
> Throughout the ferocious fighting around the trench, the 13th's carrying parties have moved back and forth across the shell-swept ground between Stormy Trench and the Australian support line, bringing up the vital supplies of grenades and ammunition and helping wounded men back whenever they can. A ... company of

the 14th Battalion occupying the original jumping-off trench in support of the 13th, is pounded with ... severity by the German artillery, but keeps up a constant stream of ammunition and grenades to the 13th. Another lull follows.'[31]

That 'lull' gave Murray a chance to consolidate his defences. Donald Fraser remembered that 'he [Murray] must have killed a lot of Germans ... that night. There was a heap of [dead] Germans ... [and] some of our blokes were sent out in a burial party ... to bury them, but the ground was too hard to dig. Anyhow, they might have got shot too. So they put them out with the good barbed wire, and a bloody shell landed there while we were digging. And it was blowing the bodies out.'[32]

At 2.30p.m., the German guns resumed firing. Following a 25-minute barrage, assault troops began advancing across no man's land. Given the likelihood of more bomb fights in which his exhausted troops would probably be overpowered, Murray ordered them to go 'over the top' to 'bayonet charge' the enemy. 'Their first wave gives way,' one report noted. 'Corporal Brown leads another charge against a second wave, and Murray joins in this one also.' The account continued: 'Roy Withers, who had been sent back to the rear to have his injured knee treated and insisted on returning to the front line, repeats his earlier heroics, flinging grenade after grenade into the German positions. Finally this German attack is repulsed like the previous ones.'[33]

Reginald Colmer commented that enemy troops 'didn't get any retreating—hardly any of them. There was more killed than what there was retreated ... It was the blood-thirstiest thing that ever I'd seen.'[34] The Australians also suffered heavy casualties. Lewis Sharp (13th Battalion) was only sixteen years old when he enlisted on 14 February 1916. The following day—5 February 1917—was to be his seventeenth birthday. Sharp sadly recalled the death of a 'really good mate,' Ernie Cranzke. 'He was in C Company—and I was in B,' Lewis said, 'it was just along the trench. And "Bluey" Melvin ... came running down, and he said "Ernie's gone!" So I went along the trench, and here he was. What I saw was his face blown away. I couldn't do anything for him. Killed instantly.'[35]

In the pre-dawn light, Australian artillery resumed its bombardment of known enemy positions. Fearing another counter-attack, Durrant told both his company commanders to remain vigilant. 'Daylight comes at last,' another account noted:

Gone was the admirable trench we had captured, and in its place there remained a boulder-strewn depression—boulders of frozen earth. The mantle of snow has disappeared for a hundred metres to the front and rear of Stormy Trench, blasted away by the artillery shells. Murray counts sixty-one dead Germans and twenty Australians over a distance of seventy metres. The company stays alert for another counterattack—Murray believes he can still deal with one more—but none comes. The other companies have held their positions through the night also.

Later that same afternoon, intelligence officers intercepted a German message outlining plans for another counter-attack for just after sundown on 5 February. At approximately 7.45p.m., enemy bomb-throwers were seen assembling. However, no counter-attack eventuated. At 8.00p.m., Durrant considered it sufficiently safe to relieve Murray's company. Of the 140 men who assaulted, only forty-eight returned. A report concluded that 'the 13th Battalion had secured its victory.'[36] Thoroughly exhausted and demoralised, the Germans would make no further attempt to retake Stormy Trench.

German prisoners captured at Stormy Trench lined up before a British Intelligence Officer for questioning. (AWM E00180)

Roll calls revealed that the 13th Battalion had lost seven officers and 226 ORs. Casualties in Captain S. Hansen's company—part of the 14th Battalion supporting the 13th—were particularly heavy. Ninety-five officers and men, from a total of 120, including Hansen, were listed as dead or wounded, most killed when the company suffered a number of direct artillery hits while waiting in the jumping-off trench during the night of 4 February. Still, Durrant was able to label the operation a success. The battalion had taken around 600 metres of enemy trench, including sixteen dugouts holding almost 150 men.

Another eighty Germans had surrendered—an unusually high number (which gave some credibility to intelligence reports concerning the 'poor' standard of the German division facing the Australians). During interrogation, a few assumed that 'they had been attacked by picked storm-troops, and marvelled at the speed and efficiency of the Australians.'[37] The 13th Battalion had captured a handy feature with glimpses over a small, albeit insignificant, part of the enemy front. Yet, in reality, the attack lacked any tactical or strategic consequence. A German report provided possibly the best account of the operation:

> The Australians attacked with a sufficient barrage; their success was greater and they inflicted heavier casualties. An immediate counter attack failed, and so did one prepared later; the *sturmtrupps* could not get through the barrage and machine gun fire. A third counter-attack was then prepared and attempted before dawn, with the same result. The success of the attacker had been complete; he had won a trench, taken prisoners, and lost nothing which afforded the Germans any information about himself. The total German loss was about 250, of which the missing comprised 100. A decision taken on February 5 to recapture

the position by carefully prepared counter-attack was later abandoned as likely to lead only to more expenditure of life and ammunition. The loss of Stormy Trench did not endanger any other German position, and the commander of the Guard Reserve Corps therefore obtained leave of the army commander to barricade the trench and let things remain as they were.[38]

However, the Germans were not quite finished. For a further four days, the Australians in Stormy Trench endured endless enemy artillery barrages on top of the worsening weather. Pioneer battalions constructed machine-gun positions and dug new support and communication trenches so as to incorporate the trench into the Australian line. Finally, at nightfall on 9 February, the battle-weary troops were relieved by the 46th Battalion (12th Australian Infantry Brigade) which continued to attack German positions around Stormy Trench. On 11 February, the 46th Battalion captured some 150 metres of German front and, during the night of the 14th, another twenty-five metres. The following evening, the 57th Battalion (15th Australian Infantry Brigade, 5th Division) took more than seventy metres while, on the left flank between 21 and 22 February—in what has been described as a marvellous feat of arms—the 45th Battalion (12th Australian Infantry Brigade) captured in excess of 300 metres of enemy trench.

***

Despite Murray's lavish praise of his men's heroic performance, he refused to take any credit himself. Durrant, nevertheless, had heard enough from survivors. On 7 February, having questioned the other officers, he recommended that Murray be awarded the Victoria Cross (VC). Durrant's report outlining Murray's 'sheer valour' in capturing and holding the trench, finished with the words: 'His Company would follow him anywhere and die for him to a man.' After the award was announced on 12 March (it was the third for the 4th Brigade), Durrant added that 'Harry Murray was not recommended for his VC because of one action. He was recommended because he gave more than brawn; he gave brains over a sustained period of 24 hours.'[39]

While recommendations for the VC for Lance Corporal Roy Withers and Corporal M. Robertson were rejected, they were awarded Distinguished Conduct Medals (DCM). In total, the 13th Battalion collected one VC, three DCMs, three MCs and fourteen Military Medals (MM) for its part in taking Stormy Trench.

Perhaps Murray's A Company deserved most of the kudos, yet the achievement was largely the result of methodical planning and preparation, from brigade to battalion through to company level, as well as a mark of the capability and resolve of the troops. Above all, it was the never-say-die leadership of junior officers and NCOs that carried the day for the 13th Battalion.

***

The attacks on Stormy Trench demonstrated that the 4th Australian Brigade, and the 13th Battalion in particular, had learnt from its previous stint on the Somme. While casualties were high in what was a comparatively minor battle, the men seemed satisfied with what they had achieved. More than ever, they understood that the Germans were a deadly and formidable adversary and that, in future engagements, victory might not come so cheaply. They also faced the problem of replacing those men killed or wounded with drafts of reinforcements who had little or no front-line experience. This experience would come quickly. In early April, while the reinforcements were undergoing training behind the line, the Commander of the Fifth Army (General Sir Hubert Gough) commenced planning an operation in which the 4th Australian Division would launch an attack against the well-fortified village of Bullecourt.

CHAPTER FIVE
First Battle of Bullecourt
'It was a Hell of a Morning'

CHAPTER FIVE

FIRST BATTLE OF BULLECOURT

'It was a Hell of a Morning'

After the taking of Stormy Trench, Birdwood considered that the 4th Australian Brigade—indeed the entire 4th Division—had done enough. On 24 February 1917, he ordered that the men be taken out of the line for a rest. On almost the same day, enemy troops began to pull back. The German High Command had earlier decided to reduce its front so as to make better use of its dwindling resources (both manpower and equipment). However, the German planners knew that a large, well-coordinated Allied offensive would, in all probability, break through the old defensive line, and developed an innovative 'defence-in-depth' system designed to reduce Field Marshal Haig's chances of taking the upper hand. In some places, the new structure called for a network of two or three main trenches with reinforced underground bunkers (where the garrison was relatively comfortable in extreme weather conditions and well protected from artillery barrages) surrounded by huge entanglements of barbed wire, usually many metres deep, and shielded by thick concrete machine-gun blockhouses and well-concealed artillery emplacements. Moreover, the line of trenches followed the lie of the terrain, allowing machine-gun posts clear arcs of fire on attacking infantry. The main trenches were connected by a maze of 'switch' (communication) trenches which—in the unlikely event of a breach—allowed enemy reinforcements to rush forward, trapping the attackers in a salient. The Germans referred to their new front (which they considered almost impenetrable) as the *Siegfried stellung*. It would become better known by its Allied name—the Hindenburg Line.

But Haig was not one to sit idly by. As the Germans withdrew, he ordered his troops to take up the chase. The 1st, 2nd and 5th Australian Divisions were to engage the enemy in the ANZAC sector while the 4th Division remained in reserve. From late February through March 1917, the Australians pursued withdrawing enemy units. As the cold, frosty weather again gave way to heavy rain and intermittent snowfalls, the pursuit continued, usually through sodden, muddy terrain. On 26 March, after an advance guard of the 5th Australian Division had taken the strategically important village of Bapaume,

Australian troops moved east and north-east, pursuing the enemy who, by the first week of April, had pulled back from their 'RII' and 'RIII Lines' to the more formidable main Hindenburg Line. The Australians also forced their withdrawal from the outpost villages. On 9 April, the 1st Division captured the final two villages, Hermies and Demicourt. From the outskirts of these villages, the Australians could clearly see the Hindenburg Line, around three kilometres away, its forward trenches guarded by thick curls of rusty barbed wire, with another two defensive lines discernible further to the rear. Assaulting the Hindenburg Line was not part of the current plan, however and, for the moment at least, Haig planned to focus his resources on offensive action around Arras.

***

The 4th Australian Division remained behind the line engaged in a program of resting and refitting, camping for almost six weeks around Albert on the old Somme battlefield. 'Nothing of any importance to report,' Lieutenant William Shirtley (13th Battalion) scribbled, 'this country is still the same. Mud deeper if anything. All's quiet on the Western Front.'[1] Percy Toft, too, remembered this as a very agreeable period, with football a popular pastime. Four states 'played the Australian Rules code', the other two (NSW and Queensland) often took part in games of rugby union. Toft described the matches as occasionally 'brutal. Goudecourt memory was still rankling. Both sides played the man, though all were fair to good footballers. One or two of the men had represented Australia and there were some Interstate representatives.' Not all the time was devoted to amusement, however, and Toft added that the troops 'practised open warfare. It was very pleasant riding spirited horses across a big plain, in which there were no shell holes.' By mid-March, newly arrived recruits from Australia had boosted the complement of all battalions to something approaching full strength. Toft wrote, with more than a little prescience, that the 4th '[B]rigade had reached its zenith, its maximum power. Never again was it so good or so strong. Since the landing on Gallipoli and the first attack at Poziers [sic], battalions had fought at an average of about 600 men. We were now to fight beyond full strength and as experienced soldiers. How proud all commanders, high and low, were of their men. Pride and a fall—how often that is true.'[2]

The Australians were unaware of the final plan currently being formulated by British GHQ. Given the heavy casualties the British army had sustained on the Somme, Haig had decided against any large-scale attacks and wanted nothing more than smaller scale 'wearing down' battles until spring, when he anticipated a major offensive by his reinvigorated army around Ypres. However, the recently appointed French Commander-in-Chief, General Robert Nivelle, persuaded Haig that the British should assist his troops, currently preparing for a massive attack on the Aisne. At first, Haig wanted Gough's Fifth Army (to which I ANZAC Corps was attached) and Allenby's Third Army to attack the Germans near the Bapaume salient. But his plan was stymied by the German withdrawal to the Hindenburg Line. Instead, he decided on a Third Army offensive around Arras. Gough's troops, meanwhile, would face the most daunting challenge of all—a re-entrant (the reverse of a salient)—from which attacking infantry could be fired on from three sides. Gough was engaged in drawing up plans for two divisions—the 62nd British (West Riding) and 4th Australian—to attack either side of the small, well-fortified village of Bullecourt.

Haig must have realised how daunting a task this was for Gough, particularly as some of his commander's heavy artillery brigades had already been detached. The movement of the remaining guns to within striking range of the enemy defensive line would be a lengthy process. Enormous demands would also be placed on the 4th Australian Division's field artillery, currently so hamstrung by a lack of horses that assembling all seven brigades at the front would take until 8 April. In addition, the difficulties that plagued the hard-pressed lines of communication meant that ammunition supply was slow and labour intensive.

***

By 2 April 1917, British and Australian troops had occupied a series of outpost villages stretching from Doignies to Croisilles. The Hindenburg Line was now within striking distance. Almost immediately, Gough ordered that 'every available heavy gun was to be pushed forward and no thought of risk was to be allowed to cause delay.' On 5 April he directed V British and I ANZAC Corps to advance 'on a front of some 3,500 yards, of which the village of Bullecourt formed the centre. The second objective included Riencourt and the third, Hendecourt.'[3]

The 4th Australian Division had taken over the sector of the British front that faced Bullecourt. On 3 April, Holmes was directed to prepare for an attack near Bullecourt 'at an early date'. After visiting the front and seeing firsthand the difficulties his men faced, Holmes decided that one of his brigades should attack the village while another moved against enemy positions east of Bullecourt.[4] Intelligence reports, usually information received from German prisoners, only compounded Holmes' preparation and planning.

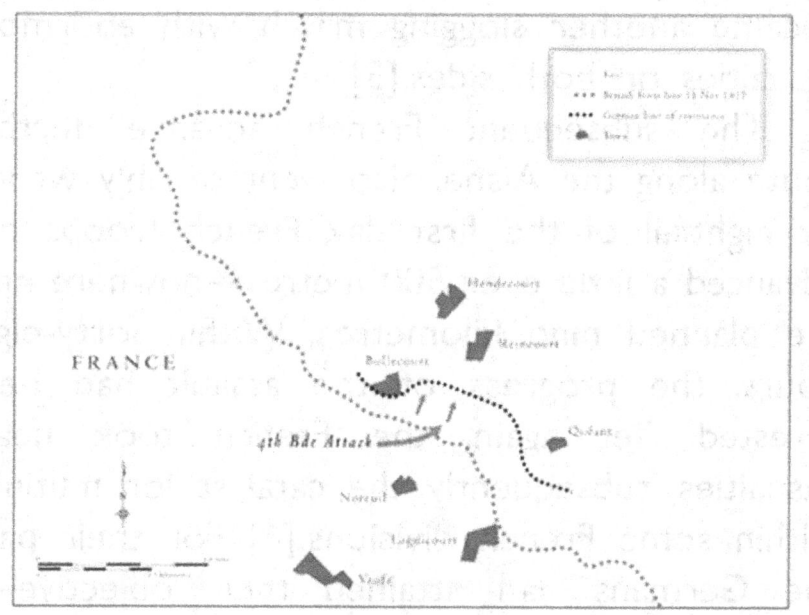

Map 3: Map showing Bullecourt and the Arras Front.

On 9 April—in a blinding snowstorm—the British Third Army attacked Arras. Initially it appeared that Haig and Nivelle's expectations for the Allies' first major offensive of 1917 were to be realised. After a massive softening-up bombardment by British artillery, the Canadian Corps, in one of the great feats of the war, took Vimy Ridge. The 9th (Scottish) Division advanced almost seven kilometres. Soon afterwards, however, British troops came up against fresh enemy units, hurriedly moved to the front from rear positions, supported by heavy artillery and machine-gun fire. The advance faltered and ground to a halt. Instead of the 'bite and hold' approach to which Haig had pinned his hopes, Arras became another slogging match with enormous casualties on both sides.[5]

The subsequent French advance, further south along the Aisne, also went terribly wrong. By nightfall of the first day, French troops had advanced a little over 500 metres—nowhere near the planned nine kilometres. Within forty-eight hours, the progress of the assault had been arrested. Yet again, the French took heavy casualties, subsequently the catalyst for mutinies within some French divisions.[6] For their part, the Germans had attained their objective—a straighter front line to defend. With most French units bled dry, the British now had to bear the brunt of any major offensive, at least until American soldiers began arriving in large numbers later in 1917 and in early 1918. The British attack on Arras was left in the balance.

An oblique aerial view of Bullecourt showing the trench lines around the perimeter of the village, 5 April 1917. (AWM AO1100)

***

The Australians continued to prepare for operations around Bullecourt, although Gough was beset with uncertainty over his lack of artillery support. Manna from heaven arrived in the form of an officer from the Tank Corps, Lieutenant Colonel J. Hardress-Lloyd, who told Gough that twelve of his tanks could achieve what the guns had failed to do—cut the barbed wire, in some places up to thirty metres thick, in front of the Hindenburg Line. Gough jumped at the idea although, unhappily for him, as the British military historian Robin Neillands remarks, from that moment 'matters went seriously awry.'[7]

At 4.00p.m. on 9 April, Holmes was told of the revised preparations. With little time to prepare new plans, he was forced to make the best of what he had, concluding that his greatest chance of success now lay with one battalion capturing the first line of German trenches, and another battalion 'leap-frogging' onto the second line.[8]

Holmes then faced the unpleasant task of informing his two brigade commanders. Two battalions (the 46th and the 48th) from Brigadier General J.C. Robertson's 12th Brigade were to move forward on the left and 'follow the tanks into Bullecourt'. Another (the 47th Battalion) 'had to capture the Hindenburg Line'. The 45th Battalion was to act as the reserve. Brigadier General Brand's orders were even more intimidating: he was to use all four of the 4th Brigade's battalions (the 13th, 14th, 15th and 16th) and also take the village of Riencourt.[9] Birdwood and Brudenell-White protested to Gough, reminding him that Australian soldiers had 'never acted with tanks before' and, more significantly, that 'tanks had never been used in the manner proposed.'[10] Gough, however, refused to sanction any changes to his plan.

Soon afterwards, officers communicated what they knew of the approaching attack to their men. The hour or so before dawn on 10 April had been chosen if, for no other reason, than because this date offered maximum surprise, allowing the slow-moving tanks to reach the starting line without being spotted by enemy observers. According to one Australian, 'In the bitterly cold early morning ... [troops] moved to their pre-prepared jumping off trenches in front of the railway embankment that had been part of their lines of defence. They knew this operation was different from anything they had previously experienced and were champing at the bit to get in and have a go.'[11] Upwards of 4,000 Australian soldiers began moving to their designated positions in front of the Hindenburg Line, in anticipation of the mechanical monsters' arrival.

But the tanks failed to show. At around 5.30a.m. the battalion officers were informed that the attack had been postponed. Instead, they were to return their troops to the safety of the sunken road near Noreuil.[12] The men needed little enticement. Fearing that, with first light approaching, they would be at the mercy of German artillery and machine-guns, they rushed back 'like the departure of a crowd from a Test match.'[13]

Not all arrived safely back. Enemy observers spotted the last groups of Australians sprinting for their lives towards the sunken road. German artillery fire accounted for what has been described as 'remarkably few casualties'. Even before those survivors arrived back at Noreuil, 'all' were said to be 'intensely soured and disgusted. The bungling that had resulted in this grotesque fiasco was evident to everyone, and confidence in the higher leadership was badly shaken. It was due more to good luck than to good management that the retirement had not ended in an Australian shambles.'[14]

16th Battalion, under CSM Fisher, marching off to the front, France, c April 1917.

Concluding that another attack was highly probable, enemy soldiers who were preparing to move north to the Arras front were instead ordered back into the forward trenches in front of Bullecourt.[15] For his part, Gough was unfazed by the absence of the tanks. Doing exactly as the Germans had anticipated, he ordered another attack, scheduled for the same time the following morning—11 April. Birdwood and his fellow staff officers at I ANZAC Headquarters were now more convinced than ever that the operation should be abandoned. Yet again, Gough refused to brook any opposition, even discounting the little time available to make proper arrangements or the exhaustion of those Australian units expected to attack, much less the preparedness of the enemy troops.[16] Any element of surprise had now been lost.

Australian soldiers greeted news of the fresh attack with incredulity. Most Australian officers also considered the planned attack nothing less than sheer bloody-mindedness on the part of Gough and his staff.[17] Brand decided that, for the 4th Brigade to achieve its objectives, the 14th and 16th Battalions would lead the attack against the first line of enemy trenches, with the 13th and 15th ready to leap-frog and advance on the second line, then capture Riencourt, a distance of over a kilometre from the first objective.[18] Similar tactics were adopted in the

12th Brigade's sector. The 46th and 48th Battalions were to lead off, with the 47th ready to pass through, then advance and take Bullecourt. The 45th Battalion was to remain in reserve.[19] While their senior officers were making those final plans, the exhausted troops—who had endured another night in the snow without proper sleep—yet again assembled in the sunken road before moving out to the jumping-off tape.

At 3.00a.m. the first tank arrived. Over the next hour, another two lined up in front of the 4th Brigade —well short of the promised six. In the 12th Brigade's sector there were no tanks at all. As had happened the previous night, many of the tanks had experienced mechanical problems. Others became stuck in the gluey mud leading to the front. The attack was ordered to proceed regardless.[20] At 4.30a.m. the tanks, now numbering four (another had arrived in the gap between the two brigades) moved forward. Almost immediately, enemy artillery opened up. German flares lit no man's land, making the slow-moving tanks an easy target for their gunners.

At 4.45a.m. the 4th Australian Infantry Brigade advanced across no man's land, 'with the 16th [Battalion] on right, 14th on left, moving in four successive waves, followed by the 13th behind the 16th and the 15th in rear of the 14th.'[21] By now two tanks were already on fire, having been hit by artillery shells. Another soon became stuck in the mud. One Australian infantryman remembered 'bullets flying off [tanks, which] ... were useless.'[22] Another officer recalled how eagerly the surviving crew from one incinerated tank 'came out and fought with their Lewis guns with us.'[23]

Under heavy and accurate machine-gun fire, the infantry pushed on towards the few gaps in the wire—the handiwork of the only surviving tank—in front of the first line of enemy trenches. Ferocious hand-to-hand combat and bombfighting ensued until finally, at about 5.15a.m., the 16th Battalion took the brigade's first objective. The assault was costly and the unit 'suffered very heavy casualties'.[24] According to Lieutenant Albert Marshall, a significant number of men were shot long before they reached the barbed wire which he described as 'awful stuff.'[25]

Finding the wire in front of the second line of trenches largely uncut, the courageous Major Percy Black sent a runner back to brigade headquarters describing the difficulties his men faced. Black pushed ahead undaunted and, finding an opening, led a group of men through until he was shot in the head, his body falling to hang limply on the wire where it was discovered by his good friend, Captain Harry Murray, a little over an hour later.[26] Ignoring the order to leap-frog, troops from the 13th Battalion were now advancing alongside their mates from the 16th. More fierce bayonet and bomb-fighting took place until around 6.50a.m. when the second objective was captured.[27]

***

On the 12th Brigade's front, conditions were far worse. The first tank arrived at around 4.45a.m. and, mistaking the Australians for German troops, fired a number of shells into their ranks. 'After much abuse from the incredulous Australians,' recalled a soldier from the 46th Battalion, 'and finally realising his mistake, the commander of the tank showed himself and asked the 46th members in which direction was the enemy.' Fifteen minutes later, the second vehicle arrived. Confused orders compounded the already dire situation. Divisional and brigade orders directed the men to 'Advance at 0445 hrs irrespective of whether or not the tanks had reached the Hindenburg Line.' Yet the battalion's CO (Lieutenant Colonel H.K. Denham) issued instructions that his 'infantry will not advance until 15 minutes after the tanks pass the jumping off trench.'[28]

Shortly before dawn, at 5.00a.m. (about thirty minutes behind the planned schedule), the two tanks began to advance. One of the vehicles soon experienced mechanical problems while the other was quickly destroyed by artillery fire before it could reach the wire. The infantry was left confused, unsure when to advance. According to the 46th Battalion's historian, with 'fear ... starting to set in ... something needed to be done to arrest this situation immediately.' Fifteen minutes later, having acquired some direction, the troops advanced. But, without support, they were enfiladed by 'heavier' rifle and machine-gun fire from the direction of Bullecourt.[29]

The Australians suffered enormous casualties crossing no man's land. Lieutenant Colonel Ray Leane of the 48th Battalion recalled that 'a machine gun nest near Bullecourt and a trench mortar on our left were giving us considerable trouble ... The right [flank] of the 46th ... was mown down in the gap. The rest of the battalion forced its way through on its correct front.' Following the 4th Brigade's lead, the two battalions from the 12th managed to fight their way into the first line of German trenches. But, as Leane added, 'The 48th found the wire in front of the second trench uncut but struggled in, bombed right as far as the "central road" in the depression and established a post there.'[30]

Leane requested an artillery bombardment of known German positions. At 7.15a.m. Murray, too, despatched a message to brigade headquarters asking for a barrage to assist the 4th Brigade which had 'established block on the right of both objectives.' He added that, 'With artillery support we can keep the position till the cows come home.'[31] The brigade commanders agreed and ordered a bombardment for both flanks, some 180 metres ahead, in front of the positions held by the Australians.

Inexplicably, other reports coming in from artillery observers and aircraft told of Australian troops and tanks well beyond the German front-line trenches. Fearing the losses artillery shells might inflict on his own men, the Fifth Army artillery commander in charge of the sector, Lieutenant Colonel R.L.R. Rabett, refused to sanction the barrage. The Australian brigade commanders were livid when informed that Rabett had countermanded their order. When Holmes heard the news, he immediately contacted Birdwood.[32] While sympathetic, Birdwood concurred with Rabett's decision; given the reports, he had little choice.

The German reinforcements being hurried forward could not believe their luck. Fearing that their positions would be overrun, numerous Australian officers were now firing off SOS flares requesting artillery support, particularly targeting the village of Riencourt, a little over a kilometre to the right of Bullecourt, from which German machine-guns were picking off their men at will. No response came. In sheer frustration, Murray despatched another runner informing headquarters to 'Look out for [more] SOS signals. [I'll] send ... as many as possible ... white flares.' This message was also ignored.[33] Soon after 7.30a.m., German infantry launched a major counter-attack. Lieutenant Colonel J. Durrant (13th Battalion) described the 'bombing from Riencourt. [We were] beaten back to 100 yards from Riencourt. [Another] counter attack on right.'[34]

A number of Australian troops had managed to fight their way into the Hindenburg Line despite a hail of relentless fire from enemy machine-gunners, artillery and counter-attacking infantry. However, most of the Australians were rapidly running out of ammunition and that most important of infantry weapon for trench-fighting—hand-grenades. Options were limited. They could either continue to fight and face certain death or wounding, run the gauntlet of German fire and attempt to return to the Australian lines, or surrender.

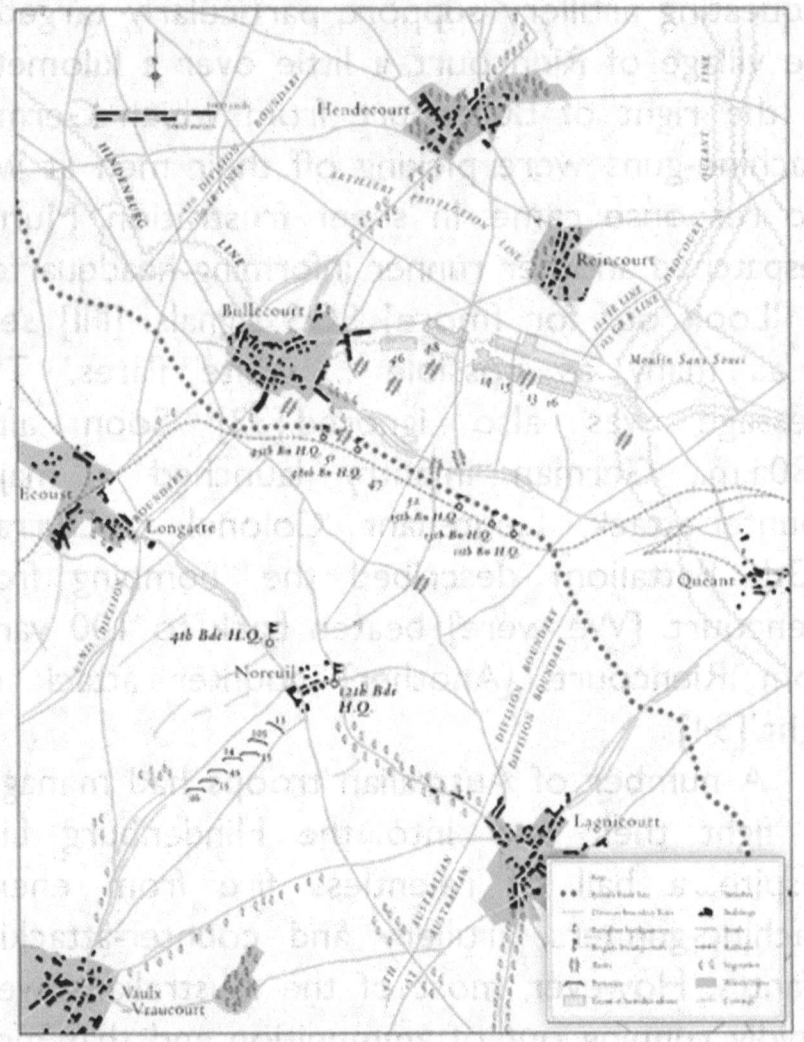

Map 4: The situation at Bullecourt at about 9.30 a.m., 11 April 1917, after the capture of portion of the Hindenburg Line by the 4th Australian Division.

At around 9.15a.m., the two brigade commanders made another concerted effort to secure artillery support. Again, none was forthcoming. Instead, British gunners were ordered to fire on enemy positions well behind Riencourt while 'not one ... shell disturbed the Hindenburg Line or the villages around it.'[35] Recognising the hopelessness of the situation, Murray led from the front and 'went along the whole line—1,000 yards [and] reorganised the Brigade front.'[36] His efforts were to no avail.

At 10.45a.m., the Germans launched a series of six concerted counter-attacks, most of which were successful. Frank Massey remembered that, in the section of German front his platoon had occupied, enemy troops 'came through the saps and communication trenches, and outnumbered us ten to one.'[37] Captain G.G. Gardiner (13th Battalion), who found himself in command of the right flank, had little hesitation in recommending that the survivors withdraw. Murray, however, refused to give up the fight. Still calling for artillery support, he told the men that they 'had two alternatives': capture or certain death.[38]

Some sections never heard the order to withdraw. Others chose to fight on to the bitter end. Corporal Jim Wheeler demanded that his men stay put and 'fight it out like Australians.'[39] A few, Murray included, managed to fight their way back. 'Scores' did not.[40] Clarence James recalled that his group 'could only frog-hop from shell hole to shell hole, because ... [of] enfilading fire ... We lost a lot of men.'[41] Many more

Australian soldiers from the 4th Brigade decided to surrender. Given the enormous number of casualties and men captured, Donald Fraser commented bitterly that 'it was a hell of a morning.'[42]

The 12th Brigade suffered a similar fate, although some platoons of the 46th and 48th Battalions were more fortunate than others: 'the centre and left ... had met with semi broken wire and the enemy defending it had fled to his second line of defences.'[43] Inevitably, the Germans counter-attacked and the 47th Battalion was ordered into the attack. Flares were fired in the hope that the artillery would respond. Each went unanswered. The Australians were now running critically short of bombs and rifle-grenades.

The 48th Battalion, which was holding part of the second line of enemy trenches, reported 'being bombed on both flanks', resulting in 'very heavy' casualties. At around 10.00a.m., the Australian position became dangerously precarious. Troops from both battalions had become disorganised. Major V.J. Waine of the 46th demanded 'more ammunition, bombs, and rifle grenades. Vickers [machine gun] requires 4 gallons water and at least 6000 rounds SAA [small-arms-ammunition]. Enemy massing in Riencourt—Rifle grenades most important.' Waine received '4 petrol tins of water'—nothing more. By 11.00a.m., the Australians were overwhelmed by sheer enemy numbers and firepower. The men's options were similar to those of the 4th Brigade. The 46th Battalion war diary noted that 'at about 11.15, our men were seen evacuating the objective.'[44] Guppy witnessed firsthand the 48th Battalion 'withdrawing in confusion and the men in retreat being mowed down by machine gun fire.'[45]

The 46th's war diary adds that, soon afterwards, 'a heavy barrage commenced on the enemy trenches.'[46] The fact that it was too little, too late, seemed to have been lost on senior British and Australian officers. To make matters worse, instead of falling on German positions 'this barrage fell on the members of the 48th Battalion who had fought their way back to the 46th's positions when they realised that their comrades had retired, without telling them.'[47] At 12.25p.m., 'a full hour after the other troops', the 48th Battalion finally managed to withdraw.[48]

At around 2.00p.m.—almost ten hours after the fighting began—the last shot was fired. Brand, possibly more than any other Australian officer, was overwhelmed by the sheer number of casualties. Of the almost 3,000 4th Brigade troops who advanced, 2,339 were listed as casualties or

POWs. Durrant noted that losses in his battalion were 'about 80%'.[49] The 12th fared little better—the brigade counted 950 casualties from the approximately 2,250 soldiers who went into battle. By comparison, German losses amounted to six officers and 132 ORs killed and another eleven officers and 520 ORs wounded. British historian Jonathon Walker commented that Bullecourt 'was a notable German victory in what had been a bad week elsewhere for the Sixth Army and its commander, Freiherr von Falkenhausen.'[50]

Percy Toft described a devastated Brand reportedly wiping tears from his eyes and yelling, 'To hell with the tanks, I've lost my brigade over them!'[51] Brand's sentiments were echoed elsewhere throughout the entire 4th Australian Division. The division's commander, General Walker, also asserted blandly that two of his brigades were virtually wiped out because of the tank crews 'failing to do their work'.[52] Tom Chataway reflected the general feeling of those soldiers who managed to return to their own lines: 'The tanks had failed,' he noted simply.[53] Ray Leane never forgave the tank crews. Twenty years later, he was still claiming that 'Tanks were of no assistance in the attack—in fact [they] proved a menace.'[54]

Two German officers with a captured British Mark II tank, serial number 586, visible on the left hand side. The tank is from British unit No 11 Company, D Battalion, which took part in the first battle of Bullecourt, 11 April 1917, and disabled near the German front trench. The image, taken soon after the attack, shows the significant shell damage sustained by the front of the tank. (AWM G01534J)

Yet, the reality was quite different. Certainly, Gough and his staff at Fifth Army Headquarters, including Tank Corps officers Lieutenant Colonel Hardress-Lloyd and Major Watson, deserved to be censured. Birdwood, too, was not entirely without blame. Had he heeded requests from officers in the field for artillery support, the captured enemy trenches may have been held. But, while some criticism of the tank crews was warranted, most was not. The majority of those young British soldiers were inexperienced and had no idea what to expect inside tanks with poor protective armour—the vehicles chosen were, in fact, little more than training vehicles. They endured not only the engine noise, but also the terrible smell of exhaust fumes and oil. All the while, there remained the constant fear of the tank catching fire from a direct hit, resulting in a slow, agonising death, or shrapnel ricocheting inside the cabin, causing shocking wounds to most of the crew—so bad, in fact, that the luckier were killed instantly. Moreover, some tank crews put themselves at risk by helping draw fire away from attacking infantry, thereby saving the lives of many Australians.[55] Instead of blaming the tanks, the British military historian, Captain Cyril Falls, was more critical of the lack of a proper preliminary artillery bombardment. 'Had Bullecourt been first unmercifully pounded by artillery,' he reasoned, 'and had the whole attack been made under a barrage, it would have succeeded, and the position could have been held.'[56]

Those Australian survivors who managed to return to the sunken road were pessimistic not only about what had gone wrong but, more significantly, about their future. Whatever their previous confidence in the British High Command, it had now evaporated. By contrast, the Germans boasted that their troops had captured 1,137 Australian ORs, twenty-seven officers and fifty-three machineguns. For some of those POWs, their ordeal on the front line was not yet over. A German report revealed that, after 'the Australian prisoners trudged out watched by our escorts several shells exploded among them, fired from our artillery, which ignorant of the sudden turn of events in the fighting situation, took these for advancing enemy attack troops.'[57]

After the horrors of Bullecourt, the survivors were allowed some rest, while the decimated battalions attempted to return to something approaching their prebattle strength. Those survivors marched through near-blinding snow to Bapaume, where they were put on trains that took them to Albert, one account noting how a few men from the 48th Battalion 'marched into "Crucifix Camp" with brave show, singing.'[58] Toft reflected on a 'meal and a sleep, how one appreciates these common things when they are much needed. One saw the reaction of the men who had taken part in the battle. They were listless and difficult to interest ... We went back to Ribemont on the Somme River and did very little work.'[59]

***

Incredibly, Gough ordered another attack on Bullecourt. On 3 May, the 2nd Australian Division, supported yet again by the hapless 62nd British Division, launched another assault—on this occasion, with artillery support. In some places the wire was cut successfully and the infantry managed to penetrate parts of the Hindenburg Line. In reality, senior British and Australian officers had learnt precious little from their earlier folly. Why, for instance, did the artillery plan of attack ignore completely the position of well-sited enemy machine guns at the Six Cross Roads? Why, too, did planners ignore flanking machine-gun fire from the nearby village of Queant? Troops from the 5th Australian Brigade subsequently paid the price for that negligence, massacred by those very same machine-guns as they moved forward.

For the next five days, German troops gamely held on. On 8 May, the 5th Australian Division replaced the 2nd and, over the following nine days, Australian and British soldiers were put through another mince-grinder. Finally, on 17 May, enemy resistance collapsed. Gough had won through. Bullecourt was occupied, albeit at great cost. A small, tactically insignificant village had claimed over 7,000 casualties. Apparently forgetting the horror Australian soldiers had endured, *The Times* in London reported that the attacks against Bullecourt were 'typical of [Field Marshal] Sir Douglas Haig's methods and thoroughly profitable for him.' The newspaper added that the small French village 'had remained German until Saturday [17 May], when the British established themselves in it.' It was not unusual for the British press to give scant acknowledgment to the Australian troops, apart from indicating that they were 'at this part of the British front', and demonstrating 'what they can do in this kind of deadly work.'[60]

The 4th Australian Brigade would never fully recover from the anguish of Bullecourt. The survivors were perhaps the unlucky ones. They were destined to endure more hideous battles. Even the POWs were, in some respects, far more fortunate, although they had certainly lost whatever freedom soldiers on the Western Front could claim. Instead, for the next nineteen or so months, those captured were forced to tolerate conditions not far removed from troops in the line, although usually without the constant fear of death or maiming, and the terrible psychological torment of artillery barrages. There were few other compensations.

CHAPTER SIX
Captivity
'At the tender mercies of the enemy'

CHAPTER SIX

CAPTIVITY

'At the tender mercies of the enemy'

In the aftermath of the horrific Battle of Bullecourt, a number of Australian soldiers who had survived the battle found themselves stranded in no man's land. Many of these men were wounded and knew themselves incapable of making the perilous journey back to the sunken road or the old railway siding to rejoin their units. The stranded survivors faced a difficult choice. They could surrender to the Germans and face an uncertain future as POWs, or they could continue their desperate attempt to cross the pitted battlefield and regain their own lines. The second choice was far more life-threatening than the first as most knew they risked almost certain death in the struggle to return to safety. Many were killed as they attempted to scramble undetected across the shattered landscape of no man's land. Those who failed in the attempt were picked up by the Germans or surrendered, forfeiting their freedom and perhaps their lives.

As the survivors made their way back to Bapaume, wounded Australian soldiers who had crawled into shell-holes, or were lying in the open, waited for the inevitable—either a slow lingering death or being taken prisoner by the Germans. Once the fighting had ceased, enemy soldiers came looking for Australian wounded. Despite sporadic artillery and machine-gun fire from the Australian side, A.G. Butler wrote of 'German medical orderlies attending the wounded in the shell-holes in No Man's Land and on the wire. The firing was therefore stopped, and, after display of a white flag, for some two hours our regimental [stretcher] bearers and fifty infantry were permitted to assist in collecting wounded. Most of those who were picked by the Germans off the wire were carried by them to their own trenches.'[1] Bean's account differs slightly. He noted that countless Australian soldiers 'were wounded and lay about the wire until captured or put to death by a merciful enemy.' Bean adds that other German troops were not so chivalrous. Some

> at first fired on the stretcher-bearers, but about 4pm upon [Lieutenant J.] Julin's taking his party boldly towards the wire with Red Cross flags flying, the sniping ceased and for two hours the wounded were collected without impediment, the Germans carrying to their own trenches most of those from the wire, but in a few

cases placing badly wounded men beyond its outer edge to be picked up by their opponents. Although they also took full advantage of this informal truce to repair gaps in their wire, the concession was welcomed by every Australian. It lasted till 6 o'clock, when snow began to fall and the Germans, probably fearing an attack under this screen, shouted 'finish hospital!' and both sides withdrew. Nevertheless, throughout the night, which was still and frosty, not a shot was fired, and for several days afterwards, odd survivors crawled or were helped back to the railway.[2]

***

Given the fighting reputation of the 4th Australian Brigade, German GHQ was mightily impressed by the large number of Australians captured at Bullecourt. Subsequent enemy reports smacked of 'the German elation at the defeat of the 4th Brigade. War Office records ... show that they specially feared our [4th] Brigade, and that their front line troops were always warned when the 4th Brigade was opposite them. Also that there was a reward of 1,000 marks for each Colonel of the Brigade and a larger one for the Brig[adier General] dead or alive. That they knew all these by name was proved to our prisoners captured at Bullecourt.'[3]

***

Ernest Etchell was one of the few who made it safely back to the Australian front line. Wounded in the left ankle, he began edging his way through the uncut wire. 'I was crawling outside the second line of wire, when a machine-gun opened up on me,' he remembered,

I took my boot off first, but I couldn't see no blood or nothing. And I thought, "Well bugger it, I haven't been hit at all!" ... I tried to get up and walk on it, but I couldn't walk on it. So I thought I must have been hit. And I had another look and there was just a little hole where a bullet had come in through the lace-holes of my boot and out my heel. The wound never bled. I decided I'd better get rid of my gun ... Not just leave it for the Germans to get and use. So I pulled the guts out of it, all the parts, and threw them in opposite directions. I hung onto my revolver. Then I had to get myself back on one leg.

Once I got back to this platoon in reserve, they looked after me. They got me on a stretcher and sent three jokers to carry me back ... We was going back down the road when a battery of 18 pounders come up the road at full gallop, and the Germans started shelling them. These jokers dropped me in the middle of the bloody road and cleared off. Well ... the limbers went either side of me, one of them touching me on the hand. After they'd gone by I rolled myself off the stretcher and got off the road, dragging my stretcher with me. When the shelling had stopped, these three jokers came creeping back. I said to them, "You're damn fortunate I left my revolver with Sergeant Lonergan, or I'd have shot the pair of you!" And I would have done. I said, "At least you could have put me off the road. But you was in too big a hurry to get away."

The stretcher bearers carried me back to a motor ambulance. When I was in the ambulance one of the doctors put his head inside. "Any 15th in here?" he asked. I leaned up on my leg. "Yes, I'm one," I said. "How are the boys getting on up there?" he said. I said, "Getting shit chopped out of them!"

Etchell was patched up by the doctor and later rejoined his battalion.[4]

The Germans continued to pursue Australian soldiers withdrawing across the battlefield and attempting to regain their lines. 'Bullecourt was the biggest mess you ever heard of,' exclaimed A.J. Whittington, 'our artillery did nothing!' He added:

> The Germans counterattacked, and we were kicked out. I was kicked out, the same as the rest of them, and from then on we were cutting across no man's land. I threw away everything I had. But when I got half way across to our lines, still out in no man's land, there was a bit of a lull. Well I got into a deep shell hole ... I was going to go home when it got dark, but when I popped up to have a look, the blighters were all over no man's land! The blighters went over attacking our lines.

Whittington's disgust at being captured was evident. 'I cursed myself after that,' he said, 'that I didn't look around earlier. I could see them collecting stragglers. They just collected a lot of us up.'[5]

Corporal Lancelot Davies was one of many men who regarded capture as a humiliating experience. 'As the alternative [to capture] meant death, and I was in a helpless position, one must naturally excuse my choice ... I was compelled to submit to the most humiliating experience of a lifetime, surrender!'[6] Every man captured also faced the grim possibility of being shot as he surrendered, whether due to misunderstanding or even embitterment on the part of the German captors. There was also some anxiety as to how the men would be interrogated, and the nature of repercussions should they fail to answer questions from enemy soldiers skilled in their art. Many soldiers preferred death to the ignominy of becoming a POW and their perceptions of having 'let their mates down'.

***

As the captive men moved further behind the line they had to endure another pounding when 'they were accidentally caught in the open by ... [a] late Anzac artillery barrage and also received a strafing by a passing British airman who mistook them for retreating Germans.'[7] The men cursed their luck; had that bombardment occurred some hours earlier, the Australians would probably have held their objectives. Horatio Ganson was adamant. 'If we'd had that barrage,' he asserted, 'we could have walked through the Jerry lines.'[8] Donald Fraser remembered: 'when the barrage came down, the Germans crouched up against the front wall of the trench as close as they could get. They didn't care where we were! Some of our fellows were killed.'[9] George Bean (4th Machine Gun Company) remarked that when our artillery opened up this is where I became separated from the main column. When this barrage started ... both prisoners and guards ran everywhere for shelter, up to this time I was being helped along owing to a bad wound in the leg, which I had received earlier in the day. We were about half-way through the village when it [artillery] opened up, and I was deserted and left lying in the centre of the road, where I remained until sometime later and was picked up by two Germans who took me to a dressing station where I rejoined a number of our own wounded.[10]

Ernie Chalk provided his own assessment of the barrage and its aftermath: 'We had to go through one of our own barrages,' he wrote,

> and this gave us to realise very vividly what it really meant to be the object of a British bombardment. It was accountable for the lives of a great many of our own boys, and of course, our Hun guards suffered very heavy losses as well. We were kept moving for about three hours after this. It was necessarily a very slow march, for nearly half of the lads were wounded in some way or other. And those that were unwounded, and those only slightly so, had to carry and

in other ways help along those who were less fortunate than themselves.

Chalk added that, after marching through a 'very heavy snow storm that was raging at the time,' they came to a tiny French village. The prisoners 'all looked a very dejected crew, and we were turned like so many cattle into an enclosure out in the open.'[11]

***

The method of capture varied across the front. Albert Marshall recalled that he 'just had to wait ... The company had no ammunition and couldn't get it. There was nothing we could do. The time came of course when we had to surrender. We had no option—no option whatsoever.'[12] Lieutenant A.V. Watkinson, on the other hand, was climbing through the barbed wire when he

> received a machine gun bullet in the arm which broke a bone. I lay in a shell hole and waited for dark as the machine gun was sweeping the ground around where I was for some time. After about two hours I tried to get back but as I had lost some amount of blood I fell over as soon as I started up. A short while afterwards a German party picked me up.

I was thrown into the front line trench and left there for five hours after which I was put into a bag and carried into Riencourt village. I was then taken to a German dugout where I remained about 12 hours. Then I was sent to a field hospital for a few hours where I received no attention.[13]

Donald Fraser received 'a couple of flesh wounds' when 'most of the men who were able, started to run the gauntlet back through the German wire ... trying to get back to the railway cutting. Dozens of splendid men were killed and many wounded.' Almost as an afterthought, he described his own section's capture:

> Most of the wounded [including himself] who were able, crawled into shell holes and were picked up by the Germans later in the afternoon. Some did manage to get back, including Captain Murray ... Most of our runners were killed that morning, while trying to get through to Battalion Headquarters with messages from our Commanders Murray, Gardiner ... The Germans simply shot them down with machine gun fire.
>
> After the Germans picked us up, all the wounded who were able, were marched back and herded into a big church, which

I think would have been Cambrai. Late that night, they brought some of the badly wounded in. The pulpit was used as an operating theatre.

Fraser was especially critical of enemy military doctors.

Anyone needing to be operated on suffered sheer hell, due to the absence of anaesthetic. The German doctors were very rough with the prisoner patients. They referred to us as "Englander Swines" and any of the badly wounded who yelled, they said to them, "Snouteer hauling dumb swine," meaning, "shut up dumb pig". Paper bandages were used as they as they had no linen.[14]

Many years later, Fraser described the events of his capture in more detail. He revealed that his section had exhausted all its ammunition and, soon after, enemy soldiers had entered the trench.

[It] was full of Germans ... There were hundreds more marching down. We could see them. It would have been beautiful for artillery. They started to shell a road. We saw them shell the road, and the Germans each side of the road ... [Enemy infantry moved] off the road. They were well trained. They didn't stop on the road when a shell came for them ... They got off the road and lay down ... I was still in the German line when I was captured. The Germans counted us. Some enemy guards then went through our blokes ... picking their pockets. If they had any money on them they took it ... I was terribly tired too. You're knocked up. Buggered-up in other words.[15]

Len Pooley was taken prisoner earlier in the fighting. 'We stayed in Jerry's trenches until about eleven o'clock,' he recalled,

> not long after that we were surrounded by a lot of Germans. They were school-boys really—very young—although the officers in charge of them were older. All I can remember then is 'Loos! Loos!' We had to throw all our equipment off. We had to leave our rifles where we stood. We had a pack on and they pushed it off us, shouting "Alles loos! Alles loos!" You had to do what you were told because they had bayonets on their rifles, and you'd get a bayonet.

The seventeen-year-old Pooley (who had enlisted under age) believed that he was about to be executed:

> They marched us out and they lined us up along the bank of a small pond. There

might have been a hundred of us. When they lined us up I thought they were going to put the machine-gun on us. I said to my mate next to me, "This looks like they are going to finish us off!" But he said, "Oh, no, don't think things like that." Anyway, it was only to count us, and ask us a lot of questions. There were about one hundred of us, and they divided us up into three groups. The German officers spoke English really well.

One officer said to me, "What made you enlist so young?" I said, "Well, I wanted to see the world." 'Mmm, mmm!" he said, "I thought so!" And he went on.[16]

Horatio Ganson was captured soon after the battle. Realising that his section was cut off from the rest of the battalion, he recognised that the men's only chance of survival was surrender. 'It was about midday when we were driven back,' he remembered,

there were seven or eight of us, although I didn't know who the other blokes were. We got that way that we had nothing at all to fight with. I know I never had a cartridge or anything. We had fired everything ... and thrown all our bombs ... In the end we were all jammed up in the end of the trench. We couldn't go any further. It was such a long way back to our lines and ... we didn't know quite where we were. There were snipers everywhere and you couldn't put your head up. The trench system was like a Chinese puzzle. We ended up in a dead-end, a lookout trench. We took the bolts out of our rifles and flung them away. The rifles also had illuminated sights, a little bar across the sights tipped with phosphorus.

We stripped those out and slung them away.

Then we flung our rifles in a heap on top of the trench, and with our last bomb we blew the rifles to smithereens. Then we just waited for about half an hour. The first thing we saw was a stick bomb poked around the corner of the trench. We didn't know whether they were going to lob it or not. But we didn't do anything and the German followed the bomb around with his hand, holding the bomb out. He was only about ten feet away.

Unsure of his fate, Ganson 'didn't know whether to say anything or not. Then we heard his first word in German, "'Loos!" That's what he said. "Come on! Get out of it!"'[17] William Groves, on the other hand, recalled little of his capture. 'I remember only that a group of young

Germans descended upon our sadly reduced party,' he wrote, 'my equipment was taken off and flung to the ground; and then conscious only of a vague ineffable weariness, conscious of the humiliating futility of all our desperate efforts, to the accompaniment of a monotonous "Loos! Loos!"... the little party moved off to join dozens of smaller groups that were beginning to congregate within the village of Riencourt.'[18]

Company Sergeant-Major Emerson was also forced to surrender his little group and they 'were marched along enemy communication trenches through Riencourt—then being shelled heavily by our own artillery—to Corps Headquarters at Ecourt St Quentin.' The same night, they 'were assembled in the village church and there were about 800 Australians. Next day we were entrained for the distributing camp at Le Quesnoy.' Emerson was among the more fortunate Australian POWs. Instead of being sent to work for the enemy in France, he was part of a 'draft' which was sent to 'an NCO Lager' in Germany.[19]

Guppy was aghast at his capture. He confided in his diary that he remained in a shell hole until about 4.00p.m., 'nearly frozen with the cold, when a strong party of Jerries with some of their stretcher bearers out looking for wounded came upon me and took possession of me.' He continued:

> I was then ordered to carry on my back to the German line a wounded man of the 15th Battalion. I found the trench full of Germans and some of them bound up the wounds of the man I brought in. One of them also gave this man a cigarette and gave me a handfull [sic] from a tin he had evidently taken from one of the many Aussie haversacks lying about. I was not molested or searched in any way. I then carried this man for some distance along the trench which was strewn with our dead and thence back to the village of Reincourt. During this journey I had the chance to look around me and was horrified to see everywhere by the bodies lying in trenches and in shell holes and in heaps in the open how terrific had been the slaughter of our boys. As I passed one shell hole I saw therein the body of a dear old comrade. Lying close to him was a wounded man to whom I said "Is that poor old Reg Blamey there?" and he answered "Yes, he just died a few minutes ago." Many of the Germans were searching the bodies and placing them in shell holes. I carried my burden down

into a very deep Red Cross dugout in the village.[20]

Captain D.P. Wells (in a statement made after his repatriation from Germany) provides a rather different account:

> After capture no attempt was made to remove the wounded till dark, when German orderlies removed them, handling them very brutally without regard to the nature of their wounds ... A German Major put himself out to aggravate me and robbed me of all my belongings and badges of rank ... Corporal Stewart craved for a drink. He died soon after drinking. Then they handed the drink, and when I found it to be paraffin, I would not drink ... The medical attention is disgusting ... Quite a number of lives could have been saved had the patients received treatment in time, whilst others, instead of being permanently incapacitated, could have been completely cured. I can quote numerous cases of willful brutality to helpless wounded men.[21]

Ernie Chalk was even more succinct. When his 'supply of bombs and small arms ammunition gave out ... [he] then automatically became at the tender mercies of the enemy.'[22]

Private Thomas Taylor noted 'the struggle [on] that memorable day', before adding that:

as the day [11 April] wore on, we found ourselves forced back by sheer weight of numbers, and late afternoon found another "Digger" and myself wounded, and, in an endeavour to reach our own lines, taking refuge from the incessant snipe ... in a shell-hole. We had got nearly three-parts of the way back, but it became too hot altogether, as they were sniping and using machine guns 'to some tune,' and were killing our boys by the score. We decided then that the shell-hole would do us until darkness should give us an opportunity to again seek safety unobserved. Our 'bolt' for the trenches occupied but a few minutes ... After lying, inactive, cold and miserable in the snow for at least three or four hours, I could see a German passing from shell-hole to shell-hole, evidently looking for prisoners. Lying low, we anxiously watched his movements, and our hopes rose as it seemed to us he would miss our haven. One of their machine guns, however, was playing over his head, and he evidently did not feel comfortable, for he stopped and signalled the gunner to cease fire. When he turned to continue his searching he had altered his direction, and was coming right towards us. Our detection was inevitable, and my feelings were indescribable. I said my prayers then, for I had an idea that he'd stick that bayonet into us. We had nothing whatever to defend ourselves with, as we had thrown everything away, even ... our overcoats, in making the attempt to escape. He came straight on to us, and it was evident he had given up all expectations of making a capture, so he got as big a fright as we did when he saw us. I believe I could have knocked him over with a stick at that moment if I had one.

Well, he made us his prisoners and we were taken back into their lines. Passing again over the scene of the conflict, we noticed a good many of our comrades lying wounded, and we were granted permission to collect as many as we could and carry them in behind the lines ... We must have carried about twelve of our mates in before it became rather dark, and, seeming afraid that we would "do a break" under cover of the darkness, they gave us to understand that we couldn't carry any more. We then collected as many waterproof sheets as we could off the dead, and covered the poor chaps up. It was all we could do under the circumstances towards making them comfortable and protecting them from the weather.

I must admit that up to this time the Germans had given us a very fair "spin."[23]

For his part, Horace Rumble felt ambivalent. Despite a badly wounded hand, he was desperate to return to his own line. But enemy troops entered the dugout in which he and a group 'of fellows' were sheltering. 'Next thing I knew there was a whole pile of Germans coming down the stairs armed,' he added, 'and [they] said—all those who can walk come up on top.'[24]

Campbell Stewart wrote bitterly that the 'day of the great attack resulted in dismal failure owing to lack of organisation, failure of tanks, shortage of bombs want of artillery barrage and loss of officers.' While he did not describe his capture, Stewart noted that he was 'taken behind German lines under heavy barrage to a village called Ecourt St Quentin ... [where he] slept in church ... Everybody cold, wet, hungry, miserable. Marched to station and travelled ... about seven hours in a cattle truck to [another] village ... Still fearfully cold.'[25]

A survivor from one of the 'bombing squads,' Jim Wheeler, recalled that 'a shell lobbed about ten or fifteen feet from me.' 'You evidently hear the last second of the shell that hits you, or is close to you,' he said, because what you do is you crouch down under the wall nearest the enemy. Of course, no trouble at all, the whole wall just rolls over you. I was thrown away like a rag doll, and the bloody swale just rolled over on top of me. I was buried up to the shoulders. I had no chance of ever freeing myself. It was the Germans who dug me out. They carried me out on a stretcher.[26]

Wheeler was treated by his captors before being moved to a hospital in Douai.

Corporal Claude Benson's 'remnant' was another group of stragglers. Although wounded in the hand, he led them through a roadway to 'take cover in a shell hole', where they were 'surrounded by Germans'. Convinced that it was 'useless sacrificing more lives', Benson chose surrender. His group was 'taken to a village [collecting station] ten miles behind the German lines ... [where] the wounded were attended to by a German "sanitator."[27] After his wound was dressed, Benson was one of nine NCOs 'picked from different battalions' and taken 'before an intelligence officer'. This 'officer questioned us about the disposition and movement of our troops, but got no information from us. He particularly wanted to know about our artillery. I told him I did not belong to the artillery and knew nothing at all about it. We remained here for one night when the [more severe] wounded men were sent to hospital.' Unlike the reports of others, Benson was adamant that he 'did not see any ill-treatment while here.'[28]

Lancelot Davies wrote that, once he had surrendered, a German soldier moved alongside him in the trench and

> made a sign that I divest myself of my web equipment, and this done, another, evidently the "leader," told me to continue attending to the wounded. This party now passed on to the attack, and others followed them, who on gaining our sap, jump in, surround and proceed to search us for arms. This done, we are ordered out, and under guard continue the "advance" into enemy territory, but not according to plan, leaving the wounded as they lay.

It seems that the fate of the wounded depended largely on their captors' whim. Some were tended by their comrades, while others—as in the case of Davies—were left behind to fend for themselves. Davies accepted that he was about to embark on 'a trek into the unknown'. Climbing 'up out of the trench' he witnessed

> a scene I shall never forget, so indelibly impressed was it on my mind. Here we

were (I say "we" because other Aussies in distress had joined in the evacuation from nearby positions.) There lay before us our previously planned objectives. Bullecourt on the left, Riencourt in front, with Queant, a German stronghold, on the right. Confusion was rife as the Huns were still coming over in great numbers to the attack. A few found time to pay their attention to us, both by remarks, but the majority appeared concentrated on their "job" of consolidating the ground we had wrested from them just a few hours previous. No ill-treatment had so far come my way. Jerry soldiers who had been delegated to the job of collecting and guarding us prisoners in their immediate vicinity, commenced to conduct us to the "rear." Our artillery had once again opened out on the positions, but the strafe was too late to be of any use to the Australians. As a matter of fact, it became seriously detrimental from our point. Shells fell among both friends and foe, the heavier stuff tumbling the houses of both villages systematically ... Riencourt was the nearer to me. I was ... plodding with others along the metalled road leading there. Light shrapnel shells hurled their pellets along this road. I could plainly distinguish the pellets hit, and roll forward, some quite close, and the wonder is none caught me. A few of our chaps were hit, apparently by the British shells ... Somehow all fear had departed; after the first shock of capture it was furthest from my mind ... Shells continued to crash. A British plane hovered around, and appeared to be endeavouring to sum up the whole position as it swooped down and then ascended again. Suddenly its machine gun rattled ... and I could see men scatter, many of our chaps among them ... The shelling from the British side continued, and on the road we were traversing it became more intense as we came closer to Riencourt. As the fire became rather hot for the Germans, and being hindered by our wounded mate, our posterns compel us to leave him to the stretcher bearers, who would get him to the aid post later ... Meanwhile the party moves on ... Looking around I ... see ... scattered units of khaki and grey ... some running as if to cover. Nevertheless onward I go with the shells persistently bursting at close quarters ... I had come by this time fairly close to the village, when suddenly ... shouts are heard from the right, and my attention is attracted to one of our worthy sentries who has now taken cover in a sap, beckoning to us stragglers in a rather flustered and threatening manner, to come his way, which we do, and the trek is then continued along the communication trenches. At one spot is a regimental aid post, around which both German and Australian wounded are gathered, and we have some difficulty in getting past. We are now in an area of much more calm, as the British strafe is not falling here.

Further progress brings us into the open again, and we come up with and are joined by many other prisoners from the lines, and are formed into a column of fours. The excitement of the battle, and its ultimate result, is now passed off, and we find ourselves in a sort of "family group". But rather gloomy, although some endeavour to brighten up the mob, and tales of the recent experience are exchanged, and opinions discussed, as we plod along to an unknown destination.[29]

***

Horatio Ganson echoed the feelings of disbelief and astonishment of other Australian prisoners:

> After we were captured it was a case of not knowing what to think. Your mind's given way. Everybody sat down more or less dumbfounded. We never thought of being a prisoner—never. That's the last thing we ever thought of ... You don't know what's going to come ahead of you, that's the trouble.

Ganson was disturbed by the way several German guards interrogated his mates.

> [they] searched you before you went out of the line. Everything was spread out on the ground. You had to empty out. They take everything off you, although they didn't take personal things. They wouldn't take photographs. But we all had knives and tin-openers, and a big spike for splicing rope. They took all of those off us, and safety razors. Anything that was dangerous. There was an officer waiting. He shooed you along once you went out. You had to move. But we were moving under our own barrage then, so it was for your own good.[30]

In fact, the Germans were more concerned with captured Australian officers who might have some knowledge of the tanks. While there were plenty of officer prisoners—for instance, not one officer from the 15th Battalion managed to return to his own line—none had any inkling of the way tanks operated. Albert Marshall recalled:

> When we were taken prisoner we were taken into a yard where we [were] interviewed and asked questions ... Well I've never seen so much torn paper. I suppose everyone had notes, you know, and different things, and they tore them up into little bits, and just chucked it on the ground. I'll never forget that. The Germans talked to all the men to see what they could get ... well, they were getting a little information from everybody.[31]

Lieutenant Garnet Veness noted that a 'small party of us [officers] ... were separated for cross examination purposes ... [which] was unsatisfactory although they did try to draw us by speaking of what others [POWs] had said.'[32] Lieutenant Reginald Sanders wrote that the Germans divided the officers from the men they led. After being taken to a French village and given a bath, 'two dozen officers were entrained under guard and eventually found ... [them]selves at the German township of Karlsruhe,' while their men were forced to tolerate 'untold sufferings as working parties behind the German lines.'[33]

***

Horatio Ganson was part of a larger group marched off to a stone church not far from the front. He recalled that the Germans had

> taken all the chairs and everything out. It was just like one big bare room. Of course, we just got pushed into it. I think there were about 200 of us in that church—all the 4th 'Divvy' blokes. We stayed there that night; we slept on the floor of the church ... The next day the Uhlans came for us. They were mounted, and had proper lances, with the square top on their hats. They were a crack regiment. They took us to St Quentin, and we were put on a train there and went to Lille.[34]

According to A.J. Whittington, 'The Germans stuck what prisoners they'd collected in no man's land into a shed' where they were organised into groups:

> We had to sleep on a bit of straw. I had trench feet at the time. Of course, your feet swell up. We were examined, and they must have looked at my feet; they sent me back to Germany. Most of the able bodied fellows were kept there to work behind the lines. But I went to Friedrichsfeld, a base camp.[35]

***

Guppy wrote that the men felt 'too much stunned with the awful day we have passed through and the realisation of what we are now. We are issued later with a small quantity of vile black bread which it seems impossible to eat. All were only too pleased to lie down on the benches and floor wet and cold and try to get some rest. Early in the morning' of 12 April, they were marched away 1 kilometre to the station. Whilst waiting here I told a postern I wanted a drink and he directed me to a tap close by at the rear of the station. A moment later a Hun NCO rushed round and commenced angrily abusing me at the same time picking up a large piece of wood, from a heap, with which I expected to be attacked. What he was talking about I did not know, however he dropped the piece of wood, perhaps it was the look in my eye, for I did not care much just at that moment what I did ... At midday we entrained and travelled to Solesmes where we were locked up in an enclosure and issued with some coffee and black bread, vile stuff which we were nevertheless pleased to partake of having had nothing all day.

The next morning was much the same. 'Coffee for breakfast,' Guppy recorded, before his group was forced to

> undergo a search, not a close one by any means and all papers are inspected though little is taken except knives, razors and in some cases the more valuable wallets. Some of the wounded who have been with us so far are taken away to Hospital also a few men of each Battalion ... are kept behind here. We are then marched a considerable distance to Le Quesnoy under the escort of mounted Uhlans. As we pass through many villages the French people bring us out pails of water to drink from and also occasionally throw to us loaves of bread. We see old women bursting into tears and many bewailing our fate as we pass along and we tell them as best we can that all is going well on our side. We reach Le Quesnoy toward evening and are at once placed in a barbed wire enclosure in which is a long terrace of houses. In the rooms in which we are crowded is a plentiful distribution of straw which is our only bed.[36]

The men remained in Le Quesnoy until suitable transport could be arranged for an unknown destination.

***

Harold Horner (3rd Brigade Machine Gun Company) was captured a few days after Bullecourt, during the Battle of Lagnicourt on 14 April. He was unarmed at the time and was surprised by enemy troops as the other members of his machine-gun company were sleeping in a cellar beside their gun. 'An easy capture,' he wrote. 'The German officer was excited somewhat, and looked around several times, as though he expected our counter-attack to come on at any minute. He told his men to move across to the church-yard, where they would meet others of their company. The men seemed eager enough to go. 'Kom! Tommy,' said the man who first smiled at me; so, of course, as there was no option I went with them, glancing round to be sure that no one looked into the cellar. I felt confident that an opportunity to slip away from them would occur ... In following the street through the village, we arrived alongside some dead Fritzes; and I wondered if they would be angry with me when they saw their own dead. They gazed on them quietly as they passed. Evidently they were old hands, and had seen hundreds of dead men. Soon we reached the church-yard, which was enclosed by a low strong wall.

Here other Germans had gathered, and I carefully looked through the different parties but found that I was still the only one in khaki! ... After spending some time in the sunken road, it became evident that the Germans were retiring; and my friend [guard] beckoned to me to follow them ... About this time our people put up a barrage—big stuff started falling thick and fast ahead of us. Fritz knew [that a] ... counter-attack was coming on ... Down through the village we passed a continuous line of Fritzes ... As I trudged on with my captors, my chances of getting away seemed to grow less and less—more hopeless as we got nearer to open country ... Soon we were clear of the town, travelling across the open country, and here it was that we met the barrage. Now I learnt that while my men had been quite undismayed by rifle-fire, they turned white when the big stuff rained down around us. Before we had gone 200 yards, they called a halt, and snuggled close behind a bank on which lay a fallen tree ... After a pause of a few minutes, my captors and I ran on for another hundred yards or more, when they decided to take shelter again ... We [then] progressed in the direction of Fritz's wire by such rushes of a hundred yards or more, until I was surprised to find that we were right on it quite suddenly, and machine guns in the trenches were looking straight at us.

We passed through a zig-zag road in the barbed wire entanglement, which was about twenty yards wide; and soon found ourselves in the German trenches ... It was not until I was safely landed in Fritz's trench that I realised that the game was up for me ... We trudged many weary miles through several villages until we arrived at headquarters. Young officers with skin like a girl's, and Iron Crosses, etc, on their breasts, questioned us good-naturedly; and we were put into a stable with a sentry on guard ... I have always made my boast that I do not worry; and I suppose the 'chronic grin' is the result; but during the first day of my captivity I experienced a state of soul, shall I say, that I have never known before; and I hope I shall never have to pass through it again.[37]

***

On the morning of 16 April, the Germans assembled Australian POWs captured at

Bullecourt for a roll call. Some of the men, including Sergeant Guppy, were 'ordered to fall out and remain here whilst all the remaining NCOs and men are marched away to the Station. We believed they are going to Germany but hear later that they are going to Lille to work there behind the lines.'[38] Guppy would remain in Le Quesnoy for a few weeks before being sent to Germany. Officers and some of the more fortunate men (such as Whittington) were immediately trucked to prison camps in Germany while wounded soldiers were treated in nearby local hospitals. The rest were marched to Fort Macdonald, the infamous prison nicknamed 'The Black Hole of Lille'.

Australian prisoners, used to savouring their freedom, were now beginning an ordeal which to most was unimaginable. They would be forced to rely on one another's courage and comradeship; on sporadic Red Cross packages; and on the Germans' respect—or otherwise—for POWs and the international laws of war. It was an enormous risk and one that did not always pay.

CHAPTER SEVEN
The Status and Treatment of POWs
'You owe your Life to his Humanity'

CHAPTER SEVEN

THE STATUS AND TREATMENT OF POWS

'You owe your Life to his Humanity'

At the time the Australians were captured at Bullecourt, there were already millions of other POWs (mostly Russians) in camps scattered throughout Germany and occupied Europe. Some of these men were living in appalling conditions, often because in Germany—as in other belligerent countries—there was little infrastructure in place to house POWs. As Robert Jackson suggests, none of the involved 'nations had given much thought, prior to the outbreak of war, to the logistical problems involved in handling and sustaining large numbers of prisoners, although the rules governing their treatment had long since been formulated.'[1]

The status and treatment of POWs had been determined largely by the experience of previous wars. Since earliest recorded times, prisoners taken in combat have been treated harshly or, indeed, executed by their captors. Well prior to the Greek wars, for example, the King of Judah ordered his troops to kill more than 2,000 captured Edomites by throwing them from the cliffs around Petra in Jordan. 'To walk beneath this cliff today,' Patsy Adam-Smith writes, 'is to hear the death cries of the young men whose only crime was to do what their countrymen had sent them to do.' By the nineteenth century—when more soldiers than ever were being captured, mostly in European wars—a number of organisations, individuals and governments had expressed anxiety over the fate of those prisoners. The future British Prime Minister, Winston Churchill, himself a captive of the Boers, confessed to being in a state of unremitting depression. 'You are in the power of the enemy,' he noted,

> You owe your life to his humanity, your daily bread to his compassion.
>
> You must obey his orders, await his pleasure, possess your soul in patience.
>
> The days are long, hours crawl like paralytic centipedes. Moreover, the whole atmosphere of prison is odious. You feel a constant humiliation in being fenced in by wire, watched by armed men, and webbed about by a tangle of regulations and restrictions.[2]

**

The Boer War also occasions the first recorded account of Australian POWs. A total of 104 men from the almost 16,000 Australians who fought in South Africa were captured and incarcerated. Given the nomadic nature of the Boer guerrillas, housing large groups of POWs was not a prospect they could entertain. Thus a significant number of other Australian soldiers taken in battle were stripped of their rifles, ammunition and other equipment before being set free to find their way back to their own lines. Most of those held captive were imprisoned in a large camp at Waterval, close to Pretoria. Inadequate food and poor sanitary conditions were responsible for outbreaks of enteric fever and dysentery. The Red Cross arranged for the Australian government to send money—through the United States Consul—to provide a more substantial diet for these men, somewhat alleviating their condition.

***

During the second half of the 19th century, the 'Quarantine Theory' had been accepted by the majority of the Western Nations. Detention for the duration of the conflict of captives taken in battle to prevent their further participation in the struggle, became a matter of reciprocal obligations, accepted by both captor and captive ... [It] also undertook to protect the capturer and treat him humanely; the captive, on the other hand, had to refrain from taking further part in hostilities and to submit with good grace to temporary passivity. The removal of captives from the battlefield and their humane treatment during their detention by the enemy had become generally accepted policy.

Basic as they may have been, the 'American Instructions' instituted during the American Civil War in 1863 provide the first instance of codifying the status and treatment of captured soldiers.[3]

In Europe, the International Committee of the Red Cross became the earliest major organisation to concern itself with conditions for combatant troops wounded in battle. In June 1859, a Swiss national and founder of the Red Cross, Henri Dunant, saw firsthand the suffering of Austrian and French soldiers at the Battle of Solferino. Five years later, he and a number of like-minded individuals were able to persuade the major powers to send delegates to the first Geneva Convention which aimed to improve the plight of soldiers wounded in combat. While little mention was made of the treatment of prisoners, more drastic measures followed. In 1870 the Red Cross founded an agency in Basle devoted exclusively to gaining knowledge of troops reported as missing or wounded.

This Red Cross agency did not have long to wait for another European conflict in which to exercise its new role. During the Franco—Prussian War (1870—71), the Basle agency, along with a smaller agency established in Berlin, replied to around 186,000 enquiries concerning French soldiers taken by the Prussians. While the unit did whatever possible to locate captured troops, it was unable to advocate for their welfare. This changed in 1899 when delegates to another conference ratified the *Regulations Respecting the Laws and Customs of War*. Effectively the announcement of a 'code of conduct between belligerents', the conventions were more clearly defined at a second Hague Conference in 1907. While not binding, the status of captured soldiers was, at least, codified. Further 'guidelines' outlined their basic 'rights':

1. He is the captive of the government of the enemy country and not of the individual who captured him.
2. He must be protected by his captors from violence, insults and public curiosity.
3. When interrogated, he is obliged to reveal only his name and rank; and no pressure

may be brought to bear to force him to give any other information.
4. His permanent place of captivity must not be in a district which is unhealthy, nor in area where he will be exposed to the fire of the fighting zone. He may be reasonably restrained but he must not be strictly confined except under absolute necessity.
5. He must be given freedom of religious worship.
6. He must be treated with due regard to his rank and age. If he is an officer he cannot be obliged to work, and, if an NCO, can be obliged to work only in a supervisory capacity. A working prisoner must not be made to work longer hours than a soldier of his captors' army and must be paid the same rate of wages. He cannot be required to do work which is directly concerned with the captors' war effort.
7. He must be allowed to correspond with home and to receive parcels of food, clothing, and books.
8. Attempts to escape shall be punished only by disciplinary action—usually a spell of solitary confinement. All forms of corporal punishment, confinement in cells not

illuminated by daylight, and all other forms of cruelty whatsoever are prohibited as disciplinary punishment; nor may the prisoner be deprived of his rank.

Although far from complete—there were numerous exceptions and language ambiguities (not least the different interpretations that could be placed on each clause)—the guidelines constituted a starting point. Indeed, almost all were endorsed and included in the *British Manual of Military Law* and the corresponding German *Kriegsbrauch* ('War Usage'), often with strikingly comparable clarification.[4]

Both manuals, for example, stipulated that questioning soldiers taken on the battlefield should no longer be limited to name and rank. Provisions allowed for 'humane' but not 'compulsive' interrogation to gain some useful response concerning numbers, movement and location of other enemy troops. However, if a prisoner provided false information which was acted upon, he could not be punished, the *Kriegsbrauch* going so far as to declare such action 'cowardly murder' although, paradoxically, it justified executing a 'requisitioned civilian guide who deliberately misled the troops'. Feeding captured soldiers was also a complex issue, and an issue of concern which, due to food shortages in Germany, would impact on captured

Australians. Like Britain, the Germans agreed in principle to the Hague Convention 'that a prisoner was to receive the same rations as the troops of the government which captured him.' The Germans, in common with the British, used the ambiguous phrasing to mean that 'a prisoner was to be fed on the same scale as peacetime depot troops, with no extras.'[5]

In 1912, a diplomatic conference held in Washington DC agreed that the Red Cross should assume the role of sanctioned mediator to provide aid to POWs. Conference delegates also ratified an agreement made at the earlier Hague Convention which decreed that the shooting of unarmed enemy soldiers was specifically prohibited. The German *Kriegsbrauch* was less prescriptive, noting that

> Prisoners can be killed ... in cases of extreme necessity when other means of security are not available and the presence of prisoners is a danger to one's own existence ... Exigencies of war and the safety of the State come first and not the consideration that prisoners of war must at any cost remain unmolested.

The *British Manual of Military Law*, practised to degrees by the Australians, was more guarded:

> A commander may not put his prisoners to death because their presence

retards his movements or diminishes his means of resistance by necessitating a large guard, or by reason of their consuming his supplies, or because it appears certain that they will regain their liberty through an impending success of their own army. Whether nowadays such extreme necessity can ever arise as will compel a commander on grounds of self-preservation to kill his prisoners may well be doubted.[6]

Whatever instructions were included in the manuals, there were occasions at Bullecourt when both German and Australian soldiers were forced to shoot unarmed combatants. For those gravely wounded Australians caught on the barbed wire, a German bullet was a merciful ending. However, Germans taken prisoner during the early Australian onslaught who could not be guarded or returned to the Australian line were executed—based on principles comparable to those of the King of Judah.

The majority of Australians had never contemplated the idea of capture, and had little or no concept of their rights as POWs. Certainly, the few hundred sent to Lille were initially poorly treated, spending their first week of captivity in the notorious Fort MacDonald punishment cells. Horatio Ganson described their plight:

> When we got to Lille we were marched through the main street ... and then they marched us into Fort MacDonald. A lot of people in Lille tried to give us food. But the Germans knocked them back ... In Fort MacDonald we talked with one another about what had happened—everybody was waiting for a feed, but we never got one. We were there for a week, and they gave us nothing at all, but a slice of bread. There were no toilets, or anything like that. They had a big 40 gallon [approximately 180 litres] drum in the corner, and you had to do everything in there. They'd take us out for a few minutes to give us a walk around the yard, and then they'd shut us up again ... All the men were talking about was tucker and women, and what they were going to do when they got home ... I think what caused a lot of the trouble was because we were starved. You lost your spirit really. You lost your interest.[7]

The men would soon become accustomed to other privations and discover the true meaning of life behind barbed wire. For most, capture represented the loss of whatever freedom they cherished as soldiers. Officers, however, fared a little better, although they, too, had lost their precious freedom.

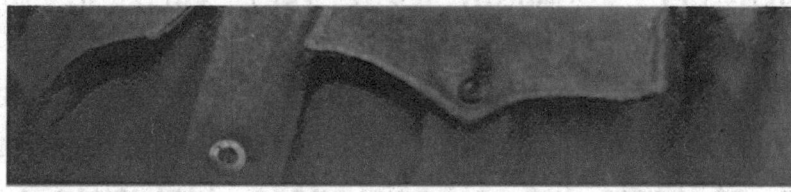

CHAPTER EIGHT
Behind the Lines
'Prisoners of Respite'

CHAPTER EIGHT

BEHIND THE LINES

'Prisoners of Respite'

Captivity has been recognised as one of the 'most stressful and persistently troubling wartime experiences' for all concerned. However, during World War I (and in the immediate post-war years) little was known—or understood—about the 'effects of the psychological trauma [POWs] ... suffered.' Further problems, 'a direct result of harsh treatment and starvation during captivity', particularly poor diet and inadequate medical facilities, saw some POWs experience 'the greatest trauma-induced weight loss, defined as greater than 35 percent of their pre-captivity weight.'[1] Certainly, from very early in their captivity, lack of food was a common cause of complaint by most Australian POWs. The lack of proper medical care was likewise close to the top of their list of grievances. However, very few had any chance to air these complaints. The more unfortunate—certainly many of those captured at Bullecourt—were kept behind the lines working for the enemy, performing such tasks as moving munitions, digging trenches, rebuilding roads and even burying the dead, all the while under fire from their own artillery.

***

Having been sorted into groups, most Australian POWs were taken to the French town of Douai. 'And soon we were marching through the city, proud to be prisoners with the French people,' noted Herbert Horner. Unsure of their final destination—a large number believed that they were going to Germany—the men were taken to the city barracks and 'locked in a large room, with very lousy straw to sleep on.' Fed the staple diet of soup and bread, the prisoners were continually questioned by German officers. 'Why did you come to fight against Germany?' Horner was asked. 'You people in Australia are alright. You are a long way from the war. Germany is a good friend to Australia. Why do you come to fight against us?' Horner accepted that his captors never understood 'why Australians, of their own free will, left a good country to go to war on the other side of the world.'

When allowed into the courtyard, the men mingled with other prisoners 'representing all parts of the [British] Empire, captured in small parties on various sectors of the front.' Horner soon realised that Douai was a distribution centre for men captured by the Germans. Prisoners were sent there to be given 'a hot bath and then distribute[d] ... wherever they were required.' Believing that 'the light had gone out of ... [some prisoners'] lives,' Horner attempted to offer some solace. 'The war could not possibly last many months,' he told them, 'Austria was breaking up, Bulgaria and Turkey had had enough, and America was coming into the war. Germany must see that it was madness to continue.' His stock reply to those less optimistic than himself was to predict confidently that 'You will be eating hot scones and butter in England in two months.' On 20 April 1917, however, several hundred prisoners were given little time to prepare and 'bundled into horse-trucks, and sent off in a northerly direction.'[2] Clearly the war would last longer than the optimistic Horner had allowed.

***

Corporal Lancelot Davies provided a detailed account of the men's experiences as POWs. As he and his fellows captives were marched from the battlefield, he noticed 'companies of Germans going towards their front line to reinforce.' Sometime later, the prisoners reach Cagincourt. 'Here in the courtyard of a onetime French farmhouse we are reviewed by the Hun officers,' he wrote,

> and in an hour are again on the road ... Truly we are objects of interest to all the Jerries we meet on the road, and especially in the villages. Taunts are hurled at us; epithets are numerous, and souvenir hunters molest us, but so far not violently. After passing through the village of Villers, we come across some British prisoners who are clearing the road, and they present a sorry spectacle, unshaven and dirty looking. The guards endeavour to prevent any conversation, but we manage to have a few words with them. Some offered some appeal for food, but we have none to give. In fact, we are ourselves hungry ... Their predicament does not create in us a very favourable impression, although I, like others, do not realise the seriousness of what is in store for us. The future is a blank, as no-one knows what it holds. Many opinions are expressed, but all is conjecture.

Davies' final thoughts were less optimistic: 'We only hope for the best.'[3]

Ernie Chalk's group had not given up hope. They were later 'again visited by the Germans in mass formation, this time to search us individually and to take from us practically all we possessed.' He wrote that the 'more civil' guards informed the men that they 'should get them back again, but it was goodbye for we never saw any of our things again.' The next morning, they were woken by their captors and

> we were each given a slice of black German bread—sour and tasteless stuff. But we were desperately hungry, so we were able to down it somehow. We naturally thought we should get some more during the course of the day. But imagine our dismay when we were told later that ... one slice was our ration for the day, and that we should get no more until the following morning ... When we at last reached Le Quesnoy, we were put into a large compound. Here we were sorted into two parties. In one party they put all those that were unwounded: in the other all those who were wounded and those who had fallen sick. We who were in the latter party were sent into a hospital, and we did not see the others again ... [A] very large percentage of them lost their lives, which was caused through lack of proper food, hard labour, and ill treatment.

Probably of more significance was Chalk's outline of the procedural system which the

Germans used for 'unwounded prisoners'. 'They worked behind the lines,' he wrote,

> until it was a physical impossibility for them to do another stroke, and when, in many cases, their number has been reduced by half, caused by sickness, due chiefly to starvation and heavy work combined. When they are reduced to this state they are sent back to registration camps in Germany. Here they are at last registered, their names and particulars going through to the British government for the first time. This of course means that a very great many have perished as prisoners-of-war of whom the people at home know nothing about, only that they are reported as "missing." And then again, it is not until they are registered that the Red Cross are able to send them any relief, for any letters they may have written are held back until such time that the official communication has been sent through.[4]

***

The men in Thomas Taylor's group 'were taken back to the village behind Bullecourt'. After staying in the village

> for a little while, we were sent with a guard over us, a long way behind the lines.

We marched very nearly all night and towards the early hours of the morning, we arrived, cold, wet and hungry at a town the name of which I never heard, and there were taken to a French church. In this were gathered hundreds of our comrades. We remained there over night and in the morning were given the order to march once more. We passed through several towns of little consequence before we came to the city of Lille, and it was here that, I think, we endured one of the worst periods during our captivity. The place here where we were imprisoned was an old fortress called Fort MacDonald. The rooms in which we were confined were really little better than cellars ... They were fairly large, being about 100 feet long by about 10 feet wide, and had two doors and two windows, the latter being barred with iron ... We were packed like flies in summer time in a flycatcher. To add to the discomfort and ignominy of our position, the only convenience supplied for nature's calls was a barrel placed in a corner of the room. Evidently this treatment the Huns considered too humane, or else they were too kind to pile on the agony all at once, for after we had been there a day or so they bricked up the windows, leaving us in almost total darkness.

Taylor was disgusted with what he was fed, 'best described as pig's food.'[5]

Chalk's account of the German attitude towards wounded prisoners was particularly resentful. 'All this time nothing had been done for those that had been wounded,' he wrote, 'and it was not until long after this that any of them were given any attention. And then it was only to bandage them in the most crude fashion with paper bandages.'[6] Campbell Stewart felt humiliated by his treatment, writing that, after a long march, he was 'wet, cold and tired and jammed into a fortress where we had to spend the night in a dark cell and on a stone floor. Officer gave us great lecture ... about escaping.' The following day he noted that he was 'still in here on same ration bread and black coffee and not allowed out for fresh air.'[7]

**

Perhaps somewhat surprisingly, ways and means of escaping captivity were already occupying the minds of some. Claude Benson recalled being taken by motor wagon to a small French village. 'Two guards who took charge of us gave me little chance of escaping en route,' he remarked. 'We were taken to a church with some of our officers and for two nights most of us had to sleep on chairs. I found a very interesting place under the altar.' Any further thought of escape was forgotten as they were taken by train to Lille:

> The German guard waiting to meet us there delighted in showing us to their own people, with the helpless French civilians looking on during our march from the railway station through the main streets of this captured town. The poor people were compelled to live under this so-called Prussianism but were not crushed. One French girl threw a biscuit to us from a window whereupon a German military policeman shook his fist at her and took the number of her house. I often thought of that poor woman and wondered what punishment she endured for her kindness to us. Shortly after, a Frenchman threw his cap to one of our men who was without a covering to his head, and suddenly, military police seized him, took him into custody and marched him off. By this time our blood was up and it was hard to watch this sort of treatment without doing something to help these poor people. They stood outside, wet through in a rainstorm, just to give us courage as we went by.

Many French girls bravely faced the risk of severe punishment in giving a slice of bread to us.

We were taken to the French prison [Fort McDonald], placed thirteen to a cell, the door locked on us and [later] we were told we were to be ready to go to work on the roads at 6am. No sanitary arrangements, a wooden floor without blankets or straw, one loaf of bread for three men and one soup a day of barley and sometimes sauerkraut and if you were lucky you might score a bit of meat the size of a finger.[8]

Despite the meagre rations there was only one recorded incident of an Australian POW stealing food. 'After several thefts and hidings which followed,' Robert Ayres wrote, 'he was caught again. This time the men agreed to deal with him in a manner which would make him think in future that his mates' rations were best left alone. Probably [never] during the whole period of the war did any man have to go through such a humiliating experience. The guards, hearing of the facts, would not interfere.' While Ayres refused to describe the 'experience' or give the man's name, he later wrote that 'he is now [1935] holding a prominent position in the Government Service.'[9]

***

After marching for 'six weary hours,' William Groves' group arrived at a clearing camp. 'In Le Quesnoy we were put through our first paces in prison routine and discipline,' Groves penned, 'a sort of beginning of strict and harsh training ... It was a concentration and clearing depot. When the count was completed and we had been officially received, we passed through the gates into the lager. There we lay down on the ground exhausted ... [Later] everything proceeded like clockwork.' The men were first fumigated then given a warm shower, while their uniforms were steamed—and also shrunk. 'We had about five or six days in this cesspool of a lager ... [a] Filth Hole,' Groves noted, 'a monotonous time with its daily routine of discipline, parades when, to our joy, our whole party was mustered and marched off to the railway station.'[10]

Lancelot Davies' group (of 'about 50 men') marched the ten kilometres to Ecourt St Quentin. In the late afternoon they were

> taken into the yard of a large chateaux, where is quartered the [German] divisional general. A surprise meets us here, for we join a large body of our own comrades, which had proceeded us. Feelings run high as mates are recognised, greetings are

exchanged, and questions are numerous ... The coming together of such a large body of men—for such we are now—there being 400 of us—seemed to revive our feelings of security, and cheered us up somewhat, that is of course, those who were not carrying wounds and disabilities ... As often happens everywhere, the individual element had much bearing on what a prisoner has to contend with. Some two hours elapsed during this procedure at the chateaux. Several men had been taken away, "we knew not where until they returned," and interrogated by the German intelligence staff, and our men were surprised at the many things the staff told them. They knew much of the British and Australian movements, and also of the various units they had badly smashed up in the battle. We were all very tired, and of course, hungry ... About 6.00p.m. we are again ordered to form up, and are counted, and then proceed to march out to the unknown.

Davies remained positive. 'I had given little thought, if any,' he remarked, 'to the fact of ever falling into the hands of the enemy, but such is the exigencies of warfare ... one has to adapt oneself to the position so created.'

Like most Australians, Davies was certain 'that we shall be sent to a prisoner-of-war camp somewhere in Germany.' A few days later, his early optimism had dimmed. 'Comrades in distress we were,' he recorded,

> and irrespective of any previous petty differences, it was now that one felt the existence of a brotherhood that establishes itself in circumstances of this kind ... A few of the men are very dejected, and appear to be losing all interest in themselves, their habits and practices not being approved by the majority. In some cases, for the most miserable reward, they cringe to the Germans for the chance of being of some service; others also, despite the fact their bodies can ill-afford the sacrifice, trade their boots and other clothing in exchange for food and smokes ... This is regrettable, but censure has no effect on the few. Most of us have resolved to maintain some sort of dignity, though tis difficult ... We begin to ask one another questions as to whether rumours of shortages in many commodities are well founded, as it does seem incredible that such a thing as soap is not to be had.[11]

Sergeant Guppy also believed that he was going to Germany. 'On the morning of the 16th a roll call is held and CSM [company sergeant-major] Garrison 46th Battalion, Emerson and Archer 15th Battalion and myself are ordered out,' he wrote,

> to remain here whilst all the remaining NCOs and men are marched away to the Station. We believed they are going to Germany but hear later that they are going to Lille for work there and behind the lines. We four were then placed together in one room in which is a stove and four bunks and issued with a pair of blankets, a gammil and spoon apiece. Lance-Corporal Benn has also arrived here and is in a room set apart as a Lazarette (Hospital). This is a receiving camp for new prisoners and others going through to Germany after having been some months working behind the lines. The English cook here is Private Pinborough ... and he was taken prisoner nine months ago and has so far not received a letter from home, so does not know if his people know he is a prisoner.[12]

***

On 16 April, Lancelot Davies discovered that he was not going to a camp in Germany. Instead, he wrote, for 'seven days we were confined in Fort MacDonald ... Each day we became more despondent in our misery ... Frequently we asked ourselves the question—"Why were we here, and why subject to such sorry treatment and neglect? Had we been forgotten by some superior officer, under whose charge we came as prisoners?"'[13] Claude Benson considered that the Australians were 'wretchedly treated ... the food ... and sanitary arrangements were awful.'[14] For his part, William Groves believed that the 'sentries were ... selected and highly trained for the job. They had shown a good deal of their suitability for this special work during our march through Lille.'[15]

Donald Fraser 1915.

'Who will ever forget that Black Hole at Fort MacDonald?' Harold Horner asked. 'In the interesting, ancient city of Lille,' he continued, 'we saw for the first time the German Military

Police—able-bodied men who were able to take their place at the Front; but to escape from it, they took the position of "bullies" among the women and children of France, who hated and despised them and did not hesitate to let them know it. Dressed in very flash uniforms, they sprang about like well-drilled artillerymen; and judging by the expert way in which they could knock women about, one was compelled to conclude that they had been trained for it.'[16]

Horner also recorded his group's departure from Douai. 'A very strong guard,' he wrote, 'marched [us] through the city to Fort MacDonald,' which was located

> on the outskirts; anyone even daring to even smile at us was very roughly handled. These Barbarians show no respect for old age, nor women nor children. Fort MacDonald was practically underground, well-built and with a touch of French beauty on the court-yard walls; but the hideous German eagle—the hungriest-looking creature ever pictured—was nailed upon the wall, while on the opposite side was a sign in German:
> GOD GIVE THE KAISER A GRIP OF THE LAND; THEN WILL WE GERMANS STAY OUR HAND!

We were marched into underground rooms. The number 104 was printed on our door, and 104 men were put in it. When lying down close together we just filled it. There was a cement floor, no bedding, no straw, no food, and no fire. We were not allowed out of the room on any account. A half-barrel in the room did duty as 'closet;' and when it was full, some sentries took four of the prisoners, who, with a bucket, ladled 'it' out into filthy buckets, which they carried out. No disinfectant nor ashes nor earth were put into the tub. We have since found that this was a fair sample of 'Kultur.' We were supplied with a liquid made with a few cabbage-leaves and water; but we were not supplied with any tin or basin to take it in; so that anyone who had no helmet had to wait for a mate's. We also received half an ordinary slice of black bread per day. I won't attempt to describe the atmosphere in the room.

After only one day at Fort MacDonald, some of the men became even more dejected. Horner was certain that because 'the second and third day showed no improvement, many became very despondent, seeing nothing ahead of them but a miserable death.'[17]

'To men mostly used to the open-air life and the wide spaces [of] "dear old Aussie" it was a terrible time,' wrote Thomas Taylor. He added that,

> as days gave place to night, and nights in turn gave place to days, to drag interminably, it seemed our tempers were completely set on edge. For hour after hour, men (more like caged beasts than humans) would pace up and down the only available space in the room—a narrow strip which seemed to have been left by tacit understanding. If one spoke or asked a question, he was answered by curses and snarls, and the wonder is goaded as we were to desperation by the impotency of our fate, that we did not fly at one another's throats. It all helped to produce an effect evidently intended by the Hun, and I have not the slightest doubt was all part of the German plan for waging war.

Taylor, too, understood that when he and his comrades 'were at last released from that living hell, we had been reduced to a state of sullen, resentful, semi-submission.'[18]

Earlier in their captivity, however, several other POWs who regarded their 'position' in the cells as 'intolerable and in desperation ... [wrote a petition] ... inquiring as to the reason why such treatment was being meted out to us.' Somewhat unexpectedly they received a 'typewritten' reply. 'Declaration to British prisoners of respite,' it was headed:

Owing to the English Government not replying to the German request to remove all prisoners to a distance of not less than 30 kilometres from the front line, it has been decided that those who will be taken prisoner in future will be kept as Prisoners of Respite, left very short of food, bad lodgings, no blankets, no water for washing, no soap for shaving, no boots, clothing, etc. The British prisoners of respite are allowed to write to their relations or persons of influence in England how badly they are being treated and that ... no alteration will occur whatever until the English Government has consented to the German request. It is therefore to the interest of all British prisoners to write to their relations and thus enable us to remove you to good camps in Germany, where you will be properly treated, with good food, clothing etc. You will be supplied with paper and envelopes, in which you will state your hardships, and then surely the English Government will consent for the sake of their own countrymen.

And, as Taylor noted: 'the above declaration they carried out to the letter.'

Donald Fraser 1985.

Several hundred Australians spent up to six days and nights in punishment cells. According to Taylor, it was 'absolute torture in that dungeon.' When they 'were at last brought out into purer air and the sunshine ... the light, after a week in darkness, had the effect of temporarily blinding ... [them].' He concluded that, while it 'was a relief, notwithstanding, to get out of that "black hole" ... we did not know what was in store for us.'[19]

By 23 April, the remainder of the men had been released. Not long after breakfast, 'we are led out from our dungeon down to the courtyard,' Lancelot Davies noted, 'where we join up with our comrades from other parts of the fort.' The Australians remained unsure of what to expect. Many hoped that they would be sent to a proper camp in Germany. Their hopes, however, were soon dashed. Davies describes how, 'after a few preliminaries,' they were taken 'out under heavy guard, passing through the streets of Lille, but avoiding the main routes, as evidently Jerry has no desire to "show" us this time, maybe owing to our wretched starving condition.' Marched to the station, Davies' group was 'bundled into' a train. 'Occasionally we heard the booming sound of guns,' Davies added,

> but little notice was taken of it, until some hours passing by, the "boom" became more distinct and caused us to sit up and take heed. Eyes tried to penetrate the

gloom around us, but apart from a glow in the sky over one particular direction, and the distinct sound of distant artillery, no sinister signs were manifest. Later on ... we were alarmed to see faint lines of light curve upwards, then down through the air, far away in the distance. Instantly the cry was raised, "Flares!" Too well we knew them, and what it signified. Although they appeared many miles away, the fact struck home to us that we were in the zone of war again.

This sensational development awakened us in two respects. Sleep was now out of the question, and we were also deeply incessed [sic] at our position, and all in accord cursed the Hun ... The boom of guns became still more distinct, but we thought this must be from those on the German side ... Approximately an hour passed, and we again halt for fifteen minutes or so, during which the facts become more apparent. Suddenly the screech of a heavy shell is heard, followed by its terrific burst of explosion and the truth flashes home to us. We are under fire! And it must be from our own side. None could but realise that our position was unenviable, and although darkness prevented us from seeing any signs reflected in each other's faces, there was undoubtedly a tinge of dread ... in the remarks one heard. Our guards showed uneasiness too. Three more shells came over and one in particular burst very close. Evidently they were meant to damage the railway line, but that portion in front was uninjured, for in a short while we proceeded on our way again. The morning had become very cold, and everyone felt it.

Not long afterwards, the train arrived at a railway dump near the village of Marquion. Ordered to disembark, the POWs were 'lined up and counted'. They were later marched 'to a large farmhouse and halted, where a German officer and his staff received us, and after a count we pass through the gateway and are deposited inside a barbed wire enclosure under guard ... We no doubt were sent here to labour for Jerry.'[20]

***

After the horror of the punishment cells, most POWs were almost pleased to work. The tasks varied. 'We worked behind the lines from April to December,' Horatio Ganson recalled,

> building huts for the army, wooden huts with a corrugated iron roof, and similar types of buildings. If a train came in with

shells, we used to unload them. We got that way that we couldn't do anything, we were that weak. We were scruffy and dirty. And when we went back to our digs—an old farmhouse or something—there were no blankets or anything. You just had to peg out on the floor ... The Germans were responsible for feeding us. But we only got ... bread and a little bit of this soup at dinner time. We used to scrounge everything. We'd eat anything. If you were walking down the street and you saw an apple-core, you would make a dive for it, and gulp it down. We used to pinch this sugar beet too. We'd nibble that all day. When you were eating the sugar beet, though, you could stay in the 'lavvie' and wee all the time, you know. It went right through you.

When we went out to work, some of the French girls would be alongside the road, and they'd run across and give you a plate of rice pudding, or something like that. You'd shove it under your coat, you know, because the Jerries used to knock them around if they caught them giving us anything. When your boots wore out, or your coat got filthy, the 'Froggies' would give you an old coat, or something like that.

> That used to be daubed with paint, you know, so you would be known as a prisoner of war, and not a French farmer.
>
> None of us had a razor or scissors. We all had beards, and our hair was long and dirty ... The British had the sea really tied up. The Germans couldn't get through to anyone. They really felt the war. The officers who used to look after us, they'd only have a piece of this brown rye bread, and a bit of grease on it—some kind of fat. That's all they used to get, you know.[21]

Taylor's group boarded a train destined for 'a village behind the lines called Brebries, situated on the Arras front.' They went straight to a camp where 'we were caged up in a barbed wire enclosure containing just a bare room to sleep in.' Still, the men considered it superior to Fort MacDonald. 'The first work assigned to me there,' Taylor wrote,

> was digging graves and burying German dead. One of their clearing hospitals was situated there, and it transpired we had been brought there for the purpose. Two of us worked together on each grave, and we thought it the most satisfactory job we had had. The more they brought for burial the better it looked for our side and nothing would have pleased us better at

that time than to bury half the German forces had they been brought to us.

A thing that mystified me while at that work was the appearance of the Germans after death. They were brought out for burial sometimes within a few minutes of having expired, and they were all, without exception, inky black. Whether it was the food they had to eat, or what it was that caused it, we could never understand. Perhaps they were only coming out in their true colours.[22]

After a short time on burial detail, Taylor was sent to work at the ammunition dump near Douai.

Claude Benson's group was 'taken off' building roads to work in 'ammunition dumps' and their 'condition got gradually worse'. At first, they were 'marched to Douai ... a distance of 30 kilometres ... under the shellfire from our own army' all the way. Benson also recounted that

> it took us two days to do the trip, camping at a farm for the night. The only food we had during the trip was ... boiled turnips ... The men were in a very weak condition and many of them were suffering from diarrhoea. Stragglers on the march were roughly handled by the guard. Civilians

who tried to give us food also got a rough time. Our guards would not allow us to accept anything from them. During the march the men were pulling up turnips in the field and eating them raw.

We arrived at Douai about 4pm, on the day after we left Lille. We were placed in a civilian prison—13 of us were packed into a cell that was originally built to hold one person, and the door was locked. Here there were no sanitary arrangements at all. When a man asked the guards to be allowed to go to the latrine, no notice was taken of his request. Men had to use their tin helmets to "evacuate" in. The food served to us was rotten—poor in quality and insufficient in quantity.

After a few days of this treatment we were split up into working parties and sent out repairing roads, working on ammunition dumps and building billets behind the firing line and within range of our guns. We were given a printed declaration to read to the effect—that Germany's request to Great Britain to withdraw prisoners-of-war 30 kilometres behind the firing line had not been complied with, we were to be treated as "Prisoners of Respite." We would be badly treated, receive no pay, work long hours, no soap would be given, and we would not be issued with blankets or straw to lie on etc. This document was dated May 1917 and was an instrument of the German War Office. Our guards and bosses did not miss an item of it, and carried out the instructions it contained to the letter. We spent three months as "Prisoners of Respite" and were then all moved to Orchies where we were again split up into working parties and sent to different places. The party I was with was sent to Mortagne where we were put to work unloading barges of sand. I think this sand was used for repairing roads at the front. Here the accommodation was very bad, the food worse and we were roughly handled by the guards. Cases of sickness were refused medical attention or an examination by the Medical Officer. Two men died here, one of them an Australian, but I did not know his name or battalion.[23]

Such treatment only increased Claude Benson's desire to escape: 'I made up my mind to try and make the best of things until I could escape.'[24] He spent another eight weeks at Mortagne and, in November 1917, was told of his imminent departure for a camp somewhere in Germany.

The Germans justified their indifference to the convention on the grounds that the British were working German prisoners less than thirty kilometres behind the Allied line. Jim Wheeler supports this claim, explaining that 'Britain was giving the German prisoners some bally rough treatment. I saw prisoners working behind the lines. They were mostly road building.'[25] Horatio Ganson, however, remarked that most Australian prisoners had little idea of what was actually happening on either side. He also revealed that

> Not long after we got captured the Germans lined us up and an officer said, 'Is there anybody wanting to go to Germany? They can if they wish.' Well, I didn't want to go to Germany. So that's when they kept us behind the lines. That was the trouble you see. We came a big thud. If we'd have gone to Germany right away, you became registered as a prisoner of war. But while we were in France, we weren't registered. Of course, if any [prisoner] died, or were killed it was a matter of 'killed in action.' The Germans weren't responsible for us. But once you went to Germany, you went through the Red Cross. The Germans then had to be responsible for you.[26]

Harold Horner's account differs somewhat. 'One day a German officer entered,' he wrote, 'accompanied by a number of sentries.' The officer addressed the prisoners: 'You see the condition you are in. You have no food. You have no blankets. You are hungry and cold. This will continue until the English Government replies to the letter from the German Government. You must write to your friends, and tell them that you are starving because the English Government will not answer our note. We will give you paper and envelopes.'[27]

***

Most groups did not stay in the same place for an extended period. Private F.W. Longwill's group was sent initially to Le Quesnoy, about seven kilometres from the front. 'Here we were making a sunken guntrack,' he remembered,

> and were continually under bombing from our own aeroplanes, though we suffered no casualties. A German pushed me over the cutting, a drop of some 15 feet. I was injured internally and sent to hospital at Douai. After a fortnight I was returned to the same Commando at Le Quesnoy. I was still bad internally, and the living conditions were awful. Our next move

was to Marchiennes, some 35km behind the lines. From here I was sent to hospital.[28]

Frank Hallihan, who had been captured earlier in one of the disastrous attacks around Mouquet Farm, was taken to Cambrai. He wrote that 'four large motor lorries ... [would call] every morning to take a working party out to the German aerodromes repairing roads.' He witnessed many acts of cruelty by his German captors. Hallihan's worst recollections were of 'men with dysentery [who] were allowed to remain in torture until they were delirious and had to be carried away. Some recovered after medical treatment, but many were allowed to die without medical assistance of any kind.' There were also 'heavy punishments' meted out to any French civilian who provided extra food to Australian POWs.[29]

Campbell Stewart noted that, when it was his group's 'turn to move, after a long dreary march of about 6 miles without a spell or a drink of water we arrived at our new internment camp at Noyelles. One of his [German] cavalry mob in charge of us, driving us along with their cavalry swords all the time. Not sorry when we arrived here.' The following day they were 'sent out at 6.30am and did pick and shovel work until 5pm. Half an hour for lunch—one of the hardest days I've ever put in working along the road from the fort.' Stewart was not sure how long he continued this often back-breaking work, confiding to his diary 'Fritz driving us a treat.'[30]

Len Pooley's recollection of his transfer to a working party near Marquion was likewise vague. Having been released from the cells at Fort MacDonald, his group was moved and

> kept in a barbed wire enclosure in [the] village ... There were about fifty men in ours [enclosure] ... It wasn't long before we started work .... They [Germans] were building a railway where we were, and we used to go and lay the sleepers and carry these heavy rails. There were about six of us to a rail, and we would carry them and dump them down. They had a fettler who used to drive them in. That's where we stopped, until we got that weak that we couldn't carry on.
>
> I remember when we were in the enclosure one day, Corporal Bradley saw a sparrow. He reckoned it was meat. "Look boys," he said, "meat, meat!"

Food rations remained meagre. 'We used to go and get this rape,' Pooley continued,

> cow feed it was. That was our daily feed. Some of the boys used to boil it down. But I couldn't see the benefit of that. They used to drink the juice, but we used

to chew the rape as we picked it ... We used to eat grass too. Grass filled us up. We boiled dandelions. We'd eat anything. All the Germans gave us was a slice of bread. That's all ... [W]hen they gave us our piece of bread, we used to put a rag or bit of paper over our knees to stop the crumbs falling on the ground. The bread was precious.

Some POWs were prepared to do anything for more food—even trade their precious clothing and personal effects. 'I swapped my boots for biscuits,' Pooley revealed, 'I also swapped my greatcoat for a few biscuits. And I sold my watch for a bit of chocolate.'[31] Lancelot Davies wrote that 'once within the [new] camp our first thoughts are of food, for we are very hungry ... Eventually we are told that no food is available just then owing to the fact that our arrival was advised only a few hours beforehand, and the notice had been insufficient to arrange supplies for such a number of extra men in time.'[32]

Other Australians were not above stealing food from their German guards. Private Robert Ayres recounted an unpleasant incident on a train taking POWs to work. At Valenciennes, a guard went to get some coffee and while there awoke to the fact that their rations were gone but evidently not forgotten. With bayonets drawn they rushed into the truck lashing out with their bayonets in all directions ... It was bedlam. The guards cursing & swearing & shouting their intentions of killing all the "Schwines" whilst we were endeavouring at the same time to protect ourselves & overpower the guard. The noise attracted other Germans who came running down to see what the trouble was & an officer appeared. After asking the cause of the trouble he turned to us seeking our version. Of course we told him everything! ... Eventually the officer exchanged the guard from our truck with another.[33]

***

Sleeping arrangements were primitive. Len Pooley used to sleep on the ground. All we had were the sacks we used to go and get the grass in.' With a touch of irony, he added, 'it wasn't all honey, being a soldier those days.'[34] Lancelot Davies, no doubt, would have agreed. His group was working at the railway dump near Marquion and was under constant fire from British artillery. They were also occasionally strafed or accidentally bombed by British aircraft on raids behind the German lines. Davies wrote that

> we were called upon to perform many types of manual labour, chief of which being that on the dump, or connected with it. Trucks had to be unloaded and their consignments stacked or stowed daily ... Arriving at our destination, the party would be split into smaller sections, and allotted to respective tasks. Needless to say, we were never ambitious to carry out our jobs. Consequently, no man done more than he was actually compelled to do ... Nothing strenuous could be taken owing to our physical condition. It became tiring to even take a short walk up and down the wire at the back of the compound. Any event or movement would stir up interest. The only part from which we could catch any view of outside objects was at the rear where no walls separated us from them. Only two rows of barbed wire, and open fields lay beyond, with scattered trees thereon, and a slow running creek. Sometimes it would be movement in connection with the guns close by, which often fired, and on many an occasion one wondered just how many times its shells were effective.

> There were times too when the opposite happened. Being in the zone we ... were quite open to the shells from the allied artillery, and many times when our own side searched for these two German guns we felt the tension of anxiety, not so much by day, because we were able to occupy ourselves in conjecturing where they would drop their shells. Fortunately we never had any into our midst, but several times it was only a matter of yards. As far as we could judge, neither of the German guns were destroyed, although sometimes their position was untenable for the crews.[35]

Harold Horner's group was transported to the village of Phalempin. 'Here in the railway yard we were drafted into working parties of about fifty each,' he wrote,

> after the officer had called for 'locksmiths'; but I don't think anyone volunteered. We were all lined up between two ranks of sentries and two of *Uhlans* [German light cavalry]. An interpreter addressed us in English, in the presence of some 'big heads.' He told us that we must do any work that the sentries ordered us to do, and give no trouble, or the sentries would shoot us ... In small parties we were

marched off in different directions, dragging our weary limbs along, always starving ... A long tramp through several villages brought us to a coal-mine head near [another village] Carvin; and we found our home to be a real prison cage, and quite a new building.

Cement floors are always cold, but at this place we could get some coal from the top of the mine, so we had two bucket-braziers burning at night. The fact that we were not far from the front line made matters a little more interesting ... Some of the German captive balloons were quite close to us; and we could see our own balloons not more than six or eight miles away. Therefore we might have been within three miles of No Man's Land, and well within gun-range. Our guns would often send shrapnel at the balloons overhead. On one occasion, without any warning, one of our 'planes glided out of a cloud overhead, shot incendiary bullets into one balloon, glided over it and into the second, then over it and into the third, and then got safely away home without a shot being fired at him. All three balloons burnt up in a few seconds, the men in the baskets swinging out in parachutes, while all other balloons for miles, both north and south, got such a scare that they came down also. One evening we saw one of our aviators round up seven enemy 'planes and drive them back. They were afraid to attack him. The German guards didn't like to see their men beaten.

In the evening we could see the flares along the front line, and the flashes of big guns. Quite close to us, Fritz had a big gun on the railway. It would fire two or three shots from one point, then the engine would pull it on to another line, where it would open up again. Our guns, in 'searching' for this gun, killed some women in the village. Many soldiers were coming and going, and guns of all kinds were moving to and fro ... We had the satisfaction of keeping a large number of guards employed looking after us.

Horner also had ambitions to escape, noting that 'one was always nursing a hope of getting away in the night.'[36]

But, given the weak condition of most of the men, escape was impossible—at least for the moment. The men in Horner's group were forced to work around ten hours a day. Horner was 'at Carvin for two months, and I ate grass all the time, and was very thankful there was grass available ... [during] our worst period of starvation, practically everyone dreamt and talked about nice things and good food—always the sweetest and the best ... A good deal of bartering was done.' Gradually rations improved. The prisoners had 'their first experience with sour vegetables. The Germans have a weakness for sour things; but they don't like this form of preserved vegetables; and it made many of our men ill ... [W]e had a little horse flesh and some tinned sausage-meat ... We also had "blut-wurst" or "blood-sausage," in tins.'[37]

Later, the men were sent to work in another ammunition dump near Carvin. 'The train would bring loads of shells of all kinds,' wrote Horner,

> and we had to unload them. There were many Germans working there also. They employed us cleaning salvaged machine-gun ammunition a good deal of the time. Many thousands of rounds had been slightly damaged, and had to be cleaned, and packed into cases, and given to the machine-gunners. We found that the bullets could easily be removed, and the powder poured out, then the bullet replaced. We treated a great many that way, and packed them with the rest! No one could tell the difference, but it would stop the machine-gun! It was my business to pack

them, and give them to the machine-gunners when they drove up.

Horner added that some German guards treated the prisoners well—indeed, one 'was living in the hope that he would be soon captured.'[38]

***

Campbell Stewart was feeling increasingly dispirited as a result of his treatment. Early June found him still working on the road near Fort MacDonald. 'Alex, one of our guards, caught me having a sleep in the scrub,' he recalled, 'and booted me a bit.' He also suffered some other punishment which he did not describe. By mid-June, Stewart's mood had changed. 'French women allowed to bring in gifts of shirts, socks etc,' he noted in his diary. On 22 June, he 'had a good day today. French people bringing us in some bread, rice and also some vegetable for our soup.' On 1 July, Stewart had his 'best day since taken prisoner, great dinner, a Tommie conducted a service and music and singing all day.' That same month, the group moved, now working 'on [a] railway job.' Finding proper food—by whatever means—remained their top priority. On 25 July, Stewart 'sneaked over to bakehouse and landed some dodger.' On the 28th he recorded that the 'work on railway finished, glad to say, so we are having a few days spell and expect to be shifted from here in a day or two.'

Prisoners were paid a small amount for their back-breaking work. Usually, however, they had little opportunity to spend the money on anything useful, except gambling. Before being moved, Campbell Stewart's group enjoyed almost a week of '[doing] nothing,' except 'played cards most of the day,' and on 'Pay Day ... had a holiday[a] a lovely day, 51 of the mob went to Templestra [sic].' On 6 August they marched to Wattingniers where, on the 10th, Stewart 'started on a new job ... carrying rails, one of the worst days we have had. Came home for dinner (coffee). Fritz knocked us about a bit in the afternoon. Carried rails until smoko and then went timber stacking. Got word tonight that our bread ration is to be increased 100 grammes. Troops issued with clogs.'[39]

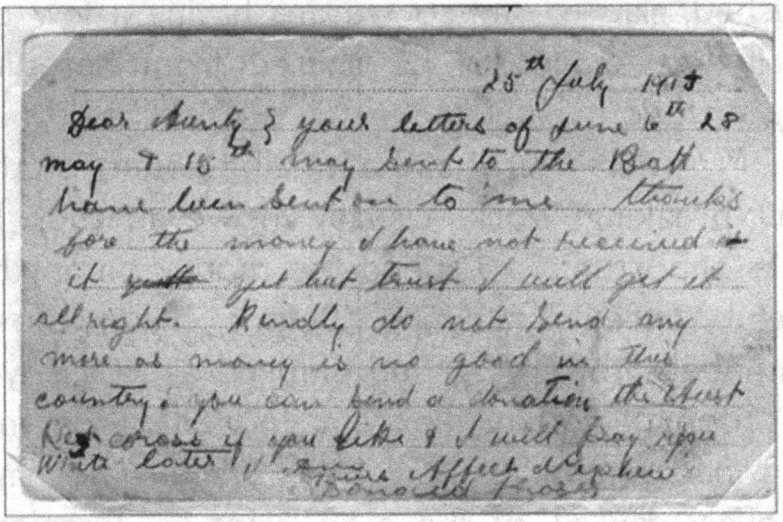

Post-card sent by Donald Fraser to his aunt, July 1917.

***

Like Harold Horner, Thomas Taylor recalled working at the ammunition dump near Douai and the constant danger from artillery barrages. Every 'time that the Allies commenced a bombardment,' he wrote,

> we had to toil like the proverbial nigger loading shells on to lorries, which were sent up to the guns to deal out death and destruction amongst our own comrades. We fared badly all through for food, but Douai was one of the worst we struck in that respect ... The quality and quantity were bad enough, but to make matters worse, they issued with our rations a day

ahead ... On rising in the morning we had our coffee, and as we had eaten our bread the night before, we had to commence the day without having partaken of any food. We worked hard all day long, lifting and carrying heavy shells, and with the exception of a little food which the French used to smuggle in to us on the sly ... we had no food whatever until we got back to camp, which was, more often than not, very late. Our next day's bread was then issued, together with the "soup," and is it any wonder we left tomorrow to take care of itself? ... On [one] ... occasion, we watched a fight in mid-air between three German aeroplanes and one British, with the German anti-aircraft guns endeavouring to get a shot home from below. They succeeded, too, but it was into one of their own machines, which they blew to matchwood. Pieces of woodwork, machinery, and scraps of human bodies fell in a scattered shower. We were afterwards told by our guards that the gunner who fired the unlucky shot was himself shot.

Taylor remained at Douai for several months. He recorded that deaths 'were not alone confined to the combatants; we had our share ... [when] a party of my companions were detailed to load empty shell cases at the railway station, and while there our own artillery opened fire on it, with the result that fifteen of our chaps "passed in their checks." Doubtless they were reported as "died of illness."'[40] Another Australian, Charles Neander, described 'bombs dropped by British airmen on [a nearby] ammunition dump and three or four Germans injured or killed also two British prisoners.'[41]

Lancelot Davies also wrote of casualties from friendly artillery fire. He witnessed the construction of enemy defensive positions and was part of a working group that was ordered

> to ... the rear ... of the village ... and set to work inside some houses, which turned out to be the making of underground defences .... We knew the German was particularly adept at underground engineering ... Day by day we learned more of its progress and plan. The central and chief portion was situated near the middle of the village, and below the commandanture (headquarters). At various points which would have dominated any enemy approach, strongpoints were in ... the making, and these would be equipped with machine guns when occasion arose for their defence. Care had been taken to hide the fact of the presence of these strongpoints, and also any

entrances to the underground passages, from allied aircraft. This was ingeniously done by allowing the skeleton buildings to remain overhead. One such place appeared to us completed, although we could only see it when passing the spot. It was situated beneath the first shop as one entered the village from the direction of Arras, and commanded the approach via the bridge which spanned the canal. Evidently this village was an important strategical position attached to the Cambrai defences. Much barbed wire entanglements were in evidence, and we also noticed that earth breastworks had been built on the edge of all low-lying positions, which seemed to pressage [sic] flooding when occasion warranted. Our part on these tunnelling jobs was to shovel the soil back along the passages, and eventually up to the opening on ground level, filling it into bags, and tipping it elsewhere. German labour was used at the face, and so also for timbering. Twice a day the party from the dump would bring the necessary timbers and leave them as they passed the spot when returning to the lager for their dinner ... and again at dusk.[42]

Keith Tamblyn's group was also working around Douai. He remembered 'quite well' being 'locked-in ... a brick place, and there were no windows in it, only one door ... with a sentry outside.' At night the group of between 'twenty and thirty' had to sleep 'on the floor' without any blankets, only 'a straw mattress, if you were lucky.' During daylight hours they dug pits for enemy guns near the side of a sunken road. He recalled that 'by the time you've got them dug out and take the guns in, it would take a day or two.' With a hint of satisfaction, Tamblyn remarked that he

didn't do too much. One time we had to dig some pits alongside a railway station at Denain, and I went up with the boys. We dug these pits. We wondered what they were for. There was just a hole in the ground, and then they'd dig a bit of a trench right up the middle of it. There were ... two shelves, one on either side. And ... to make them weatherproof ... the Germans covered them over with ... some sort of material they had. Anyhow, they'd just got them finished, and we came up the next day. Didn't know what to do or anything else ... Train pulled in, full of ammunition. A German officer came along and he said, "Unload them and put them down there." I said, "Not on your life." I said, "No." And he looked at me and said, "Why?" I said,

"Look, mate we're not going to kill our own men just to suit you!" And he looked at me. I said, "Your men are not allowed to touch anything like that over that [Allied] side." He shot us back to the camp. "Get out! Get out!"

But the Russians did it. The Russian prisoners-of-war, they did it all ... for an extra loaf of bread a day ... And they unloaded it and loaded it up onto Jerry ammunition carriers to go up the line.

Shells. I wasn't going to do that, not on your life.

Tamblyn believed that his rank—corporal—should have precluded him from any physical work, and that NCOs were generally treated no differently to privates. Soon afterwards the group 'split up', although not before they had ostracised an NCO named Lochel. 'He could speak German,' Tamblyn said. 'He used to act as an interpreter, but he also used to crawl [to German soldiers], and that's one thing those boys couldn't stand.'[43]

***

Towards the end of June, Harold Horner's group was moved to work in a foundry near the village of Raismes. Horner remembered the pleasant scenery—so unlike 'our own sunny

Southland.' Waiting for a change of train at Phalempin, he 'met those with whom we had parted some weeks before; and it was hard to recognise them. Some had faded to skeletons.' Arriving at Raismes, Horner continued:

> about 300 of us were housed in a large foundry, from which Fritz had removed most of the machinery ... Here we received our first welcome donation from organised charity. It consisted of half-a-loaf of French brown bread, and a piece of soap per man, from the French people ... Several working parties were taken away, until we numbered only fifty, when we were ... domiciled in a Girl's High School; but, of course, the girls were not there. The prisoners at the school numbered 150—mostly Tommies; and with our contingent, which was still practically Australian, the total was brought up to 200. The school was a very pleasant change from the foundry, as we had plenty of fresh air, and a good view of a large garden ... After a few days the 150 party left, and our men again selected me as "cook," which ... was the highest position of trust in which prisoners of war could place any man, because food was so precious ... Here we received a better variety of food; but actually no more in quantity ... June 28th

was a memorable day. We marched through Raismes and Anzin to Valenciennes, for a bath and fumigation ... [where] those wild street scenes with which we had become so familiar were the order of the day ... The Germans had mirrors fixed at an angle ... so that they could see along the street either way. There were officers always on watch, and machine-guns were placed in suitable positions.

We marched through the city to the bath-rooms, which were on a hillside from which we had a splendid view of beautiful Valenciennes at its best—mid-summer. With so many trees among the houses, it reminded me of Subiaco in West Australia. The Germans thought it was theirs forever. Many of the French thought that the Germans would secure the land as far as the Hindenburg Line permanently.

Horner's time in this idyllic part of France was all too brief. On 1 July he 'entrained for Audenarde, in Belgium, passing through Douai and Lille again.'[44]

***

By early June, Lancelot Davies had become bored with the monotony of the work. He noted how 'little distance separated us from our own friendly trenches,' although any thought of escape had long been out of the question—presumably because, on the few occasions it was attempted, 'the culprits were caught' and received punishment of 'anything from seven to twenty-one days detention ... served in the filthy conditions in a "clink" made up from what had been the pig-sties of the farmhouse.' Instead, according to Davies, 'we had long since resigned ourselves to a miserable existence until the end of the war and felt that anything was liable to happen to us, and at any time, even to meeting our doom by the unfortunate action of British artillery ... We just lived from day to day conscious of the fact that anything would happen, as our lives were in the Huns hands. "Hope" was our only benefactor.' Not long afterwards, news came through that inspired hope in the men.

On 9 June, Davies heard that 'the German staff had confirmed the orders ... we were to leave the next day.' Davies' first thought was of a move 'to a proper *gefangenenlager* (prison camp) in Germany.' He wrote that the night before the move was the kindest we had experienced for some weeks. Sleep came happy in the thought of quitting this "hell" ... Next morning we were up not quite as early as usual.' Later the same day they were 'moved out under guard and marched to Sauchy-Lestree, a railway town ... About 1.00p.m. we boarded the trucks and set out for the unknown destination.'

The group travelled for almost four hours before they reached Denain, the main centre for the mines around Angin. The men were astonished by their new 'quarters [that] were inside a very large building known as The Institute of Engineers,' which Davies considered

quite spacious and clean, and after what we left at Marquion, it inspired us somewhat. Although ravenous, no more food was issued us that day, but we were given blankets, a welcome addition indeed ... Next morning saw us roused up in a much better frame of mind and body than on previous mornings at Marquion ... Shaking ourselves free of slumber, and convinced that we were really transplanted into more congenial surroundings, our new diversion came with the cooked breakfast ... The general consensus of opinion was that we were sent here temporarily prior to being sent to Germany, and the thought pleased us ... Certain facts ... we elicited, such as being quartered in the same town as the 6th German Army Headquarters, and approximately 35 kilometres (22 miles) from the front line trenches.

> Our billet ... [occupied] a fair area of ground within the town. It was surrounded by a paling fence with barbed wire mounted on top ... The first thing undertaken as soon as opportunity offered on the morning after arrival, was a good wash—body and underclothes.

Other surprises included a hot shower and fumigated clothes. With expectations rife of a move to Germany, they 'looked upon things rather light heartedly.'

However, after almost a fortnight they 'became restless and again gloomy.' While the men 'had not been called upon to work,' exercising was a necessity, something 'naturally to be expected, and ... considered necessary for the welfare of ... us in "idleness,"' Davies wrote. After another week they had developed an 'extreme desire to get outside the lager, so penned up did we feel.' Rumours of another move began circulating through the camp, as well as talk 'of the possibilities of prisoners being drafted to farm work ... A job on the farm was stated to carry many liberties or advantages.' Davies was one of the lucky NCOs to be selected. 'Gathering up our blankets and other incidentals,' he wrote,

> we eventually moved off for the promised land. After a two hour march,

which landed us at the village of Hornaing, we are taken into the new quarters, a building which had been prior to the war, a brassiere (wine brewery). The top part of the two-storey structure contained bunks, and this was our living quarters. Below was occupied by the Jerries as storehouses, guards quarters and workhouses ... The whole was surrounded by an eleven foot brick wall, which made it an ideal enclosure for prisoners. Our party comprised 60 men, in addition to a staff of about fifteen Germans. The afternoon of arrival was taken up by the usual preliminaries connected with such "kommados" (working parties), and evening left us free to explore the surroundings and debate on things in general.

Next morning we were aroused at six ... and received ... the usual "fruhstuck" (breakfast) of coffee. Roll-call came next, after which the "kommando" was divided into smaller sections and taken out under guard to the "maire," headquarters of the commandant, although in pre-war days it was the local council headquarters. Here we met with numbers of civilians conscripted for labour, but no fraternising was allowed ... Having received our definite instructions ... we were taken out to our respective jobs ... returning for lunch to the lager, and then out again afterwards.

The group worked on the farm for almost six weeks, sometimes 'in fields of growing crops ... in particular ... hoeing and weeding a plot of potatoes,' some of which 'found their way into the *gefangener*'s larder.' On 27 July Davies was told that he would be leaving the following day. 'Needless to say, the usual "furphies" floated around,' he noted, 'and many of us had visions of a nice NCOs camp in Germany, which ... was our one objective.'

Davies would again be disappointed. The unknown destination 'turned out to be a place called Bouchain.' Arriving in late July, they were immediately put into 'a pre-war barrack for French soldiers, that was situated on the main street of the village.' Davies described the accommodation as

> a two-storied structure of stone and enclosed with barbed wire ... [W]e dumped our kit in the possie we each chose, although ... the choice was very limited as usual—just a space on the floor, or, in the case of the fortunate ones, an elevated bunk similar to those in the British billets in France.

These hardships ... we were by now quite able to tolerate ... Nevertheless, after Hornaing, this place made us glum and cranky, and the environment seemed to foreshadow trouble ... The Jerries seemed very arrogant. After the usual roll-call, [they] lined up for the "essen" distribution (coffee and bread), the portion of bread being one loaf to five men ... [W]e were ... very hungry and tired ... Some of us who felt more active than the rest indulged in a short constitutional round of the "platz" [parade square] and discussed our next move and what it held for us, prior to turning in.

Next morning reveille sounded at six ... and after coffee issue came the morning parade and roll-call ... followed by the procedure of sectioning out the working parties. Following the agreed plan we NCOs took our allotted places with the privates ... I happened to be with about 60 others ... which terminated their march at a huge sawmill a mile or so from camp. Here we were split up into small sections, and delegated to various parts of the mill. I ... another corporal ... and five privates, were set to work on two circular saw benches under the supervision of a German "gefreiter" [lance-corporal].

A few days later, a number of NCOs—including Lancelot Davies—refused to work. The 'strike' soon spread throughout the camp. 'Through our senior noncommissioned officer (a British sergeant-major),' Davies wrote,

> we put our case that in being forced to work as privates, our rank was not being respected, and such action was contrary to the recognised rules of war. To us Australians who looked upon non-com rank as merely nothing of importance, this was at heart no great blow to dignity, but ... the German view of his men of similar rank was more elevated, and we set out to gain as much as possible in concessions, and having resolved to show our enemy that although in subjection, we possessed pride, our duty was to assert ourselves always.
>
> Jerry very well knew that he was overstepping the bounds, but evidently for reasons known to themselves and presumed by us, he sought to gain his own ends by fair means or foul. The commandant refused to accept our view of the matter and told us "we had to do as we were ordered." Our senior rep replied that we had no objections to being detailed as NCOs in

charge of parties, but we still refused to go out as workers. This only aggravated the wrath of the German "Comm" and the parade was dismissed without compromise. The 'strike' continued unresolved for another four weeks. Davies described the

> respective experiences of the past few weeks, the various moves and countermoves. The smaller parties had come in for the hardest time, and the few men [NCOs] we had see march past our lager ... were from a village ... where they had been in prison for the past nine days. Their officer commandant took himself this extreme step after continuous threats, which failed to coerce his charges. Unfortunately ... this meant that as a working party they were a useless asset to the job, for the few remaining privates constituted the only active part. Naturally Jerry was not going to tolerate such a drag on his resources, and he declared war "on the boys." Into clink went the strikers, and they were told "No work—no food." And he kept his word too, for officially no rations were issued to these men, although their pals, who were not going to see them starve, found ways and means of getting some food passed in by using strategy and bribes.

The German commandant, however, had reached the limits of his patience. On 26 August, Lancelot Davies and other 'striking' NCOs received 'news of a return to Denain'. According to Davies, 'it was not until the German officer received orders to return the "nicht arbeiters" [non-workers] to Denain that he gave them food.' [45]

On their arrival in Denain, Davies and another eighty-four NCOs refused to give in and again went on 'strike,' refusing to work. Instead, they endured the 'monotonous cloak' of camp life—usually exercising for between four to five hours each day in the 'platz'. Within a week they were all as 'glum as before, tired of the uncertainty of the future, which became aggravated by rumour after rumour.' On 7 September they were told that they 'were to go into fresh quarters in the town.' Later the group was ordered to 'the bathhouse,' where they had 'hot showers but minus soap, had ... clothes fumigated, and took up abode at a cottage which was filled up as a billet.' Yet again rumours were rife of movement to Germany. 'The following day brought definite news of our transfer to Deutschland,' Davies noted, 'which pleased us immediately, and on the morning of September 9th we ... joined a train bound for the "promised land."'[46]

***

Keith Tamblyn also recalled the time he spent at Denain alongside POWs from England and Canada. Initially, he worked in a 'colossal foundry, about a kilometre long and half-a-kilometre wide,' manufacturing 'anything from ploughshares to railway engines.' Then came a stint in a storage depot. 'I never worked, I didn't want to work,' Tamblyn said, 'I didn't want to help the cows [Germans].' Instead his thought turned to ways of assisting 'mates' at the front. While others filled

> machine-gun belts ... I used to just poke around and ... look around, and sit around. They'd take a bullet out and empty the powder out of the case. Put the bullet back in and stick it in. They'd do about four or five like that. See, put the powder in ... their pocket and take it away. I wouldn't like to say how many machine-gun belts that they did like that. I used to watch them ... Well that went on for ... two or three weeks ... I was nosing around one day and I came across a lot of [captured] Lewis machine-guns. And I said to Roy, "God! He's got a few Lewis guns in there." ... "Oh," he said, "we'll fix them." And there's a little spring in the Lewis machine-gun called a pall

spring. Once that's out the gun is useless. So one or two of them had had a bit of experience. This one particular chap was a machine-gunner ... Anyhow, I kept my eyes out for him. He took all the pall springs out. There was about thirty or forty Lewis guns in there, all ready to go into the line. Took all those pall springs out ... and put them down the toilet. Those guns were made useless then.

Tamblyn's satisfaction was evident. He commented that 'we were doing a bit of good even there.'[47]

***

Sergeant Guppy was still in Le Quesnoy where the men relied on even smaller food rations:

A few days after coming here a large party of Frenchmen who have been working up near the line came in here making over 600 in the camp. The soup boilers in the kitchen are only large enough to allow a pint to 300 men so before issue at midday half is taken out into barrels and the lot filled up with water to make it go round. This soup is made with barley, macaroni or dried fruit with a little bony meat—horse flesh it looked like—boiled in it till the meat falls from the bones. I have often seen the German Unterofficers take out in the Lager yard and scramble amongst the starving Frenchmen, meanwhile standing laughing at the poor wretches scrambling on the ground after a bone which barely smelt of meat. We had a go at the Feldwebel in charge here over the food but of course did no good. The Commandant of the district, a lovely Prussian, often comes into the Lager and with a roar like a bull orders everyone out on parade yelling all the time to men to hurry. The German posterns and NCOs seem to be far more frightened of him than the prisoners.

Other conditions were far better than those experienced by prisoners closer to the front. 'There is a big bathhouse close [to] here,' Guppy added,

> where we can go weekly for a bath. Almost daily trains pass through here with material and munitions for the line and others come back laden with French and Belgian civilians. One day I ask to be taken to the town to visit the Doctor at the barracks there and a postern takes me. The town I found large and well built with a huge wall and moat enclosing it, having in times past been very strongly fortified. I

have in my possession 100 francs which I get exchanged for 80 marks but there is little chance of spending any of it as there is no possibility of buying anything in the way of food.

We are given postcards and paper to write letters but find out later that they are not sent away as in the majority of cases no letter is allowed to go from a prisoner behind the lines. Prisoners are not registered or reported until they reach Germany so if any die, whilst at work behind the lines they are never reported prisoners.

Daily we see parties of women of all ages being marched past here under armed escort from the town barracks, where they are imprisoned, out into the fields to work. One girl living in the town was, whilst we were here, thrown into prison for trying to give a parcel of food and clothing to one of the prisoners whilst passing through the town.

It is the enforced custom for all men civilians to lift their hats and all women to bow to the Commandant (German) of the district. There are a number of young French girls working in the laundry at the bathhouse ... About the end of April the

Frenchmen here are sent away and another party of French and English from Cambrai, about 800, come in. These men tell us that the Germans have had them employed in Cambrai and Douai for some time removing all metal fittings from the houses and roofs, all machinery from factories etc and carting same to trucks on railway, also in smashing up what furniture and wooden fittings the Germans did not want. We often see many truckloads of this metal and farm machinery on their way to Germany.

The men were paid for their work. While a pittance, and in a currency that could only be used inside the camp, they still looked forward to pay day. Campbell Stewart wrote of his pleasure on receiving his payment although, realistically, he knew there were very few worthwhile items to purchase.[48]

***

After almost four months working behind the lines, the prisoners' rations were reduced again. 'We were very hungry,' Claude Benson recalled,

> and on the way to work the men would pick up cigar or cigarette butts from the street and smoke them just to try and satisfy the craving for food. Very often the

French civilians would place bread on the road for us to pick up but they had to be very careful not to let a German officer see them do it. I have seen German guards, when food is placed this way, kick it into the gutter so the prisoners wouldn't get it. One poor Frenchman, noticing one of us without a cap, took the risk of placing a cap in a little boy's hand, directing him to give it to us; the German guard deliberately snatched it from the boy and threw it into the canal.

On returning to our cell after a long day's hard work, very hungry, we'd lie down and wait for our mangle soup (a root vegetable fed to cattle) to be dished up and often the German guard would offer us half a loaf of bread for a watch and I have seen gold watches and rings go for less than half a loaf of bread, anything to satisfy hunger. We were becoming so weak from want of food that whenever we got the chance to gather nettles, we'd take them to the prison, make a fire as best we could from sticks gathered from our various jobs which we had concealed under our coats, we then boiled the nettles and mixed them with our watery soup which we drank from tins we'd collected by the roadside. Those who weren't fortunate enough to possess a tin had to use their steel helmets. When English shells fell in our vicinity, they would often kill birds and we were glad to eat those that had died by concussion.[49]

Sergeant Guppy and his mates were faring little better and thoughts of escape were constantly on their minds. Guppy suspected that a few Australians were passing information to the Germans in exchange for increased rations. 'With more men coming in the food gets scantier every day,' Guppy wrote,

> One is always hungry and I feel very depressed and desperate but though we watch there seems to be no chance of escape, as we are closely guarded especially at night. L/Cpl Benn and a few other men are sent away from here and then I am told by the cook, Pinborough, who received his information from a German in the office here with whom he had found it convenient to become friendly, that Benn had not really been ill at all. This German says that when Benn came here a few days after us he was accompanied by a letter from a high command saying that he was to have special treatment. He affirms that Benn gave away any amount of information and even in his sight drew maps of parts of our side of the

line, also that each day when he went over to the Office he was provided with a substantial meal.

However, Guppy was not entirely convinced by the cook's story. He concluded: 'Personally I saw nothing and thought him genuinely ill.'[50]

***

The Germans continued their practice of rotating POWs. 'After some months of hard treatment,' Claude Benson wrote,

> we were sent to yet another camp in France. We were marched off, many fainted through weakness and in many cases the guards would kick those who fell and shout at them to get up. I saw one of the guards using his bayonet on a poor French woman who had given one of our party a biscuit. She stuck on her feet, put her hands to her face and went limping and crying into her house. I thought I would rather die from starvation than see this woman so ill-treated. I wished the poor creatures would not try and help us. I never admired a woman's pluck and spirit more than that of the French woman of about twenty-two years of age who noticed us coming and ran back to her house and returned, running towards us with a bag of biscuits and as

she came near the road she shouted, 'English, sweeties.' The German guard rushed to intercept her and lifted his rifle to hit her when she raised the bag of biscuits and let it fall with all her force on his head. He was about to give her a swing with his rifle. We all rushed in and wrenched it from his hand and threw it away. My heart was in my mouth and I wondered what would happen next but some Germans in charge of transport shouted out to the guard, he mumbled something in German, picked up his rifle and left her.

The French population could only stand on the footpath, smile at us, touch their caps or nod their heads. Towns having suffered severe bombardment at the beginning of the war, were full of roofless walls with holes in them, reminding me of an ancient city crumbling to ruins.

The new camp was close to Montaigu. The following day Benson was sent out to work. From 11.00a.m. to 8.00p.m. the party worked solidly, only to return to a hut with beds comprised of wood shavings. While it was late autumn, they were not provided with any blankets against the cold. Benson remembered that they were marched out every day to work on barges and sandhills. Four men from the barge threw the sand by shovels to the first platform built of planks and two men would throw it from the platform to the wharf. It would be taken away in small trucks by three prisoners. I often jumped on to a barge from the wharf for bread offered by the barge people.

The hardest part was when a man was too ill to keep working because it disorganised the whole system, and the guard would stand over weak men, knowing they were exhausted and knock a prisoner down for not being able to keep up with the others. I very often advised the boys when they were sick or too weak to work just to lie down and stand a few kicks as the guards willingly kicked the men who were down, but if unable to frighten the men to work they generally left them to lay there.

Lack of food, no warm bedding, unhygienic sanitary conditions and no proper medical care caused more illness. Dysentery became prevalent. The treatment offered by German guards was to starve dysentery sufferers for a whole day. Benson added: 'This was ridiculous as the men were already starving.'

Some died of dysentery. As if to punish the survivors further, German officers ordered French peasants to bring in small amounts of vegetables or biscuits whenever a prisoner succumbed to dysentery. The Australians owed a great deal to the audacity and goodwill of the villagers, as Benson explains:

> [The] French took great risks to help us keep alive. I shall never forget a little French girl in Montaigu, our village. I had managed to climb the fence just as the guard was enjoying a smoke and the wind was rustling the trees which prevented my movements being heard. On the other side I came upon his little French girl who brought me some bread immediately and told me to come again. Before I left she gave me her photo and on it wrote, "My pa has been a prisoner for three years. All I give you is from my heart."

As the autumn weather turned colder, they endured further hardships. Their 'clothes were covered in vermin and we found delight in picking them off ourselves and flicking them on to German officers. The German guards tried to frighten us by opening and closing the bolt of their rifles and pointing them at us.' But the Australian sense of humour prevailed and, as

Benson commented, 'It made them very angry when we laughed at them.'[51]

***

Guppy and his group were now behind the wire in Germany. Before departing Le Quesnoy, he described seeing

> a copy of 'The Continental Times' a paper now published for the French and Belgian people on this side of the line. In it was an account of our stunt and capture. It said that there were two Divisions of us engaged and that we had no food for three days previous to the attack, were given a large issue of rum and driven into the affair by our officers at the point of revolvers. Another small party of English and French including a French Sergeant—Armedie Menier—came from Cambrai where they have been working. Menier speaks good English and tells us that he has made three attempts to escape on the last occasion after 21 days hiding and travelling, succeeding in reaching a village within 3 kilometres of the Dutch border where he was given away by the Belgian people. Some of these latest incomers have some food stuffs with them and one day Menier brings one up to our room with a bag of rice and

a request to be allowed to cook some over our fire.

On 10 May, Guppy was 'told that the whole camp now numbering about 1,000 was to go to Germany tomorrow.'[52]

Thomas Taylor had 'received the joyous news that we were to be taken back from the front lines, the British Government having, we were told, consented to the German demands.' He added, somewhat ruefully, that it 'did not take us long to obey the order to collect our things and prepare for a removal.'[53] Before going to Germany, Taylor and his group were sent to work at a veterinary hospital in Conde where he saw horses being put down daily. After being 'cleaned' and 'dressed,' the better part of the carcasses (heart, liver and stomach, for tripe) was given to German soldiers. What was left went to the prisoners. 'Every disease known to veterinary science' was there, Taylor wrote, 'and we were compelled to work amongst them [horses] ... and ate their lungs.' He eventually became ill with the same disease that killed the horses.

Having recovered from his illness, Taylor was sent to work at Tournai, where he remained for 'a little over a week.' While there, he witnessed an incident that he had previously dismissed as propaganda. He noticed that 'the Germans dragged off all the young Belgian women from their homes, and marched them off, for a purpose it is not hard to guess at. As our German guards were heard to callously remark, "They were laurels for the soldiers."' Not long afterwards, Taylor was informed that he was to spend Christmas 1917 in Germany.[54] Similar news was conveyed to other Australian prisoners still working behind the lines. By early December, the majority were behind the wire in Germany, or on their way to POW camps.

***

Despite protocols of the two Hague Conventions (1899 and 1907) which prohibited captured combatants from working close to the front, large numbers of Australian soldiers had been forced to work behind the German lines for almost eight months. Other provisions of the conventions dealt only briefly with prisoners' rights and never permeated through to influence POW conditions. Work, discipline, food, even pay were constantly on the minds of the captive men. Most, however, displayed little concern for religious freedom, also a provision of the conventions.

To a greater degree, the Germans' behaviour could be attributed to ill-will and the desire for revenge. It was true that the British were forcing some enemy prisoners to work close to the front line and thus the German use of Allied prisoners as a form of 'reprisal' is perhaps understandable. In fact, both sides utilised whatever labour was available for the 'operations of war' regardless of the vulnerability of those men to shellfire from their own artillery. Others who found themselves further back from the front often enjoyed better conditions, particularly those captured Australians confined to German hospitals. Yet, as always, the conditions of their captivity varied, based, more often than not, on the whim of the captor.

CHAPTER NINE
German POW Hospitals
'I Think they Gloated at Our Plight'

CHAPTER NINE

GERMAN POW HOSPITALS

'I Think they Gloated at Our Plight'

Depending on the severity of their condition, wounded or very ill Australian POWs were sent to various locations to receive medical treatment. Shortly after their capture, the men were sorted into groups and—usually—despatched to facilities where they could receive appropriate medical care. The quality of care, however, varied considerably. Those whose wounds were not considered serious were immediately moved to hospitals in Germany. Severely wounded POWs were treated at enemy casualty clearing stations before being sent to hospitals further behind the front, either in France or Belgium. As with those POWs working behind the lines, luck played an enormous part in the quality of care afforded to these men. The more fortunate received appropriate treatment at well-equipped hospitals with qualified and caring medical staff. Others languished in poorly equipped and often primitive facilities with little attention from rude and callous doctors and orderlies.

***

William Barry was one of many Australians captured in the badly planned attack at Fromelles in July 1916. Barry's experiences as a POW, however, were characterised by the special care he subsequently received which contrasted starkly with the accounts of many other POWs. After German soldiers found the wounded Barry, he was initially refused treatment. Instead, an enemy officer 'said something in German to a couple of soldiers standing nearby and I got one of the worst beltings that it was possible to give a man, in fact I was knocked unconscious for more than four hours.' He was finally

> handed over to two ... German [soldiers with] Red Cross [patches] who carried me to their dug out and gave me a piece of their black bread ... with a piece of bully beef and a drink of black coffee. The German who could speak English asked me if I felt cold. I told him "Yes" and he brought me a German military coat. It was wet with blood, but that didn't matter ... [He] left me propped up against a heap of earth ... I was able to look around me and to my horror I was in a place where all

the dead were being stacked. I was sitting on the edge of a hole about forty feet long, twenty feet wide and fifteen feet deep and into this hole the dead were being thrown without any fuss or respect. Friend and Foe being treated alike, it was pitiful to see the different expressions on their faces, some with a peaceful smile while others showed they had passed away in agony.

Barry was taken to a dressing station and 'laid on a stretcher ... for some hours.' He was also questioned. 'About midday, half a dozen of us wounded chaps were put on a horse ambulance and were driven to a hospital a few miles away.' There they were

> taken in and left waiting in a very small room ... I was now suffering great pain and was very thirsty and as there a plentiful supply of soda water, we were given plenty to drink ... Our wounds were not attended to at this hospital, and the following morning we were ... [taken to hospital in] Valenciennes ... The following day two Russian prisoners carried me on a stretcher to the operating theatre and lifted me onto the table and all the bandages were taken off. I was able to see my injuries, which were a gaping wound in the left calf, right knee smashed and a nasty wound in the big

toe. In the room besides the doctor and nurse was a German Officer who could speak English and a clerk who wrote down in shorthand, everything that was said. After my name and address were taken, the officer wanted to know if I was sorry that I came to the war. I said "No." Then he wanted to know why I came to the war, as Germany was not at war with Australia, and I just told him that an Australian stood by an Englishman always. As this officer found he could not get any information out of me, he sneeringly remarked, "Well, you have come a long way to get your knee blown off," but I didn't take any notice of what he said. After the doctor had finished with me, I was taken back to the ward ... One Sunday I was taken down to the operating room and as soon as I was laid on the table, without any warning of what was going to be done, a cap or mask was put over my face. I had no idea what had been done until two days afterwards, when my leg was being dressed by the German orderly. I noticed that a rubber tube had been put into my leg above the knee. My health gradually got worse.[1]

Barry initially thought that he was going to die. After a few weeks in hospital he had recovered sufficiently to write that 'my health was by now broken down, besides being light headed, was suffering from fever and weakness and to make things worse the cowardly orderly used to twist my leg around to make me sing songs for him, which I always did.'[2]

Eventually, Barry was moved to another hospital in Germany. He remembered clearly being 'delirious and in a raging fever', recalling also the help he received from enemy doctors. On 23 September—almost two months to the day after his capture—he was taken to

> the railway station and ... put on a Red Cross train ... [We travelled] for three-and-a-half days through Germany and along the valley of the Rhine, which by the way the scenery was beautiful, and we were kindly treated by the German staff on board. The train arrived at the town of Kempton, in the South of Bavaria. After the Red Cross had got all the wounded off the train and sent them to various hospitals, my eight comrades and I were taken off and put on a motor ambulance wagon and sent to a large, three storey brick building and put straight to bed. During the afternoon, a German [Professor Schultz] who ... could speak very good English ... told us that ... he was the censor and that we were

allowed to write home one postcard every week and two letters a month.

William Barry was fortunate that the hospital employed a number of well-trained German doctors. The next morning he was examined by three specialists and later by six nurses and two orderlies. He was not surprised when the staff all 'spoke German', but rather concerned that 'it was impossible to understand anything they said.' He was 'put on Number 2 *Kost* [diet], while the other chaps were ordered Number 1 *Kost*.' The food ... was good and wholesome, but of course was morish. Number 1 diet received one pound of rye bread and two litres of beer per day. Besides the ordinary diet, I received six ounces of white bread, 1 plate of boiled ham at 10am, two cups of fresh milk and one pint of wine every day.' Barry's 'wholesome' diet was possible only because of the reasonably good supply of food in Germany in late 1916 as the Allied blockade of the Atlantic had not yet fully taken hold. By mid-1917, however, when those captured at Bullecourt were in camps or hospitals, the blockade was causing dire shortages for all Germans. By this time, Barry was too ill and 'couldn't eat anything for days ... One afternoon another doctor came and saw me. I afterwards found out that he was a Specialist [Dr Septz].'

Dr Septz ordered another operation. 'I was taken downstairs to the operating room and put on the table and lay there for some time.' Barry recalled,

> watching the doctors and specialists washing their hands. The matron, Schwester Franka ... came along side of me with a mask in her hand and as she placed it over my face, I remembered her saying Nix pain, Nix smarten De Barry. On the following morning when the doctor did his round and I was being dressed, I saw three more tubes had been put in to drain the poison from the wounds. When Doctor Septz used to move these tubes the pain was fearful ... [W]ith all the kind attention that I got at this place, my condition was getting worse every day ... I can remember one night in the middle of October, Professor Schultz, Schewster Franka and a pastor, coming to my bedside and telling me that Doctor Septz had done all he could to save my leg and the only thing that could be done was to amputate, as I would not live another three weeks with it as gangrene had set in. They gave me till the next evening to decide what I intended to do, and on leaving me ... the Lutheran pastor gave me a New Testament

with different chapters marked for me to read.

On the following evening they visited me again and enquired what I intended to do. I told them that I was in the hands of the doctor and he knew best. Then Professor Schultz produced a form and asked me to sign it, giving my consent to have the operation performed. When the form was signed, the Pastor asked me if I would take the Holy Communion in the morning. On the following morning October 25th, at 7am, the Communion was administered. Soon afterwards I was carried downstairs to the operating theatre and put on the table. The leg was amputated. I was back in the ward before 11am, and I heard afterwards that the doctor did not think I was going to pull through.

Barry defied the doctor's prediction. Within a few weeks he was attempting (unsuccessfully at first) to walk with the aid of crutches. By December, his 'health and strength were improving daily.' Perhaps because he felt a degree of compassion towards his captors, Barry's spirits were also uplifted by a visit from the German Field Marshal, Paul von Hindenburg:

One morning in the middle of December a great commotion was caused throughout the building, all the orderlies and sisters were very busy cleaning up the place for they told us that ... von Hindenburg was coming that day to inspect the hospital ... At 11am the door of the ward opened and in walked an elderly man with a grey moustache looking about sixty years in age, dressed in civilian clothes, closely followed by an orderly who called out ... attention, and we all obeyed the order but ... [Hindenburg] waved his hand and said "Sit down."

He went to each bed and spoke to its inmate and when he came to me he said in splendid English, "I see young man that you have had the misfortune to lose your leg." I answered him "Yes, but it is all in the game." He replied, "This war is awful for everybody who is concerned in it," and went on.

On 24 December, the doctors presented Barry with gifts, including two packets of cigarettes. On Christmas Day he received a more welcome present. Matron Franka 'came and said she had some good news to tell me. I would be sent to England to my people very shortly and that news seemed to put new life into me.' But Barry's hopes were to be dashed. After periods in other camp hospitals—first Ingolstadt, then

Aachen—he was transported to a POW camp. He realised then that it would be many months yet before he tasted freedom. In the meantime, he was to receive rougher treatment at the hands of German guards.[3]

***

Hugh Anthony was also wounded and captured in an earlier battle—at Mouquet Farm on 18 August 1916—the same day he had been promoted to full lieutenant. Immediately after surrendering, Anthony's

> shoulder straps were taken. My pockets were emptied. The Germans bound my wound, put me in a small dug-out, gave me a drink of cold coffee and a small piece of chocolate. Later taken to Brigade HQ. Here they started to ask me questions. I nearly fainted so they gave me two small cups of tea instead, then put me on the steps of a dressing station to await transit. We arrived at a larger dressing station where my arm was dressed and I received three small glasses of brandy ... and was given some straw and a blanket to sleep on, in the corner of a shed ... On 20/8/1916 we were herded into a cattle truck which had straw on the floor. There was not sufficient room for us all to lie down. I was the only

officer. The men belonged to various English regiments. We de-trained at Cambrai, [then] took hospital train to Caudry Hospital. I was put in a ward of sixty beds.

Hospital wards fairly clean; operating theatre ditto; sanitary arrangements bad; wounds dressed every 4 days with rewashed bandages; a little chloroform used for bad operations; wounds never washed ... On 5/9/1916 we left Caudry in hospital train, arrived Munster Lazarette 7/9/1916. Temperature taken twice daily. Diet consisted of coffee, barley water, black bread, fruit skin jam, soup and sometimes a stew. This was number 1 Diet, the general diet for patients, although some were put on Diet number 2 which was more substantial food. My uniform was taken away at this hospital. Given different clothes including a French overcoat.

Anthony's opinion of Munster was not flattering. He wrote of 'crowded wards; medical treatment very rough and ready; civilian doctor; sanitary conditions bad; half Lazarette Venereal cases; food same as Caudry.'[4]

A solemn occasion. Funeral of a fellow POW, who died of wounds or from illness. Note German officer in centre of photograph

Sapper Leslie Barry (1st Field Company Engineers) was captured in November 1916 at Delville Wood. Barry recalled being 'particularly struck by the physique and soldierly aspect of my captors,' as they transported him to a field hospital at Bapaume. Four weeks later, he was moved to better facilities at Cambrai. 'After a week in the Citadel, at Cambrai, converted into a hospital, I was moved off into Germany in a hospital train to Dortmund, where we ... were taken ... to the local *Krankenhaus* [Catholic hospital].' Barry was impressed by the large ward's 'cleanliness', although the food—'boiled turnips in the absence of potatoes'—was unappetising. 'Medical treatment by way of operation was impossible,' he wrote, 'one of the Englishmen had a shrapnel pellet ... removed without anaesthetic, a cheerful enough sight to make a Russian, who was waiting his turn to go under the knife faint.' By February 1917 Barry had recovered sufficiently to be transferred to the POW camp at Dulmen, in Westphalia.[5]

***

Following his capture at Bullecourt, Donald Fraser and the other less severely wounded POWs 'were hurled into a train.' The men 'still hadn't been given anything to eat, and we were not told where we going to.' The next morning, when the train called at Liege in Belgium, they were given what passed for soup—'boiled cabbage water, with a little cabbage floating around in it.' Fraser recalled that the wounded 'were becoming very weak and hungry.' On 14 April, the train arrived at Munster. The wounded were immediately taken to the camp's hospital and provided with beds, which Fraser described as 'quite good and clean.' His primary concern was food, which

> was still very scarce—one slice of very sour heavy black bread, which we thought comprised of part sawdust, and a bowl of sauerkraut a day. Some of the German

doctors could speak a little English. I think they gloated at our plight. One of the fellows close to me was a South Australian and had a German name. One day a doctor told him he should be shot for being a traitor to his Fatherland. He replied "Thank God the name is the only part of me which is German." The doctor told him he was a swine and left.

Fraser described the hospital as 'only one storey. In the centre of the ward was a big heater to put coal in. It was quite a big ward, which had thirty or more [beds].' He spent another two weeks at Munster and wrote that he wanted nothing more than to get out of hospital. By now, Fraser 'was becoming very weak' and had lost 'a fair amount of blood,' his weight being a mere 7 stone. We heard rumours on the grape vine that we were to be sent to Soltau, the main Internment Camp. When our wounds were healed, all were keen to get away from Munster, as we heard rumours that the Red Cross had a packet staff there, conducted by Switzerland, Holland and Sweden—all neutrals. I remember one of our fellows, "Red" O'Shea, who had a nasty wound on one of his hands.

When the German doctor came around and asked him how his hand was, he said it was healed. He kept the bad hand behind his back and showed the doctor the good hand. The doctor grunted and walked on.

According to Fraser, O'Shea's 'hand was bad. It swelled up, and he wanted to get out of hospital. He wanted to get to Soltau to get something to eat.' They had both heard 'on the grape vine' that Red Cross food parcels were being distributed at the Soltau prison camp. To their relief, O'Shea and Fraser were told that they would soon be moved to Soltau.[6]

An Australian soldier captured at Bullecourt recalled having his wounds dressed by a German orderly at a casualty clearing station near the French village of Solesmes. 'Those of us who remained,' he wrote,

> were put on a train and taken to various hospitals in Germany ... [where] I found the "Fritz" quite straight, except when one departed from regulations and then ... one laid himself open to anything. Some of the doctors were kindness itself, some were not. On the whole I reckon I had a square deal. However I have seen the wrecks of men who sometimes drifted into the hospital from working parties in France and one could only be thankful he had not

endured their hardships. Thanks to the Australian Red Cross, we had at any rate sufficient food and clothing, and were able to give them some help until their food parcels arrived.[7]

***

Having had his wounds bandaged at a German field hospital, Lieutenant A.V. Watkinson was put on a 'very dirty hospital train', his destination Gutersloh in Westphalia. 'Several men died on the journey,' he remembered,

> owing to lack of medical attention. A doctor was on the train but did not bother about any of the wounded, many of whom were badly in need of dressings. On the third day the hospital was reached. Medical attention there was fair as it happened to be a civilian hospital. We were given little food and one bath during the two months I was there. Before my wound was healed I was sent in a dirty 3rd class carriage for a two days journey, being put into numerous railway cellars en route, which were in a filthy condition. Most of my clothing and boots were stolen at different times.

When he had recovered sufficiently, Watkinson was moved to an officer POW camp in Germany, first at Karlsruhe then Freiburg (both in Baden).[8]

***

G.W.D. Bell was wounded in the knee while attempting to return to the Australian lines. He was moved to a hospital where the injury was treated, although this did nothing to improve his opinion of his German captors. Later, he was transferred to a larger military hospital at Valenciennes. 'I submitted to the inevitable,' he wrote,

> and merely lay gazing at my surroundings. About twenty Australians, numerous Englishmen and an assortment of Russians, French and Belgians occupied the ward. The Hun orderlies assumed control of this forlorn crowd of approximately 150 prisoners ... The Doctor (a young Hun under-officer) visited us later. He spoke a few words of "Pidgin" English. This creature strutted round the ward, finally coming into the English section. "Pain? Yes? No?" and before one could answer he would run off to another bed. He is truly a most absurd despicable creature.

Once his wound had healed, Bell was moved to another, better equipped hospital in Germany. In May 1918, he was repatriated to England.[9]

Horace Rumble's attitude towards his captors was more philosophical. 'We went first of all to Munster Lazarette, not far from the Holland border,' he recalled. In fact, Rumble was lucky to survive complications from his damaged hand. For several days the wound remained untreated. Eventually, it became gangrenous. More problems followed. Almost 'a week after capture I developed tetanus,' he added.

> My jaw shut with a bang ... The old doctor who had looked at my wound, he gave me 24 hours to live, that's all ... I wouldn't move ... I thought, I must keep on my back. If I roll on my side, my spine will snap. I felt just like a fish would when it's thrown in a hot pan and starts to curl up. I was weighing fourteen stone [90 kilograms] then, and do you know, I dwindled down to ... six stone [38 kilograms]. Instead of pegging out, I was helped by a young German army doctor who was working in a hospital nearby. He was a tall fellow with a big sabre slash across the side of his face. He wasn't even supposed to have anything to do with us. But he'd been wanting to have a go at an experiment with a tetanus case ... He came over with two Russian prisoners and they put me [on] a stretcher, and took me over to the hospital. They put

me on the table and the doctor put these injections into the lumbar region of my spine.

He did nothing else at all. He didn't make any arrangements at all about feeding me. No, none of that. The Russians just brought me back again and put me back in my old plank bed. This doctor kept repeating that, and in five months he cured me of this tetanus. He was very pleased. He had me before a big German board of elderly doctors with Iron Crosses on their chests. He had a big book and he read out all that he'd done to me. I was "Exhibit A." After he finished he turned around and tapped me on the shoulder, and he said, "You very lucky boy, Rumbley!" I never knew his name, and I never saw him again after that.

Rumble was doubly fortunate that the efforts of a good friend, John Brennan (16th Battalion), helped pull him through the crisis. Rumble never forgot the countless times Brennan fed him 'strained watery mangelwurzel soup.' Eventually he was able to move freely and take more notice of his surroundings. 'The lazarette was a wooden building,' he remembered, 'it was only for the wounded,' and it was supposed to be a hospital, but there was no proper sanitation. At the end of the ward there was a room which had been walled off, where they had a long seat with holes in it. The pit underneath could be emptied from outside. It was open ... [Occasionally] they'd get some fellows down there shovelling it all out and taking it away in a cart. There were no showering arrangements. You know after I was captured and got into Germany, it was five months before I got a shower ... What they did do when we arrived there, was to make us all strip off, and they brought in a tin bath, about three feet long. It was full of dirty water. They made every one of us, wounds and all, wash in this stuff. There was blood and pus in the water, but we all washed in it. But before we dried down, two Russians got through and shaved everyone of us all over all over. Completely. Every bit of hair came off. They shaved us with an open razor; a pretty rough one too. They made cuts all over us, but we had no soap. Nothing ... Then they only gave us a thin cotton gown. They took away our uniforms and clothes. Put them in a fumigator thing. I had sheepskin coats and those things, all ruined ... They gave them back to me five months later.

Not all wounded prisoners were as fortunate as Rumble. A great many succumbed to their wounds and were buried by the Germans. These men were listed simply as 'killed in action'.

During his convalescence, Rumble saw many young soldiers suffer terribly before dying a merciful death. 'There was one fellow there who had a [three-inch] hole in his chest,' Rumble wrote:

> We had to tip him up to tip the pus out. And put ... a big swathe of paper around his chest. He was a Queenslander, and he was always talking about going back. You know, he died [after] about five months with this huge hole in his chest. There was never any nursing or anything like that. If we had too difficult a bandage to put on, they had two Russian stretcher-bearers who were prisoners, and they used to send them in to see if we had a good bandage. Most of us were bandaging ourselves, but if we had any difficulty, these [two] Russians ... they'd come along and say, "Good bandage?" And you'd say "Yes." The paper was easy to bandage.

Conditions in the hospital were less than hygienic. 'I used to burn the paper in a little pot-bellied stove in the middle [of the ward],' Rumble added, 'where we burnt all the bandages.'[10]

Private F. Longwill was assaulted by a German guard while working behind the front and his wounds never healed properly. 'I was sent to hospital first at Denain,' he wrote, and then at Mons. At Denain the French residents were distinctly friendly to us. The Mayor and other French gentlemen sent me in clothing and other gifts, which were smuggled into hospital. A French attendant ... also sent me in daily gifts of food.' Longwill was sent back to Marchiennes to work in the same *Kommando*. A few weeks later, he was part of a group of Australian and British prisoners sent to Friedrichsfeld camp.[11]

Edmund Sadler (16th Battalion) was wounded in the right arm by a bullet but managed to staunch the bleeding with a handkerchief. Along with other captured Australians, he was taken to the nearest German field hospital. The wound was dressed and he was put on a train to Munster Lazarette where a German doctor amputated his now gangrenous arm. A number of Sadler's German guards spoke reasonable English, and the medical staff 'always treated him well, although ... their food left much to be desired, especially the endless sauerkraut and "black" bread.' Red Cross parcels arrived frequently. After eight months of captivity, Sadler was among the wounded POWs to be exchanged for their German counterparts. Having completed the formalities at the exchange centre at Manheim, he crossed into neutral Holland. Waiting Red Cross ships took Sadler and other wounded POWs to England. Having recovered sufficiently at the Australian base hospital in Southall, he boarded a ship, the *Dunkirk Hospital.*

Instead of returning directly to Australia, however, the *Dunkirk Hospital* sailed to Alexandria, in Egypt. Sadler was told that 'It was unwise to send [me] directly home as people "high-up" did not want many "wounded cripples" sent back home.' He dismissed this reason as nothing more than 'political propaganda'. A base hospital had been established at the Sultan's Palace near Montassa, and Sadler stayed there for 'quite a few months, almost to the finish of the war.' Activities included 'swimming, walking and other gentle games.' Red Cross parcels and letters and parcels from family and friends were welcome distractions.[12]

Jim Wheeler was sent to a hospital in Douai—the same town in which his comrades were working. 'I was in Douai for a week to ten days,' Wheeler recalled,

> The hospital was crowded with British wounded ... I was practically a cot case in

Douai. I was in bed most of the time. I was not hit at all. It was just the force of the explosion ... I was practically a mass of blasted bruises from the shock of the explosion. The first week I was damned crook. I hardly knew whether I was alive or dead. But there were worse cases than me. I saw some terrible cases from bloody shell explosions. The whole body was shaking. Their nerves were gone. And bruises! Practically the whole body was blue, and not a hit on them—not a metal hit. The concussion from the shells was terrific.[13]

So 'terrific' was the concussion of the shells that some of these men eventually died. In fact, any man within ten metres of a shell explosion was usually killed by the concussion from the blast. While the body showed no external signs, the kidneys and spleen were often ruptured. Other soldiers within the extended blast radius, such as Wheeler, suffered significant internal injuries which sometimes led to an unpleasant death.[14]

Not all deaths resulted from wounds sustained in battle. Private Hubert Demasson (16th Battalion) was recovering from surgery at Langensalza Lazarette in Thuringid. One of his mates, Private T. Sloss, had previously informed

AIF Headquarters in London that 'all I know of Demasson is ... when he left the trenches about 12 noon [on] 11.4.17, after receiving the order to take our choice of surrendering or retiring, Demasson decided to stay behind as he was then wounded. I expected to hear he was taken prisoner.' A few months later, Demasson died. AIF Headquarters was told that 'shortly after arriving at this Camp, [he] contracted dysentery. He was treated for this complaint, in hospital, but without avail, he passed away ... on 19 September 1917.' A later report noted that he died 'at 5.15a.m. from inflammation of kidneys and chronic inflammation of the bowels.' Contrary to popular rumour concerning German treatment of Allied POWs who had died, the Germans gave Demasson a decent burial service and marked his grave with a wooden cross. They also provided details of the grave's whereabouts to the AIF.[15]

***

It took five months for Horace Rumble to fully recover from his battle with tetanus. During his treatment, he persuaded John Brennan to write to another friend in England. 'He told him that I had tetanus, and couldn't open my mouth.' Rumble added:

So he got the Red Cross to send through a dozen tins of milk. And they never got to me ... They were a big prize in Germany. Germany was very short of food ... It was a long time before I got a Red Cross parcel there. And I didn't get any clothes from the Red Cross. I still had this cotton gown. But just before, when I did heal, they brought me along a parcel with two sets of grey flannel underclothing and boots and socks and things. And a cap made in England to the design of the Germans for their prison uniform. And they were black and brown. And a proper double breasted coat. A decent button-up tunic and pants ... [The clothes] were good, but it was five months before I got those. And when I put them on I was terribly prickly and hot. I thought, "What goes on?" Anyhow, when I was cured there and got fitted out, they sent me down to a working camp. See I was healed. I went off to a big working camp [Soltau].[16]

Despite being on crutches, Claude Benson worked as an orderly at a military prison hospital in Germany. There he cared for a number of POWs who had suffered shocking wounds. He remembered the disheartening ordeal of waiting for men to die:

Poor fellows with gunshot wounds were in terrible condition, some of the wounds hadn't been dressed for five days, so I went to the inspector of the hospital and he said I could look after these men. I found the British wounded were placed in the same beds that had been used by the Russians suffering from consumption and all sorts of infectious diseases. I washed the place out and thoroughly disinfected it, separated the contagious patients and gave them strict orders to keep themselves clean.

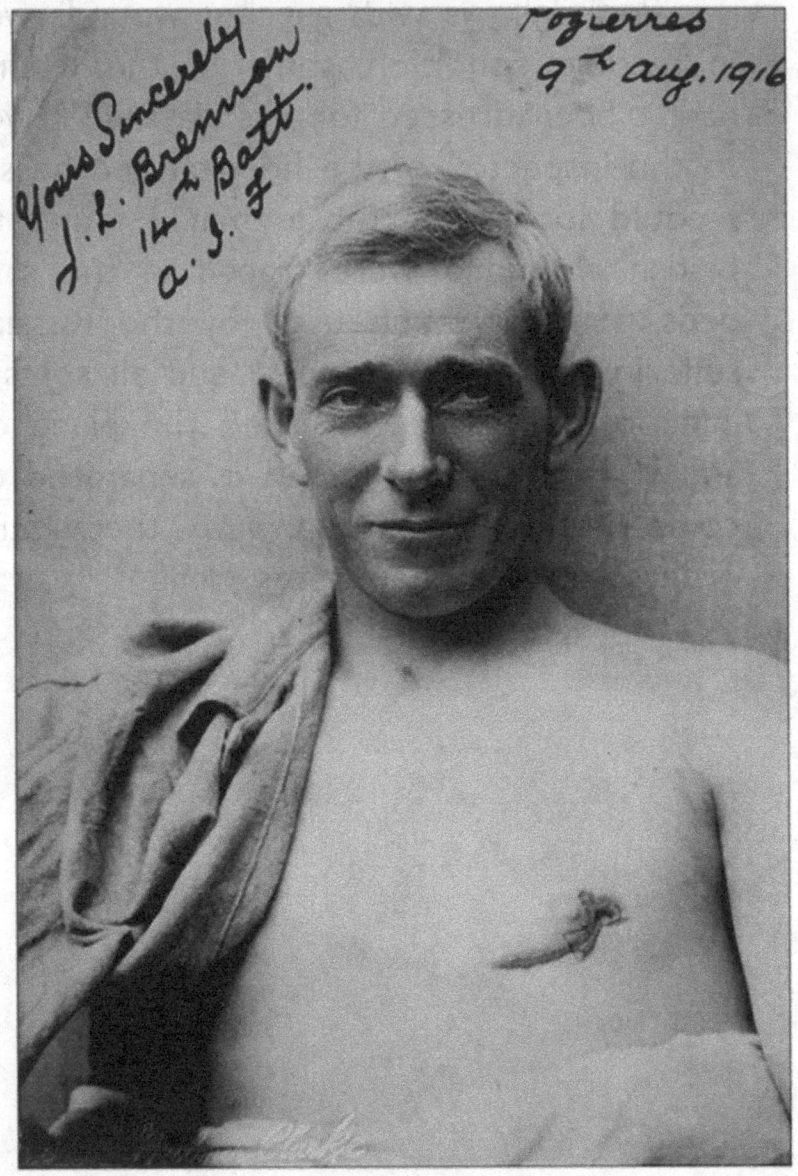

Photograph of wounds inflicted on J L Brennan, 14th Battalion, 9 August 1916.

Washing and re-applying bandages on badly wounded soldiers was another unpleasant task. As there was no proper bath, Benson had to physically move a patient, laying the man onto a table so that he could wash him with a bucket of hot water which he obtained from 'the cookhouse'.

Benson later spent time working in a nearby exchange barracks where Australian and English prisoners recovering from wounds waited to be swapped with German prisoners who were behind the wire in British POW camps. Appalled by the conditions, he recalled:

> One poor fellow who'd been wounded in three different places had his kneecap blown off and his leg in a splint. His wound was discharging more than it should and I discovered a piece of bone projecting from the side. Once inside this barracks men belonged to the transport office, to be sent to Aix La Chapelle, England or Switzerland, therefore the hospital didn't want to have anything more to do with them and it was hard to get advice from a doctor, but I managed to get this man to hospital and they removed a piece of bone two and a half inches long. He was sent back to me feeling much better and finally reached England. I learnt that after arrival there his leg had to be amputated with good results.

As essential supplies were required for front-line troops, the hospital was given halfstrength medications and no proper wadding. Instead it received 'paper bandages and wood-wool for use on wounds where plugging was essential, or for large wounds.' The wounds soon became 'saturated with pus and [would] become very stiff and any movement of the body or limbs [would cause it] to come out.' Benson added that it was not unusual for Allied soldiers 'to wait sometimes for weeks before an operation could be performed because of the lack of instruments.' The worst cases usually ended in a painful death before an operation could be performed.

The commencement of the German army's spring offensive meant that Benson's gut-wrenching work only increased. At times he had more than eighty patients in his care—yet, he still could not obtain proper dressings. When, at last, he 'received some from the British Red Cross ... [he] was able to keep wounds clean until the men were sent to England.' He believed that 50% of these boys would have died otherwise.' Lack of proper medical training did not prevent Benson from being asked to perform minor operations. 'The majority of these men didn't want to see a doctor because it may delay their exchange and they begged me to fix it up myself. I'd treat an abscess or splinter of bone not far from the surface. I would only operate when I was sure that by taking the risk the patient would not miss his exchange and perhaps wait for months before getting away.' Those who managed to 'get away' told authorities in England of Benson's minor miracles, performed without the aid of proper instruments. To ensure that his good work continued, the Red Cross despatched 'a case of surgical instruments'.

Photograph showing damage to Brennan's personal items – which, most likely, prevented more serious wounds or even death – including the size of the piece of shrapnel that caused the wound.

As the number of wounded increased, Benson was handicapped by the small number of spare beds available. The worst cases were sometimes moved to hospitals that were better equipped. 'Straw would be thrown into the fourwheeled army transports,' Benson remembered, for the patients to lie on and when it was full the remainder were allowed stretchers. They were given a portion of bread, taken to the railway station and placed on the hard wooden seats of third-class compartments without even a blanket. Sometimes they went for more than two days with their wounds not being dressed, a distance sometimes 500 miles from Hamburg, Bremen and Cologne. I asked at these stations for the necessary dressings for the patients but I was refused outright.

Constantly reminded of 'the hopelessness of it all', Benson recalled the occasion he visited an Italian prisoner who had cut his own throat. After treating the wound, Benson saw that another prisoner had attempted to disembowel himself. It was all too much for the Australian, who decided there and then to plan his escape.[17]

***

Richard 'Dick' Chalk and his big brother Ernest 'Ern,' c 1916.

The incarcerated Ernie Chalk would have been unaware that, on 12 June, in his home town of Burnie in Tasmania, the local newspaper reported that 'another brave Burnie lad had made the supreme sacrifice "somewhere in France" fighting for King and country. Last Thursday Mr. A.G. Chalk received official news that his eldest son, Ernie T., was wounded and a prisoner-of-war at Dulmen, Germany.' More significantly for the Chalk family, the paper also revealed that

> last evening the Reverend A.V. Ballard had the painful duty of advising them that

their second son, Corporal Richard George ("Dick") had died of gunshot wounds on the 13th May at the Second Australian Casualty Station ... He was home on final leave for his 19th birthday, and was [sic] 20 on the 7th of this month. He left England for France on 3rd November, and his letters from the front were always bright and cheery. The deepest sympathy is extended to Mr. and Mrs. Chalk and family in their hour of great bereavement.[18]

Soon after, Ernie Chalk recalled being 'parted' from his mates—'the larger party going on to Lille, and we who were left, about 200 of us, going into hospital at Le Quesnoy.' Chalk was cared for by

> two Belgian sisters who were doing the nursing work. We were very fortunate in ... [having] them, for they were very kind to us, and gave us things which otherwise we should not have had. They also told us that they, like ourselves, were held as prisoners by the Germans. They had been taken away from their homes by the Germans in the early months of the war, and had since been through some very terrible hardships. And their hatred for their captors was very intense indeed.

But we were not destined to rest in peace here. In a few days after being admitted, we were ordered to get up and get ready ... as we were going to be sent to Germany. I shall never be able to adequately describe the journey that followed ... We were put into five closed-in cattle trucks and one open truck ... I was fortunate enough to strike the open one, so was not denied fresh air, as most of the party were. It took us four nights and three days to make the journey, and this under the worst of conditions. The train was a goods train returning to Germany, and at some of the stations we were shunted into the sidings for hours at a stretch, and all this time we were confined to the trucks. The only food we were given for the whole ... journey was a piece of the German bread ... and also a very watery soup at one of the stations in Germany. We also went a very roundabout track ... Minden being our destination. Some of the boys who were wounded badly suffered terribly all this time. One brave little chap I remember very distinctly. He was only about 18 years of age, and he had had half of his hand shot away. He ... only had it dressed once, and that was with the paper bandages. He was sitting next to me during the whole trip, but I did not hear him murmur once. I shall never forget the way in which he silently suffered.

The group arrived at Minden shortly before dawn. 'This rather picturesque old town looked very fine as we passed through the streets in the early morning light,' Chalk observed,

> for everything was covered with about nine inches of snow which had fallen during the night and had not yet been disturbed. But we were not in the humour to look upon the beautiful. One thing we all noticed though was the bareness of all the shop windows. There was ... [no] food for sale in any of them, and this we tried to cheer each other up with. "Well cobbers, we won't be here for long, anyhow. Jerry can't last much longer. Why look, he has nothing left to eat. He will soon be starved into giving in."

He quickly recognised the irony of his situation. Sooner, rather than later, the food shortage would affect the POWs' own well-being: 'if Germany starved we should do the same.'

The walking wounded had to march over seven kilometres to the hospital which was located inside the prison compound. Chalk described it as once having been a military barracks ... capable of holding many thousands of men ... [A]bout 150 of our party were put into a camp hospital, after we had undergone a thorough fumigation. In the hospital Russian orderlies were doing most of the work. At least they were supposed to. But they would not go out of their way in the least to help our boys. And very often they would cheat us out of our meagre allowance of rations, which here consisted of one thin slice of bread per day and two very watery soups, which was sometimes made out of sauerkraut, "a kind of cabbage which had been preserved in large casks," and at other times it was made from dried mangels and swedes.

As Chalk predicted, some Germans did not treat the prisoners well. Recognising the shortage of medicine and 'proper' bandages, he was probably unaware that the Germans were drastically short of essential medication, even for their own wounded. He recalled that, whenever necessary,

German doctors did the operations, but they were very cruel to some of the boys. I saw quite a number of operations take place, but in not a single case was any narcotic given, or anything whatever to alleviate the pain. A West Australian who was lying next to me had a bullet deeply embedded in his leg, and he was just simply held down by a couple of Russians while the German doctors probed at his leg, which they did in no gentle fashion. So it can be easily imagined the pain that the poor fellow needlessly suffered in consequence.

Ernie Chalk was held in the camp for two more weeks before he, along with others who had recovered sufficiently, were moved to a smaller camp at Dulmen 'not many miles past Munster'.[19] Other wounded Australians, left behind in France, did not fare quite so well.

German doctors diagnosed Campbell Stewart as suffering from haemorrhoids, yet he was forced to continue working. On 20 August he was 'still very bad with piles. Went on sick parade this morning and got two days light duty.' The following day he was 'still bad ... [and] expect to be going to hospital tomorrow. Doctor down to "clink" to see a few of us.' On 22 August he was 'sent on to Tournai, was given a bath, clean clothes and a haircut and admitted to hospital ... In with Ruskies [Russians], French, Portuguese, Canadians and all sorts.' He added that another Australian prisoner, who died the previous day, was buried before he left, and 'all our fellows [were] at the funeral.' The food was much better at this hospital; for breakfast, Stewart was given coffee and bread, while barley, macaroni and meat were provided for dinner. On the 25th he wrote, 'Feeling well today, examined by doctor.' However, over the next few days, his condition deteriorated. 'Piles very sore today,' he wrote, 'can't get anything for them ... Had a very bad night, never slept all night. Our planes over Tournai there about midnight and dropping bombs, some which fell very close to us, here.' German doctors considered his condition so serious that, on the 28th, Stewart was moved from 'Tournai [bound] for Deutschland [Germany]. Carried down from top on a stretcher and waited in yard for ambulance. Put on train at 12.30 [p.m.] and given basin of soup for dinner ... [A] slice of bread and barley soup for tea. Two Russians in our carriage looking after us.' He also disclosed that another Australian prisoner, 'Snowey, died this morning.'[20]

More fortunate POWs who became ill while working behind the front were usually sent to the nearest German military hospital. Keith Tamblyn had only recently been moved to Condi when he was discovered to be suffering from 'a bout of scabies.' First transported to Denain to a hospital for factory workers, he was later moved to another, better equipped hospital in Mons.[21] Tamblyn stayed 'there for a while amongst the patients. It was a prisoner-of-war hospital, four or five Australians, and these chaps were getting Red Cross Parcels, they never made a meal for themselves without they did one for me. So I was in the winning. I picked up remarkably well and a German doctor soon cleared up my scabies with sulpha and Stockholm tar and a little bit of soap.' He remained in care until early November when he was discharged and returned to Denain.[22]

Len Pooley was another more fortunate POW. Pooley fell ill, his condition deteriorated and he became too weak to continue working on railroad construction. The Germans chose to send him to a hospital in Lubeck. 'I was very sick when I went there,' he recalled, 'very weak. I know I was longing to get out of the hospital at Lubeck, because I couldn't eat the sauerkraut they used to bring.' At Lubeck approximately 50% of the patients were prisoners, while the other 50% were enemy soldiers in poor health. 'One day the German officers and a couple of orderlies came along the ward,' Pooley remembered, they pointed to me, and the doctor said, "We'll be carrying him out in the morning." I got a shock. I said to myself,

> "Be buggered they will!" And I got up, and I walked out the door and up to where the German wounded were. There was a wire mesh netting separating us ... I pulled myself up on this wire mesh as far as I could, and I just hung there. I did that for a couple of days before I went away. I was only there for another day or so. And I started to recover. It was determination, I suppose. If I had just laid there in bed, that would have been the end of it.

Pooley remained in hospital until the German doctor considered him sufficiently fit to be moved to a POW camp.[23]

Thomas Taylor contracted his illness while working at a German veterinary hospital. His condition worsened and an unfavourable diagnosis saw him taken to a military hospital where he 'was the only Allied prisoner there.' He recalled that some German doctors

> proposed to make short work of my complaint by removing my arm. I strenuously objected, and at length prevailed upon one doctor, who could speak excellent English, to try an operation on [my] hand. They lost no time over it; I was bundled on to an operating table, and without an anaesthetic of any kind they opened my hand right from my fingers almost to the wrist. The shock

was rather severe, but I saved my arm ... After spending about a month in that German [military] hospital, I was transferred to a hospital for prisoners of war, and there the effects of the bad food and black bread were very evident. Dysentery was carrying off the invalids in scores, especially the Russians, who seemed to be accorded worse treatment than other Allied prisoners. I counted as many as 150 deaths in the Russian quarter in one week ... Their ward was in an upper floor of the building, and each unfortunate, as he died was taken by the legs or an arm and dragged down the stairs and thrown into one huge common grave. Even now I can hear the dull thuds and bumps of those lifeless bodies. Several English Tommies died at the same hospital while I was there, but they were treated with more respect, and were carried out decently and buried in separate graves.

Once doctors believed that Taylor had made a satisfactory recovery, he was taken, under guard, to another veterinary hospital in Tournai, where he resumed his work with horses.[24]

Bible, with 40th Battalion Colourpatch, belonging to Richard Chalk, photograph of Chalk as a Corporal and Memorial Booklet to Corporal Richard Chalk who died of wounds, in France, 13 May 1917. Photographed by David Chalk.

***

Conditions for wounded or sick Australian POWs varied considerably. Ultimately, their fate depended on the hospital in which they were treated. Generally, the further the medical facility from the front line, the better the medical treatment the POWs received. Overall, however, their chances of recovery were quite good. Certainly, those men sent to Germany for treatment were cared for in a more benevolent manner. Wounded or sick prisoners usually fared much better than their healthier comrades who had been forced into labour. Food—though never adequate—and a warm bed were the norm, unlike working prisoners who existed on meagre rations and were rarely given blankets. For all POWs, the arrival of a Red Cross parcel was greeted with joy and recognised as both a means to supplement their often parlous diet and as a boost to their flagging morale.

CHAPTER TEN
The Red Cross Society
'That Noble Institution'

CHAPTER TEN

THE RED CROSS SOCIETY

'That Noble Institution'

The International Red Cross was formed in 1864 by Henri Dunant as an adjunct to the Geneva Convention. Items in its charter included assistance to soldiers wounded or captured in war. Delegates to the Second Hague Conference (1907) agreed that:

> Relief societies for prisoners-of-war, which are properly constituted in accordance with the laws of their country and with the object of serving as the channel for charitable effort shall receive from the belligerents, for themselves and their duly accredited agents every facility for the efficient performance of their humane task within the bounds imposed by military necessities and administrative regulations. Agents of these societies may be admitted to the places of internment for the purpose of distributing relief, as also to the halting places of repatriated prisoners, if furnished

with a personal permit by the military authorities, and on giving an undertaking in writing to comply with all measures of order and police which the latter may issue.

However, the Red Cross did not gain proper recognition until 1912. A conference of international diplomats held in Washington DC ratified the earlier agreement and added another clause which authorised the organisation to act as an official intermediary to assist POWs. Every fighting nation had an obligation to notify the Red Cross that a soldier was being held prisoner. Likewise, if a POW died in captivity, the authorities were obliged to inform the Red Cross which would convey the information to the soldier's family.

After war was declared, the Red Cross immediately established an International Prisoners of War Agency with its headquarters in Geneva. Individual units came under the auspices of four main departments. The first department gathered information concerning POWs which was passed to their families. Eighty-three staff attached to the British section worked various shifts, ensuring that the department never closed. Another department handled letters, parcels and money. The third supervised conditions in all camps. 'Inspectors' from neutral countries (most notably Switzerland), acting as representatives of the Red

Cross, visited camps to ensure that POW conditions were satisfactory. The last department looked after repatriation and the men's welfare as they were released to neutral countries.

Initially, the society's most fundamental and difficult undertaking was to persuade all nations to provide a list of prisoners. Some—most notably Germany—provided the information readily. Others—particularly Russia—were slower. As the huge lists of prisoners (mostly taken on the Eastern Front) arrived in the departments, staff compiled an index of names. The Red Cross typing pool required 100 women, working full-time, to complete that job alone. The agency also maintained standard information cards which listed details of each POW including name, rank, home address on enlistment, camp address etc. The French section produced 2.5 million cards during the war, the German section 1.5 million, the British section almost half a million. That task was made somewhat simpler by the close cooperation of POW information bureaux established by all the belligerent governments.[1]

***

The Australian Red Cross Society was inaugurated on 13 August 1914 and soon claimed 100,000 members (80% of whom were women). The society's initial purpose was to raise funds to provide comfort supplies for all soldiers of the AIF. Members also contributed by making clothes—in particular socks, shirts and gloves. Some women worked with a subsidiary organisation, the Voluntary Aid Detachments (VAD), helping in hospitals and convalescent homes. Of more significance was the formation of a POW section in London to 'look after the interests of Australian POWs and large numbers of parcels and sums of money were sent to prisoners. The POW section was the official link between prisoners and their families, and maintained full casualty lists for each State.' The section also provided a link for British citizens to 'adopt' or sponsor an Australian POW. The society would then arrange for food parcels to be despatched with the sponsor's name attached.[2] Once they were registered, Australian POWs were administered by the London section, led by one of the many women on the staff, Miss E. Chomley.

The Red Cross' most important undertaking—and one which affected each and every Australian POW—was the parcel system. At first, the British took responsibility for sending parcels to captured Australians. But they were soon overwhelmed by the sheer size of the task, and had problems simply maintaining the flow of parcels to their own troops. Large numbers of

British soldiers had been taken in the early battles of 1914 (such as at Le Cateau) and subsequent offensives in 1915—16, culminating in the disaster that was the Somme, which only added to the strain on the already stretched resources of the British Red Cross. Britain was also busy making overtures to the German government concerning suitable 'parcel systems' and a mutual exchange of POWs—particularly sick and wounded—through a neutral country such as Holland or Denmark. The Germans initially baulked at the proposal, but subsequently acquiesced when a 'one-for-one' exchange was proposed. Despite unfair criticism (most notably by POWs who would have been unaware of 'behind-the-scenes' negotiations) Germany and Britain eventually agreed to a scheme that would also allow their prisoners access to Red Cross parcels.

***

A British officer, Captain G. McMurtrie (Somerset Light Infantry), provided a comprehensive account of the way parcels—and their contents—were distributed in a POW camp:

> Once the parcels and letters began to come regularly we were all right, especially as large consignments of shirts, socks, pyjamas etc were sent by the Red Cross.

Meanwhile a large number of cases of biscuits and "emergency" parcels were also sent to the camp by the Red Cross. If any officer did not get a food parcel for a week then he was given one of the emergency parcels. The biscuits were ordinary hard biscuits which were kept as a reserve in case the frontiers were closed (as they were for about a month, once or twice a year) and thus we still had food to carry on with, even though our parcels had stopped coming. Later as more food came into the camp we gave a great many biscuits to the French officers' camp at Graudenz who were badly in need of food.

The procedure for parcels was as follows: One English officer and three English privates went down to the post office each day with a guard. There they picked up the parcels and the officer checked the numbers. When the parcels got to the camp they were immediately taken to a "parcel house," a small building with about six rooms in it. Here they were unloaded and the parcels for half the officers in the camp went to the "right" rooms and the other half to the "left." They were all set out in order, numbered, and then the number was put against the officer's name on a printed list which was posted on the notice boards.

The next day those officers for whom parcels had come would queue up in the required "margarine style" queue and would get their parcels in alphabetical order. There was always a German officer, one or two sergeant-majors and four German privates watching. The parcel was opened and all tinned goods were put in the officer's tin locker (every officer had a tin locker in the parcel house). The number of tins would be entered in a book. The rest of the parcel the officer could take away unless there was some forbidden article, which would be confiscated. In the case of clothes, all civilian clothes were either kept by the Huns until the Armistice was signed or, if the officer wished, broad stripes were sewn into the clothes. All clothes parcels were carefully searched by the Boche before being passed.

Candles, compasses and books were kept by the Boche. Books were censored and then returned. There were about eight English officers in each room doing the work and running everything to do with parcels. The Boche simply cleared away the rubbish and saw or did not see that tins were not taken out unopened. Tins were not allowed to be taken away unopened; I suppose for fear of compasses etc being hidden in them. Once or twice a day, officers could draw their tins. They came with plates and stated their locker number and the tins would be opened and deposited on their plates. Needless to say, all these queues were a constant source of annoyance. There were many exciting moments when officers, with the assistance of confederates inside the parcel room, would get their parcels out whole or tins unopened. If an officer knew that a parcel contained something that could be used to assist escape, it was smuggled out.

The food that we were given was ample to live on; however as soon as we had got over our starvation period and were used to food, the continual tinned food, tinned everything, began to get on our nerves. There is something about the ordinary tinned food which you cannot get away from, unless you have flavouring and we had none.

From our Red Cross parcels we got Quaker Oats, tea, milk, cocoa, bully, maconochie cheese, biscuits, jam, marmalade, tinned puddings, milk puddings, margarine, potted meat, bacon and sugar; but all of it tasted of tins. We also received at first white bread, which was mouldy, but at that time we were too hungry to throw it away. Later we received boxes of hard biscuits from Berne and towards the end white bread was once more sent which was quite fresh.[3]

Similar systems were common in all German camps where Australian soldiers were held.

Campbell Stewart, for instance, recalled receiving his first Red Cross parcel in late August, not long after his arrival in Germany. He noted with delight, 'three packets of Hambley Palmers biscuits issued to us today from the ... Committee, which was very good also a clean sheet and a sort of quilt.' His greatest pleasure was reserved for the following day. 'Lovely day today, finished our ration of biscuits, got an issue of a packet of Woodbine cigarettes.' And, a few days later, even better: 'got an issue from the Committee including four packets of biscuits per man, cigarettes, tobacco, raisins, lollies, chocolate, bully, fish, quaker oats, rice, macaroni, tinned fruit, so we are not having a bad time here now.'[4]

Douglas Grant also appreciated the parcels' contents. 'The Australian Red Cross send me three packets of groceries a fortnight,' he wrote, 'which contain oatmeal, rice, bacon, cheese, butter, cocoa, coffee, tea, cigarettes, tobacco and other articles. I also get two loaves of bread and a tin of biscuits a week from the Red Cross in Switzerland. I also have good boots, shoes, slippers, socks, shirts and a prison uniform.'[5]

Red Cross Society workers packing 'comfort' items for Australians who were being held as POWs in German camps. (AWM H00507)

Australian POWs certainly looked forward to (and could not do without) their parcels. The diligent work of the Red Cross prevented countless numbers from starving to death. Usually, however, it was only *after* they arrived at a camp in Germany that the men's names were conveyed to the Red Cross in England. In some instances, this process took months. POWs who were sent to Germany almost immediately following their capture were, however, a notable exception. Sergeant Guppy, for example, wrote that, in mid-May, 'we had to fill in identification and registration cards and [were] also each given a card on which to write a notification to the

Australian Red Cross, London, of the fact of being a prisoner.'[6] When their names were registered, the men's families in Australia were informed that they were still alive. Following the disastrous Battle of Bullecourt, a large number of men had been listed as missing. The news that they had not been killed provided untold relief to their families.

***

Corporal Lancelot Davies was well aware of the way the system worked. Nevertheless, he believed that the Germans were holding back some food parcels. 'There were aspects unfavourable to inhuman and shrewd Jerry,' he wrote,

> parcels of food and other things had been entering Germany per medium of the Red Cross subject ... to German censoring ... Every soldier officially reported as a prisoner-of-war was provided for on equal terms ... They were known to us as grocery parcels ... really they were cardboard boxes, size about 12x10x10 inches ... and contained tinned meats, butter or margarine, jam. Fish, soups, vegetables, biscuits, tobacco [and] cigarettes and all the necessities of life ... The contents were distributed over a series of boxes, which arrived at six day intervals

... Clothing also was sent every six months. Consignments went by steamer to a head base in Holland, and from there distributed in truck loads to the various lagers in Germany. Neutral and German Red Cross commissioners accompanied the consignment to the rail destination where posterns guarded same until they could be taken delivery of by the camp authorities, who sent a working party of prisoners to draw it to camp ... Regular parcels of specially made white bread were also sent from Denmark or Switzerland every six days ... Special lots of medical supplies were sent from London and also a limited amount of goods on behalf of newcomers.

Davies noted that, when he first arrived, a Red Cross committee had been 'established, and assumed control of the stuff for distribution.'[7]

Jim Wheeler recalled that 'it was probably at the Stargard hospital, [that] a Swiss man, a Red Cross man, came along and took your name. That's how your name got to England, and you'd go on the list for Red Cross parcels.'[8] Other Australians had similar recollections. 'I was at Friedrichsfeld [POW camp] about three months I think, but we were starved.' Whittington noted disconsolately, 'We had no Red Cross parcels. The Red Cross hadn't got in touch with us. But after they got in touch—I think it might have taken three months—then they sent us foodstuffs. They kept us alive. Oh, we were well fed ... we used to get three parcels a fortnight.'[9] Horatio Ganson remembered otherwise. 'They rigged us out there at Friedrichsfeld,' he said, 'they gave us Red Cross parcels from surplus kept for prisoners coming in from outside. They'd give you everything, you know. You got soap and sugar and biscuits, and an army razor—although that was like trying to scrape yourself with a brick.'[10] Parcels weighed around five kilograms and went into a central storage area where they were opened. 'About four or five Germans opened this bully beef tin,' Rumble recalled, 'and cut up all the meat to see that there was nothing in it. I also had a loaf of bread, and they chopped that up too. They wouldn't give us cigarettes. If we got any cigarettes, they pulled all the cigarettes to pieces.'[11]

Representatives from the Red Cross periodically visited the camps to check on the men's welfare and ensure that parcels were properly distributed. On these occasions, the Germans usually ensured that the men were being reasonably fed. Representatives were prevented from witnessing the appalling situation that POWs endured in the mines, nor did they visit farms. Donald Fraser mentioned that, during his time at Soltau, 'Swedish ... Red Cross people ... used to come ... to the camp and look through them ... I didn't actually see them myself, but they came here. I know that from other fellows that did see them.'[12]

Sometimes problems arose when a few men became over-enthusiastic. Harold Horner remarked that parcels were waiting when he arrived at a camp in late November 1917. 'Many who came with us were dreadfully thin,' he wrote. However, an English NCO 'came out and warned us not to eat too much when we received the packets ... He told us that numbers of starved men had killed themselves by over-eating when their packets were given to them. I have seen men eating rolled oats and jam straight from packet and tin. Sometimes bread and other food would be mouldy. But many men ate it.' Horner noted sadly that, for some, food parcels were too late. 'There were several deaths in camp [while] ... we were there,' he added. 'One young fellow in our hut was too far gone to rally when he received his packets. Four men carried him to the doctor, who said there was nothing wrong with him ... Next morning he was dead.'[13]

The men also began receiving letters from loved ones in Australia. 'Those letters brightened us all up wonderfully,' wrote Thomas Taylor,

> and soon after that our Red Cross parcels arrived. While we were in France a few found their way through to one or two of the prisoners ... And what a blessing those parcels were. You, Red Cross workers, could have witnessed the joy they brought with them, I am sure you would feel amply rewarded for all the loving patience, time and care you bestowed on them. It is not exaggerating in the slightest degree to say that the contents of your parcels saved many a prisoners life. I believe also that the arrival of those parcels in such numbers and afterwards so regularly had [a] big influence on the morale of the German people; at any rate, where we were.[14]

Parcels began arriving almost six weeks after Lancelot Davies arrived in Germany. 'At about the same time ... letters also filtered through,' he remembered,

> and glad were the hearts of those recipients on getting possession of mail from their loved ones. Naturally the Englishmen (Scots, Irish etc) were the first to receive, owing to their close proximity ... although we Australians and other Dominion men were not kept long in suspense, as our mails had been accumulating in England since we had been temporarily lost to sight and

record. None of us ... were aware of just what had happened regarding ourselves (officially) since that eventful day of 11th April 1917, although we conjectured much.

It appears that I.... like many others, was posted "missing," and after the stipulated three months had expired, "dead" was written against my army records. To be officially posted missing in the casualty lists of the war struck a severe blow to those at home, who were continuously carrying the burden of anxiety, all through the period of absence ... Only those concerned know the true feelings experienced on learning that a loved one is missing, and such it was in my case, for nigh on five weary months a blank existed as regards to my fate since the First Battle of Bullecourt.

In September 1917 the letter for which Davies had been waiting finally arrived. Despite his unenviable situation as a POW, 'the fact of our being alive sufficed for the home folk.'[15]

***

William Barry's recollections were not so pleasant. 'I had been ... [at a hospital, in Ingolstadt] two weeks when I received a letter from the Australian Red Cross Society,' he wrote, informing me that they were sending parcels of food and clothing. One can just imagine how delighted I was at the news, for I was practically starving, but it was my luck as usual, those parcels never came to hand ... Several of the chaps were now receiving parcels of food from the various Red Cross Committees in England. I was not among the lucky ones, until one morning a parcel of tobacco and cigarettes came for me and needless to say I was delighted at receiving it and wrote at once to the Australian Red Cross Society in London, thanking them for their kindness and not forgetting to give my new address. Barry, however, had still not received any food parcels. When he and other prisoners indulged themselves in a three-course dinner, he wanted to know where all the food came from ... and they told me the Red Cross Society in England sent them parcels of food and white bread every week, while the potatoes were sent to Mick Moylan [a British POW] from his wife. When I told them that I had never received a parcel of food, "Darkie" [Green, another British POW] laughed and called me an "orphan," but consoled me by telling me not to worry as they would look after me as long as they were able to.

British prisoners continued helping Barry—not only with food, but also blankets and warm clothing—until one afternoon while the names for Red Cross parcels was being read out, to my delight I heard my name ... I was as happy as a school boy. "Darkie" laughed and said I wasn't an "orphan" now ... Thanks to the kindness of my "Tommy" pals, my strength was coming back and after "Darkie" had drawn the parcel for me containing groceries weighing ten pounds and was taking them out of the cardboard box, I managed to climb up onto the top row of bunks and sit with them ... I knew now that I was sure of receiving my parcels of food from the Australian Red Cross Society, which amounted to six parcels, each weighing ten pounds, of groceries per month, besides two, two ounce tins of tobacco and one hundred Major Draphins cigarettes every fortnight. Besides the groceries I received from Switzerland thirteen pounds (six loaves) of white bread a fortnight, donated by the Australian Red Cross. I was now well off for food and smokes.

Not long afterwards, Barry received other parcels containing 'two flannel and two flannelette shirts, two pairs of flannel underpants, three pairs of knitted woollen socks, ... two towels, one pair of braces, two handkerchiefs, ... a comb, complete shaving outfit with a safety razor ... a pipe ... a blue military overcoat and a pair of boots' as well as other useful items. He considered himself 'now well supplied with clothing ... [and] was now receiving my Red Cross parcels regularly.'[16]

If an Australian POW died in camp, his food or clothing parcel was not wasted. In most camps a committee was formed to distribute it among the others. 'The committee ... composed of six sergeants ... took charge or claimed all parcels of food and clothing sent to any man who had died,' Barry wrote. 'These parcels were known as dead men's parcels.' The committee was given a storeroom by the Germans in which to keep parcels until the food or clothes were needed. Barry added that he was advised 'to go to them [the committee] and after giving them all the information they wanted, I received for several weeks a small supply of tinned bully beef, fish and biscuits which I handed over to my pals.'[17]

***

The Red Cross, along with the Army Pay Office, also took responsibility for ensuring that Australian POWs received an adequate allowance. 'Arrangements had been made ... for a POW to draw 4p per day of his pay,' Barry wrote, 'and so I applied for the amount and after waiting six weeks, I received the amount of 15 marks, worth in English money ten shillings.'[18] POWs were also paid a meagre amount by the Germans—usually only for use in camp—provided they engage in some work. The Red Cross sent all POWs a special uniform to wear when working. 'It was a very dark navy blue with a brown stripe down the leg of the trousers,' Wheeler recalled, 'they'd send you a great parcel with two suits of clothes, and an overcoat and cap.'[19]

German officers and guards generally respected POWs' rights to their parcels. Only occasionally would they steal anything—usually a bar of soap, or a tin of bully beef. Wheeler even 'admired' the Germans for their honesty. They were 'starving themselves,' he said,

> and they let those tons of parcels come through untouched without thieving anything. By god, they were envious of what we were getting. They didn't try to trade, though. Well, they had nothing to trade ... They lived poorly—on bloody black bread and

> some sort of bloody sausage they had ... Even when I was in the hospital, it was still poor. They had no anaesthetics, and only paper bandages.[20]

After the Australians left camp—some to work on farms, others in factories and mines—the Germans not infrequently continued forwarding the parcels.

By February 1918, Australian POWs were, in most cases, better off for food than German civilians, thanks largely to Red Cross parcels. Harold Horner, for example, described a period in early 1918 when he and another nine prisoners were waiting to change trains in the 'large railway refreshment room' at Mecklenburg station. 'The room was well-filled with women and children and a number of [German] officers,' he wrote,

> Our boys love a joke at the enemy's expense whenever opportunity offers; so as some of those who had received [Red Cross] packets had a lot of conserves and white bread, we took the largest table in the centre of the room ... A tall Australian, who entered thoroughly into the joke, brought out tinned meat and salmon, jam and butter, biscuits and cheese, preserved fruit and milk and beautiful white bread, ... things that the Germans had not seen for

years, and many of them never in their lives. And yet prisoners-of-war could carve it up as if it were the cheapest thing in the world, thanks to that noble institution, the Red Cross Society! The lads gave one of the waitresses a packet of tea to make some for us, and of course have a cup themselves. It was something new for them.[21]

***

The Red Cross provided a number of essential services to Australian POWs. The most significant, the parcel system, worked extremely well and the parcels made an important contribution to the men's health and well-being. Food parcels may have fed the men; however, what is often overlooked is the substantial amount of medical equipment and medication provided by the Red Cross to enemy hospitals, which frequently saved the lives of sick and wounded Australians. Significant, also, was the service of supplying letters and cards to men, thereby providing them an important link to their families in Australia. The society also assisted them with extra money. Without the help of the Red Cross, a good number of Australians would never have survived the war. Donald Fraser was one who considered that 'if it had not been for these Red Cross parcels ... none of us would have survived to come home.'[22]

CHAPTER ELEVEN
Attempting to get Away
'The Hopelessness of it All'

CHAPTER ELEVEN

ATTEMPTING TO GET AWAY

'The Hopelessness of it All'

Provisions for escaping POWs had been included in the Hague Conventions which decreed: 'Escaped prisoners who are retaken before being able to rejoin their own army or before leaving the territory occupied by the army which captured them are liable to disciplinary punishment. Prisoners who, after succeeding in escaping, are again taken prisoners, are not liable to any punishment on account of the previous flight.' The Germans adhered strictly to the first part of the article—a fact quickly recognised by escaped Australian POWs.

Working close to the front in France was particularly harrowing for those captured Australians. Yet, there were few recorded instances of attempts to escape. In camps located in Germany, the POWs were usually allowed out to work, either on farms or in mines, some of which were located close to the border with neutral countries. In these places, the number of escape attempts by Australian POWs was relatively high. For those imprisoned in camps further away from neutral countries, the prospect of escape was rather more difficult, especially for those with no knowledge of the local dialect or of German customs. Some attempts were made, either through the digging of tunnels or by subterfuge while, in a few notable camps—mostly confined to officers—sophisticated escape plans were developed. The most successful plans required an extraordinary level of patience: the POWs collected and stored civilian clothes and established tool shops that fashioned crude saws, wire-cutters and files, while the planners awaited the perfect opportunity.

***

Captured British officers were masters of the ingenious escape plan. At Neuenkirchen they established an unlikely 'escape factory' in the top storey of a house, built originally to house a Catholic club. 'Escape kits' were manufactured virtually under the noses of German guards, despite the fact that fashioning many of the items in the 'kit' required prolonged hammering. POWs used inventive methods to mask the noise, one of the most remarkable a Wimshurst machine, a contrivance used for generating static electricity. When detectives from Berlin were called to

Strohen—a camp in Hanover reserved exclusively for officers—to investigate (unsuccessfully, as it turned out) who was responsible for planning the large number of escapes, their identity cards were stolen. One cheeky POW even left a message, '"You know my methods, Watson!" pinned to a [detective's] coat tail.'[1] Australian POWs were far less organised than the British, and relied instead on pluck and guile—attributes they possessed in abundance.

Being held captive played uncomfortably on the psyche of some Australians. From the moment they were taken prisoner, escape was uppermost in their minds. Astonishing, and sometimes bizarre plans of escape were hatched—forty-six of which ultimately succeeded. Many did not. Some POWs tried more than once. While never guaranteeing success, sound planning and preparation were essential. Certainly, Australian POWs in 1917-18 entertained far higher expectations of escaping from Germany than their counterparts in the next great conflict. Several factors favoured the men of the earlier conflict. Most of the German guards at that time were older men, incapable of serving at the front. The greater part of Western Europe was unoccupied by German forces—unlike World War II which saw a significant portion of the continent under German rule. For those

Australians held captive in camps in the north of Germany, escape to the neutral Scandinavian countries and Holland presented the best prospects. Australians interned in central and southern Germany looked towards Switzerland.

Private Fred Allen was captured at Fromelles in 1916. He was moved through a number of camps in Germany before making his successful bid for freedom from Munster, on 11 September 1918. On reaching Holland, he was confined to a quarantine camp in Vidam. 'You see it happened like this,' he wrote,

> three of us, a Canadian, an Englishman and myself broke away from our sentries having about two minutes start. That occurred on Wednesday September 11th about 9.15p.m. And then the fun started. We were six days on the way to the border travelling by compass and by night, while by days we tried to snatch a bit of sleep, but as it rained five days, always during the day, the amount of "shut-eye" we obtained wasn't worth mentioning. After many adventures both funny and serious, we managed to get by the guards on the border. We covered about 125 kilometres in all and when we disclosed to a Dutch farmer, our identity he hastily told us we were in Holland and from then, that is early

Tuesday morning 17th, we have had hospitality showered upon us. We are undergoing a period of quarantine here after which we shall go to England where I hope to spend a few weeks with the Old Folks and then rejoin my battalion.[2]

However, Allen was never able to rejoin his battalion. He reached England on 5 October and, three weeks later, died from influenza and bronchial pneumonia most likely contracted while he was on the run.

**

Claude Benson hatched his first primitive escape plan soon after being released from Fort MacDonald. 'One day I was walking near a German aerodrome,' he wrote, 'and got within 12 yards of a Taube flying machine when the engines were going while waiting for the pilot. Seeing nobody near, I was trying to judge how the thing worked and my heart started to throb as I really thought for a moment I might be able to escape, but not knowing anything about the machine I had to give up the idea.'[3]

In June 1917, Lancelot Davies was also plotting his means of escape while working near Marquion. He wrote that 'escape was out of the question, except under cover of darkness ... [even though] little distance separated us from our own friendly trenches.' Davies soon recognised that his weak physical condition was a 'disadvantage' and changed his mind about escaping—more so 'when escapees were caught and ... sentenced to twenty-one days detention ... in the filthy conditions in a "clink" made up from what had been the pig-sties of the farmhouse.' However, this punishment did not deter everyone, as Davies explains:

> The most determined attempt made from Marquion was one in which four men were involved, all 16th Battalion chaps AIF. It became history, as for two of them successfully negotiated the blockade. The event was broadcasted by news from England ... The plans were engineered by one Corporal Percy Job, who feigned sickness at a time when certain repairs were being made to the wire round our lager. Getting possession of a pair of wire cutters, he made a breach, and carefully concealed the cuts during the day. At night when the posterns [guards] were simultaneously at their maximum beat extremities and not alert, the four "nobles" took departure. By dint of strong will and diplomacy, a little extra food had been gathered and they made fair progress to the point where the last good judgement was required—the

garrisoned trenches. Here, with pulsating hearts ... they divided, two going in one direction, and two in another. Shortly afterwards Job and his companion, in crossing the trenches, unfortunately slid into one which contained Germans, so this ended their flight. Later in the day they were brought into camp under guard, looking very dejected and weak, and covered in mud ... The other two men were in a precarious position for a time, and exhaustion struck them down, to be found later on by British patrols, who succoured and led them to our lines.[4]

***

Generally, the more ingenious and successful plans were put into practice after the men joined camps in Germany and were sent out to work. The arrival of Red Cross food parcels meant that the health of many improved and they were in a better state of mind and body. Being able to speak fluent German—which very few Australians could—was a definite asset. The camps were usually guarded by old men of the *Landsturm* (the German territorial reserve) who treated POWs with courtesy. However, strict regulations prohibited any contact between prisoners and their guards. Security precautions varied in different camps and at different places of work. Sometimes there were few sentries employed. If an escaped POW was challenged, there was a good chance that the German would not know the correct documentation the man was obliged to carry. Providing the documentation resembled something official and was written in German, the POW often would be allowed to continue.

Prisoners seeking escape from camps close to the borders of neutral countries stood the best chance of success. However, for those who sought to escape through Holland—and had the misfortune to be questioned by over-zealous Dutch frontier guards—there was the added risk of 'being sold back to the German sentries.'[5] Wesley Choate was captured at Fromelles in 1916. His plucky escape attempt from a camp near Dusseldorf soon after his capture was atypical. Choate quickly made friends with another Australian prisoner, Sapper Leslie Barry (1st Field Company Engineers). Both men had an eye for pretty young German women. This proved an unlikely boon to their escape bids as they became romantically involved with four women, two of whom were single while the other two were married with husbands absent at the front. While the women were 'entertaining' them 'in a comfortable drawing room', the POWs were more interested in acquiring maps and information about escape routes to Holland. 'Our visits to our friends were frequent,' Barry recalled,

two or three night a week, and our progress in the "romancing direction" was by no means backward. The ladies were particularly fond of our tea and English cigarettes from the Red Cross parcels. Occasionally a bottle of choice wine would be awaiting us and we always had tea with fresh goats milk served with our supper, a real treat as it was the only milk other than condensed I'd tasted in Germany. Saying "goodbye" to our friends at about half-past-four in the mornings, we would reluctantly make our way back in the dark to our barracks the way we came out and managed to get in about an hour's sleep before being called.

Once sufficient information had been collected, the next hurdle was locating suitable civilian clothing. In Barry's words: 'They had to be made out of our prison clothes and it was only during the few hours of night that we could do the work without fear of being disturbed.' After persuading civilians working at the camp to exchange headgear, collars and ties for biscuits and bread, the two were ready to put their plans into action. According to Barry, before 'leaving we were given supper and biscuits and fruit by the girls. This kindness touched us deeply, we knew the hard conditions and the little extra meat they obtained with their coupons, and high prices for luxuries such as tea, coffee, cocoa, butter which was smuggled in through Holland.'

Under cover of darkness six men—in two groups of three—attempted to make good their escape. According to Barry, they were all

> in pretty fair condition thanks to our Red Cross parcels. We had accumulated a good supply of biscuits, chocolate and dried fruit. We colonials broke out of camp successfully because during the past few months we'd become proficient at getting out to visit the girls. Our lady friends had given us the time and instructions on how to catch the train that left shortly after midnight from Dusseldorf. Choate, one Canadian and myself were in the last party to leave the barracks. The first three got away but we were a few minutes behind time and when we arrived the train had gone.
>
> We spent the night on the ground in a spare allotment and at three in the morning we made our way back to the station, not being too sanguine as to our

improved civilian clothes passing the censor in the daylight. However, Choate got the rail tickets all right and we got on a platform to find our train wouldn't start until 7am, which was very risky because by this time our escape from camp would have been reported. If the corporal in charge of the station had been sharp he would have stopped us.

We waited anxiously to hear the rumble of the wheels over the Rhine Bridge because then we would know we were on the right train and the biggest barrier had been passed; but ... the train switched off in a different direction. We got off and set out to walk the 20 kilometres which hadn't been included in the plans we'd set ourselves.

Aware that the German government had offered a reward of thirty marks for each captured POW, the men remained cautious. They were stopped by a German policeman, but were able to convince him that they were Belgian citizens heading off to work.

'We reached a swamp and dug in,' Barry added, 'as we'd learnt our lesson as regards walking in the daytime, and set off again at dusk, and astonished the villagers at one town [Kaidenkirchen] when they found us washing ourselves at the village pump.' After a hurried exit, they continued on, travelling to within sight of the border with Holland. But the alarm had sent German soldiers in hasty pursuit. Before the three men could reach the border, they 'heard the command, "Halt!" We were not across, we were still a little way on the wrong side. The Canadian with us was taken away and given some kind of third degree and let the cat out of the bag, so they learnt we were prisoners-of-war.' They were crammed into the town's tiny gaol cell, and Barry 'asked the sentry how far we were from the promised land and he said Holland was only ten minutes easy walk.' Sentenced to fourteen days' solitary confinement and a diet of bread and water, the trio was escorted to Munster camp.

Having served their time and been released, the men quickly began to plan another escape. According to Barry, an extraordinary level of 'graft went on at this camp.' They soon secured 'compasses, civilian clothes, maps, everything needed in the escaping line, even some civilian money.' Before they could 'hop over' the wire, however, the Germans returned them to Dusseldorf camp. Barry heard later that this was due to the large number of British prisoners trying to get into Holland. However, they were able to take the precious 'escaping gear' with them. Yet again, Barry and Choate contacted their female conspirators. Unable to visit the women, they nonetheless obtained a more detailed map and new train timetables. Confident that they were well prepared and knew the exact timing of the guards' shift changes, Barry decided that, in order to 'prepare for our next attempt I needed "sick time" so I poisoned my left hand by rubbing rust into a blister which through the swelling necessitated being lanced by the doctor. This piece of swindling got me a fortnight in the barracks.'

Others from the group had managed to secretly supply Barry with strong wire and extra food. On 12 December 1916—after two of the men were discovered with a map—Barry and Choate realised that they needed to bring forward their day of escape. With a limited supply of food 'and no cigarettes', they managed to climb onto a roof outside the camp's perimeter. 'Six of us made the attempt,' Barry recalled,

> each of us "old hands" taking a man in tow who had not attempted escape before. My pal on this attempt was an Englishman somewhat thick in the vicinity of the belt and he had trouble getting through the bars of the windows which were 10 inches apart. After several gymnastic contortions and a

good push from one of those who stayed behind he got through and joined me on the roof. Choate and Pitts got through the window, shook hands with me and by the time we hit the street they were out of sight. Within an hour-and-a-half we were on the train. We left it at the first station across the Rhine, walked into the frozen fields and lay down in the ditch among winter-stricken trees. We were covered by snow in a few hours and took turns at the one and only pipe in our possession. At about three o'clock an elderly civilian gathering firewood walked on top of us. We lay low on the off chance that the old man would not raise the alarm. An hour passed without interruption and we were beginning to think we were safe when two armed soldiers charged in on our position, taking us in front and rear and we were once again prisoners, after some twenty hours of liberty. Back to Munster to do two months in the cell in solitary confinement.

Barry was reunited with four of his mates who had also failed in their bid for freedom. Only Choate and Pitts eluded the guards and successfully crossed into Holland. On his release from solitary, Barry prepared yet another escape attempt. But his captors had reached the limits of their patience, and sent him to a more secure camp further inside Germany.[6]

***

By the time those Australians captured at Bullecourt arrived in Germany, most—although not all—of the camps had some escape mechanism in place. Some camps presented more opportunities for escape than others. The Hague Conventions allowed guards to fire on POWs attempting to escape. If they were recaptured before reaching a neutral country, the rules permitted some form of punishment (but not execution). However, any disciplinary action for a prior escape attempt was strictly prohibited. Punishment could also include 'hard labour'. The Germans—in common with the British—preferred a lengthier sentence of solitary confinement (without hard labour), believing this to be a more effective deterrent against future escapes. Given that the work POWs were routinely expected to perform was 'hard labour', additional work could hardly have comprised a realistic deterrent. If a POW made a number of escape attempts and was recaptured each time, he was inevitably sent to a *Strafelager* (punishment camp) such as Harburg, Strohen, Ingolstadt or Holzminden. At these camps, escape attempts were inevitable.

Strohen, for example, was crisscrossed by numerous tunnels dug by POWs and also claimed the record for the largest number of successful escapes.

Captain John Mott suffered five bullet wounds at Bullecourt and was partially paralysed by a bullet that touched the spine near his neck. Lying helpless on the ground, he was quickly captured. By September 1917 he had recovered sufficiently to attempt an escape. Armed with a compass and an antiquated map which he had acquired from fellow POWs, he waited for an opportunity when the sentries were distracted. Mott's escape experience was particularly daunting. He dodged guards, dogs and townspeople while hiding in drains and sewers and swimming rivers—all with one arm virtually useless. At times he back-tracked—sometimes in putrid water—to erase his scent and escape vicious dogs. Thoroughly exhausted after six days and nights on the run, he finally neared the border. 'I had been hoping it would rain in torrents and blow a hurricane,' Mott wrote,

> but it was a perfect calm, starry night and the slightest sound could be heard at a great distance. I seemed to be making a fearful noise as I walked slowly through grass and heather; so I took off my boots and crept along the last two miles

barefooted. I stopped every few yards and lay flat to examine the sky line for silent sentries. Time after time I imagined I saw a sentry creeping stealthily towards me, only to curse myself for a fool when, after wasting a precious quarter of an hour watching, I found it to be a harmless bush. After creeping and halting like this for three hours, I came upon a road which was not marked on my map; but I knew I must be quite close to the border. Crawling carefully across this road I noticed that the country on the other side had quite a different aspect; and I had just come to the conclusion that I was safe at last when I saw against the side of the road a sentry in a crouching position, moving towards me. I screwed up my courage for a last fight for freedom, and waited. He was certainly moving. I wondered why he was coming at me like that—why he did not challenge or fire. Then I saw that it was the road that was moving, not the sentry, and recognised the enemy this time as—nerves.

I stretched myself with a fine feeling and looked around. The country seemed different from what I had come through. The trees grew high, the houses were built in a different style, and if I had been followed there was now plenty of cover. But I felt in my heart that I was free.[7]

Mott was the first Australian officer to escape from Germany. When he reached AIF Headquarters in London, he was warmly welcomed by senior officers. Soon afterwards he was granted an audience with the King to whom he presented a bound copy of his escape experiences. Mott then persuaded senior officers to allow him to return to the fighting in France. He was promoted to major and returned to the 48th Battalion. By war's end he was the battalion CO.

Albert Marshall took part in his first and only escape while at Strohen, 'not far from the border.' The unsophisticated plan was hatched at the last minute. 'I was told that it was going to take place ... at night,' he recalled, 'and I said I'd go. There were only three of us ... I don't know where they got their pliers from to cut the wire.' The escapees cut a wire mesh covering that hid the opening to a drain. 'I went down in a drain from the kitchen, all muck stuff ... was in it,' he continued, 'we crawled along ... this big drain ... [which] went under the guard fence ... I had a real army compass ... from Gallipoli, that they didn't take from me ... to travel at night.' Marshall 'was caught when I got out,' and sentenced to seven days' solitary confinement.

After his release, he was sent to Holzminden *Strafelager*. 'I never heard of the other two again,' he said, 'I don't know what happened.'[8]

Holzminden had gained notoriety for the large number of escape bids, usually through tunnels dug by British POWs.[9] One successful escape, in the summer of 1918, involved several Australians—but not Marshall. 'I didn't see the tunnel,' he recalled, 'I knew all about it but I wasn't in it.'[10] Other Australians had helped dig the tunnel—planned to the minutest detail by a Canadian officer, Major Colquhoun. Another officer, Lieutenant Cecil Blain (Royal Flying Corps), recorded the dig, which had a carefully concealed tunnel entrance located beneath a staircase, and measured a mere forty centimetres in diameter:

> We dug with table knives where there was soil, and prodded about with a cold chisel and bits of rake through the stone. The soil and stone collected was drawn back in a basin on to each side of which a rope was attached so as it could be pulled backwards and forwards. This was one of the biggest tunnels that I had worked on. It was some sixty yards long, and as wide as the average fireplace ... The soil and rubble was disposed of by filling mattress covers stolen from our quarters ... By the

time digging was finished the chamber under the stairs was packed to the limit with these "sacks" of soil and rubble.

Running about eight to nine feet below the ground surface, the tunnel twisted somewhat tortuously ... The main illumination of the tunnel was candlelight, and a very creditable device was constructed for ventilating it ... We used wooden bed-boards stolen from our beds to revett the tunnel.

As the tunnel neared completion, the 'escape committee' met to decide who to select from the eighty-six prisoners who had submitted their names for the bid. The thirteen men who had been part of the tunnel working party were automatically chosen. Finally, as Blain noted,

> it was all settled ... and on one wet night—23/24 July 1918—the tunnel was opened, and figures with big bags streamed out as in one huge crocodile, heads and feet all touching, to crawl behind beans, peas, and through high standing corn, to break away each party for itself, and in its own special direction ... Twenty-nine got away that night, and one thing I regret is that I was not in the camp the next day to see Herr Hauptmann Niemeyer's face when

the roll was called—I expect it was a wonderful show.

Unfortunately, the tunnel collapsed before they could all emerge to freedom—some, indeed, were lucky not to be buried alive. Of the twenty-nine men who managed to escape, very few made the journey to Holland safely.[11]

While Australian officer Lieutenant Veness took no part in any escape attempts, he kept a detailed chronicle of the frequent bold break-outs from Holzminden. Not long after arriving, he described 'quite a number of daring attempts to escape. The usual manner is to watch the beat of the sentry at dusk and then to slip up and cut the wire. It is a pretty slick job. Tunnels are another method of escape, but it is slow, dangerous and weary work.' On 25 July 1917, he recorded 'several daring escapes last night.' Two days later, Veness noted that

> several officers have been recaptured. One Australian officer still out. One recaptured officer who demonstrated how he got out by climbing the wire was rewarded with a present of a bottle of beer from the Kommandant. Extra sentries were posted at this spot. Needless to add he did not escape that way, but everybody is satisfied.

The collapsed tunnel at Holzminden officers' camp, excavated by the Germans the morning after the escape on 23 July 1918

And, a few weeks later: 'Tunnel discovered in this Barrack. The occupants of the room were "clinked" including an officer who only arrived yesterday.'

In mid to late August there was a spate of break-outs. 'Another attempt to escape,' Veness recorded on 20 August,

> an Australian officer concealed himself in the bottom of a rubbish truck. He was wheeled out but the usual bunch of kiddies and soldiers at the rubbish dump prevented his escape. After any attempt to escape we are always "strafed" with two or three extra Roll Calls daily.

Three days later he wrote:

> Six more officers missing. Still greater excitement. Are kept on Roll Call for three hours. At last the six officers are discovered and the mystery is solved to the great jubilation of the Germans. The manner of escape in this case was to go in (with escape kits etc) for a cold bath with waterproofs on. Some two days previously an officer had cut an ingenious hole in the floor of the bath-room and on coming in, promptly got down underneath the floor while someone else replaced the boards. They stopped there until night then crawled out. The bathroom was situated outside the "lager" but the pathway to it was wired in.[12]

***

Having recovered from a bullet wound to his thigh, Jock Williamson was transported to Friedrichsfeld camp from which he attempted to escape on at least two separate occasions. On the first, he was recaptured soon after slipping away from a working party returning to camp, shortly before sunset. Wading 'along creeks to throw the prison dogs off the scent and utilis[ing] a map supplied to him by a French POW cook at Friedrichsfeld,' proved insufficient to elude his captors. The second attempt came in late winter. Within reach of the border, Williamson's 'footsteps in the snow' were noticed by Dutch locals seeking a reward for captured POWs. By now, Williamson, who 'had been living on raw swedes and turnips ... [was] starving.' He was 'apprehended by pitchfork wielding farmers whilst sleeping in a haystack.' Handcuffed by German guards, he was sent back to Friedrichsfeld and denied food for the duration of the train journey. Only the intervention of 'German women on the train,' forced a change of mind and resulted in his being given 'something to eat'. Arriving at the camp, Williamson was informed that, if he made further attempts to escape, he 'would be shot.'[13] The threat appears to have worked as, during the following nine months, he remained a compliant POW.

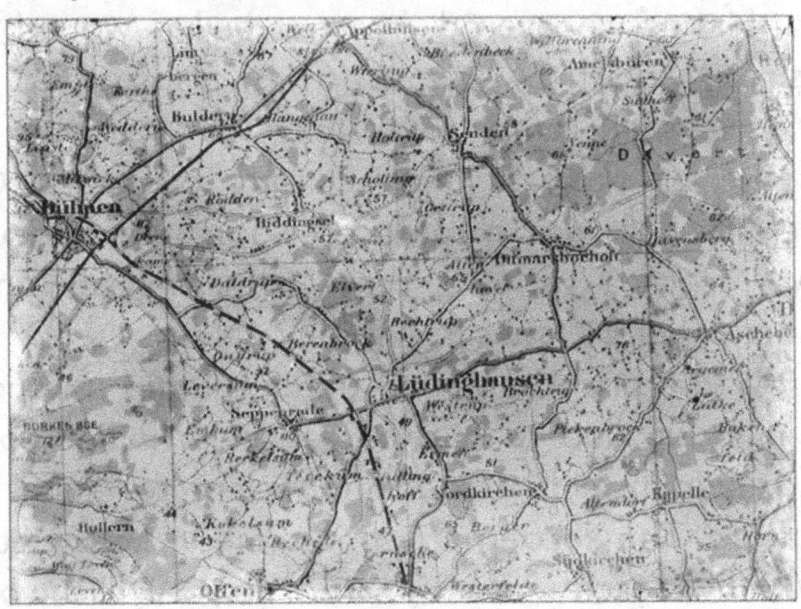

A section of a map of Germany, made by Private John Richard Cash, made to help escaping prisoners of war from Holzminden Camp, in July 1918. (AWM PO3473.008)

It was only after Harold Horner arrived in Germany and commenced work on a small farm that he put his thoughts of escape into action. 'Before going to Weitendorf I had been carefully laying plans for escape,' he wrote,

> and soon after making my home there I secured a map of the country from there to Denmark—about 200 miles. The chances of getting enough to eat on the way gave me some concern, and I had no way of ascertaining how the Kiel Canal was

guarded. Those were the only problems which worried me. I decided that the best time to go was the middle of July [1918] because it would be necessary to swim the twelve rivers and canals that lay between; and as I would have to live on grass and vegetables on the way, I must wait for that time. I took the keenest interest in anything I heard about others who had attempted to get away, so that I might avoid any mistakes they made. There was plenty of evidence to convince me that it was useless thinking of going by sea, even though Denmark and Sweden were comparatively close. The coast was too well patrolled, and all boats would be carefully guarded. A Russian fisherman got away safely as far as Stettin, and there started building a boat, but he was found. Three Frenchmen and an Englishman got as far as Warnemunde, on the coast; but a boy who was bathing saw them, and informed the guards. A Scotch sergeant I knew and his mates went to the same place; but they could not get away and had to give themselves up. Several others of whom I have heard made the attempt, but it was unsuccessful. Our own sentry at Weitendorf was in high glee one day because he had seen three Russian runaways in the woods.

However, I was satisfied with everything except the food question and the watch on the Kiel Canal. As midsummer approached, another problem presented itself. As I had to keep clear of roads—not only because someone might be passing at night, but because there were houses and villages along all roads—I must travel straight across country in the night, through crops of all kinds. I found that the commonest crop was a mixture of barley and peas—a terrible tangle to drag through ... However, I made up my mind to give it a trial. We often worked close to the river Recknitz, and whenever possible I would go in for a swim, just for practice. If the Germans were not near, I would fix my clothes in a bundle in the recognised style, tie them on the side of my head, and swim across with them.

To get away from the farm without arousing suspicion, I selected a path through the rye ... I took to the bush. I carried with me what little food I could, which, of course, would not last me very long. Before I had gone two miles I found myself on a rush-covered bog, in the dark ... I had to pick my way out very carefully ... I found that I made an awful noise walking through the ripe crops and I was afraid it would attract attention, because the farms were very small and close together, and as prisoners were employed everywhere, there were sentries at practically every farm, always looking out for runaways ... After travelling for about three hours, I saw something which reminded me of war. In the direction of Rostock, I could see searchlights.

Horner knew that, by midnight, the farm's foreman would notice his absence and alert authorities. But by daybreak he still had not been spotted. He observed that

> there was a good stretch of clear country ahead ... After crossing the cleared area, I turned into a green crop of oats, and lay down, dead tired, after about fifteen miles weary drag. I was not a minute too soon, as I heard a rattle of milk buckets, and girls talking ... I was very soon sound asleep ... When I woke soon after mid-day, I heard children talking and laughing at the farm house close by; and I lay quietly in the crop for the rest of the afternoon ... After a good rest ... I started off to take another night's gruelling; but I found that ... the previous night had taken a lot out of me

... I found that I could not keep it up all night, so I decided to sleep, and try daylight travelling; but ... there would be a big chance of being recognised ... I travelled several miles, but knew that everyone who saw me knew that I was a stranger ... They would tell the sentries at their farms, and I would not have a hope of getting away ... so when I saw a sentry I went up to him, to save him the trouble of running after me ... He roared at me, but I could see that he was pleased that he could record a "capture" to his credit.[14]

***

Jim Wheeler also realised that working on a German farm provided the best opportunity to abscond. Camps, on the other hand, were a far more difficult prospect. 'They had guardhouses on the corner, and an eight foot-high fence,' Wheeler recalled of Hestinmoor camp. 'It was not electrified, but they had a lot of barbed wire. On the corners, and at two or three places along the side, there'd be these guardhouses looking over the camp. There was generally a man or two in it with a machine-gun, and a man patrolling from guardhouse to guardhouse all night long. The first place I got away from was well back in Germany, I think it would be in the province of Hanover.' He added that it was somewhere about the centre of Germany. I didn't have very good maps, you know ... I got to the Ems. It would be late January [1918] by the time I got there, and there's a bridge across. That's what I was after ... about half-a-mile up there appeared to be shallower water, and a sand-spit ran nearly halfway out into the river. I thought this damn bally river must be shallow. I might be able to walk across it ... So I went into the river. But it dropped into deep water almost immediately. I was up to my neck, and by God it was cold! There were sheets of ice like big platters floating down with the current. I'll never make this I thought. So I turned back and made camp.

It was one of the best camps ever I had too—and in Germany. It was up against the abutment of the bridge. It had all been cemented, of course. The bridge was fifteen or twenty feet over me. Someone had been up there before, and made a camp up against the embankment ... I was as wet as a shag—and cold ... I always carried a complete change with me—boots and all. I took everything off and got into dry clothes. There was a lot of bally driftwood there ...

and I lit a fire ... I was only a few miles from Holland.

The second night I waited until 2 or 3 o'clock ... [and] I went up onto the embankment of the bridge, and laid there for nearly an hour. I thought that at 3 or 4 o'clock in the morning there would be no traffic. Well, I crossed the bridge at a trot, and got across alright ... I'm travelling in the dark, on the soft side of the road, to get off the metal ... so my boots don't sound; and I ran straight into two bally "gendarmes" on pushbikes with no lights on! Goddamn it! If they'd had lights, I'd have been sweet and gone. They told me that they were on watch—not for me—but for their own young men escaping into Holland to dodge the war ... I had a poor understanding of German, and what they said didn't mean much to me. One of them got a great cartridge and waved it in front of me. I knew what that meant—if I tried to run, I'd be shot.[15]

***

Claude Benson, fed up by 'the hopelessness of it all' and his terrible treatment at Gustrow camp, made a number of unsuccessful attempts to escape. However it was not until the war was almost over that he made his final—and successful—bid for freedom. Benson and a Belgian sergeant were accompanying wounded POWs on a two-day train journey from Gustrow to the hospital at Aachen, not far from the border with Holland. Having already secured a compass for travelling at night, they decided to make their attempt once they had delivered their wounded charges to the hospital. 'We arranged that I should go into the town of Aachen and engage rooms at one of the hotels,' Benson wrote,

> a guard accompanied me. The sergeant who would also be in the charge of a guard was to join me later on. I succeeded in getting a room and waiting till 2am on the 30th [September] for the sergeant, but he did not turn up. At 7am a runner came to the hotel with a note for the guard ordering him to take me back to the hospital. When we got back I was paraded before the chief doctor who asked me if I was English, I told him I was. He told me I would not be allowed to live in the town, but must remain in the hospital. I saw three English officers who were waiting to see the exchange commissioners and I ... told them that I intended to make my escape and asked ... if they could give me any information about the Dutch border. They

could not tell me anything and wished me luck.

The sergeant and I decided that we must make the attempt from the hospital. We approached the corporal of the guard and offered him a packet of biscuits if he would allow us out for two hours to visit some Belgian friends. He agreed at first, but on seeing two German "Sanitators" [hospital guards] near him he was afraid to let us go. We had to give up the attempt for that night and return to our quarters on the top floor of the hospital. Next night, 1 October 1918, we succeeded after some difficulty in getting clear of the hospital. We made for a hill a short distance away where we consulted a map and got compass bearings and then decided to go right into Aachen and take the border tram to Vaals. We had no difficulty in boarding the tram and travelled on it about halfway to Vaals and then got out and walked the line for the rest of the distance, passing three sentries without being challenged, but the fourth man was standing in the middle of the track and we decided to go round him. We took to the fields without being seen. It started to rain just then. We passed through several barbed wire fences, through a cabbage patch, and passed another sentry box.

About 3am we noticed a flare go up in the direction of Aachen. I took this to be a warning to the guards on the frontier that we had escaped. About half-an-hour later we crossed the border and were safe.

Their ordeal over, the men were 'interviewed by the Consul-General' at Rotterdam and given 'a change of clothes and accommodation.' On 4 October they arrived in London.[16]

A.J. Whittington was another who made several attempts to escape. On the first occasion, he joined three other POWs (two Frenchmen and a Belgian) absconding from Ohlig camp. According to Whittington, the Belgian suddenly 'got scared and pulled out of it. We had it all worked out nicely.' Unfortunately, the Belgian was the only one who knew the route,

> but anyway we still decided to go. We thought we could follow the Belgian's instructions ourselves. We got away at night easily enough, and we got on the tram alright. One of the Frenchmen said to the conductor, 'Drei, bitte'—three for Dusseldorf. But he didn't know that we had to change trams to get into Dusseldorf. So when we got to the end of the change, we all just sat there, long enough to arouse

suspicion, unfortunately. The two Frenchmen were on one side of the tram, and I was sitting over on the other side. I wasn't supposed to walk with them. I trailed behind. Eventually the two Frenchmen got out and walked down the street. I followed along at a distance behind them; but we had hardly gone anywhere when I saw the Frenchmen look round over their shoulders. At that moment, someone behind me yelled out, "Halt!" A German soldier was chasing us! But I didn't look round. I was pretending I wasn't with the Frenchmen, and the German raced right passed me, chasing these Frenchmen. As soon as he went past—it was wartime, you see, and the streets were not well-lit—I ducked down a side-street, still not looking round. If I had looked round I might have aroused suspicion. I walked down this side-street going north. There was snow all over the ground, and as I walked out of the town, I came to a field, white with snow. I still refused to look round. All of a sudden I heard a fellow calling out in German, "Come here! Come here!" But I still didn't look around. I thought, I'm sure to be caught! I expected to be grabbed at any moment. Almost at the same time, I saw a dog running through the snow—and there was a fellow coming behind on a bike. He was calling his dog! He rushed past me. I kept going, and of course, he and the dog kept going too. But if I had looked behind, and panicked, it would have alarmed him.

Whittington's luck eventually ran out long before he approached the border.[17]

Donald Fraser engineered his escape while working at the *Kieselgour* works near Melbeck, alongside ten other Australians, an Englishman and some Russians. 'It was very much against our grain to work at this sort of job,' he commented,

> so some of us planned an escape bid. We did not have much trouble with loosening one of the bars on the window [in the hut]. Unfortunately, we did not possess a map or compass, so we had to be content to be guided by the stars. This was ok providing the nights remained clear. We knew we would have to go west to reach the Dutch frontier. The hours of darkness are very short in Germany during the summer months. However one clear bright night, 4 of us slipped out through the window ... We lay low in the shadow of the building for a few minutes, and then took off across an open paddock,

barefooted, carrying our boots so that we would make less noise. We reached a clump of timber without being seen. We then split up into twos, as four was too big a party ... We walked all night and laid low in scrub at day break, not far off the main road. We also found that we were very close to a large village ... We saw a column of German soldiers marching along the road during the day ... When night eventually came, we set off again. We tried eating raw potatoes and cabbage, which were abundant in the country-side.

It became very cloudy that night ... so we didn't know if we were going in the right direction or not. At about mid-day the sun came out. We decided to risk the daylight, and started to walk again, keeping off the roads as much as possible. We eventually came out into an open field, where we saw some British prisoners working ... No guards were in sight, so we decided to approach and speak to them. No sooner had we done this, when a German sprang up from behind a bundle of hay, rifle in hand, and yelling ... "What are you doing here? Running away are you?"[18]

Fraser and his mates were locked in a barn overnight and taken to Soltau camp the following day.

Thomas Taylor's escape was better organised. Taylor had made his plan in October 1918, after settling into a camp in East Prussia close to the border with Poland. 'We were distributed among the various farmers around,' he wrote,

> I found myself on a farm with two Russian prisoners, the three of us working for a woman whose husband and two sons were at the war. Because I was so young she used to make sure I wrote to my mother to tell her I was safe, and she fed me in her kitchen. She didn't worry at all about the Russians ... For some considerable time several of us had been thinking seriously of making a bid for freedom. One Russian prisoner had secured a compass, whilst another had a map, and together we studied and discussed that map. From information we got ... from Russian prisoners who had escaped and had been recaptured, we decided that our best course was to make for Minsk, which was situated on the border of Poland and Russia. Once over that border we thought we would be safe. Our German guards had ... told us that the Russians had deserted their Allies,

and that the country was in a state of chaos, but we did not believe anything ... We figured it out to be well over 400 miles to Minsk and so had to stint ourselves as regards food, and save enough to see the journey out if possible. The Red Cross parcels helped me there, as the bully beef and biscuits they contained were just suitable. Every week I put something by and in a few months I had quite a store. We chose a Sunday night for the venture ... [3 November 1918], and there were four of us set out—three Russians and myself. A nastier night we could not have chosen, but undeterred by the weather ... we started off at about seven o'clock in the evening, making for the Polish border, which was about eight miles east ... marked by a high barbed-wire fence, and which we knew to be patrolled by Prussian cavalry.

Managing to avoid German patrols, they slipped into Poland. 'One of the Russians spoke the Polish language,' Taylor added,

and he cautiously went out to make investigation, with a view to discovering our whereabouts, and when he returned ... we found we had only covered a little over eight miles ... We travelled on without mishap, always at night where cover was scanty, but chancing it in daylight when we came upon forests of any extent.

When we reached the vicinity of Sawalki we had no cover whatever, and travelled for a considerable distance over ploughed fields ... That went on very well for a good few miles, but the heavy going and continuous plodding had made us all very tired, and we rested for a while on the roadside ... How long we slept I don't know, but we were rudely awakened by the sound of approaching horses, which were so near ... We ... did the most natural thing ... nothing. And it was well we did ... They were a party of Uhlans patrolling the road ... One of them remarked as they were opposite to where we were lying that "those black objects looked like men," ... and to our unbounded relief, they ... passed on ... As we got well into Polish territory we became a little bolder, and often spoke to the Polish peasants. They were afraid to give us shelter, though ... we received a fair amount of food from them ... We plodded along through many small villages, always on the alert for treachery and German patrols, and ... we were forced to go from place to place cadging for food.

For almost two weeks they moved through Poland dodging enemy patrols, until their progress was finally halted by the Niemen River. 'For another three nights we walked up and down ... searching as best we could in the darkness for anything that would be likely to carry us across in safety. On the fourth night we were despairing of ever getting across, when we suddenly came across an old abandoned boat, which had evidently been regarded by the Germans as too crazy a vessel to float. After a close inspection of it, we decided to give it a trial, and quickly launched it ... and at length we "passed" it as seaworthy. We were all ready ... but [had] nothing with which to propel it, and nothing about us that we could use as oars. The only thing that seemed likely ... were a few stunted trees ... We decided to try to fashion something out of a few branches ... and to "give it a fly."

Now, we had become rather engrossed in our task ... We prepared for eventualities by stripping off our clothing ... Much as we feared it, there was nothing else for it but to commence our hazardous voyage ... However, we accomplished it without accident ... We travelled many miles after that without any hindrance ... We approached a house on the outskirts [of a town, Vilna], and asked ... if there were many German patrols about. We were ... told that the bridge was very often guarded ... It happened to be unguarded at the time, so we crossed and entered the town ... I was all nerves. Two of us walked well ahead of our two comrades, and we kept to the middle of the street, so that we would not come too closely in contact with any Germans ... My companion kept up a conversation in Polish to allay suspicion, but I did not know anything of the language except "da, da" ... our luck stuck to us, and we got through safely, much to our relief.

After hiking through 'a beautiful stretch of forest', the four escapees were within reach of the Russian frontier and their destination, Minsk. However,

> we had been told by recaptured prisoners before leaving Germany to be beware of electrified wires near Minsk and we were keeping a sharp look out for them. That we would also have to be extra careful when approaching the Russian frontier we knew, and one night ... a command from the darkness ahead suddenly halted us. We did not notice for the moment the person

spoke Russian, but immediately jumped to the conclusion he was a Hun. As he advanced towards us and again spoke the realisation that he was a Russian soldier, and what it meant to us suddenly dawned on us. We had evaded the German outposts, and had crossed the twenty miles of no man's land, or neutral territory, without knowing it ... Germany, with all its horrors, and Poland, with its haunting and hidden dangers, were behind us. Russia and freedom (as I thought) were before us.

Taylor was the only Australian POW to seek refuge in Russia. Instead of returning to Australia, however, he was sent to Moscow, becoming embroiled in the Bolshevik 'reign of terror [where] soldiers were a law unto themselves with rifle, revolver and sword; the hue and cry of a chase and promiscuous shootings in the streets went on day and night.'[19]

***

For those POWs caught attempting to escape, the punishment varied. Usually, they were sentenced to from seven to twenty-one days' solitary confinement. 'After they tried you, you were punished for attempting to escape,' Whittington recalled, and they'd give you solitary confinement—a fortnight. The first time they put me in a local gaol in Ohligs. I was put in their solitary confinement cell—on starvation rations. One of the sentries from the working party used to have to come up with my starvation allowance—two slices of black bread and water. That's all you got for two days. On the third day you got one slice of bread and a bowl of soup ... one of the soldiers—he must have been off-duty from the front—he could be bought. My cobbers, the Canadians, could bribe this fellow to hand me a packet of biscuits or something. They'd give him a bit of food, if he'd deliver a bit to me in the clink. I would have been tortured with starvation, only they sent me food. The other two times [caught attempting to escape] were at Friedrichsfeld. You had two days dark cell, and one day with lights on. But you still had this starvation allowance. In the dark cell, I could tip the bunk over and get up near a crack in the window and read. I must have had a book from one of the other boys.[20]

Some recaptured POWs found the Germans unexpectedly sympathetic. Others were not so lucky. In an attempt to discourage further escapes, a number of camp commandants treated the men inhumanely. At Clausthal in Harz, for example, the commandant was one of the notorious Niemeyer twins (some POWs believed he modelled himself on the Kaiser, as he had a waxed moustache with upturned ends). Niemeyer yelled insults at the prisoner before posting 'two sentries outside each window and four on the door.' He personally 'proceeded to tear the clothes off' a prisoner before the man was 'escorted down ... to a new cell, in which ... [the POW] was locked with a sentry ... [with] fixed bayonet.'[21] For his part in a botched escape attempt at Christmas in 1917, Lieutenant Atkinson received 14 days in cells ... and a few other times for making holes in the walls for the same reason. English food was stopped several times for supposed breaches of German laws.'[22]

While he was more disobliging to his captors, Jim Wheeler's story was somewhat similar to Whittington's. Following his recapture, he turned his wrath on his guards. 'It was a temporary gaol, with a wooden floor,' Wheeler remembered,

> and I put my clodhoppers on one night, about midnight, and I started tramping across the floor stamping my feet and singing, "In the Heimat, in the Heimat, where the Kaiser wears a kilt!" That was

the blasted German army marching song. That was the English version of it, of course—where the Kaiser wears a kilt! You didn't know daylight from dark. But I would reckon, oh, it must be dark now. Everyone will be asleep. So I would start singing. That would bring the guards raving to the bloody door. "What's this? What's this? Quiet! Quiet!" When they came in I said, "I'm an opera singer."

But there was nothing they could do. You're only on bread and water, and they couldn't cut you down much on that. Two or three of them came looking into my cell, with the idea, I think, of giving me a hiding. But I used to roll my blanket up very tight and stand on it when they came to the door. They thought better of it when they saw me—an unshaven old bastard about seven foot high! They were generally old men anyway, finished with further service. They'd open the door and see a man about seven foot high, and they'd chicken out. You'd stop for about an hour, and then start again. It was damned hard, though, on that lean ration.[23]

Keith Tamblyn recalled an incident in which two recaptured American airmen were confined to a tiny punishment cell because they refused to 'give a word—parole, that means that they wouldn't attempt to escape.'[24] In any case, German officers knew that any American, British or dominion soldier taken prisoner was forbidden to give 'parole'.

At Soltau, Donald Fraser was 'paraded before the Commandant and sentenced to 14 days strong arrest in a tiny cell about 7 foot 6 inches by 4 foot.'[25] Having surrendered himself, Harold Horner was taken to a nearby farmhouse where he 'was well treated'. He was then returned to Weitendorf camp, resuming work at the farm from which he had recently escaped. 'On Sunday, August 4th,' he wrote,

> I had to appear at a court-martial, held at a neighbouring farm, where I was asked to explain my conduct. There was an interpreter present. I believe a decision was not arrived at until nearly a fortnight later, and as our men had been crumbling up the German army during the fortnight ... there was no doubt that I got off easier than I might have done. My farmer also stated that his harvesting was not yet finished, and asked that I might be permitted to stay for a while. It was decided to give me seven Sundays on "starvation diet." A man is taken to the cell on Saturday night, and kept without any food or water or bedding until

Monday morning. My farmer knew that I would not do much work on Mondays, so he persuaded the sentry to take me quietly on Sunday morning and bring me home on Sunday night. On August 18th I was marched off to a cell at a neighbouring farm to put in the day on "starvation diet" ... On the following Sunday a Belgian ... brought me some biscuits; so that I fared well. But the sentry was getting tired of having to stay near the place because I was under arrest; so on the third Sunday he came to tell me quietly ... that if I stayed in our room all day, and did not let anybody see me, especially the under-officer, then I would not be taken to the cell again.

That Germany was close to defeat was not lost on enemy officers and guards. Horner had little doubt that he 'got off very lightly, thanks to the boys who were smashing up the German army.'[26]

The consequences of a successful escape could be dire for the remaining POWs who lost certain 'privileges' as the Germans sought to deter further attempts. Lance Corporal Arnold Mason, who suffered extensive wounds at Fromelles, was interned at Dulmen camp. He confided to his diary that, on 10 October 1917, '2 Russians and a Frenchman cut the wire and escaped last night so we are being punished by having to stand on parade from 8a.m. to 11a.m. and 4p.m. to 8p.m., not being allowed to smoke and all tobacco taken out of our parcels and canteen closed until the "cutters" are given up, but I think they will get tired of it before us.'[27]

***

Would-be escapees recognised the chances of being wounded, or even killed in the attempt. Donald Fraser related the story he heard from a 'mate, "Yank" Buchanan', in Soltau. Buchanan told him

> that he was sent to work in a coal mine, which was sheer hell. He and a Russian escaped, and were very close to the Dutch border, when they were seen by a patrol. The Russian said, "Run comrade," which they did. The patrol opened fire, and the Russian was shot dead, and "Yank" collected a bullet through his upper arm, which broke the bone. He fell down and stayed put. The Germans came up, gave him a kick and told him to "Up stand swine."
> They bandaged his arm and took him to the doctor, who sent him back to Munster hospital by train. He said that he got a lot more abuse and kicks en route,

but his arm had set and healed quite well, and only the scar remained.

During the last few months of the war, as the guards' morale plummeted, escape became a far easier prospect. Captain Honeysett certainly encouraged escape although, somewhat paradoxically, he believed that 'from a military point of view it was deplorable to observe the general slackness of discipline that undermined the morale of the German soldiers.'[28]

Earlier, on 2 November 1917, Honeysett had made his own valiant bid for freedom. Lieutenant Veness, who was a witness to the attempt, wrote that he was

> standing by the main gate tonight when I noticed Honeysett (an Australian officer) being escorted through. A minute after I heard four shots fired. Presently Honeysett was brought in wounded. It seems the Kommandant sent for another officer. Honeysett saw the guard and impersonated the officer in question, detecting a chance of escape by hopping it when outside the gate. I believe it is a flesh wound only.[29]

***

Not all POWs tried to escape. Although they were reluctant to admit it, some may have been afraid of the consequences if caught. Others were more pragmatic, believing they were better off in captivity and had a greater chance of survival away from the carnage of the Western Front. Captain J. Ackerley wrote that he 'never even thought of doing so. Perhaps the fact that I was taken rather late in the War—in the middle of 1917—had something to do with that, for by that time I may well have been too stunned and frightened to do anything more than "stay put."'[30] Some POWs considered that they were never presented with 'the right opportunity'. Len Pooley made no attempt to escape. 'I've often thought of that since,' he commented, 'now, why didn't I try? What would I have done? I suppose we could have made a go of it when we were working out in the open [behind the lines] on the railway.'[31] Robert Henry believed that 'it was hardly feasible' to abscond. 'It was not a very easy matter to escape,' he remarked,

> We were too far away from any borders ... you couldn't get food to get away ... And food was so scarce. It was not much good getting out of the camp [Schneidemuhl] unless you know where you are going to get the next meal from. If you are a prisoner ... in a camp you are not getting much food. You're in a pretty weak state. You're not fit to be travelling long distances on an empty stomach ... You'd be

picked up. We was in shelter. Several people made attempts, I think, but I don't know if I heard of anybody getting through. What was the use? You might be shot ... I heard of one fellow, he could speak five or six languages, he didn't manage it. He got caught.

Henry also made no secret of the fact that he 'wanted to come home alive.'[32]

Keith Tamblyn was another who never attempted to escape. During his time as a prisoner at several camps he witnessed some daring attempts, usually from working parties near the border with Holland. 'There were quite a number of chaps used to escape,' he wrote, 'and they had a scheme the Germans never seemed to wake up to.'[33] Tamblyn later commented that he

> didn't have much chance [of escaping]. I mean, you were too well guarded ... but in Friedrichsfeld the boys that were [in a] working [party], they would go out on a job and two or three of them would stick together ... one bloke would go off right on his own, and these two would expose themselves. And of course, then Uhlans [guards] who rode around on horseback would grab them ... and take them off; the other bloke would get across the border

into Holland ... It was only a matter of a hop, step and a jump, you might say, and they'd be across into Holland. Well the other two, they'd draw lots as to who was to go next, they'd work it so that either they'd go just the two together, or they'd pull another bloke in ... And they worked it that way. It was always one escaped ... Jerry never woke up to it. There was always that one bloke escaped. Most of them were British troops—Tommies. They were shrewd enough.[34]

***

Escape for a POW depended on three circumstances. First—and most significantly—was the desire to escape. Some were content with their lot, particularly as they were away from the hellish conditions on the front. By contrast, others not only wanted to escape detention but, more importantly, were eager to regain their reputation as soldiers and return to fight for what they regarded as 'a noble cause'. Military honour and patriotism were overriding motivators for these POWs. The second factor was location. POWs interned close to the border of a neutral country stood a reasonable chance of succeeding in any escape attempt. The more successful escapes were from work *kommandos*, where it was simpler to abscond and remain concealed. The third factor involved the method of escape. Most attempts by Australians were enterprising in their planning, although the men were almost always recaptured. The more daring POWs would immediately plan another escape. If caught, they would try yet again. Ultimately, however, the vast majority of Australian POWs—including those captured at Bullecourt—remained in German camps until after the signing of the Armistice.

CHAPTER TWELVE
In Germany
'My Blood Run Cold'

CHAPTER TWELVE

IN GERMANY

'My Blood Run Cold'

As the war entered its fourth year, the number of POWs (particularly Russian and British) in Germany increased significantly. The primary reason for this escalation in numbers was the bloody nature of combat, which drove more troops—particularly conscripts—to simply refuse to fight. When presented with the opportunity, they chose to surrender. While this practice was rare among Australians, it was common in British units.

By the end of World War I there were 167 known *Gefangenerlagers* (primary, 'parent' or registration POW camps) scattered throughout the German states. Over ninety housed ORs while approximately seventy-five were reserved for officers. Hospitals were attached to some of the larger camps. William Barry described a typical *Gefangenerlager* (at Langensalza) as 'composed of a number of wooden huts the inside was fitted with rows of bunks and resembled a cattle boat. Although they were lighted by day, at night one small electric light in the centre of the barrack was all we were allowed.'[1] Over 100 more *Arbeitskommandos* (satellite or 'working' camps) were attached to, and administered by the 'parent 'camp. Many POWs were never sent to those 'parent' camps but, instead, were sent immediately to a 'working' camp.

Some 'parent' camps contained *strafe* (punishment) camps where prisoners who committed minor infringements or more serious breaches (suchas attempting to escape) were confined. Punishment varied according to the offence and the whim of the camp commandant. Captain J.E. Mott, for example, considered the treatment 'very bad indeed'—so bad, in fact, that he believed many of his fellow officers 'were "queer and quiet," although not actually insane.'[2]

Due to decentralisation (Germany was divided into twenty-one military districts, each analogous to an army corps sector), administration of the camps was cumbersome and by no means uniform throughout the states. Bavaria, for example, retained control over its own army. Thus, Bavarian corps commanders—rather than the German Central Ministry for War—were responsible for looking after camps within that district. The Hague Conventions stipulated that officers, NCOs and ORs were to be housed in separate camps.

While there were around seventy-five camps for officers and over ninety for ORs, this separation was not always possible.[3]

A group photograph of German officers responsible for guarding prisoners of war.

Conditions and quality of life varied according to the location, size, quality of the administration and number of POWs in the camps. By mid-1916 there were 1,646,233 POWs, comprising 1,200,000 Russians, 355,000 French and 40,000 British. The remainder were Serbs and men from other combatant countries. By early June 1918, the number of British POWs had risen dramatically in the wake of the German spring offensive. Almost 90,000 British soldiers (including Australians) were taken into captivity during this period of Allied reversal. Many of those POWs shared one thought—of life beyond the camp's perimeter.

Characteristically, larger camps such as Friedrichsfeld (near Wesel, approximately 100 kilometres north of Cologne, in the Rhineland) housed between 30,000 and 40,000 POWs 'attached to the camp; all with the exception of 7,500, are in [adjoining] working camps.' An American, Daniel J. McCarthy (at the time—1916—a neutral observer), provided a comprehensive description of the Friedrichsfeld camp which he considered

> one of the best camps in Germany on account of the attitude of the commandant and by him and through him of his staff, noncommissioned officers and guard. While the commandant insisted on the most rigid discipline throughout the camp, his intense interest in the welfare and everything that pertained to the prisoners was reflected by everyone in the camp. The camp was organised with the prisoners own non-commissioned officers assigned to full duty and control of their own men ... This trust and confidence placed in the prisoners' non-commissioned officers coupled with this strict military discipline, the practical kindly attitude of the commandant and his staff, make the atmosphere of this camp one of

cooperation and, if not contentment, at least a minimum of discontent.

The camp was an old camp with antiquated barracks, low and forbidding looking, and with relatively little ventilation. Changes were, however, made in these barracks which made them comfortable and cheerful. The very long barracks were divided into two by partitions, reducing them to moderate size, a wall was run along one side of the barrack and partitions erected to give moderate-sized rooms. On these partitions lockers were built to hold the clothes and food packages. Instead of the usual bunk system [one on top of another] low cots made of wood, large enough to hold a small mattress and the two blankets, made a comfortable bed which could be easily taken out in the air for cleansing or piled up against the wall during the day to give a maximum amount of floor space.

The walls of these barracks were whitewashed, as were likewise the long corridors left at one side. In this corridor facilities for washing, basins, etc., were placed ... The camp was one of the earliest camps constructed. It is divided into three separate camps, designated as Camps No.1,

2, and 3, within the same enclosure. These camps are arranged as battalions in the general form of an irregular triangle. Each camp has ten large double barracks; at either end of which is a water pump, with a large permanent laundry trough, used for hand laundry and washing purposes. The water supply is drawn from isolated, protected wells sunk at either end of each barrack.

The hospital is situated in a separate compound about one-half kilometre from the camp. The general administration, the store houses, the post office, and the guard[s] are all housed in a separate compound at the entrance to the camp. The quadrangle has an unusually large amount of space, some of which is devoted to exercise, etc. The camp is tastefully decorated with flower beds in front of each barrack [looked after by POWs]. An open air concert hall has just been completed for band concerts. In addition to this, there is a theatre, a cinematograph barrack, a church barrack, a photographic studio, a printing office, an art room, a physical-culture room, a school for language study, a science room and a large barrack devoted to the re-education of injured prisoners ... The kitchens are placed at one end of the long barracks and the latrines at the opposite end of the camp.[4]

A Currency Note for exclusive use of POWs at Gefangenenlager.

POWs were usually transported by train to Wesel station before being marched the five or so kilometres to Friedrichsfeld camp. The typical routine began with reveille at 6.00a.m. when the men were served a bowl of coffee. Roll calls took place before the prisoners went out to work. At around midday they were given a bowl of watery soup. Another roll call preceded the afternoon's work. Shortly before dusk they were provided their main meal—an issue of black bread and more of the same watery soup or sauerkraut, mangolds, cabbage and the occasional potato. For the more fortunate, there was a little meat—usually taken from the carcass of a dead horse. The day ended with 'lights out' at around 9.00p.m. The men slept on straw mattresses covered by two thin blankets—even in the depth of winter—unless they were ill, when they were provided with an extra blanket. Without Red Cross parcels, many POWs would never have survived.

A group of Australian POWs trying to look happy for the camera.

Prisoners at Friedrichsfeld usually worked in a nearby chemical factory. While work was supposed to finish at 6.00p.m., it was not unusual for the men to work 24-hour shifts before being rested for a short period. Then it was back to work. They were paid in a currency which could be used only inside the camp. The paybook of Private Alexander Joseph, for example, showed that his income was a paltry sixteen pfennigs, plus a 'stipend of 14.50 Pfg' each month.[5] POWs also received 'extra pay' through the Red Cross. Nonetheless, it was not uncommon for their pay to be 'strafed' two to five pfennigs for any minor offence they might commit.

***

By December 1917 most Australian POWs were sharing the privation and indignation of being held captive alongside prisoners from other Allied nations. The Germans mixed the Allied soldiers deliberately in an attempt to challenge whatever goodwill and harmony that may have existed between the allied nations. Prisoners were interned without allowance for cultural differences. For instance, Australians found themselves in the same huts as men from such diverse backgrounds as Russia. Not unexpectedly, this engendered a sense of disorientation given the unfamiliarity of such critical aspects as language and personal habits. Officers usually found themselves separated from the men they led, and were sent to camps such as Crefeld in the Rhineland. Unlike ORs, they were not expected to work. Yet, whatever their circumstances, most Australians were generally much better off in German camps than behind the lines in France and some were pleased to be away from the carnage of the Western Front. The vast majority, however, remained unhappy with their plight.

'Australian Boys' photographed at Friedrichsfeld Camp, 3 March 1918.

John 'Bertie' Giles was taken prisoner at Fromelles in 1916. As was the practice, the briefest of information was relayed immediately to Giles' next of kin: 'To Mr J.C. Giles, Regret to inform you that Private J A Giles, 53rd (late 1st) Battalion is officially reported missing 19th July. Should any further particulars be received, you will be informed immediately.' Some families had to wait over six months for information—all that time living in hope that their beloved son had not been killed. Giles' family, however, was more fortunate, having to endure only a few months before they were informed that 'Private J.A. Giles, previously reported missing now officially reported prisoner of war Germany.' One of Giles' friends, holding back from writing, was now able to inform the Giles family of a letter he had received, written around the time their son went into battle:

> Dear Mr Giles, How glad I was to get your note today and hear dear "Bertie's" safe even if a prisoner. Any news is better than the terrible uncertainty of these last weeks. I never knew so much dread and horror could be held in this one word "missing" and I know what you have gone through. We had a letter from him last week but as it was dated 26 July, I would not let anyone tell you as I knew it would surely mean only added pain.[6]

At that time Giles was at a sanitation and distribution centre close to Munster, in Westphalia.

Corporal Harry Still was also captured at Fromelles and was initially sent to Dulmen. Located north of Essen, in a desolate part of Westphalia (about twenty-five kilometres south-west of Munster), the camp was surrounded by a three-metre-high barbed-wire fence. Constant patrols by well-armed guards meant that cutting through the wire was close to impossible. The commandant attempted to break the POWs' spirit and determination to escape through a 'systematic course of near starvation.' Apart from the appalling diet, Harry Still regarded the camp as 'comfortable'—most Australian POWs 'stood up well under the strain, relying on the mateship and good humour of their friends for strength.' After four weeks of having 'no work to do', Still was moved to Minden (also in Westphalia) which was

> vastly different in most respects ... The camp was closed, the barracks forming the walls of each compound or group of which there were six laid out in square formations. Surrounding the barracks were barbed wire entanglements with patrols of guards. There were ample exercise yards but apart from the tree tops showing above the twelve foot barracks we could see none of the outside world ... The food was as scarce and unpalatable as at Dulmen and Lille, hence the continuation of hunger and dysentery.[7]

Wesley Choate was another Australian taken at Fromelles, and like Harry Still, also sent to

Dulmen. The reality of his predicament as a POW soon sank in, especially when his first meal 'was brought to us by two of the boys who undertook orderly duty and so avoid working for Fritz.' Choate was not so charitable in his assessment. As living conditions deteriorated and he was forced to labour for the Germans, Choate wrote: 'It was an awful thing to realise one was powerless to "carry on," and in addition there came the heart breaking order that you must work for the enemy against whom one would naturally rather fight, and if any of the boys could get a chance of working for brothers in distress, of course, they would jump at the chance, and so relieve their conscience by the fact that they at least were not doing anything to benefit the Hun.'[8] Soon after, Choate began to plan his escape.

Some prisoners were assigned to work on large farms known as lagers. This photograph shows sentries detailed to guard the POWs and, as the annotation points out, the lager's machine gun emplacement.

Robert Henry was wounded at Fromelles and quickly captured by the Germans. One month later, when his wounds had healed sufficiently, Henry was transported to Dulmen. Most of Henry's work was in the wash house or 'doing some little job, or other.' He, too, complained that 'we didn't get much to eat there because the conversation amongst all the blokes was about what their sisters and mothers could cook up.' He remained at Dulmen for several months and was permitted to write a postcard to his family explaining his circumstances. 'We ... were allowed to write a postcard every week,' Henry remembered,

> and two letters a month ... You know, that postcard got there [Australia]—I was missing for five-and-a-half months. That postcard actually got home before the War Office let my father know that I was a prisoner-of-war ... I wrote to the High Commissioner for Australia in England [Andrew Fisher] telling him we didn't have much to eat, and all that. The Germans jibed this over that [sic] because they reckoned we were getting what the civilians got, and that ought to have been sufficient.

View of Clausthal POW Camp showing wire fences and huts. A lake and woods are in the distance. (AWM AO1579c_

Henry was also interrogated during his internment. 'Of course they [the enemy] were told a whole lot of lies,' he said,

> which, of course, they dropped too. Some fellows told them they were in different units from what they were. The Germans, they knew what units were over there before we jumped over the top. Got their spies out—marvellous. They jibed us ... for being volunteers. "Man you must be verucht," which means mad, to volunteer. "Why did you go in the army for, and all the way to fight?" They [the Germans] were all conscripts [sic].[9]

***

Private Raymond Embrey, who had been captured in the fighting around Mouquet Farm, recalled that 'about ten days later', after some questionable treatment, he

> arrived at Gottingen POW camp in the same condition as when they pulled me out of the shell-hole. I had slept in my dirty and wet clothes and never had a wash, I wasn't worth two bob. After some time a Doctor came to the camp and had a look at my arm and said "It will have to come off." He pulled out a pair of scissors and cut it off. They had very little medical supplies and no anaesthetics ... After some time I was able to walk. The camp was made up of sick and wounded soldiers ... It took the Germans six months to report that I was a POW and that I was seriously wounded. Somehow I lived on ... [meagre] German rations ... No one could survive on ... [that] diet. I occasionally got a little help from prisoners who were getting their parcels, but they couldn't spare much as the parcels were their only means of survival.

Probably of more concern—particularly for those POWs on their way to camps in Germany—was Embrey's observation that 'anyone who was fit was sent to work in coal mines, road repairs and farms, the latter being the lucky ones as there was food there.'

A large group of POWs, of different nationalities, at a camp in Germany. Note German guard with rifle in bottom left hand corner.

Others, like Embrey, were unable to work because of their wounds or due to poor health. 'Life in the camps was boring as we had nothing to do,' he added, 'I got hold of a Frenchman who could speak a little English and we taught each other our languages. We had soldiers of all nations who were at war with Germany, but mostly Russians and Italians. They were captured in big groups but didn't last long in the camp as many of them were not wounded and they were sent out to work.'[10]

POWs of different nationalities in Dulmen Camp's Library.

Frank Hallihan was also captured at Mouquet Farm and was sent to Dulmen towards the end of September 1916. According to Hallihan, the camp was divided into three separate sites, with new arrivals housed in Number 3 Camp. 'The censors went through everything we had in our possession, and our money was exchanged,' Hallihan wrote. 'After being inoculated three times we were sent to the Doctor and marked fit for a working party. Although hardly fit to stand on our legs, we were shifted to Number 1 [Camp], and it was there that we found out to our sorrow that some of the English NCOs were only too pleased to get rid of us as early as possible into working parties, and were helping the Germans to do so.' Despite his condition, Hallihan was sent to work in the Wulfrath stone quarries, 'recognised by all prisoners-of-war and sentries also, as absolutely the worst "Kommando" in Germany.'[11]

Hamilton Warrell was wounded while fighting at Mouquet Farm. He was treated by German doctors and transported to Nurnberg camp in Bavaria despite the fact that his wounds had not healed completely. 'We were indeed a forlorn sight, with sunken cheeks, clad in rags, and as pale as death from cold and weakness,' he wrote:

> Our first few days in camp were cruel, and our prospects were ... poor. Our daily bread ration ... was a two pound loaf of black rye bread for twelve men in the morning, and at mid-day we received one ladle of sauerkraut soup ... It was enough to break the spirit of the most optimistic. For men just released from hospital, ill and physically weak, with tender wounds, these hardships seemed too much, yet there was always a hope that the war might end, so we were in a measure living in hope, but in misery from the conditions endured.[12]

William Barry was another Australian captured prior to the First Battle of Bullecourt. Held at Langensalza in Thuringia, Barry's description of the camp and account of camp life portrayed an experience typical of the Australian POW. His first sight of his camp was a double row of barbed wire, behind which were numerous huts. Towers containing machine-guns were located at strategic positions around the compound. 'As soon as we disentrained [sic] we were hurried off to the camp,' he wrote,

and the sentries were pretty quick about it. We were taken into a building and the roll was called and ... we were escorted into the Lager ... and there saw what prison life was like. The first glimpse I got made my blood run cold, for of all the ungodly places to put men in, I thought this was it ... We were taken along a brick path ... there were several inches of mud and slush covering it ... We all arrived at the ... hut where the Englishmen were and soon were taken to our quarters which, as only could be expected, were anything but pleasant. While I was sitting on a bit of wood, wondering what next was going to occur, a Tommy (English) sergeant put his face through the window and told us to go into the next barrack and get our tea.

The first that I noticed was the clean and tidy way the Tommies were dressed. Every man wore a blue serge uniform and cap with the usual military brass buttons and everything about them was spick and span and they were themselves the picture of cleanliness ... I could hardly believe my own eyes when I saw a plate of mashed potatoes and bully beef before me ... After the first course was finished there was white bread and butter and jam, not to forget strong tea with milk and sugar in it. I did enjoy that meal, in fact felt ashamed of myself at being such a glutton, but my new friends told me that they had suffered starvation and knew what it was to be hungry. When the meal was over we had a little talk together, these three chaps had been taken prisoners just after the Retreat from Mons and the first battle of the Aisne and had been in Deutschland ... for three years and were anxious to hear the latest news ... We had two [German] officers over us who were tyrants and were known as Ginger and the three stripes. One morning Ginger came into the barrack and caught some of the chaps having breakfast. He at once drew his sword and with one stroke cleared everything off the table.[13]

***

In June 1917, Albert Marshall was in an officers' camp at Strohen in Hanover. He recalled that 'as officers, we didn't have to work. That was the only thing we had. But camp life was no good. We just ate what they gave. I lived on sauerkraut and "mangelwurzels" ... It was awful damn stuff. There was very little to eat. I suppose they'd call what they gave us, a stew. Well, if I got a potato in it, I used to wash it, and then heat it up again on the stove ... And I swear that in their brown bread was sawdust.'[14] Marshall had every reason to complain. An investigative committee established by the British government in 1915 heard evidence from almost 4,000 officers who had been repatriated or who had escaped. The committee's scathing report on Strohen was indicative of conditions in the four camps examined, all of which were administered by General von Hanisch:

> The camp at Strohen Moor was some two acres in extent. It comprised three large, two medium and three smaller wooden huts or sheds, a hospital, dining and reading hut—all in a bad state of repair—within a double barbed wire square enclosure, the whole situated in the midst of four swamps. In the centre lay two stagnant pools. On the east side of the camp, close to the trench latrine, the foul

condition of which was a continuous infliction on the prisoners, were two pumps, one with fresh water of indifferent quality, and the other with water of a dark colour. The camp in wet weather was a morass; in hot weather a place of dust-storms and stench. Strohen, it is said, had been a camp where Russian and Romanian officers had been treated with exceptional severity. Its commandant, Major von Kichton, was a savage man, unrestrained either by feeling or reason. The attitude adopted by the guards throughout the period when von Kichton was commandant, and during the six weeks subsequent to his departure when Hauptmann Niemeyer, afterwards commandant at Holzminden, succeeded him, was uniformly threatening. [This Niemeyer was the twin brother of the commandant at Clausthal, and equally unpleasant].

The cells were always full, while a long list of officers sentenced awaited their turn for confinement. Punishment was given on the word of a guard without appeal, and with the most arbitrary indifference to justice, as when a teetotaller was sentenced for drunkenness, or an officer was shut up for an offence of which a comrade admitted himself to be the author. No reason was given for the denial of this slight solace for prisoners penned up in a camp too small for customary exercise.[15]

Despite a change of camp commandant, by December 1917 conditions in the camp remained largely unaltered.

Officers were separated from other ranks after capture. Unlike other ranks, officers were not expected to work and were usually housed in separate camps. This group of Australian officers was photographed at Crefeld in May 1917.

R.E. Sanders (14th Battalion), captured at Bullecourt, was 'a lieutenant ... attached to the 4th ALTMB [Australian Light Trench Mortar Battery].' Having been subjected to the usual formalities in France, he was taken to what previously had been a large hotel in the German city of Karlsruhe in Baden. Sanders noted that a few of the men who had some French money tried unsuccessfully through a German orderly to buy some extra food but were informed that no extra food could possibly be purchased as the town of Karlsruhe was rationed and food could only be obtained through a food coupon. This same orderly also told us that we were receiving the same food rations as an ordinary civilian.

After eight days in the hotel, the men were taken to a camp 'about half a mile from where [they] had been staying.'[16]

On 17 April, less than a week after his capture, Lieutenant Garnet Veness was also taken to Karlsruhe camp. Subsequent reports indicated that the location of the *Gefangenenlager* was deliberately determined by 'various [air-] raids upon the city ... It was installed ... near the royal residence and the railway station, in order that the danger to the French and English officers concerned might lead to a cessation of their compatriots' air attacks.'[17] Veness noted that, 'For the first time we are allowed to send a card stating that we are prisoners.' A few days later, however, reality began to hit and Veness wrote that the POWs 'have no money, consequently am very hungry as ration issued is insufficient.' A week later he described the tragic aftermath of a British air raid:

We now get war news from the German officials. Discover the "Continental Times" for the first time. An anti English rag! I find that several holes in this camp were caused by bombs from aeroplanes and that over 100 children were killed in one raid. This is used as a clearing camp for French, British and Belgian prisoners ... All arms of the Allied services are represented here. The only work or discipline that officers undergo is to attend two parades a day in order to answer their names. Time hangs very heavy and we look forward to parcels from the Red Cross as we are slowly starving.

The following day he noted: 'One cannot help commenting again on the unfortunate appearance of officers. One half have been wounded and their clothes are blood stained and minus sleeves and legs of breeches in some cases.' He also described regular searches for any tools that could lead to an escape attempt, particularly wire-cutters and compasses. On 29 April, Veness appeared more settled, writing that 'We drew cheque for ... about 295 marks today, that being the amount that individual officers are allowed to draw per month as prisoners-of-war, we are told.' Nonetheless, he was dismayed at the cost of cigarettes in the camp's canteen.[18]

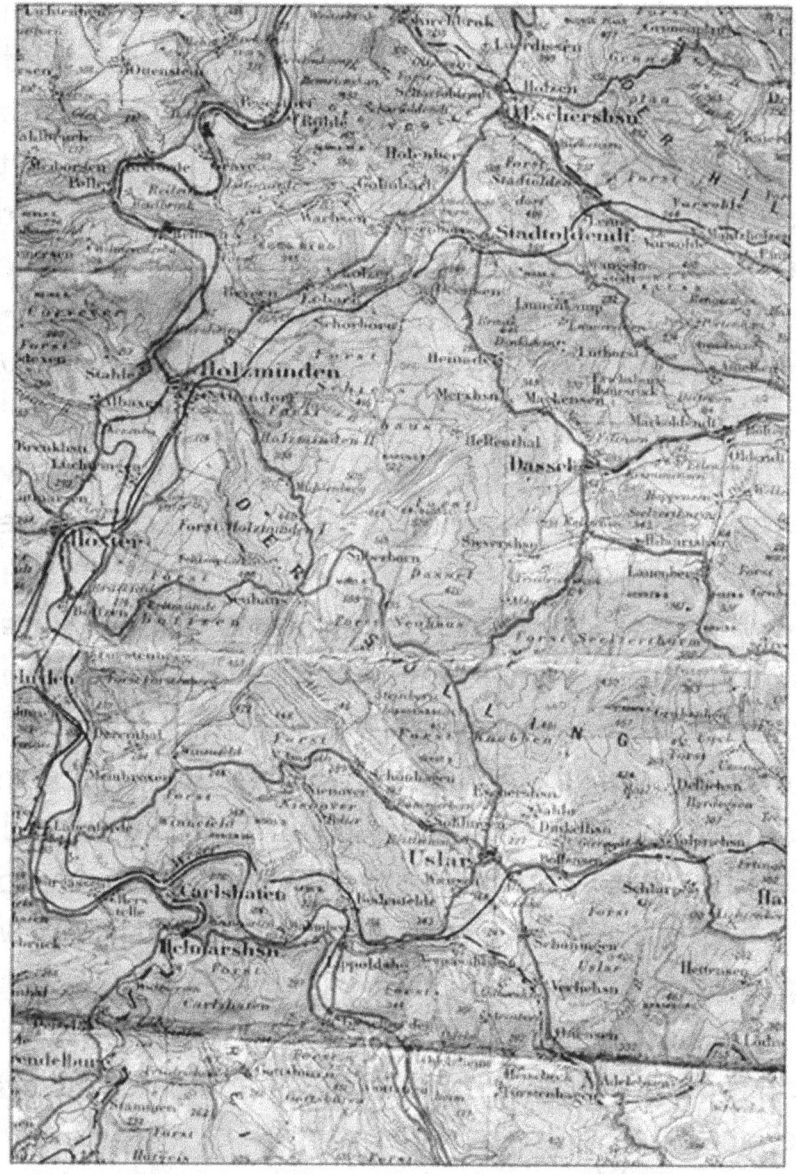

Map outlining location of Holzminden POW Camp.

After two months of captivity, the brutality of some German guards was beginning to tell on Veness. 'Several [POW] officers are daily sentenced to fourteen days in "jug,"' he noted, 'very often they do not know what for ... [One] received 6 days "jug" because he received a letter in which his sister referred to Germans as "Huns"... Officer (Downes) bayoneted yesterday for disobeying a trivial order.' Captain David Dunworth (15th Battalion) echoed Veness' sentiments, adding that 'the Germans took advantage of our ignorance of our rights by giving us no walks or parole during our stay at Karlsruhe.'[19] A week or so later, it was Veness' turn for a spell in solitary confinement. 'I am in "jug" for 3 days', he wrote. 'I do not know what for but I think it is for a missing poker which I afterwards discovered. I am not troubled. We receive no baths, parcels or exercise whilst in jail. Smoking is "verboten." Also no books are allowed in.'[20] A few days later he was transferred to Holzminden camp.

Captain Max Gore (50th Battalion) was captured at Noreuil on 2 April 1917. In a letter to his mother, he described the routine at Holzminden, highlighting how far removed from the action the men were:

> Well, mother dear, the time drags slowly on here, much the same day after day; it is extraordinary how restless one gets after a while—you feel that you must be doing something, yet cannot settle down to anything. But we find plenty to amuse

us; playing patience has its attractions even, and there are times that I would sooner do that than play Bridge. This is an ordinary day's routine: 8am; get up, have a shower (if the showers are running), if not have a wash. 9am; roll call, commonly known as "appel," finishes at 9.15 usually. After "appel," cook breakfast (we do all our own cooking); my part is usually making the water hot, then making tea. Finish breakfast at about 10am. 10-12; anything: mooching about, starting rumours or gleaning them, then discussing them, have a look at the previous day's war news. 12-1; nothing in particular—perhaps read. 1-2; play baseball or watch baseball. If wet, perhaps read some more, or if not do nothing in particular. 2-3; play Bridge or watch more baseball or mooch about or read or do nothing in particular. 3-3.30; afternoon tea instead of lunch. 3.30-5; read the war news, then look at the parcel list, then read some more or do nothing, or perhaps discuss the war news, telling each other where the last attack should have been made and why it was not successful. (We are all Generals here). 5.00pm; another "appel." After "appel" rush to the stoves to get our dinners or put them on or save them from burning. Many dinners are lost this way. Having cooked or received dinner, we proceed in the customary manner. 6.30-8.30; walk about, talk, or do anything or nothing. 8.30; inside—read or talk some more. 9.30 "appel" in rooms. 10pm; lights out. On the whole a very interesting day.[21]

Gore added a physical description of the camp as

> two well constructed cavalry barracks known as Kasernes A and B—each of three storeys with attics and basements—the weatherproof rooms were not for us. As escapees, we were ensconced once more in cells: underground ones in the basement with walls so thick that one could only communicate with a person in the adjoining cell by shouting at the full capacity of voice and lungs ... This time the "abort" [toilet] was not in the cell. We had to press a bell to notify the guard of our requirements, and he acted as companion and guide ... It was during one of these parambulations that my guard acquainted me with the news of the Russian capitulation.[22]

Albert Marshall remained at Strohen until November 1917 when he was transferred to Holzminden. 'I never left the camp the whole time,' he said, 'except when they ... had the football match.' Because of the large number of escapes (and attempted escapes), camp security was increased. A barbed-wire fence and wired 'pallisade' encircled the main part of the camp, while huge brick walls defined the outer perimeter.[23] 'I don't know what was outside,' Marshall remarked, 'you couldn't see over that wall.' He added that Red Cross parcels were received frequently, although the distinctive POW clothing was never issued. He saw no Russians at the camp, 'they seemed to be all Australian and English,' he said, 'there were a lot of airmen there.' Despite the number of escapes, Marshall recalled that 'there were no young guards ... Some of the prisoners ... talked to them [guards] or were friendly with them. But I never bothered.' Occasionally, and without prior warning, the guards would conduct searches. 'They'd look at everything,' he said, 'under your bed and ... anywhere at all they would look for something ... I don't think they found anything at all.' Food remained poor. Forced to queue outside the cookhouse, Marshall remembered that 'it was always the same'—a slice of black bread and watery soup. Like so many others, he relied on his Red Cross parcels for sustenance.[24]

***

A set of photographs outlining different forms of 'entertainment' put on by POWs for other prisoners. This activity proved to be very popular with the POWs, and was a good way for them to take their minds off of being held in captivity.

According to Robert Henry, inside Dulmen camp the main form of relaxation—and 'fun'—was a hand of cards. 'Cards was the only game you played,' he said, 'we used to play gambling games ... I used to play Twenty-One ... [although] I didn't join in any gambling there.'[25] The opportunity to participate in sports competitions—whether as a competitor or a spectator—was also generally well received. Private Frank Sturrock (16th Battalion) described a relaxing day of 'No work. Afternoon Australians played a game of [Australian] football. A novelty to the Pommies and French. Evening had a dance to music supplied by piano.'[26]

On stage portrait of members of 'Splash,' a play produced by POWs at Schneidemuhl Camp, Germany. (AWM PO3236.106)

Concerts were a popular form of relaxation and entertainment. Australian POWs usually held a regular show each week, providing fancy programs from ink they made themselves. Not everything went smoothly. 'When we got to Friedrichsfeld ... we used to have concerts there,' Keith Tamblyn recalled:

> They had a concert hall ... and different nations would put on their own—like French or Russian ... put them on. And ... the British they'd put one on too, occasionally ... They were all quite good ones too. Yes, they had quite good talent in amongst some of them ... I remember one night ... eight or nine of us got some tickets to go to an English concert. And we were in our own particular area ... It was quite a good variety show too ... Someone would sing or give a recitation ... When we came out, after the concert was over—and there was a German there. And we lined up at the gate to go back with the rest of the mob, and he wouldn't let us go through. He put us in the clink [cell] all night. We sat in there, and ... the guards never got any sleep because we sang and made all the noise we could, we did it all night ... The next morning we were brought before the officer in the camp ... He said, "I can't punish you because you haven't done anything wrong."[27]

The performance was usually well received. Max Gore at Holzminden wrote of the time 'our artists produced a revue so excellent that half a dozen ... [German officers] attended ... When the "Kommandant" walked onto the stage ... they involuntarily sprang to their feet ... However, upon realising it was only one of us, they resumed their seats and very nearly fell off them through laughing at the antics of their 'Herr Hauptmann," for they liked him almost less than we did.'[28] Frank Sturrock also noted the number of concerts 'given by old prisoners', usually with a 'very good turn out.'[29]

Cast and crew from a 'stage show' put on to entertain other POWs. Note the uniforms of different nationalities, including (top left) Russian and, next to him, British.

The bigger camps, such as Crefeld and Friedrichsfeld, boasted what passed for 'large and very good orchestras and choirs'. Charles

Hoffman, who visited camps on behalf of the YMCA and Red Cross, described how 'on going on the rounds' in Ruhleben camp, he

was surprised to find an historical club, a science club, a music club, two or three theatrical societies, and the like. One of the main thoroughfares between two of the barracks was known as Bond Street. Here were shops of the most varied type where one could purchase everything from cooking utensils and toilet articles to clothing and books. A shoe shop and a tailor shop were also to be found. Most unique was the camp police force made up of British prisoners of war who were responsible for the maintenance of order and the prevention of thieving in the camp...

The Grandstand University so named because of its origins underneath the grandstand where the first classes were held had grown to large proportions, with faculty and students and catalogues of courses ... many a prisoner prepared himself and passed the entrance examinations for Oxford University.[30]

Conditions in Ruhleben were among the best. Yet, by late 1917, those conditions had become the exception, rather than the rule. When Australian POWs from Bullecourt arrived in camps, they found little such infrastructure in place.

Football game at Springhirsch POW Camp, Schleswig-Holstein, Germany in 1918. (AWM PO3236.279)

Probably of more significance to Australian POWs was the camp newspaper or journal. The quality of the articles, all written by prisoners, varied somewhat. While a few were of reasonable literary and intellectual standard, others were poorly written. Some attempted humour; some were raunchy. At Doberitz (in Brandenburg), for example, a newspaper/journal, *The Link,* was published by POWs on at least four occasions. A larger and more cerebral journal, *TheBritish Times,* was produced by British POWs at Schneidemuhl, and often included articles and comments by Australians. The newspapers also allowed POWs the opportunity to glean news of the front, although usually from the enemy's perspective.

POWs at leisure. Top Scottish prisoners show their skill at Highland Dancing while, bottom, a group of British prisoners (without tops) ready to take part in a football (soccer) match either against another team of prisoners or, even, their guards.

***

Lance Corporal G.W. Bell suffered extensive wounds at Bullecourt and was treated by his German captors. Bell was one of the first Australian NCOs captured at Bullecourt to be transported to Germany. The severity of his wounds precluded him from work and Bell quickly became bored with the monotony of life behind the wire. He later recalled his 'desire to kill time' by 'devouring books [from the camp library] and studying French.' Bell even intimated that he would have preferred to have been part of a working group rather than having an inactive 'mind' and a tendency to be apathetic.[31]

Sergeant Guppy was also a member of the first large group of Australians captured at Bullecourt to arrive in Germany. On 11 May

> after a check roll call and issue of a day's ration of bread with a small piece of pork sausage per man we were marched to the station and entrained. We travelled northwards into Belgium and then eastwards passing through many large towns including Namur, past many great coal and iron mines, retorts and smelting works. Many of which are now idle. We saw very little evidence of the great destruction believed to have been caused by the Germans in their progress through this part of the country in the early days of the war.

We passed through the long tunnel which runs through the range on the frontier of Belgium and Germany. This tunnel was at the outbreak of war already mined to be blown up but owing to treachery in the Belgian forces this was not done thereby giving the Germans an easy passage into Belgium. Had this tunnel been destroyed it would have delayed the Germans many day[s] and perhaps have made a vast difference to the whole future of the war. Travelling on we pass through some most beautiful country along the Rhine Valley. At one station where we stopped for a few minutes to see a number of German children singing 'The Hymn of Hate.' On the evening of the 13th we receive our first meal of the journey consisting of a bowl of soup, issued to us at a station. The travelling is very slow and we stop sometimes for hours at stations. On the morning of 14th May we are, at another station, given a mug of coffee and a sandwich apiece. Here we see a train load of Belgian civilians travelling to work in German factories. We also speak to a Nun who originally came from Scotland and having been in Germany many years has almost forgotten her native tongue. At 11am we are detrained and marched 11 kilometres to Dulmin[sic] Lager, which we reach at 3pm.... Here we are issued with 2 blankets, gammil and spoons and given a meal of soup. The following morning we were searched and had our German money changed for notes and metal coins which are useless outside the Lager. Later we "Britishers" numbering about 200 are given a bath, have our clothes fumigated and our heads clipped very close. After ... we were given a change of blankets and placed in Number 3 Lager. Here we had to fill in identification and registration cards and also each given a card on which to write notification to the Australian Red Cross, London, of ... being a prisoner. This is a fairly large camp capable of holding many thousands of prisoners in its 3 Lagers and is one of the receiving camps for new prisoners coming from the front.

Guppy also discovered that, at the time, 'NCOs are not sent out to work on farms, commandoes[sic] in mines, but are kept in separate Lagers.'[32]

Ernie Chalk was another member of the first contingent of wounded Australian POWs from Bullecourt to arrive in Germany. Having been declared sufficiently recovered to leave the military hospital at Minden, he was transported to Dulmen. Chalk would spend most of his time in the one camp. 'On arrival here we found our new quarters to consist of an especially constructed prison camp,' he recalled, 'capable of holding from twelve to fourteen thousand men ... Dulmen camp was used primarily as a registration camp ... And a fairly large staff of Germans and also French and British prisoners were kept here for the purpose of carrying on this work.'[33]

Len Pooley arrived not long afterwards. Having been released from hospital in Lubeck, his good fortune continued when he was given relatively easy work as a storeman in the unloading sheds at Cologne station. He recalled being 'marched across to a camp called Lackenzohlen [sic] by a soldier from Alsace-Lorraine.' At the camp:

> There were a lot of Russians ... and they were dying from tuberculosis. They used to box them up, and we had to carry them on our shoulders, one man to each side, down to the burial yard. But I didn't last long there, because I was suffering from a nervous complaint called neurosthenia. There is no shaking ... it's just a nervous complaint in the head mostly. So I said to a German attendant, "I shouldn't be here

at all. I'm suffering from neurasthenia. And within a couple of days I was sent to another camp, and from there I went on to Cologne.

I was working in a goods shed called an "umladenhof" at the Cologne Railway Station, right alongside the Rhine. On the other side was the beautiful Cologne Cathedral ... right on the edge of the Rhine. The guards used to take us out to the cathedral now and again, half-a-dozen at a time ... They used to take us over in a punt ... The priest would put his hand on your shoulder. And a couple of times they took us out for a walk ... I was living in barracks there over the railway station. We were busy. There was a lot of stuff that used to come through there. We had a German boss—we used to call him "master"—and I was one of three men working for him. There was a gang of Frenchmen working for him too. He was just like an old father to us ... He couldn't go to the war, so they gave him this job ... I was quite happy there. There was a young girl in the office I was very fond of named Anna Brass, and I used to pass there as often as I could to see her.

I was wheeling one of these trucks along with ... potatoes and mangelwurzels, which they used to make their "marmeladen." They had no jam. The potatoes were used for ... making bread, making soup, and making stew. Everything was mangels and potatoes. But we didn't worry about their food by that time [on account of receiving three Red Cross food parcels a week]. We gave our food to the Russians. It was mostly sauerkraut, and sometimes there would be a bit of horse meat floating on the top. It was tough as the devil ... but they ate it, the poor old Russians.

Security at the camp was lax, and Pooley noted 'six guards ... and they worked in shifts, afternoon and night. Three at a time used to come on. They were men too old for the army.'[34]

Lancelot Davies arrived in Germany around the same time as Pooley. 'Morning of the 10th [September] found us well on our way through Rhineland,' Davies wrote, 'arriving at Koln [Cologne railway station] about 2p.m.... we became objects of great interest, as we became mixed with members of the German civilian population, who crowded round us in their eagerness to view some of the hated Englanders.

Reception was none too polite, either, and many were the scowls and insults thrown at us.' At Wesel station they 'left the train and marched to ... [Friedrichsfeld] lager

> arriving about 7pm, while it was still daylight. As soon as we came inside the main entrance enclosure, but outside the inner wire, we were greeted by many Britishers dressed in neat dark uniforms, who shouted words of cheer ... Here we were, a party of miserable dejected half-starved and tired creatures who had passed through five months purgatory, and to look upon those inside the lager who seemed happy and well-dressed, and who promised us a good feed and plenty of good English "brew" [tea] caused us to wonder whether we were really awake or dreaming.

By late 1917, the camp had two barbed-wire fences; the inner perimeter about five metres high, while the outer fence (approximately 1.8 metres high) was charged with electricity. Strategically placed towers contained machine-guns and lights powerful enough to illuminate the camp's outer edge. Guards constantly patrolled most parts of the enclosure.

A number of POWs attempting to keep warm – note elderly, unarmed German guard on the left, with stick.

Inside the main compound, Davies' 'broken spirits were revived' when he was taken to the hut that he would share with thirteen other men. 'The surroundings ... were so comfortable-looking,' he related, 'with their electrically lit cubicles ... each [man] had a wooden trough-like bunk with straw palliase (bedding) two blankets (certainly a thin material) a locker for each person, wooden table and forms, while in the passageway which ran through the wooden barrack stood a continental stove for warmth.'[35] William Groves was also impressed by his first sight of Friedrichsfeld. 'The large camp looked clean and well-organised,' he noted, 'and very inviting to us. We were marched, stiff and cold, into the search compound, just outside the main gates ... Within the next few hours we were inside the camp, in the middle of a group of fellow Australians, who plied us with questions as we ate.'[36]

Horatio Ganson recalled that most of the new arrivals were pleasantly surprised by what they saw inside Friedrichsfeld's 'perimeter'. He noted that there were 'three or four thousand [sic] men' already there (mostly Russian French and Italian, as well as around 250 British and Australians). He thought the 'camp was a beauty ... They had football grounds and tennis courts.' Ganson added that

> the guards marched us through the railway station and up to the camp, and I tell you, we were filthy. We were only kids ... about 21; but we had beards a foot long ... and long hair, all stringy and dirty; wooden clogs, green pants and blue pants; some had old frock coats ... Then they stripped us all off—everything—and burned it, and put us through the showers ... you had to stop, and this German would daub you all over with this big brush with something like whitewash; on your head, and on your arms, and under your beard. Then you'd hop under the shower. But when you tried to rinse yourself, all your hair came off! You looked like a new-born baby; a real shocker! But it was good for

us. It cleaned us up. Then when we went out the Red Cross uniform was waiting for us. The Red Cross rigged us out at Friedrichsfeld with new uniforms, clean singlets, new boots and socks. We thought we were made really.[37]

Some camps and most places of work had little in the way of security. 'We were allowed much greater freedom at Heilsburg Lager,' Thomas Taylor wrote:

> There were no barbed-wire enclosures, no guard continually watching us. Evidently the Jerries thought that our geographical position was a bar to any attempts to escape—and, indeed, it seemed hopeless to try. Consequently we came in touch with the people, and saw more of the Hun "at home." We found that they were almost entirely ignorant of the true state of affairs beyond Germany, and even in Germany ... They were deliberately misled, and we soon became aware of the efforts that were being made by persons of authority, and also their newspapers, to "bolster" them up. To us they seemed to be awfully gullible.[38]

***

William Howard was still recovering from treatment for haemorrhoids at a military hospital in France when he was told that he would be transferred to better facilities in Germany. The news came as a welcome relief to Howard who recorded the daily deaths of other seriously ill Australian POWs around him. On 28 September 1917 he 'left Tournai for Deutschland.' After an incident-free two-day journey, he arrived at Cassell railway station. Howard's relief soon turned to anguish. 'Carried on stretcher from station by Russians, French and our fellows,' he noted, 'and dumped in [what] they call a hospital in the prison camp on a bit of straw and one blanket only had a thin shirt on, put in a fearful cold night. Lots of Russians dumped in with us later.' The following day he discovered that he was 'isolated here for 23 days on account of coming from Tournai where they had fever.' After a 'warm bath,' and having been issued a 'shirt, and sleeping clothes' he felt more cheerful. The Russian POWs, however, proved troublesome. 'I got into a brawl with the Ruskies,' he wrote, 'I stouched a Ruskie tonight. They are fair devils to get on with, just like a lot of pigs.'[39]

Some Australian POWs relished the opportunity for a stint in the prison hospital, particularly for a minor injury. Others disliked being confined to a hospital ward where death and suffering were their constant companions.

Captain Joseph Honeysett wrote of the discomfort he experienced while in hospital recovering from a minor wound and how 'it was a treat to have the company of my fellow prisoners again,' when he returned to Strohen camp.[40]

Delegation of civilians from neutral countries talking with POWs as German officers look on.

***

A group of POWs, of different nationalities, sorting through Red Cross Parcels for distribution to other prisoners.

Following his successful escape, Claude Benson retained 'some fugitive memories.' In November 1917 he was sent to Denain and, the following month, transferred to Friedrichsfeld. During his two weeks there he was forced to exchange his boots for a pair of clogs (customary for all POWs in 'parent' camps) complete a proper 'registration form' and undergo a thorough medical examination. He was then transported to Gustrow. 'I was admitted to hospital here suffering from boils,' he wrote, and

> I was punished for not giving up my pay-book. I got seven days in cells on bread and water and a bowl of soup every fourth day. After I was discharged from hospital, I was placed in charge of the Exchange Barrack. My duties were to dress the

wounded and look after the sick. This barrack was a ... collecting station where prisoners-of-war of all nationalities picked for exchange, were lodged. These men came from the camps at Gustrow, Hamburg and Limburg. The men were only examined by a doctor when running a temperature. The beds here were very often used by Russians, and others who were suffering from infectious diseases. At times I found it difficult to procure disinfectants and antiseptics necessary for carrying out my work properly. In many cases men marked for exchange were admitted ... crawling with lice and vermin and had not had a wash for months ... While at Gustrow a detachment of German troops arrived there from the Eastern Front. They were given a few days rest and then ordered to go to the Western Front. They threw down their arms and refused to go and were put to work in factories. Some of our prisoners-of-war have told me that they have seen German soldiers placed in barbed wire enclosures for refusing to fight. They did not know what eventually became of these men. Another thing that I learnt ... [was] the Germans were billeting their prisoners-of-war in places that were being bombed by our aircraft and artillery.

The scarcity of food in Germany is very noticeable especially among the civilian population. People in Gustrow were stealing food from one another. I learnt from Germans working in the camp that the civilian prisons were overcrowded with people who had been guilty of stealing foodstuffs ... I received my Red Cross parcels at Gustrow ... They came to hand regularly and in good order.[41]

***

Harold Horner recounted his last few dreadful days in France before he, too, left for Germany. 'A British prisoner at the next camp was shot dead for picking a beetroot—starving, probably,' he recorded. 'On November 26th we packed for a three days' journey to Germany through Louvain and Liege and on to Verviers, in the hills, approaching dawn revealed storks on their nests on the house tops ... As we steamed into Verviers East, the engine "missed the tunnel" and crashed against the rocky hill side ... A number of men were killed, including two German sentries, while ... there were some remarkable escapes. One man was pinned in a corner, where he could not move a finger, but he was unhurt. This delayed the train considerably ... While the train wended its way slowly through those pine-covered hills, the fact that I was actually in Germany dawned upon me quite suddenly ... [which] with mixed feelings I contemplated; but ... it seemed that a great door closed behind me—no more friends, no more waving hands, no more kisses, no more of our own language nor the French that we had learnt to love ... Yet we could not expect any friendship in Germany. We came to Europe to fight against them, and we must take the consequences ... We crossed the Rhine at Dusseldorf, and ... arriving at Friedrichsfeld, we were reminded at once of war, by the sight of a dead man on a sack-truck on the platform. Some Russian prisoners arrived just before us, and this man had died on the train.

German guards marched the men to Friedrichsfeld camp. Horner recalled that, before they 'were allowed through the barbed wire we were all carefully searched; waiting outside the wire for hours in the snow. Many who came with us were dreadfully thin, while some inside the wire were just the reverse!'[42]

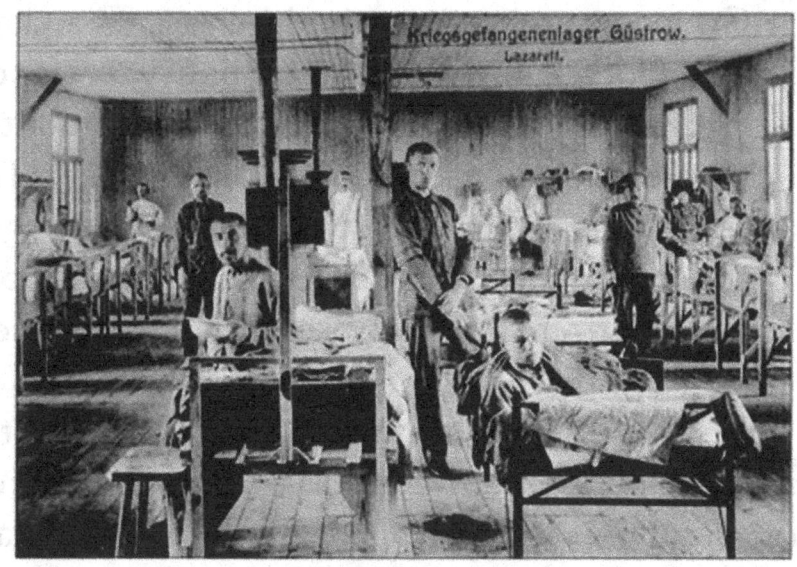

The Hospital at Gustrow POW Camp. Claude Benson worked in this hospital.

Donald Fraser was among the less fortunate, sent to Soltau camp in Hanover. 'On arrival ... we were placed in long army huts,' he wrote,

> similar in many respects to the huts in the camps in England. We were given two very thin single blankets and a sack of straw to lay on during the night. One of our own sergeants was placed in charge of each hut ... The Germans held the sergeants responsible for all in their huts. Much to everyone's relief ... we were issued with Red Cross food, which saved us from the expected fate of death, due to starvation. Soltau was a real league of nations. I think every nation which was at war with

Germany was represented here ... The camp was fenced in by a high barbed wire fence. A German machine gun team was mounted on a mound just outside the wire ... The fence was brilliantly lit-up during the night, so that the guards could see anyone attempting to make a break and shoot them down.[43]

Fraser was one of many who suffered the worst punishment for any minor infringement—fourteen days in solitary confinement. After his release—and nearly six weeks in camp—he was informed that he was to work in the *Kieselgour* near Melbeck.[44]

The Cookhouse at Gustrow POW Camp.

Having recovered from his wound, Horace Rumble was also sent to Soltau. 'I was healed. I went off to a big working camp,' he explained,

They must have had about 30,000 prisoners there. Portugese, French, Belgians. There was one Belgian who was a millionaire, and he'd got one of his huts there finished off ... Inside it was beautifully finished. I went there one night to a party, and we had weak beer and everything. We had a sing-song. Some of his fellow Belgians were in female evening clothes and everything. But this fellow had imported all this into the camp. His money bought things. He was living in comfort in the camp ... he'd bribed somebody, but he managed to get everything in because he had tons of money.

More significantly, Rumble recalled receiving a Red Cross parcel comprising 'two sets of grey flannel underclothing and boots and socks and ... a cap made in England to the design of the Germans for their prison uniform, and a proper double-breasted coat [as well as] a decent button-up tunic and pants.' At first, Rumble was required to work and his wounded hand again became infected. 'I wasn't required to work on account of my hand,' he added, 'but I was pretty knocked about then.'[45]

Claude Benson in blue POW uniform at Gustrow POW Camp, February 1918.

According to Rumble, Soltau camp had 'only the flat ... hard mud.' His thoughts often turned to one of the few pleasures available in the camp.

'Most weekends ... in that working camp there would be some very good professional football,' he said:

And we had no grass ... And the Red Cross sent through goal posts, and footballs. And the fellows; a lot of professional footballers from England were in the army, and they used to get up a good match every Sunday afternoon. We weren't required to work on Sunday unless there was an emergency. I used to go down and watch these football matches there. It was quite good. On rare occasions a guard came in armed to the teeth and wanted a working party. And you ought to have seen all the spectators scatter. They all rushed out of the huts and came around. And they'd tear around with fixed bayonets to get their working party. But that didn't happen that often because they were against working on Sunday ... And the Red Cross sent us through some books too. In the working camp our bunks were terrible ... They had these sheets of galvanised-iron up in two tiers ... And we only had a thin palliasse on the damn thing ... And then we only had one very thin blanket. We went through the winter with that. And the snow used to seep through the hut wall. They were not lined! We had no lining or heating. It was pretty tough. That's why we used to go for a walk around the camp to get our circulation up.[46]

POWs enjoying a mid-winter snow fall at Gustrow POW Camp.

***

Harold Horner was at Friedrichsfeld for only seventeen days. During that time there were a number of unpleasant deaths among the POWs. On the eighteenth day he was moved to Gustrow in Mecklenburg which, according to Horner, was 'a large military camp. A main road passed through it—on the one side was the prisoners' camp, and on the other side that of the German soldiers.'[47] Horner's story was not unlike that of other Australian POWs. While some stayed in the one camp for longer periods, most were moved on, usually with little notice.

Receiving Red Cross parcels at Gustrow POW Camp. Corporal Benson is marked with a cross.

Lancelot Davies, for instance, remained at Friedrichsfeld for a little over three months. During that time his health and physique improved—when he first arrived, in September, Davies weighed 'just seven stone five pounds' (forty-seven kilograms); by mid-December he was 'nine stone eleven pounds' (sixty-two kilograms). In his view, 'discipline was always strict'. Davies, apparently, was aware of the clause in the Geneva Convention specifying that officers and NCOs were exempt from manual work In some places this did not deter the Germans from ordering NCOs to 'volunteer' for *Kommandos*. Regardless of his 'steadfast assertion of our rights as NCOs', Davies was forced to join a working group.[48] Jim Wheeler was another NCO forced to 'volunteer' to work on a farm. In his words:

> I'd been getting Red Cross parcels some little while at Hestinmoor, and started to feel well. So I suggested to a mate, Bill Graham, that we do a bit of a tour. Bill ... was a piano tuner, if you please. It just shows who ends up in the army. I was a farmer. NCOs weren't compelled to work anywhere; you had your pick of what you'd volunteer for. Of a daytime, there were always jobs to be done around the *lager*, but if you were a toiler, or a private, you didn't stay long in the *lager*. You were sent out to labour, anywhere. They'd be going out to different jobs; the salt mines and the coal mines—they were tough.
>
> Well, with the farm jobs, there was practically no guard over you. The old farmer took you over. You probably ate the same tucker as the farmer ... So I said to Bill, "volunteer to get a job, but ask him to get it as near as you can to the Holland border. The people on the German farms were pretty good to you ... It was just the farmer and his wife. There were no young men. All the men had gone [to the front]. The girls were practically running the farms with prisoners-of-war, especially Russians.

There were millions of Russians. But I was mostly working with Englishmen—and Scotsmen.[49]

Prisoners of different nationalities 'working for the enemy.' Note unarmed German officer and elderly guard at right of photograph

***

On 17 December Davies and another 102 NCOs were moved to Parchim, in Mecklenburg, arriving at the camp after a 29-hour train journey. Accustomed to the comforts at Friedrichsfeld, his first reaction was one of disbelief. 'It was mid-winter, and snow lay everywhere,' Davies recorded,

the look of the camp and its surroundings did not inspire confidence either. It was large, quite three times the size of the one we had just left, and appeared deserted. Labouring along the snow we entered the enclosure and paraded for inspection and counting, the prolongation of which added to our discomfort. After this ... we were allotted to barracks, procured bedding and blankets ... None of us possessed very happy frames of mind that night ... [as] future prospects looked disappointing ... Six am next day reveille sounded ... [At] our first line-up we were able to become acquainted with the German staff ... The most significant personage met with was the *feldwebel* [sergeant-major] who impressed us ... with his huge stature, soldiery bearing, waxed moustache, fierce features and a rattling sword at the side. Right from the start he ... made us feel we had a tyrant to deal with ... I like many others wandered round the lager ... the "new home" was extensive in size, but not to be compared with Friedrichsfeld as regards administration and comfort ... bunks, lockers, tables, good lighting facilities and the many others were all conspicuous by their absence ... Time dragged on ... and was whiled away reading books and indulging in ... games such as draughts, ludo, etc ...

Coming in contact with [the] ... few ... British staff ... we gleaned some information regarding the lager and its surroundings, information that tended to create glum forebodings within us ... The whole lager was practically destitute of human beings for apart from a few Frenchmen and Belgians, about 100 Russians (the majority being workers), there were but sixteen other Britishers besides ourselves, and these comprised the staff, who looked after the interests of British prisoners attached to the lager *Kommandos*. Many thousands of prisoners were on the rolls of this lager, but all were distributed throughout the country, even as far as Schneidemuhl in Poland.

Although he had been 'fairly well-hardened by past experiences', Davies was anxious to learn where he might be sent to work, and how he might live in this bleak, distasteful part of Germany.[50]

***

ORs were usually sent to work on farms or in factories. Douglas Grant was one of approximately 500 Aboriginal soldiers who fought in World War I. He was captured at Bullecourt, although the precise details of his capture are unknown, despite the fact that he wrote 'a censored letter' to his 'adopted father'. Writing positively about his work, he noted, 'I am well and as comfortable as the circumstances will permit. I am working every day, which helps to pass the time away. I often weary of home and hope to be back soon ... I had my photograph taken the other day, and I am sending you a copy by which you will see I am looking well ... You really cannot understand what happiness the receipt of letters affords me.'[51]

Prisoners were assigned to kieselgour works in Germany where diatomaceous earth was extracted from the bottom of swamps, dried and powdered for use in the production of dynamite.

The most unfortunate POWs were forced to labour in *Kieselgour* (mines), where diatomaceous earth was extracted from the bottom of swamps, dried and powdered for use in the manufacture of dynamite. Donald Fraser's misfortunes continued. After the forbidding conditions at Soltau—where prisoners were subjugated to the point of self-destruction—anything was preferable. Fraser was taken to the *Kieselgour* near Melbeck. 'There were eleven Australians and one Englishman in the group,' he wrote, By this time we started to receive Australian Red Cross food parcels—on the average, I per man each week, also some clothing. We had to open the parcels in front of the guard, who examined and took possession of all tin meats etc ... The empty tins were washed, flattened out, bagged and sent to a factory to be used in the German war effort. This ... was a very sore point with us.

We were housed in a large Barrack at the *Kieselgour* works, similar ... to the old Australian shearers' huts—double decker bunks. Each man was given a large hessian bag which he filled with straw to be used as a mattress, also two old single blankets. For pillows we used any spare clothing.

All twelve of us "Englanders," as the Germans called us, were allotted one room, which had one window, which had iron bars across the outer side, to deter any escape ideas.

There were also 4 Russian prisoners, who were housed in a similar, but smaller room next door. An old Polish civilian and his one-eyed wife were also held in a small room at the back of the Mill ... There were also a few old German civilians and some women working mainly at the Mill.

The *Kieselgour* is a shaley sort of light clay substance dug from a swamp. The water was pumped out into a channel and drained away. A steam engine worked around the clock to keep the water down so that we could load the trucks, which ran on a light railway, pulled by a horse ... which emptied their load on a flat, similar to a large clay pan, which was near the mill. Here the *Kieselgour* was spread and dried by the Russians and civilians ... After the material was dried, it was raked up and stacked in large heaps and set on fire ... Each heap took a few days, sometimes weeks, to burn into a fine ash ... It was [then] put through the Mill, which made it as fine as flour. It was then put into paper bags, and carted to the railway, to be sent off to ... big Industrial towns, such as Hamburg.

We laboured 10 hours each day, and 5 on Saturday. In the beginning we did not know what the *Kieselgour* was used for, but we ultimately learnt that it was used in the manufacture of explosives, such as binding for nitro-glycerine, in the making of dynamite.[52]

Donald Fraser (back right) was sent to the village of Kleine-Hostlingen to work in a salt mine.

Despite the constant danger of working underground, the POWs were allowed certain privileges including working alongside German women. Some Australians became quite familiar with some of the females. Due to the customary poor security, romantic liaisons—even sexual intercourse—were not uncommon.[53]

Robert Henry's experience contrasted enormously. Having endured Dulmen camp, he was moved further east to the misery of Schneidemuhl camp, close to Posen (later Poznan). This he recalled as a 'very big camp ... [with] a lot of prisoners there—French and Russian.' The POWs were housed in barrack-style accommodation, with about sixty men to a room. However, Henry's luck had changed. Arriving in the freezing cold of early winter, he was assigned to a group assisting with work at a large farm near the camp, managed by a German nobleman, Baron von Gerke. 'A lot of people worked there,' Henry said,

> about a hundred prisoners ... There were a lot of civilian prisoners-of-war—Russian, Polish ... The Germans brought all the people who could work, and were available, into Germany to help the work on the farms, and that kind of thing. Let the Germans [men] go away to war. [The farm] was two or three thousand morgens [acres] ... they had about forty or fifty horses there. Used to milk cows there too, had a herd of seventy cows

and a lot of sheep ... [They] all had to be brought in every night. In winter time [they] all had to be housed. And there was hundreds of acres of rye grown. Rye was the principal crop ... for bread. Oh, yes, they grew some wheat ... There was another Englishman and myself, and both of us could use a scythe ... Well, they had plenty of modern tractors. They used petrol, but petrol became that scarce they couldn't use them. They used to have a whole lot of these civilians with scythes, cutting down ... rye or oats. Anyhow, we were given a scythe—the Englishman and myself ... and you'd have a [Polish]girl behind, binding up what you cut.

Von Gerke used to drive round with a pair of horses, supervising. He had other foremen as well ... It was a mighty big farm ... Von Gerke didn't own the farm, he leased it from the German government. [We lived] in a building ... where we slept was down below the level of the ground. Yes, it was pretty cold too, we didn't have much bed clothes. Two or three of us used to have to huddle together to get enough clothes—in the winter—to keep warm.[54]

Henry remained on the same farm through two extremely cold winters. He was still there in November 1918.

Horatio Ganson was sent to work on a railway. 'Friedrichsfeld was only a head ['parent'] camp ... We were only there about a week, and we were all booted out of there,' he remembered:

> Everyone was sent out to different places. We went to Getdorf. There were about 200 of us at Getdorf. It was a German naval barracks near Kiel on the Baltic. It was getting near winter, and by gee it was cold. The snow would be two or three feet deep in places. The tucker was a bit better ... for Christmas dinner we had pickled herrings ... At Getdorf we was put working on building a railway running to the coast near Stettin. The Germans had built the ground up about twenty feet high across a valley so that it was level for the railway, and four of us carried sleepers for a labour battalion of naval men. The Germans laid the sleepers and fixed the rails. But everything was frozen stiff when we were working there, and when the first train came along the thaw had set in, and the ... railway engine went about six feet into the ground.

Ganson's good fortune appeared to have held when he was chosen to work on another farm still close to the Baltic. 'When we came back to camp one day,' he explained,

> they were asking for farmers ... Bill Marshall and I said we were farmers. Bill ... wasn't a farmer. He was from parcel delivery at Perth station. Anyway, they put us in with a group of other prisoners who were farmers. Five or six of us got on this farm list. The next day we were all sent to Sonderberg on the train ... In Sonderberg, all the farmers came in from around the district to pick prisoners up for work on the farms. A big baron picked us all out and took us into a farm near Flensberg to work for him. Flensberg is about 10 kilometres from Denmark. There was a bridge running across to an island called Alson ... I don't think the baron owned the whole island ... but he had the biggest part ... The military was really in charge of the island, and the baron had a sergeant-major doing all his work.[55]

The work was not overly strenuous, although Ganson was treated badly. Any thought of escape was out of the question. Ganson and his co-workers decided instead to sabotage the farm's workings. 'The baron was a pig,' Ganson said:

> The first morning we were there we brought the "super" out of town with the horses. We saw the baron coming along the road. He had a little trap, a sulky affair. So we stood on the side of the road, and as he went past we said *"Guten morgen"* to him, you know. *"Schweinhunds!"* he said. Well, we "schweined" onto him; cripes, we did. We damaged some stuff of his. The baron would have murdered us if he could.[56]

Ernie Chalk continued to enjoy his run of good luck, remaining in the camp at Dulmen. 'At the time of our arrival here they happened to be wanting more men on the washhouse staff,' he explained,

> and I happened to be among those set aside for this work. I have always considered myself very fortunate in this, for had I not been kept back for this work, I should have been sent to the coal mines within a fortnight, as most of our party were. During the time I was at this place over forty-five thousand prisoners passed through the camp for registration. I was in a good position ... to see some of the terrible aspects of German frightfulness ...

As a rule they [POWs] came in, in the very last stages of exhaustion. Some of them were total wrecks, and almost incapable of moving about. All interest in life seemed to have departed from them. They were but walking skeletons. A party such as this arriving would not be kept in camp longer than three weeks. By this time they have been registered, inoculated five times, vaccinated once, and allotted to the working commando to which they will be sent as soon as they can be got away. During the first six months I was here, no provision was made by the Red Cross for helping men such as these, only parcels being sent to men whose names they had received. Latterly, however, emergency parcels were sent in bulk for distribution among men such as these arriving at the camp ... They would get their own parcels from two to three months after being in Dulmen, as it takes that time for the official notification to be sent through ... One thing for which we were thankful for here was ... that we were left fairly well alone by the Germans. We had two roll calls each day, but apart from that we were not troubled by them, and for this we were very thankful indeed. But ... the rations we had to live on were indescribable. The first two or three months I was there we had no Red Cross food, and all we were given to live on was two watery cabbage soups and one thin slice of the black German bread per day. As a consequence of this we must have certainly all succumbed if relief had not eventually come from the Red Cross.[57]

A French POW, Gustave Etienne, a 'hut mate' of an unnamed Australian POW at Gustrow Camp.

Harold Horner had settled into camp life at Gustrow. While he had become accustomed to French winters, this was a whole new experience. 'The climate at Gustrow was much like Russia,' he wrote,

> There was a foot of snow on the ground; and even though the sun was bright

at mid-day in mid-winter, it was only about twelve degrees [Fahrenheit] ... Although we had a fire in the hut, there was thick ice on the inside of the windows day and night ... At Gustrow the soup was poorer than ever—just a few cabbage leaves in hot water ... While we were there, working parties were continually being sent out—some in twos and threes to farms—and others in larger numbers to factories and mines.

On January 2nd 1918, orders came that 150 men were to be sent to Gustrow Sugar Factory at once, and I was one of the motley crowd comprising many Russians and Rumanians, with a few Belgians and French and British, which struggled along the road to the town of Gustrow, a few miles away. When nearing the town, we passed the Field Artillery at practice. They were mere boys, and looked shy when they noticed us. "Germany's last hope!" someone suggested ... No doubt many of them were thrown away in the big German push three months later.

At the factory, the ... vegetable soup was much better, and the bread also, though there was no greater quantity; but we enriched the soup with sugar ... My work was interesting and easy ... I had plenty of spare time to ... study the process of refining beet-sugar ... We were told that before the war all sugar from these factories was exported to England ... In the room in which we slept, there were eight Rumanians and eight Britishers. We got along very well together ... After spending 16 days at the factory, the supply of coal ran out, and work ceased ... Ten "Englanders" were required for the forest, so I volunteered with others, and we were in the train once more, bound for fresh fields and pastures new.[58]

***

Despite language difficulties with the Russian prisoners, most Australians formed a strong bond with their fellow POWs. Fraser recalled that he 'made some friends among the Russians,' in Soltau, Not many amongst the French or Belgians. The Russians were the best allies we had. The only ones you could trust anyway [but they received] frightful treatment ... and were dying at the rate of five or six a day ... They [the Germans] were burying them alive, I'm sure of that. Almost dead, and they'd take them away and bury them. I seen one fellow pull his leg over. He wasn't dead, but they buried him though ... There were thousands of Russians ...They were dying at the rate of five or six a day. During my stay there, they used to carry the bodies out in a box, tip it into a hole, and then go back for the next one. They did not however succeed in breaking down the Russians spirit.[59]

At Dulmen, Guppy was repulsed at what he saw. 'In the Lager were a large number of Russians and Serbians, and it was terrible to see them,' he wrote,

> They were absolutely starving though they weekly received a quantity of foodstuffs from Britain. They used daily, at meal times, to crowd round our huts begging for some bit of food and wandering round searching the ground for scraps, fighting like beasts for anything any of the boys gave to them. They were dying in the Lazarette at the rate of about 30 per day from starvation and tuberculosis and ptomaine poisoning as a result of eating bad foodstuffs. I have seen these poor fellows scraping out meat and other tins which have been lying on the rubbish heap for weeks and eating stuff out of tins which have been thrown out by Englishmen as unfit to eat.

Tens of thousands [sic] of Russians were sent from here in 1916 to work during the winter digging the Hindenburg Line. Few of them came back, they dying in thousands there from cold and starvation. Of those that did come back the majority have since died. Tales I have heard here and things I saw would make a strong man shudder.[60]

Two POWs (most-likely Russian) happily boiling water, to make cups of tea, at a POW Camp in Germany. Note prisoners of different nationalities in background.

Len Pooley also had a soft spot for one particular Russian he encountered at Koln. 'The Russians were in one section [of the barracks] on their own,' he remembered,

We liked to listen to the Russian music. The Russians would play the concertina. They used to play a little waltz tune that I've never forgotten ... Number seventy used to play it. We used to call him number Seventy—"Siebzig." We didn't know his name. We used to call them all by their numbers. Number Seventy was a cut above the others. He seemed to have a better education. He was a really nice fellow. He escaped from the barracks. He never came back one night ... But they caught him and brought him back, and put him in the dark cell for six days.

When 'Number Seventy' was released from solitary, Pooley gave him whatever food could be spared to help him recover.[61] Robert Henry also remembered his relationship with Russian POWs. 'We didn't like the French prisoners at all,' he said, 'we got on a lot better with the Russians ... we had a good bit to do with them in the camps. They used to come and do odd jobs for the English prisoners ... [and] they would get a bit of a reward. Food or something like that. Because they didn't get any parcels. A lot of them died. There wasn't enough to eat.'[62]

A British prisoner, Able Seaman James Byrne, also described the inhumane treatment meted out to Russian POWs. At a camp in Brandenburg, British prisoners

> were mixed with Russian and French POWs. We were there for a month, and during that time two Russians were shot. As far as I could see the Russians had no-one to look after their welfare in Germany and the Jerries took advantage of this, bullying them all the more. It was agonising to see the way they were treated—worse than dogs. Most of them used to offer prayers each night ... Half the Russians couldn't write their own names, most of them being large strong peasants; they told me they had to wait in their trenches for their comrades to be killed or wounded before they could have a rifle or machine-gun.[63]

Australian POWs (and their Russian 'mates') were well aware of the German habit of attempting to 'plant' a spy within their ranks in an endeavour to find out whether any escape attempts were being planned. Fraser explains:

> The German guards brought a dirty looking Russian prisoner in one afternoon. They kicked him in the behind, and threw him into one of the Russian huts. We couldn't help but notice the cold shoulder treatment the Russians were giving him. I

asked a Russian, who and what was their comrade. He replied, "Nix Ruskie Deutsch speaon," meaning, not a Russian but a German spy. Apparently he could not speak Russian well enough ... He did not stay long—the Russians would have bumped him off if given a chance in a dark spot, out of the sight of the guards.[64]

Australian and Russian POWs generally despised working, believing they were assisting their mutual enemy's war effort.

Horace Rumble recalled that 'there were a lot of Russians in Soltau'. Because they were not receiving Red Cross parcels, the Australians assisted them whenever possible. 'We used to see the Russians,' Whittington remarked, 'from what I saw the poor blighters were starved, ill-used, and treated like animals. Just as I left, there was the start of that epidemic of "flu," and we used to see the Russians taking half-a-dozen coffins out to be buried.' Rumble added that, whenever 'we made any tea and threw out the tea leaves on the ground, the Russian prisoners came along and ate all those tea leaves. They ate everything, and would even pick over the dirt. No grass grew in that big camp at Soltau, because as soon as any grass appeared, the Russians ate it.'[65]

***

Donald Fraser was among a group of POWs moved from Melbeck to another *Kieselgour* at Kleine Hostlingen. He had heard distressing stories about working conditions and the excessive number of accidents. 'We'd heard that they [mines] were pretty bad,' Fraser recalled. After being 'picked out and told [where] we were going to work,' Fraser entertained ideas of escaping from the train when it arrived at Kleine Hostlingen station. 'We were going to try and knock the sentry out and give it a go,' he commented,

> We thought we were going to die, so we thought we might as well die fighting ... It was Jack Faull who saved us. If it hadn't been for him we might have all been dead. Jack was a ... miner from Kalgoorlie. He was a lot older than us, thirty-five or more. He said, "No, we'll give it a go. I've worked in a mine. It might not be as bad as they tell us." It wasn't either.
>
> They put us in the Ammonia Drive. There were three of us—Sandy McNab, Arthur Greasley and myself. There were four or five drives, each with a different type of salt. They used to get white table salt and red rock salt. The Ammonia Drive was the worst because it was further in and had less air. They blasted in all the

drives ... After blasting ... there would be a mist of fine salt floating about in the air—what air you had—and you were breathing the salt in. The mine went down in levels, a level every 450 metres. We were on the 450 metre level ... It was hot down there—about 90 degrees fahrenheit ... it never changed ... The air was pumped in, but it wasn't any good unless you were close to the shaft. The Ammonia Drive went in a long way, a quarter of a mile I'd say. It wasn't shored up at all. It was just a tunnel. The other drive I worked in, where they got the table salt, was not nearly as long. It was a lot closer to the shaft. There were light railway lines going in. We'd pick up all the broken lumps of salt and load them into the wagons, and then shovel up what was left ... My hand used to get all eaten from picking up lumps of salt...

There would be four or five wagons, and about fifteen prisoners—three to a wagon. They were mainly Russians, and a few Frenchmen ... We had to do 20 wagons of table salt a day. We'd start at six o'clock in the morning, and knock off about half-past two. We had a hot bath when we knocked off, to get rid of the perspiration and the salt. The bath was the best part of it.[66]

Following a 'bad accident' in "Ammonia Drive", Fraser was transferred to easier work at Stilne, where extracted material 'was put through a machine ... and ground into fine table salt.'[67]

***

Horatio Ganson worked for the German baron for almost six weeks before he was accused of inciting a 'strike'. A German sergeant-major told striking workers that 'You've got to do what you're told, or we'll shoot!' Ganson recalled

> The next day they pulled all the Aussies and Tommies out of the dining room lined us up and marched us into Sondenberg. The baron was getting rid of us; he wanted a new lot. In Sondenberg there were a lot of Danish farmers picking the blokes out. They were only picking Russians and Poles to go to the baron's farm. He could bluff them, but he couldn't bluff us ... Our group finished up living on a farm owned by a Dane named Jorgen Schmidt ... I said to him, "We don't mind working. As long as you treat us okay, we'll work; but if you don't treat us okay, no work." He said, "You'll be alright." We were too. It was

home away from home there. All the other Danish farms were good, but ... we had the pick of the bunch ... There were two girls on the farm, about 23 or 24, and there was a maid named Anna. All the other farms had girls working for them. We all had girlfriends ... I was the best boy of the family. Dora, the married daughter, was the one I looked after ... I used to go and help Dora with the milking, and things like that, dodging around about the house. I got attached to Dora. The island was under German rule, and her husband had been called up and was on the Russian front. I used to go out every night with Dora. One night we ... walked into Sondenberg and went to the pictures. The old Jerry waited up for us to come back. He wanted to warn the girls to be careful ... Dora was about twenty-five ... and [her sister] Christina nineteen ... There was no such thing as being bashful. You could go into the bedroom when they were changing their clothes. They thought nothing of it. They used to sleep with their boyfriends of a night.[68]

Ganson was still working for the same farmer—and still having his usual serve of sex with Dora—on 11 November 1918.

Harold Horner's new work took him further north, to labour in a forest close to Billenhagen belonging to another wealthy German baron. Travelling by train to Rostock—the largest city in Mecklenburg—Horner was forced to wait in freezing weather conditions for six hours before boarding a 'train to the forest, about twenty miles east.' He wrote that

> the party comprised four Australians, four Englishmen, one Scotchman, and one Irishman ... at 5pm, our train took us to Sanitz, the little village near Billenhagen ... the home of the Baron in charge of the forest, which was the property and hunting ground of the Grand Duke of Mecklenburg .... We found the prisoners' quarters occupied by sixteen Russians and five Englishmen and one Irishman ... The six old hands were receiving their Red Cross packets regularly, so they did not require much of the food supplied from the Baron's kitchen ... My stay ... at this place was interesting, because I am fond of the bush life; but the fact of being a prisoner "gets on one's nerves," and one welcomes a change. Close to our quarters was the grave of a Russian prisoner who had committed suicide! I had to stay near the old civilian who was in charge of the work. It was a

good thing for me, as I had to follow him about and do only light work. We became quite fond of the old man, who had been a soldier himself in his younger days, and was quite proud of us ... The sentries did their best to persuade us to take off our hats to or at least, salute the Baron; but the reply always was that, as the Baron was not a soldier, we were not required to salute him ... On February 10th I had the inexpressible joy of receiving three letters from home—the first since capture; and two days later six Red Cross packets came for me!

Horner worked in the forest for a little over three weeks before he was moved to a smaller farm, near Tessin, approximately fifteen kilometres from Billenhagen.[69]

At Soltau, Rumble was receiving treatment for his deteriorating wound. The infection rapidly worsened. 'I would have had to work, but for my hand,' he said, 'I got right down and didn't care whether I died much or not. I got so thin. I got bed sores all over me ... There was rumour of an exchange,' Rumble explained:

> They were going to arrange an exchange of four Germans for each Englishman. It was all fixed up ... All those ... who weren't working. And we went up

before a board, and they passed me, after a bit of hesitation ... It was rather funny ... the transport they gave us. We were three miles from the siding at Soltau, out in the woods ... All you looked out at were fir trees. They decided to let us go by train to Holland. Now they supplied us with a great big farm wagon ... [but] nothing to pull it. And we had to ... go and get hold of these chains ... and away we went. At the crack of dawn, from prison camp to the siding ... And we were all singing "Its a long way to Tipperary"... It was a terribly heavy wagon. A hard job. And we pulled that wretched thing right down into the village of Soltau ... and they bundled us into a train and went across the border into a Dutch train. And that's the first time we ever had seen nurses. They were rosy-cheeked Dutch nurses there. We'd never seen anything like that. And then we went down to a hospital fairly close to the border, beautiful hospital, and we arrived there about 10.30 in the morning.

Rumble's ordeal was not yet over. He recalled that the men were now marched before another committee. Those judged to be 'as mad as hatters' were sent back to Germany. Rumble was more fortunate. He was told that he was to be moved to Rotterdam, where he would be put on the first available hospital ship to Britain.[70] After enduring five months in Soltau, Horace Rumble was finally to be free.

***

By 1918, the Allied naval blockade of the North Atlantic had taken hold. The historian Paul Vincent argues that the blockade caused the 'physical deterioration' of the German people and led to 'political revolution.'[71] However, food difficulties in Germany were not caused solely by the blockade. Before the war the country had been reasonably self-sufficient. As the war progressed, Germany simply did not have the manpower and resources to produce food and simultaneously maintain an army. One consequence of this was that NCOs held in POW camps were forced to work. The German army's requisition of farm equipment and horses only aggravated the situation. Worse still, where food production was maintained, distribution became a significant problem because vehicles of any description were commandeered for military use. Donald Fraser expressed compassion for the German civilians, considering that the lack of food 'beat the Germans ... Once the population started to starve, they were finished. When the Americans came in, it made the blockade all that much worse. They couldn't get anything in at all.'[72]

Some German senior officers and politicians still believed that they could force a negotiated peace settlement—in their favour—if not win the war. With the revolution in Russia and the release of thousands of troops from the Eastern to the Western Front, Germany could field 192 divisions in the west, compared to 156 Allied divisions. On 21 March 1918, the German army commenced its last great offensive of the war. Enemy troops described trenches littered with the bodies of 'dead Tommies'. Survivors, it was said, 'begged for quarter and showered us with cigarettes, food and the like.' It took the Germans only five days to retake all the 'British gains from the bloody, attritional campaigns of the previous three years.' After the disaster that was the Somme in June 1916, the retreat of March 1918 was the worst defeat in the history of the British army. Almost 1,300 artillery pieces and 90,000 prisoners—including many Australians—were captured. According to witnesses, 'many more were deterred from surrendering only by the threat of summary execution.'[73]

Hamilton Warrell was interned in Nurnburg camp. He wrote that, 'following the news of German successes, the [nearby] city bells would ring, the purpose ... to foster and develop the German morale and raise the people's hopes for a speedy, victorious end to the war ... Every day during ... March, April, May, June and July, the bells would peal out the news of more victories. During one morning in July 1918, the bells pealed continually, as news was received that Russia had entered into peace negotiations, acknowledging defeat.'[74] The morale of the German guards soared. For the first time in eighteen months it appeared that Germany might be heading towards victory. Australian POWs noticed the sombre look on the faces of new arrivals. Fraser was still working in the salt mine at Kleine Hostlingen when twenty-two British POWs, captured during the German 'push', were brought to the town. 'We caught up on the latest war news from the new prisoners,' Fraser recalled.[75]

With the huge increase in the number of POWs, conditions in the camps gradually worsened. In-camp amusements such as the playing of football, cricket and hockey were curtailed, while walks, which prisoners were permitted to take outside the camp—provided they gave a 'parole' that they would not attempt to escape—ceased. Despite the men's 'parole', they had always been accompanied by armed guards. By June 1918 the number of POWs in the camps had peaked. The German advance had been halted. However, by now, the old hands had begun to exhibit a degree of resentment towards the new arrivals.

***

Harold Horner had settled into work on the small farm at Tessin, located to the rear of one of the town's bakeries. With more freedom than he had previously experienced, the Australian soon made friends with Richard, the baker's son. 'A nice white-haired boy of twelve,' Horner noted,

> he was interested in my [Red Cross] packets; so I gave him some of the chocolates ... The baker had no one else working for him at the time, except a servant girl, Augusta; while his wife looked after the shop.
>
> My work consisted of feeding about twenty head of cattle ... I also had to look after two horses, and take the wagon out to the woods twice a day for firewood ... At night, about eight o'clock, Augusta would call me to go with her through the town to another baker's shop to bring bread; the girl would pull a little four-wheeled wagon full, while I followed with a German yoke and two baskets containing eighty pounds of German black bread. There was a time

when a machine-gun team followed me ... During the first three or four days my boss was proud of his Australian prisoner. I was the only Britisher in a town of 5,000 people ... There were many Russian prisoners, and two or three Belgian and French; but the nearest British prisoner was an Englishman two or three miles away ... I soon found out from Russians that my boss was a slave-driver. He had had several Russian prisoners before I came. He started very well with me, but after doing my best for two weeks to please him, I could see that something would happen.

That 'something' happened a few days later. Horner was waiting for some women to pick up their supplies of 'briquettes' when, in Horner's words, the baker

rushed towards me and pushed me in the back two or three times quickly, as if he would force me into the crowd of women, some of whom were aged frail-looking creatures. This was the first time he had actually touched me ... I lost control of myself completely, and whipped round like a flash and "bogged" into him. He backed out of the crowd, calling out, "Nay! Nay!" He looked such a sorry picture that I stopped and picked up my sacks again

... He got no sympathy from anyone ... He kept away from me and walked on the footpath as I drove the load up to the town. As I thought over the incident, I decided that now I had a pull on him I had better keep it. I had found it impossible to please him; henceforth I would do the work in my own way.

Horner believed that his behaviour must have delighted most German villagers. Children would 'dance with joy,' when he approached them, while older folk would try to converse with him. However, he soon discovered that there was another reason for the new-found cheerfulness and goodwill. 'On March 23rd [shortly after the commencement of the huge British retreat] my employer came to the stable door with the open newspaper in his hand

"Herbert," he whined, "six hundred Australians captured! Sixteen thousand English prisoners!" His tone and manner suggested that he wished to be more friendly; he judged by the news that Germany would soon win the war, and that British countries would be in such a bad way that prisoners would be glad to stay in Germany ... This disaster to our troops was the most humiliating pill that we had to take. We had tried to convince the

Germans that our side would win, and now Fritz was walking over them. What was wrong with the boys? What was the cause of the disaster? They had had plenty of time to make a strong line.

Horner had little time to seek answers to those questions. Soon afterwards, he was ordered to work on a larger farm near Weitendorf.[76]

***

By mid-March, William Howard was working on a farm near Blankenheim and was enjoying the daily grind. He was fortunate in that the elderly female farmer allowed him more privileges and latitude than many other prisoners. 'Up at 6a.m., cutting wood nearly all day, not a bad joint for grub,' he confided to his diary on the 11th. And, two days later: 'Out in the old bush again today. Took the wagon out and carted home three loads.' The relationship with his overseer was not always agreeable—'Cutting wood nearly all day today, got a bit of hurry up from the old girl, but never take any notice of her,' he noted on the 16th. Despite the occasional disagreement, it seems that he could go into the nearest village (Isendorf or Blankenheim) in the company of other prisoners, almost at will. 'Lovely day today,' he wrote on 24 March, 'went to Isendorf, got the old boots mended and three Froggies [French POWs] and me went for a walk. Met an Englishman in the boozer.'[77] For William Howard, the war was a distant memory.

Harold Horner soon settled into his new surrounds at Weitendorf. He recalled sharing a room with three other prisoners—Fred Wilson, an old English friend, and two Russians. 'The food was no better than we were accustomed to at other places,' Horner commented,

> but as Fred and I received packets, we "mucked in;" Russians as well. This place proved to be my home until the Armistice, except for two days that I ran away. The little village comprised five farms, a smithy, a church and half-a-dozen dwellings which were the homes of labourers ... On the other farms, French, Belgians, Russians and Poles were employed. The Poles were not treated as prisoners, yet they were not allowed to leave the district. Our room became the rendezvous for all prisoners in the village, in the evenings before locking-up time, which was 9 o'clock ... My Australian Red Cross packets were well supplied with beef-dripping, a tin of which made a splendid lamp, and lasted for weeks, giving light to sixteen prisoners, comprising Russians, Belgians, French, English and Australian! ...

The Germans didn't like to see us burning fat, when they could not even get fat to eat. The Red Cross packets convinced them that the Allies were not in such a bad way as the German papers stated.[78]

A few days later, Horner made his unsuccessful bid for freedom.[79]

Donald Fraser, still working at Kleine Hostlingen, was kept abreast of what was happening on the Western Front by newly arrived POWs. The 'Germans' joy [of their spring offensive] was short lived,' he wrote:

> The Western allies counter-attacked. The Australians recaptured Villers Bretonneux, and many thousands of German prisoners ... We learnt after the war, that this was the turning point in the war ... I think it was in August, that the Germans moved all the British, French and Belgian POWs to new and better quarters in the village. The Russians were left at the stables. The Germans, including the guards were ... becoming more friendly towards us. About this time, I got a cluster of boils on one of my ankles. My foot was swollen to about twice its normal size, and I found it very difficult to walk. The Feldwebel sent me to a doctor at Grocer Hoslingen ... I had a German Alsaceian escort, who was in no

hurry, thank goodness. The doctor turned out to be an old fellow with a flowing beard. He could speak a little English, and he asked me how I came to get such a foot ... He poulticed my foot, and gave the "post" (guard) instructions as to what to do, and also told him to take his time going back. This was right up the Alsaceian's alley. He asked me if I drank beer. I replied, "A little." He said, "Cummings ze mit" (come with me). We went into a beer garden, sat down at a table under a tree and waited for the waitress to take the order. She ... returned with two big frothy pints of Deutsches Ale. After drinking these the guard repeated the order, passing a few jokes with the waitress ... He said to me, "Sight genau" (plenty of time). We managed to arrive back at the compound before dark.[80]

Following his recovery, Fraser worked on one of the mine's lifts. He was engaged in the same work at the time Germany surrendered on 11 November 1918.

***

Keith Tamblyn recalled that he spent the majority of his captivity in France. Unlike most Australian POWs, he came across very few

Russian prisoners. According to Tamblyn, in September 1918 he was still working for the Germans, close to the old fortified town of Conde, near the Belgian-French border. 'We were working in a factory there ... about nine or ten sergeants and corporals with us,' he recalled, when 'they said to us ... "going to send you to Germany." All [of us] went on this train to Friedrichsfeld.' It stopped at Cologne on the way. 'We stayed there for an hour or two,' Tamblyn wrote, 'and had a look at their beautiful Cathedral and had a few beers with the German soldiers in their canteen ... We [then] had to go through Essen, a big manufacturing works and I said you could see to read a newspaper from the reflections from the furnaces at night.' Tamblyn gleefully added that he

> got another thirty parcels when we got to Friedrichsfeld ... All at once ... Of course he [Germany] was getting a thrashing then, and our people were getting nearer and nearer ... All the Red Cross parcels came through Holland, and they were put in Holland trucks, Holland Government seal on the trucks ... I never had anything to do with the Russians at all, outside that I'd seen them. They were in the same camp in Germany, but not in the NCO section ... They were over in the working party

section. They used to go out and do work. They'd do jobs for [the Germans] ... they dug the Hindenburg Line for an extra loaf of bread a day. Well, that's the sort of thing they did. Of course, there was no Russian Army ... in those days [it] was gone.[81]

***

In late August, Australian POWs noticed that their treatment was visibly improving. Lieutenant W.S. Missingham (15th Battalion) wrote that, when he was transferred to Bad Colberg camp in late May, he 'was not treated too well for the first few months, but after that things changed very much for the better.'[82] In early September, William Howard was still working on the farm near Blankenheim. He heard of the Allies' rapid advance during one of his visits to the town. However, little had changed. As was his custom, every Sunday he went into the village. 'Quite a number of our allies [POWs] here today,' he wrote on 22 September, 'but had bad luck and run into [a] gendarme [policeman] at the boozer. Got a lovely parcel from [his sister in Australia] Lyla.' Howard was still working at the farm when he heard of the Armistice.[83]

In September, Horner, too, was informed that the Allies had the German army on the run.

'From the end of August, Germany was ripe for Revolution,' he revealed:

> Her army was beaten, and the country was in a very bad way. Quite naturally, the effect was felt even on a quiet farm ... There was trouble of all kinds. "La Grippe" was busy everywhere. At the neighbouring big farm, which employed forty-two hands, forty of them were down with influenza. We were told that at Hamburg victims were being buried all day long. Girls in tears were looking for work—or for slavery ... because they'd do anything ... Germany was poverty stricken; our farmer's son wore the boots of two dead English soldiers, taken in the big German push.
>
> On September 23rd I put a neat handle on my box, and packed it carefully. I showed it to the sentry and the farmer's sons, and told them I was ready for Australia, and I was soon going home. About the beginning of November, the Revolution spread very quickly. In places like Kiel, Wilhelmshafen and Hamburg it was a blood-red Revolution; and even in our quiet country town of Tessin there were machine-guns used ... "Deutschland ist krank" (Germany is ill), said the farmer's son to me. This young man spent a good

deal of his spare time talking with me about different countries. Soon after getting him interested, I asked him to bring me the German papers. He said that he was not allowed to give them to the prisoners; so I would not converse with him. He soon came to, and brought us the papers.

On 11 November, it was all over. The German government had agreed to unconditional surrender. Horner, like thousands of his comrades, would be going home. 'When the Armistice was signed, we threw away the padlocks, and locked the sentry out,' he wrote, clearly delighted.[84]

While conditions, generally, were somewhat better than behind the lines in France—Australian POWs could not be killed by their own artillery, for instance—they still had to cope with extreme deprivation. Whether in camps, or working below the earth's surface, the men had to endure terrible winters and the less fortunate died from hunger or hypothermia. Certainly, without Red Cross parcels containing food and warm clothing, a great many more POWs would have died. For those who fell ill, medical treatment remained primitive. Others endured the crippling boredom of living within the perimeter of camps. Those prisoners sent to work on farms fared better, particularly those on smaller properties where, occasionally, they were accepted as part of the family. There, the men received better food (although still subsidised by the 'parcels' which the more generous shared with the farmer's family) and were provided with warm clothing. Some Australian POWs, including William Howard, were glad to leave the carnage of the Western Front behind. However, after 11.00a.m. on 11 November—when hostilities formally ceased—the Australians looked forward to a quick return to their homeland. For most, this was not to be the case.

CHAPTER THIRTEEN
Peace
'The Jerries Were Furious'

334

CHAPTER THIRTEEN

PEACE

'The Jerries Were Furious'

Fighting on the Western Front may have ceased on 11 November 1918 at 11.00a.m., but Australian POWs were not officially set free at that moment. Moreover, finalising their repatriation and return to Australia proved lengthy and protracted, with bureaucratic bungling in London ensuring that some men were forced to remain in camps for an indefinite period. The POWs received news of Germany's speedy capitulation with ambivalence. Some sought reprisals against their German captors, particularly the more brutal guards. The majority, however, harboured no ill will—to them, the guards were simply doing their jobs. Instead, the men wanted nothing more than a speedy return to their families and their loved ones back home. Some were anxious about their repatriation—especially those few who had 'spied' for the Germans. A smaller number had even collaborated with their captors by providing information (which turned out to be useless) concerning Australian positions at the front. Those men's future appeared bleak.

For others, boredom was to become the number one enemy, particularly those forced to remain in camps for a lengthy period.

The conditions of the Armistice specified that POWs should be freed from the camps within fourteen days. This was virtually impossible to achieve. Somewhat surprisingly, the Germans were given responsibility for arranging and providing transport for the POWs. In some of the better organised camps, small groups began their departure within the fourteen-day time-frame. At Friedrichsfeld, for instance, representatives of the Dutch government arrived in mid-November. Their principal task comprised dividing the POWs into manageable groups, usually by nationality. The first groups departed almost immediately. Contingents of fifty or more men walked to Wesel and, following a five-hour train journey, reached Zevenaar in Holland. Buttressed by a hearty meal, they then left for Rotterdam where an overnight ferry took them to England and freedom.

***

In Friedrichsfeld in early November, Keith Tamblyn noticed 'there was something happening because ... the guards had a more friendly attitude.'[1] On 10 November the men assembled for the evening roll call. A German interpreter announced: 'I don't want you to make much noise, but Germany has lost the war and it is finished.' A British soldier, Corporal Arthur Speight, takes up the story:

> The next morning we found that some bold spirit had nailed a Union Jack and French flag to the tops of two arclight poles. The Jerries were furious ... There was a distinct change of atmosphere now. Nobody would take any orders from the guards and some of the guards themselves, especially those with the machine-guns, packed up and went home. The German officers did not have much hold on them now and this led to a visit by the officer commanding the lager who was an old dug-up General[sic] or something. He was furious at the slipshod way everything was being done ... The Germans now dropped us altogether as regards rations and we had to live on the parcels which had been stored in a large building in the lager ... Our German corporal was also badly off for food so we used to stand him his grub too. In return he used to take us down to the town of Wesel nearby, and armed with a tin of cocoa or a couple of bars of Sunlight soap we used to descend on the pubs which, for the price, would supply six men

with beer for as long as they cared to stay. The lager was visited every day by German civilians begging for bully beef and biscuits.[2]

Tamblyn was among the first prisoners repatriated to England, most likely because of his medical condition—his scabies had recurred. In his own words, he was part of 'the second lot' who left Friedrichsfeld. 'I spent a night at a place called Sevenar [sic] in Holland, and then we went to Rotterdam the next day where we spent another night ... and then had to cross the North Sea in a fishing trawler.' By 19 November, Tamblyn was at AIF Headquarters in London. Having been issued a new uniform, he was given four weeks' leave and permitted to travel anywhere he chose in Britain.[3]

Due to ongoing problems with his amputation, Raymond Embrey was another hastily sent back to England. He was initially 'taken to the Tooting Military Hospital' before being moved to another hospital in Britain. Embrey was also among the first repatriated POWs to arrive back in Australia. He was immediately booked into Caulfield Military Hospital where the botched amputation to his arm was 'fixed-up'. Despite having only one arm, Embrey was able to secure employment with the Melbourne & Metropolitan Tramways Board as a wages clerk. Soon afterwards, he and Ruby—whom he met while convalescing in England—married and purchased a house in Camberwell.[4]

***

Group of ex-POWs at unveiling of a memorial for Australians who died during internment at the Parchim Camp, Germany. The Memorial is inscribed with the words 'IN LOVING MEMORY OF' – followed by two columns of twenty-six names, and along the bottom – 'COMRADES IN CAPTIVITY PARCHIM 20 NOVEMBER 1918.' (AWM PO3236.340)

Len Pooley was living in the barracks above Cologne railway station. On 11 November, he remembered 'an announcement over the loudspeaker at the station at eleven o'clock. We all downed tools, and jumped up in the air. We danced around on the platform where we were … We went upstairs and had a bit of music. The

Russians had an accordion, and played some music. The guards came up and wanted to "loos" them down again ... But we said, "No the war's over."[5]

Lieutenant R. Sanders was at Strohen. He recalled that the Australians were to be questioned by the camp commandant (an elderly looking lieutenant colonel) before they could leave. When it came Sanders' turn, the German was

> sitting busily at his desk but upon me entering rose to his feet and offered me his hand. I shook hands and he asked me to be seated. He expressed extreme regret for the way we Britishers had been robbed and put to inconvenience ... The revolution [within Germany] had upset everything and the control of the town had been taken out of his hands. He was still ... the custodian for the government of all government buildings and military stores and equipment in the town and he gave me an order for ... the supply of forty undervests, underpants and shirts from the military supply store. While talking to me the Commandant caught sight of the Australian [badges] on my shoulder straps and showed some amused excitement. He told me that he had been in charge of a brigade of

Wurtemburgers in early April 1917 who had succeeded in capturing a good number of Australians, which to the best of his knowledge had never happened previously and had never happened since. I then asked him whether this had been at Bullecourt ... Of course this is where it happened and I told him that I was one of the Australians captured by his regiment. When the old Commandant learned this he was very enthusiastic and excited, and he again got up, shook hands again with me and made some very complimentary remarks about the wonderful fighting ability of the Australians.

In the course of our conversation he told me how our attack on April 11th had been anticipated, and how the first and second lines had been only thinly held whilst large reinforcements had been brought into reserve including large numbers of machine-guns. We chattered away for a good half hour and I learned that his wife had been educated in England.[6]

Lieutenant John Ingram was at Freiburg camp. 'After the Armistice,' he recalled, Australian 'officers were at liberty to move about in the town of Freiburg from 10a.m. to 5p.m. This time was mainly occupied in walks, and watching troops passing through. All German troops ... were disarmed on entering the town.'[7]

***

Donald Fraser's account is not dissimilar. He read the terms of the Armistice in the *Berlin Tagablat*, translated for him by a Frenchman. During the night of 10 November, meetings were held throughout the camp. The men decided collectively that

> if the Germans called us for work in the morning, we would refuse to budge, and we felt quite certain that they would be too afraid to do anything drastic to us for refusing to work ... [N]ext morning we were called out at the usual time ... Someone yelled out, "Go to hell you square-headed bastard—Englanders finished arbite [work]." Whether he understood or not I do not know, but he remained at the door saying "Yah, yah." [Another Australian] picked up a wooden clog ... and threw at his head. It missed him, but hit the wall above the door, splitting in half. The German slammed the door and said "Donra Vetra" ... As a result, we did not see him again.
>
> We all got out of bed at about 6a.m., dressed in our best clothes, and waited for

developments to occur. A little later we saw the Feldwebel with a Captain and another German coming into the compound. The other German could speak English, and ... told us that the Germans were sorry, but if we did not work, they could not give us anything to eat. We said OK, we do not want your sour crout [sic] anyway. We will survive on our red cross parcels, and besides you are obliged to send us home within 14 days. He replied by saying that he did not think this possible, due to the shortage of railway carriages, which had been taken by our people.

After a bit more haggling, he finally asked us if we would go to the mine and speak to the mines manager. We agreed ... [and] all fell in and marched to the mine gate, halting outside. [The spokesman] told the Feldwebel ... that we would not enter the mine property, and that if the manager wanted to speak or apologise to us, he could come out on the road and have his say. We saw him look out of a top window in his office, but the bandy-legged bastard did not come out. I think he may have been afraid of collecting a punch on the nose, which was quite on the cards. We about turned and marched back to our compound followed by the French and Belgians.... If we had done anything like this a few months previously, the Germans would have not hesitated to use a machine gun on us. Things were different now, however ... The German Officer told us that it could be a week or more before he could get a train to transport us back to Soltau ... but in the meantime ... we would be free to go where we liked, as long as we were back in barracks by 9p.m. We had to give the Feldwebel our word of honour not to clear off, which we didn't mind, as there seemed to be no point in doing otherwise.

Every day for over a week, Fraser and his mates walked into the village. The German people 'appeared to be glad that the war was over, and tried to be very friendly towards us.' On the ninth day, Fraser was told that a train was ready to take them home. That afternoon they marched into Soltau camp. 'There were thousands of prisoners of all the allied nations here at this stage,' Fraser wrote, 'Russians, Serbs, Rumanians, Italians, French, Belgian and *we British*. Each had their own sector. There were about two thousand British—some had been captured in the retreat from Mons in 1914 ... We met up with quite a lot of old mates. All had different tales to tell—some very grim, others not so bad.'

Fraser expected that it would be only a week or so before he could enjoy real freedom—but it was not to be. Frustrated at being in camp for over two weeks—and with winter beginning to set in—he recalled that 'time was dragging on ... and still no sign as to when we would be going home.' In desperation, a 'deputation' visited the Commandant. Told that 'German authorities were doing their best ... but transport was the trouble still', the 'deputation' responded that the men were ready to 'walk' to freedom. The Commandant was not prepared to risk any casualties. 'For God's sake do not attempt that as most of you would die on the road-side,' he pleaded, 'as it is too far. Have patience a little longer.'[8]

***

Five unnamed ex-POWs photographed with the nurses who looked after them, after the men's release from a POW Camp in Germany, c 1919.

Harold Horner wondered how long it would be before he saw his family in Western Australia. He knew that it could take some time, accepting that the priority list to get on a 'boat-roll'—which gave precedence to men who had been captured in earlier battles—was the most equitable system. This, of course, meant that British troops who had been captured as long ago as 22 August 1914 (at Mons) would be on the first ships to reach England. While the priority list appeared sound in theory, its practical application was often quite different. Wounded and seriously ill prisoners were usually first to leave—after that, the system collapsed. While the biggest headache was transport, which was certainly inadequate, there were also insufficient support staff to ensure that the system ran smoothly.

Nonetheless, Horner was impatient to leave Weitendorf. 'The [five] prisoners in the village gathered ... [and] decided that as the under-officer would not help us to get to Gustrow by giving us railway-passes, we would go on our own,' he recalled,

> We arranged to meet at our farm at 2am ... and move off an hour or so later, so that we could reach the little town of Laage to catch the train. So at that early morning hour we bade "farewell" to Weitendorf ... and started the ten-mile tramp to Laage. We had a good macadamized road to travel on ... The watchman at Kammine tried to stop us; but we reminded him that the war had finished ... Boarding the train without tickets ... we were soon in the old camp at Gustrow.
>
> In the camp there were many thousands of men ... Russians, French, Belgians, English, Colonials, Japanese ... We five Britishers were housed with our French friends, and as most of us had learned a little French, we had a very happy time, thanks to the abundant supply of Red Cross stuff. We met scores of old friends, and were very

pleased to find that they had come through alive; but there were many deaths in the big camp, even in the little time we were there. A number of Russians who were tramping into camp one night were cut up by the train, which passed close to the camp gates.

Horner did not have long to wait to be listed on a 'boat-roll'. 'At last we were ... leaving Germany,' he wrote, 'no one was a bit down-hearted at leaving the land of "arbeit"; so it was a jolly train-ride through Gustrow, Schwann and Rostock.' At Warnemunde they boarded the Danish steamship *Koch* for Copenhagen. Six days later, Horner was sailing through the North Sea on a 'big ship the SS *Frederick VIII*', bound for Britain. 'The send-off at Copenhagen was the most enthusiastic we have seen at any place,' Horner mused, 'and they treated our men so well that when we were in camp in England, and it was found that we could get a month's holiday, some wanted to go back to Copenhagen.'[9]

***

Yet again, lady luck seemed to be smiling on William Howard. On 11 November he confided to his diary that he received 'excellent news today. Armistice starts from today. Expect to be home for Christmas.' The cheeky young Australian showed little courtesy to the middle-aged woman who managed the German farm where he had worked. He made it clear that he would come and go as he pleased. On 14 December, Howard wrote that he 'got word tonight that we are going in the morning.'[10] Like Howard, Keith Tamblyn reached England by way of Holland. 'When we got into Holland,' Tamblyn recalled, 'we discarded our prison uniforms ... and we were issued with British uniforms—British not Australian ... And we had to go back to England in these [uniforms and] ... we didn't like them.... We went to Rotterdam ... [and were] put on a ... fishing boat ... only a small thing—and shot across the North Sea to Hull.'[11]

Robert Henry had just finished harvesting and expected to be sent to another farm or, worse still, a mine to work over the winter. He also heard rumours of an influenza epidemic that was taking hold throughout Europe. 'Well there was rumours about,' he remembered,

> because we got information through the priest. I remember the morning ... and one of the Polish foreman coming out, and he said, "Wilhem ist weg!" [loosely, the Kaiser has run away]. "Machen sie weg kommem!" Get out of the way ... Things got a bit lax

then. We were on a big farm ... when the armistice was declared. We wondered when we were going to get back to the camp. There didn't seem to be any hurry to take us back there. That was in November ... We were greatly excited ... When we got back to camp in Scheidemhul, everything was in a mess. See, they'd had influenza ... and men were dying in wholesale, the prisoners-of-war. Some men had been there ... four years, and they died just before they went home. Anyway, I kept healthy, and went back to camp ... I was in the camp ... until December ... then they took a trainload of us to Danzig.

A small ship took Henry to Leith in Scotland and, after a short stay, he continued on to London.[12]

***

At the time Germany's surrender was announced, some of the badly wounded prisoners who had previously been 'exchanged' were still recuperating in London. Horace Rumble was in a British military hospital

for the armistice, and I'd been having a lot of physiotherapy ... During that time we went out to Windsor Castle and we had afternoon tea there ... we had a wonderful time out there. They arranged a lot of things for the POWs. I went to about 30 live theatres while I was in hospital—for nothing. The Red Cross gave me the tickets. The Anzac Club, in London gave us free tickets. We used to avail ourselves of these and go and see the shows. I saw the "Better Hole" three times ... It was a really good laugh.

Rumble was in the West End hospital for almost a year before returning to Australia on the hospital ship *Karoola* in late 1919.[13]

For others, repatriation came more quickly. Ernest Etchell, who was wounded at Bullecourt but managed to crawl to the Australian line, 'was in the first draft home. I was about the only Gallipoli man left.'[14] Edmund Sadler was recovering from having his arm amputated at the Australian base hospital at Montassa in Egypt. In May 1918 he was among a group of amputees who arrived in Perth, Western Australia. After a medical examination and further treatment culminating in 'a final assessment and medical review', Sadler received his discharge papers.[15]

***

In November 1918, Horatio Ganson was still working on the farm belonging to Jorgen Schmidt. Considering his frequent dalliance with Schmidt's daughter, Dora, and his easy work, Ganson's reaction when Jorgen told him that 'the war will be finished tomorrow', may have been understandably mixed.[16] After bidding farewell to the Schmidt family—and having his final night of indulgence with Dora—Ganson was sent to a large holding camp near Lubeck. 'There must have been thousands there,' he recalled

> It was three or four days before we set off to come home. From Getdorf a crowd of us went by train to Stettin, on the Baltic, and from there we went by ship to Leith in Scotland. When we got home they sent us ... to Horseferry Road. They took our name and number, and we had to tell them about the Bullecourt stunt ... Then they gave us a month's leave ... So I went home to Ashton-under-Lyne. I never saw London ... [After] our second leave ... I went to Weymouth, waiting for the troopships. I put in for a job with the YMCA ... But while I was at Weymouth a troopship was loading, and they wanted two more to fill her up. So I cancelled my YMCA job, and came back home on the *Leicestershire*.[17]

Arriving in Perth later in 1919, Ganson travelled by train to his home at Hines Hill.

Unidentified Australian and British POWs passing through a Base Depot, receiving a change of clothes. Most of these men were captured at the struggle for Bullecourt on 11 April 1917. (AWM EO4234)

***

On 22 December, Donald Fraser was finally told that the British and Australians still at Soltau were to leave the following day. 'Early on the morning of the 23rd, all the British who could walk—1900 all told—marched out the gates for the last time,' he wrote,

> and boarded a train for Hamburg, where we arrived the same afternoon. To our great joy we could see the Union Jack flying from the flag pole on a fairly large merchant ship tied up at the wharf. A

British destroyer was also anchored out in the harbour. On leaving the train, our sergeant formed us up into companies, and marched us down onto the wharf. A Naval Officer addressed us, telling us that he was very sorry, but the ship had accommodation for 1,200 only ... The ship's Captain ... told us that if we were prepared to rough it, we could all come aboard. It would mean that some of the men would have to lay on the decks, but he would manage to keep us supplied in enough eats to keep body and soul together for the short voyage. A wild cheer immediately followed the Captain's address, with many of the Aussies yelling, "Oh you beaut."

After we all boarded—British and Australians—and just before the ship was due to leave the wharf, a party of French and a couple of Russians ... broke away from their guards, and came running onto the wharf. They pleaded to come aboard, and the Captain replied, "any allied POW was welcome to come on my ship, providing they were prepared to rough it the same way as our own boys." They lost no time coming aboard. There were a few German guards around, but they made no attempt to stop them—perhaps the sight of the destroyer had a sobering effect on them.

The ship, together with its escort, the destroyer, pulled downstream that evening, and sailed out onto the North Sea. The following day, Christmas Eve, many of us just lazed around on the decks. We were supplied with plenty of eats—bully beef, and beautiful bread rolls ... We had a smooth crossing, and at one stage passed very close to the island of Heligoland—this was a German Naval Fortress during the war, but was now dismantled.

Fraser had hoped to celebrate Christmas 1918 with friends and family in Scotland, but the ship did not make port in time. Instead, he 'celebrated Christmas Day on the North Sea.'[18]

On Boxing Day, Fraser arrived at Hull in Yorkshire. His next destination was an army camp not far from the cathedral town of Ripon. 'We immediately disembarked and walked along the wharf to a railway station,

where a train was waiting for us. As we walked along the wharf, each man was handed buns and tea by scores of Red Cross ladies, who had set up stalls for this purpose. Cigarettes were also handed out ... Eventually the train pulled out, with all hands on board. After about an hour ... the train stopped at ... Ripon, where we were ordered to form up into units [by country] ... We then marched off to Ripon Camp ... We were told ... that we would have to stay ... for about a week, so as we could have medical checks, be issued with uniforms and so on. None of us had any money, so we were told that we would be paid one pound each ... At the end of our week's stay we were issued with rail passes ... to London, and told to report to Australian Headquarters at Horseferry Road in London ... From here, each man was on his own, so to speak.

After drawing £50 from his army back-pay, Fraser visited relatives and friends in Glasgow. Over the following seven weeks (Fraser managed to 'fix things with the local doctor' for three weeks' extra sick leave) he travelled to Inverness with a cousin 'who was in the Cameron Highlanders ... to look at the capital of the Highlands.' Disappointed when his leave was over, Fraser 'said farewell to the most friendly and hospitable people ... [he] had ever met.' During the following week he took the opportunity to explore London. Proud of his British heritage, he wrote of seeing 'the changing of the Guard at Buckingham Palace, and lots of pageantry, including the wedding [of] Princess Pat, the Duke of Connaught's daughter. I was becoming very fond of London by this stage.'[19]

Harold Horner also felt a fondness for London. He recalled being on the same train line, between Grantham and London, 'the day we left ... to go to France, over two years before.' Travelling through Finsbury Park station, Horner's thoughts turned to 'our friends in France—those who had starved themselves and their children so that we might have a chance to live. What had become of them and their quiet little village?' When the train arrived at King's Cross Station, an officer announced: 'these men are ex-prisoners-of-war ... and the gate-keeper swung the gates as wide as he would for the King!' After registering at AIF Headquarters, Horner rejoiced in finding his way 'to that magnificent building in the Strand, Australia House', where he joined other Australians in 'a nice quiet writing room ... and penned a few letters to our good friends at Hamage.' While he enjoyed taking in the sights of London—particularly Big Ben and the Houses of Parliament at Westminster—the most engrossing incident occurred when he 'saw a crowd near Westminster Bridge. They were interested in a surrendered German submarine below the bridge.' Horner remained in England for two months. On 18 April, after 'a lively send-off', he was among hundreds of Australian soldiers who boarded HMAT *Marathon* at Devonport. 'In waving "farewell" to England,' he wrote, 'there were not many tear-dimmed eyes. We have nothing against England; but the Greater Britain under the Southern Cross has the stronger pull.'[20]

Other Australians had similar stories to tell. When Fraser met up with friends while billeted at a camp near Weymouth in Dorset, he noted that their 'experience was similar to my own.' Although it seems unlikely that he ever took up the offer, Fraser was provided with the opportunity to participate in numerous educational courses offered by the Australian Department of Repatriation and Demobilisation (led by his old brigade commander, now Lieutenant General Sir John Monash).[21] During the last week of March 1919, Fraser was one of around 1,000 men who heard the news for which they had so keenly waited. With little notice, they departed England on 'a rather small ship', the *Armagh*. With his 'deferred pay' to look forward to, Fraser arrived in Sydney on 23 May. 'It was some time before we left the wharf,' he recalled, 'we had to file past a team of Officers, who took all our particulars, and then gave us 1st Class rail passes, which ... were in force for about 6 weeks. We also had medical checks, and finally, our discharge from His Majesty's Forces, were given to each man, after filing through in alphabetical order. The army was now finished with us.'[22]

Edward Pinnell remembered returning 'home on the *Brehem*. It was a German boat that was in one of the ports that was held up while the war was on. Then they turned them into troopships ... to get [us] home. And that was pretty lively, we had a lot of fun on that. And, of course, we were coming home and were a happy lot.'[23] Before being allowed ashore, all the men (on every ship) were lectured by their CO on 'what will happen to them, and what will be expected of them after disembarkation.'[24]

Frank Hallihan felt that returning POWs 'did not need cheers' for their homecoming. He wrote that his ship

> arrived in Melbourne [for the march and celebrations] on Anzac Day, 1919. As we left we stepped into cars that were awaiting our arrival and were taken through the City to our Headquarters at Caulfield. The people of Melbourne turned out for the occasion to welcome us home ... [W]e would have been prepared to come home in the dark, because we fully realised that amongst that multitude of people there were many who belonged to those we had

left behind. It was not a day of rejoicing for us, but rather a day of sadness ... We could see so many changes in our own people. The years of suspense had left their marks upon them. We understood the position more clearly. We were always face-to-face with death, and even when under fire, we became used to it and did not take any notice. It was a matter of take things as they come.

Despite the deprivation he had endured along the way, Hallihan remained positive. He considered himself 'lucky' because he had 'learned to look on the bright side, and there was always someone to give encouragement by his actions when face to face with danger.'[25]

***

Now back in Australia, most men started the search for suitable employment. For some, after the blood-letting in the trenches and their time in captivity, readjustment to civilian life was decidedly difficult. The same government that lauded them as heroes when they left, was not prepared to honour the promise of keeping open their jobs. Instead, it offered only a minimal amount of financial assistance. Their pride dented, others looked unsuccessfully for alternative fulltime work. With limited cash, they were forced to take on menial part-time employment. If not for the Herculean effort of senior officers—including the Commander of the 5th Australian Division, Lieutenant General Sir Talbot Hobbs—and the work of the Returned Soldiers and Sailors League of Australia (RSSILA), a larger number of returned soldiers would have become destitute. Certainly, when he returned to Australia (after commanding the Australian Corps), the welfare of repatriated soldiers became Hobbs' number one priority. He told each and every one of them 'that if they were badly in need of a meal to come to the family house. This they did and there were always returned men calling at the door of the kitchen for many years [in the 1920s and 30s].'[26]

More problematic was the lack of psychological counselling. Certainly the trauma associated with being a POW was not as readily identified in the immediate post-World War I period as it was in the aftermath of later conflicts. As Australian POWs were being repatriated, a Swiss surgeon, Adolf Vischer, was among the first practitioners researching the problems associated with captivity. Vischer had visited and worked in many POW camps of different nationalities where he interviewed 'hundreds' of subjects. In all probability he was the first doctor to examine the psychological condition or neurosis which became known as 'barbed wire disease'. He discovered mental problems suffered by POWs that were entirely different to those of prisoners in 'ordinary jails'. Not only did 'the barbed wire wind like a red thread' through the POWs' mindset in camp, it produced despair in these men when they were released. These were men who were routinely uncompromising with family and friends.

Some of Vischer's other findings corresponded with later, more substantial research. For instance, the men's insecurity had been heightened by the knowledge that they were imprisoned for an indefinite period. They had no idea how long the war would drag on. This differed from the experience of men incarcerated in 'ordinary jails' who were there for a defined term. Vischer concluded that the neurosis occurred in degrees of severity and prompted symptoms of increased irritability, a desire to quarrel, inability to concentrate, difficulty with memory, discontentment, pessimism and insomnia as well as recurring nightmares. Moreover, the disease did not necessarily disappear with release. Instead, it could follow those unfortunate men through the remainder of their lives. Somewhat surprisingly, POWs who were employed were found to be less affected by 'barbed wire disease'. Working—particularly on farms—was regarded as 'real therapy for the ills of captivity.'[27]

More recently, psychologists have discovered that, for a large number of returned POWs, 'the most stressful and persistently troubling wartime experience' was being locked up behind wire. A small proportion of men were able to adjust to that stress—more so if they were involved with a 'supportive group'. For those unable to adjust, symptoms (similar to Vischer's diagnosis) were 'often extensive and commonly included anxiety, insomnia, headaches, irritability, depression, nightmares, impaired sexual potency, and functional diarrhoea.' The psychological trauma inwardly harboured by the returning POWs was initially masked by feelings of hope and joy at their return to their loved ones. In a significant number of men, those feelings quickly vanished. Instead, as subsequent research has demonstrated, 'even when there was little evidence of residual physical pathology ... survivors of prisoner-of-war camps commonly showed impaired resistance to physical illness, low frustration tolerance, frequent dependence on alcohol and drugs, irritability, and other indications of emotional instability.' There is no evidence to suggest that those returning during 1919 and 1920 would have fared any better. Indeed, it is more likely that, due to inadequate psychological treatment and support at the time, their situation was worse. Quite simply, those men could not readjust. Some attempted suicide—a few successfully. Many more than 'would have been expected' in the same age group of 'civilian life' succumbed to medical disorders such as tuberculosis, gastrointestinal disorders, cancer and heart disease.[28]

Ernest Etchell recalled a cousin (referred to only as Cleaver) who returned to Australia in mid-1919. 'He had tuberculosis,' Etchell said,

> he'd had it before he was a POW, and was in hospital most of the time when he came home ... The Germans had been treating him for tuberculosis, but Cleaver told me that the Germans had also injected needles into his leg. He'd lost a leg, and his mother reckoned that the Germans injected this chemical into his leg, and that's what made him lose it. But it wasn't. The doctors had his medical records in Germany. They were treating him for an ulcer. He was on treatment all the time in Germany. Even when he was with the battalion he always used to complain about his sore knee. He could get a day off duty anytime he went to the doctor with his knee. I said, "Oh, you're only bloody malingering!" We didn't think anything was the matter with his knee.

Etchell added, somewhat regretfully, that 'it killed him ... He died at Christmas time 1919.'[29]

Some ex-POWs were subsequently retrained in a wide variety of skills. But it was often a matter of too little, too late. Schemes such as the Soldier Settlements were established by the federal government which advanced funds to the states to provide land for farming. Some ex-POWs took up the offer believing that they could be successful, providing they were given suitable land to cultivate. Usually 'too little attention was paid to the suitability of the land or the aptitude of the settler' by the responsible department.[30] Far too many men failed to adapt. With few financial resources to support their often limited farming prowess, they usually ran up huge debts which they were unable to repay. Most returned to the cities more destitute than ever, while the RSSILA lobbied federal and state governments to give the men a fairer go. Another organisation, the Sailors and Soldiers Aid Society, also helped. In 1921 the federal government decided to pay all ex-soldiers—including POWs—a war gratuity of 1s 6d for every day that they were overseas and for time they spent awaiting demobilisation.[31]

Others, like William Barry, enjoyed better luck. A gas fitter and plumber with a government organisation, he was guaranteed re-employment on repatriation. Despite having had a leg amputated, he was provided a clerical position with the gas company. Horace Rumble also 'promptly went back to [his] old office,' in Perth, although only 'after taking enough time to purchase a house and furniture, and get married.'[32] Ernie Chalk returned to his family farm near Burnie in Tasmania. On 22 September, he married his childhood sweetheart, Corrie. With financial assistance from his family, he was able to purchase a property of his own close to Burnie. The Chalks 'began their married life in a cottage farmhouse on Hill Farm.'[33] Horatio Ganson also resumed work on the family farm near Hines Hill in Western Australia.[34] Edmund Sadler joined the Limbless Soldiers Association in Perth, receiving a pension of £2.2s a week for six months (reducing to £1.10s a week). The association assisted Sadler to find permanent employment with *The West Australian* newspaper where he operated a manual lift until he reached retirement age at sixty-five.[35]

Harold Horner had little difficulty finding work. He returned to his family farm near Lake Grace in Western Australia. Horner had arrived in Perth a few days earlier and wrote enthusiastically of his homecoming:

the first land that I clearly saw was about thirty miles south of Fremantle—probably a part of the Darling Range. Presently, two or three black seapigeons could be seen coming towards us ... Rottnest Island soon showed like a row of trees on the water; and a squadron of pretty little white gulls came to escort us in. A big porpoise also entered into the spirit of things, and kept bobbing up and down close by.

As it was late in the evening, we anchored outside the South Mole, with the lights of Fremantle to gaze at; while in the distance the clouds over Perth showed us the light of the city. In this ruddy glow there was an occasional lightning flash, caused by the electric trams.

In the morning a crowd waved to us from the wharf, as the *Marathon* tied-up to a buoy close to HMAS *Australia* ... But it was not until the train glided through that pretty suburban scenery between Fremantle and Perth that I really knew that I was home; I heard the magpies in the dear old bush.[36]

Horner's time as a POW was now a distant memory and gradually became something that he preferred to forget.

Thomas Taylor was one of the last Australian POWs to arrive safely home. Taylor, who had earlier escaped through Russia, was still in Moscow when he heard of Germany's surrender. Virtually a prisoner of the new Bolshevik regime, his release was finally secured through the diplomatic efforts of the Danish Consul General in Moscow—'charged with the protection of British interests'—and clearance papers, signed by no fewer than three doctors, certifying that 'This man is an English prisoner escaped from Germany to Moscow. He is in very bad health, and ought not to have been passed for a soldier at all.' After a journey through the Scandinavian countries which impressed him with their sheer magnitude and the region's 'beautiful surprises', Taylor finally reached England. 'How often I had longed for, had dreamed of, the day when I would at last set foot on British soil again,' he wrote, 'to have above me once more the Union Jack. My travels, my troubles and tribulations had made me mighty thankful and proud of one fact—that I was a Britisher. It was a remarkable coincidence that I should land in England on the 11th of April, exactly two years to the date of my capture.'[37] When he had recovered sufficiently, Taylor boarded a ship to Australia, returning to his pre-war occupation of bushman around the Gippsland Hills in Victoria.

✷✷✷

Captain Albert Marshall also returned safely to Australia. Over the years he became a pacifist—a strong believer in the futility of war. He never accepted that human life could be regarded as expendable in the attainment of military and political objectives. After all he had experienced—on Gallipoli, in the trenches of the Western Front, and as a POW, and despite his advancing years, Marshall was ultimately philosophical about war: 'Well they [governments] haven't learnt much in the wars, have they? Still haven't ... Why can't ... the army say, "We are not in this. We won't fight." What could they do if ... all the nations' men wouldn't fight? What could they do?'[38]

Postscript

Australian soldiers relied heavily on their mates while fighting on the front line and, indeed, during their time behind the lines. While not unique to the AIF, this was a special bond that those who have never experienced the industrialised killing in the trenches of the Western Front could not be expected to understand. The same applied to Australian soldiers who became prisoners of the Germans and who also depended on their mates to help them through their ordeal. Private P.J. Hogan penned this verse 'somewhere in France 1917' to describe that unique friendship. He called his poem *Jim*—named in honour of Private Jim Shaw, Hogan's best friend. Both served in the 15th Battalion at the First Battle of Bullecourt where Jim was captured during the fighting.

Jim
He has gone from us now—how we miss him!
In years he was only a lad,
But he'd won our respect and affection
With the brave many ways that he had.

All we know he is listed as missing
At night my eyes they grow dim
While I'm lying awake sadly thinking

Of what Fate held in store for poor Jim.

Jim always was ready and willing
Either for work or for fun.
Just a boy when out of the trenches,
But in action a man at his gun.

We had been boxing on all the winter,
But the weather was now getting fine
So with luck there was nothing could stop us
From breaking the Hindenburg Line.

Beaulencourt was to be our objective
And the lads took the news with a smile,
For artillery support we'd been promised
A thousand guns on the front of a mile.

We lads never knew who blundered
But I know at the time our hearts sank
When we heard our barrage was a '-mirage—
They were going to do it with tanks.

It was early one morning last April
The Fourth charged the Hindenburg Line,
One hundred yards of barbed wire
Of cruel Hunnish make and design.

The tanks, as we feared, proved a failure
Had they put a barrage there instead

It would have chopped the German barbed wire
Which is now thickly hung with our dead.

The Fourth Brigade charged and they broke it
Now we lads realise what it cost
When we look around for our comrades
And find those we loved best are lost.

Each had in the stunt lost some comrade
Who meant more than others to him,
And how I miss the laughter and mischief
And the bright cheery smile of poor Jim.

But although our dead comrades were many,
And the prisoners were but a few,
I am hoping that Jimmy was captured
And pray my hopes may come true.[1]

APPENDIX I

The Chalk Collection

The Chalk Collection

This book has been based largely on the research and intentions of David Chalk, who died in January 2002. David, it seems, was inspired by reading the papers of his grandfather, Ernie Chalk, a World War I POW, and Ernie's recollections of his time in captivity are used quite freely throughout the text. His brother, Richard Chalk, also enlisted, but was killed in action in May 1917.

Ernie's father was George Chalk, a prominent farmer from Burnie, in north-west Tasmania, who was a member of the early Burnie Road Trust. George Chalk was also elected to the first Burnie Municipal Council. Ernie—who died in 1964—was a member of the Burnie Council from 1946 until 1949.

David Chalk's interest in his grandfather's war service also spurred his determination to preserve that record for posterity. Over time, this interest expanded to encompass the Australian World War I POW experience as a whole—particularly as he began to realise that, while the hardships endured by Australian POWs in World War II were well documented, there was little written about those captured in the earlier conflict. As a result, he interviewed almost forty old soldiers from the 1st AIF, a significant number of whom were also prisoners of the Germans. For more than fifteen years, David combined his work as a town planner living in Sydney, with travelling the length and breadth of the continent, interviewing and photographing those men, now all deceased.

David Chalk's interviews with the old soldiers have all been transcribed (thanks to previous funding from the Australian War Memorial in Canberra) and bound. Those copies, as well as a photographic portfolio of the men and a number of other relevant images and personal papers that constitute the Chalk Collection, are now deposited at the School of History and Classics at the Hobart campus of the University of Tasmania.

David Chalk undoubtedly possessed one of the most comprehensive and valuable personal collections of World War I artefacts and memorabilia in Australia. This collection of more than 300 items—including weapons, uniforms, medals, gas helmets, recruiting posters and trench maps—was accumulated during the same period that he conducted the interviews. He also acquired a large library of books (almost 130) on World War 1. In accordance with David's final wish, the memorabilia and books have all been donated to the Pioneer Village Museum in Burnie, Tasmania.

APPENDIX 2

Notes from the interviewer

Notes from the interviewer

In the process of interviewing World War I veterans, David Chalk collected 'before and after' photographs and details of the men's service records. In addition, he compiled some useful and pertinent points about eight of the men whom he interviewed. Why he chose those particular old soldiers is unclear—perhaps he believed that these were the more significant interviews. While I—and, I suspect, some readers—do not agree with all of Chalk's assessments, I have included largely unedited extracts to provide a 'feel' for the personalities of the men and Chalk's interviewing technique. Not all of these 'assessments' or 'stories' have been included in the book.

Before and After

Bill Bradnock, 1917

Bill Bradnock, 1985

Albert Marshall, 1914

Albert Marshall, 1986

Horace Rumble, 1916

Horace Rumble, 1988

Charles Devers, 1915

Charles Devers, 1985

John Doggett, 1916

John Doggett, 1986

A (Dick) J Whittington, 1914

A (Dick) Whittington, 1986

Ernest Etchell, c. 1917

Ernest Etchell, 1985

Jack Cunliffe, 1915

Jack Cunliffe, 1987

Len Pooley, 1988   Jim Wheeler, 1985

A note from the interviewer (Bill Bradnock)

The Bradnock interview was one of the first undertaken as part of a series with 4th Brigade veterans ... The interview suffers from a lack of structure, and later interviews with veterans developed a better context through following a natural chronology. I was unaware of Bradnock's service record until 1990, and the interview therefore contains no reference to Bradnock's desertion in 1918. From a reading of the Record of Court Martial ... I have formed the opinion that Bradnock's reasons for deserting are sincere and in character.

In my opinion, Bradnock had the commitment, but not the nerve for extended front-line service. He served with some distinction at Gueudecourt in February 1917 ... but, as he says, he 'nearly went mad over it'. He appears to have lost his nerve at Bullecourt (where he was wounded in the eye), and I speculate that he failed to perform his duty and was sent back to England on training duty. From what I know of First Bullecourt, I believe the likely scenario is that Bradnock was hurt in a minor way during the Bullecourt attack, and failed to cross No Man's Land. I believe the medical reasons for desertion are slight. After some months in England, the prospect of being sent back to France was too much for him.

In terms of truthfulness, in my opinion the material gained from Bradnock is generally accurate. Bradnock was ashamed of deserting, and makes no mention of it for that reason. Similarly, the limited nature of material from Gallipoli may be explained by Bradnock's reluctance to admit that he had venereal disease. Some aspects have been exaggerated, particularly Bradnock's rank. He was never a King's Corporal, it is unlikely he had any special ability as a sniper, and no record can be found that he was recommended for a DCM. The issue about rank has no doubt been fabricated to hide the fact that he was reduced to the ranks following court martial. In general terms, however, Bradnock was competent, which appears to have been recognised by the battalion, and he had a genuine view that he did not wish to be responsible for other men's lives (which is not uncommon).

I regard the Bradnock material as an excellent contribution towards understanding the 1st AIF experience, particularly taken in context of the service record, and for the impression it creates about service in the line.

The transcripts have been edited here into 'polished' stories. The transcripts may be used in a different and—some oral historians would argue—better way. However, the edited stories set out here were my purpose, and repetition in the transcripts is explained by this 'storybuilding approach.

David Chalk
9 September 1994

A note from the interviewer (Ernest Etchell)

The Etchell interview was one of the first undertaken as part of a series with 4th Brigade veterans ... The interview suffers from a lack of structure, and later interviews with veterans developed a better context through following a natural chronology. The first part of the interview, made on 26 February 1985, was in fact the first oral history interview made in this series. The approach of focusing on names in the Lewis Gun Section was largely mistaken, and better material would have been gained from Etchell if the focus had instead been on subject matter. This understanding was, unfortunately, gained from experience.

Etchell had not talked about the war, and did not have a well-developed set of stories to tell, or have a particular gift as a story teller. There were, however, certain highlights which had remained with him, such as the story of avoiding capture at Bullecourt by getting a German to carry him back across No Man's Land, or the story of stealing the cooker for Colonel Cannan, and this material is developed here by persistence.

In terms of truthfulness, in my opinion the material gained from Etchell is generally accurate. He was, however, prone to exaggeration, and suggests for example that he was at The [Gallipoli] Landing, or that he was always in charge of the Lewis guns. Through 1916 he carried ammunition for the Lewis gun operated by T.P. Chataway and E. Chalk. He was made a Number One on 21 March 1917, and went into Bullecourt with his own Lewis gun. The impression I have is that he was young and immature, but conscientious and determined. Although he would not admit it, I believe his nickname 'Shiny' came from the fact that he took to soldiering with great interest, and was always cleaning his uniform and equipment. In an unpublished narrative written by T.P. Chataway in the 1930s ('Death Rides Abroad'), Chataway refers to Etchell with some affection as 'that old sinner', which seems to me to confirm Etchell's strong character.

I regard the Etchell material as a useful contribution towards understanding the 1st AIF experience, particularly for the insight it provides through such examples as the wounding of Captain Cooper, the disappearance of Lieutenant Nevin, attitudes to the Germans, and the way he always comments whenever Pozières is mentioned, that 'Pozières was a bad place'. The transcripts convey a strong impression of Etchell's attitude to the war.

David Chalk
7 August 1995

A note from the interviewer (Len Pooley)

The Pooley interview was made in 1988 during my second visit to Perth. The purpose of the second visit was to do follow-up interviews with veterans I had located during my first visit in 1986. During the second visit I went through a register of names held by the 16th Battalion's Secretary, Horrie Ganson, and I located Mr Pooley from this register.

Pooley was captured by the Germans at Bullecourt on 11 April 1917. Pooley had talked very little about the war, and proved to be a limited source. He was only sixteen when he enlisted, and Bullecourt was his first action. He was in general too young to have much understanding of what he was going through, and he suffered from a nervous condition which exaggerated this. It was evident even during the interviews that he found the experience more than he could cope with. Because of his youthfulness and lack of experience, he had limited ability as a soldier and was unable to display much initiative. His comments about Bullecourt, for example, and the fact that he traded his boots and greatcoat for food while a prisoner, reflect the concerns and judgement of a teenager.

I regard the Pooley material as providing a small number of very good examples of the POW experience, and the fact that Pooley was so young only adds to this perspective. In terms of truthfulness, in my opinion the material gained from Pooley is accurate.

David Chalk
15 October 1995

A note from the interviewer (Frank Lawrie)

Lawrie had a good memory and retained a strong interest in the war. The material contained here could have been quite easily expanded if more time had been available. Unfortunately in both 1986 and 1988 I was limited by a full agenda interviewing several 16th Battalion men in Perth over a period of less than a fortnight. All the same, the material contained here captures the essence of Lawrie's experiences. The structure of the second interview—in 1988—is chronological, particularly in the first part of the interview ... and was useful in placing Lawrie's character and experience in context. But it also shows that Lawrie had developed a particular set of stories about the war which caused the chronological approach to lose direction. He had told the stories so many times that he tended to trip over himself telling them again, and for this reason it was hard to keep a focus, or go deeper. At times the full nature of what he is saying is unclear.

Lawrie appears to have been popular in the battalion. The impression I have is of a man with an easygoing sociability, a ready interest and few inhibitions ... His experience is also of interest for the obvious difficulties he had with his small size and general health. He was so small that he had great difficulty enlisting, and I believe that the spirit he showed to compensate for this helped him make a lot of friends. Although there is some substance to his view that he would volunteer to get out of the drill and heavy work, I think a stronger reason is a genuine desire to prove himself and be involved. The material also has a strong local context, centred on his ties to his brother and his mates from Collie, and I have the impression that Lawrie was largely buffered by this. He seems rarely to have gone outside the group he was in, although this is typical of the general experience. The focus was one's mates.

In terms of truthfulness, I believe the material is accurate. Occasionally the order of a story is inverted and the details change, but the sense still remains. I believe the transcripts contain some rare material, such as the sex story about being in Wassir. This kind of experience is unlikely to appear in correspondence, but gives a real impression of what did in fact happen in Cairo.

David Chalk
27 January 1996

A note from the interviewer (Horatio Ganson)

Ganson was first interviewed in March 1986 as part of a group of interviews with 16th Battalion veterans in Perth, and these interviews were subsequently followed by a second series of interviews two years later. Between 1986 and 1988 it became apparent to me that the focus of the book would be very much on the personalities and experience of the men I was interviewing, rather than on an historical narrative, but I found that the first series of interviews had not covered this ground adequately. A primary purpose of the second series of interviews was therefore to develop a background and context for each veteran.

Ganson proved to be a valuable source. He had not married, and so had found the time to take on the role of secretary to the 16th Battalion Association. As a result he had a detailed knowledge of the men in the battalion, and his First World War experience remained a constant part of his life. I have the impression that, being an immigrant, the Battalion Association became a kind of surrogate family to Ganson. He never lost his Lancashire accent—few do I think—and although he clearly identified with this country, his personality seemed largely untouched by a lifetime in Western Australia.

The war was of interest to him, and he never seemed to tire of repeating his stories, but I don't believe he was affected as some men were. His front-line service was brief, and apart from several months working behind the lines as a POW, I believe he generally avoided the shock of trauma experienced by others, particularly those who went through heavy shellfire. But this was also a factor of his personality. He seemed to me to be an open and selfless man, yet there was also a wilful and determined side to his character. He was short and wiry with a strong constitution and few sensitivities, and I believe many of his experiences just passed over him, or were a source of humour.

His active interest in the Battalion Association meant that his experiences had already been focussed into stories ... Like the Frank Lawrie interview undertaken at the same time, it was a case of repeating old stories rather than searching out the raw impacts. All the same, Ganson makes no attempt to embroider his experience, and what comes across is a fresh and simple understanding. The material on the POW period in Germany is particularly valuable.
David Chalk
18 February 1996

A note from the interviewer (John Doggett)

The Doggett interview was limited by Mr Doggett's age, difficulty in hearing and failing memory. It was really a little too late to be conducting interviews. He had already recorded his experiences in his own memoirs and there tended to be a set of stories that he told, and told in a certain way. This tended to mean that—combined with his forgetfulness—the stories would be fragmented and not easy to understand. He would tell part of them, but not the full story. But in general this was overcome.

I remember him particularly for his sensitivity. His stories are characterised by a quality that is not evident in other veterans—his candour about the effect of shellfire, his memory of the cornet player on Gallipoli, his fright at the closeness of near misses—provided an interesting and revealing perspective. He was quite right that he was better suited to be an administrator than a front-line soldier, and his honesty reveals his intelligence. He asked me when I left to 'be kind to him' meaning, I suppose, that at Mouquet Farm he had really found it all too much, and this was something less than what is needed in a front-line soldier. But I feel rather that his own understanding is the right one—that he was better suited to an administrative role, and this was recognised by his unit.

The stories gathered here provide rich, if limited, material that is really new in the context of the stories obtained from other veterans in the ... project. It provides an angle that reflects Doggett's sensitivity.
David Chalk
11 September 2001

A note from the interviewer (Charles Devers)

Devers' memory was good, although a little mixed up at times concerning names and places. His experience was limited to some extent. He missed events in France during 1916 and 1917, and did not return to the unit until early 1918. He was lucky, being injured in the legs by wild holly during the Hill 971 attack, an injury that turned septic in the next few days and resulted in his evacuation from Gallipoli. Because of his Class B level of fitness, he found himself working for headquarters in Cairo and then at Tidsworth in England. He avoided all the fiascos in France at Pozières, Bullecourt and Polygon Wood. He provided an interesting perspective on life aboard the troopship *Kyarra,* and in Cairo working for Headquarters.

The oral history is supported by a useful set of letters written to Chrissie Easton, a girl he met in Brisbane just before sailing from Australia.

He was in the same group of reinforcements as James Wheeler (5th Battalion) and John Doggett (15th Battalion), who were also interviewed ... The Devers transcript is honest and accurate for the material it covers, and is interesting for Devers' perspective as an orphan.

As he says, he enjoyed his service because he was young and did not have to worry about parents. Devers' service record had not been seen at the time of interview, and he was therefore not asked about the long period in 1919 spent in hospital with VD.
David Chalk
19 September 2001

A note from the interviewer (John Cunliffe)

There were two interviews with Cunliffe, the first made in February 1986 and the second made in 1987. Unfortunately, the first interview, about an hour in length, is missing ... What remains is the interview recorded on 12 December 1987, which at least has the benefit of the chronological structure followed in the second series of interviews. That is the tape transcribed here.

Cunliffe's period of service was brief. He lost his right arm as the result of a shell explosion only eight days after landing—during the Bloody Angle attack—and was returned to Australia in late 1915. He was a 13th Battalion original. Although the material is limited by the loss of the first tape, there is nevertheless a small collection of good stories obtained as a result of the 1987 interview.

It is worth noting that Jack Cunliffe suffered from phantom pains for the rest of his life as a result of losing his right arm. At times when I was speaking with him, he would be in pain from the loss of his arm. But he was pragmatic about it. His perspective was to point out that the two men on either side of him were killed by the

shell that wounded him. His experience with the cadets meant that he was soon promoted—to sergeant only three weeks after enlisting. The impression I formed is that he was a quiet, dependable soldier with considerable skill.
David Chalk
20 September 2001

Endnotes

Introduction

[1] Patsy Adam-Smith, *Prisoners of War: From Gallipoli to Korea,* Viking, Ringwood, Vic., 1992, p.45.

[2] A further 200 Australians were captured by the Turks. The figure represents approximately 1.2% of the men who embarked for war.

[3] See Appendix 1 for more information on David Chalk and the 'Chalk Collection'.

[4] For a well-rounded account of Sir Edward's life see S. Ebury, *Weary: the life of Sir Edward Dunlop,* Viking, Ringwood, Vic., 1994.

[5] Ariotti, K., Captive Anzacs: Australian POWs of the Ottomans during the First World War, Cambridge University Press, Port Melbourne, 2018.

[6] Pegram, A., Surviving The Great War: Australian Prisoners of War on the Weatern Front, 1916-18, Cambridge University Press, Port Melbourne, 2020.

Chapter One

[1] R. Bennett, *Australian Society and Government*, MM & B Book Co., Sydney, 1992, pp.27—8.

[2] P. Dennis et al. (eds.), *The Oxford Companion to Australian Military History*, Oxford University Press, South Melbourne, 1995, p.108.

[3] D. Stevenson, *1914-1918: the history of the First World War*, Penguin, London, 2005, pp.32—3.

[4] Bipartisan support was essential as, on 30 July 1914, both houses of the Australian Parliament had been dissolved by the Governor-General following the rejection of two bills which Cook's government had attempted to push through Parliament. See E. Scott, *The Official History of Australia in the War of 1914—1918*, vol. XI, *Australia during the War*, Angus & Robertson, Sydney, 1936, pp.15—19 and J. Laffin, *Digger: the legend of the Australian soldier*, Sun Books, South Melbourne, 1990 (1959), p.37.

[5] P. Adam-Smith, *The Anzacs*, Penguin, Ringwood, Vic., 1991 (1978), p.21.

[6] E.M. Andrews, *The Anzac Illusion: Anglo-Australian relations during World War*

I, Cambridge University Press, Oakleigh, Vic., 1993, p.15.

[7] J.G. Fuller, *Troop Morale and Popular Culture in the British and Dominion Armies 1914-1918*, Clarendon Press, Oxford, 1990, p.314.

[8] Andrews, *The Anzac Illusion*, p.42.

[9] These exact words 'right or wrong' were uttered by Edmund Barton. See N. Meaney, *A History of Australian Defence and Foreign Policy*, vol.1, *The Search for Security in the Pacific, 1901-14*, Sydney University Press, 1976, p.4.

[10] Andrews, *The Anzac Illusion*, p.43.

[11] B. Gammage, *The Broken Years: Australian Soldiers in the Great War*, Penguin, Ringwood, Vic., 1987 (1974), p.3.

[12] *The Sydney Morning Herald*, 6 August 1914.

[13] J. Barrett, *Falling In: Australians and 'Boy Conscription' 1911-1915*, Hale & Iremonger, Sydney, 1979, p.67.

[14] J. Mordike, *An Army for a Nation: a history of Australian military developments 1880-1914*, Army Department, Canberra, and Allen & Unwin, North Sydney, 1992, p.247.

[15] F.W. Perry, *The Commonwealth Armies: manpower and organisation in two world wars*, St Martin's Press, New York, NY, 1988, p.151.

[16] C.E.W. Bean, *Anzac to Amiens*, Penguin, Ringwood, Vic., 1993 (1946), pp.26—7.

[17] J. Grey, *The Australian Army*, vol.1 of *The Australian Centenary History of Defence*, Oxford University Press, South Melbourne, 2001, p.39.

[18] Barrett, *Falling In*, p.228.

[19] Bean, *The Official History of Australia in the War of 1914—1918*, vol. I, *The Story of Anzac: from the outbreak of war to the end of the first phase of the Gallipoli campaign*, UQP, St Lucia, 1981 (1921), p.49.

[20] G. Seal, *Inventing Anzac: the digger and national mythology*, UQP, St Lucia, 2004, p.10.

[21] Gammage, *The Broken Years*, p.8.

[22] H. Horner, 'Reason or Revolution', unpublished manuscript, Chalk Collection.

[23] L.L. Robson, 'The Origin and Character of the First AIF: some statistical evidence', *Historical Studies*, vol.15, no 61., October 1973, pp.742—3.

[24] R. White, 'Motives for Joining Up: self-sacrifice, self-interest and social class, 1914-1918', *Journal of the Australian War Memorial*, no.9, 1986, p.3.

[25] J. McQuilton, 'A Shire at War: Yackandandah, 1914-18', *Journal of the Australian War Memorial*, no.11, 1987, pp.7 & 10.

[26] Gammage, *The Broken Years*, pp.8—10.

[27] Lieutenant A.W. Edwards, MM, 1st Battalion, AIF, quoted in Gammage, *The Broken Years*, p.8.

[28] John Cunliffe interview with David Chalk, Chalk Collection. Details of all interviews are cited in the bibliography. All subsequent citations will name only the person interviewed.

[29] John Doggett interview.

[30] Bill Bradnock interview.

[31] Frank McGinty interview.

[32] Victor Groutsch interview.

[33] Reginald Colmer interview.

[34] R.A. Goldrick, notebook, 'Introduction', papers of R.A. Goldrick, Mitchell Library, ML MSS3013.

[35] Groutsch interview.

[36] Donald Fraser interview.

[37] Frank Massey interview.

[38] P. Toft, 'Playing A Man's Game', *The Queensland Digger*, 1 November 1935, p.4, Chalk Collection.

[39] R. Kyle, *An Anzac's Story*, Penguin, Camberwell, Vic., 2003, p.123.

[40] F.W. Taylor and T.A. Cusack, *Nulli Secundus: a history of the 2nd Battalion AIF 1914-1919*, New Century Press, Sydney, 1942, pp.35—6.

[41] L.L. Robson, *Australia and the Great War 1914—1918*, McMillan, South Melbourne, 1969, pp.5-6.

[42] Grey, *The Australian Army*, p.39.

[43] Diary of Archibald A. Barwick, 2nd Battalion, Mitchell Library, ML MSS1493/1, quoted in Coombes, 'The Greatest Rat: a biography of Lt-Gen Sir Leslie Morshead', PhD thesis, University of Sydney, 1998, p.42.

[44] Anonymous, 'Brief Summary of the 15th Battalion AIF, 1914-1918,' 30 June 1964, 15th Battalion AIF, Newsletter, Chalk Collection.

[45] Ernest Etchell interview.

[46] S. Brugger, *Australians and Egypt 1914-1919*, Melbourne University Press, Carlton, 1980, p.20.

[47] Diary, Company Quartermaster Sergeant A.L. Guppy, 14th Battalion,

	22, 29, 30 & 31 December 1914, Chalk Collection.
[48]	Gammage, *The Broken Years*, pp.36 & 40.
[49]	Toft, 'Playing a Man's Game,' *The Queensland Digger*, 2 December 1935, p.4.
[50]	Robert Henry interview.
[51]	Guppy diary, 1 January 1915.
[52]	Toft, Playing a Man's Game', *The Queensland Digger*, 2 December 1935, p.4.
[53]	C.E.W. Bean, *What to Know in Egypt: a guide for Australasian soldiers*, Societe Orientale de Publicite, Cairo, 1915, p.16.
[54]	Diary of R.L. Osborne, Mortlock Library of South Australia, D 7145(L).
[55]	Kyle, *An Anza' Story*, pp.124—5.
[56]	Toft, 'Playing a Man's Game,' *The Queensland Digger*, 1 January 1936, p.10.
[57]	Cunliffe interview.
[58]	Twenty-four soldiers with sexual diseases and 131 rabble-rousers were humiliated and returned to Australia. Gammage, *The Broken Years*, p.37.
[59]	Bean, *Anzac to Amiens*, pp.65—6.
[60]	Diary C.W. Avery, Mortlock Library of South Australia, PRG 500 (6 & 7).

[61]   J. Ross, *The Myth of the Digger: the Australian soldier in two world wars*, Hale & Iremonger, Sydney, 1985, p.41.
[62]   D. Winter, *Making the Legend: the war writings of C.E.W. Bean*, UQP, St Lucia, 1992, p.25.
[63]   Ibid.
[64]   J.L. Williamson, 'Scottish Anzac: the story of Jock Williamson MM of the "Old 16th" Battalion Australian Imperial Forces 1914-18', unpublished manuscript.
[65]   Guppy diary, 25 & 26 February 1915.
[66]   Toft, 'Playing a Man's Game,' *The Queensland Digger*, 2 December 1935, p.5.
[67]   Bean, *Anzac to Amiens*, p.75.
[68]   Gunner Ray Brownell, 9th Battery, quoted in D. Horner, *The Gunners: a history of Australian artillery*, Allen & Unwin, St Leonards, NSW, 1995, p.87.
[69]   Toft, 'Playing a Man's Game,' *The Queensland Digger*, 1 January 1936, p.11.
[70]   Guppy diary, 15 April 1915.
[71]   J. Grey, *A Military History of Australia*, Cambridge University Press, Oakleigh, Vic, 1990, p.94.
[72]   Quoted in Kyle, *An Anzac's Story*, p.128.

Chapter Two

[1] John H. Morrow Jr., *The Great War: an Imperial History*, Routledge, London, 2004, p.91.

[2] P. Guinn, *British Strategy and Politics 1914 to 1918*, Clarendon Press, Oxford, 1965 p.63.

[3] Morrow, *The Great War: an Imperial History*, p.91.

[4] Hamilton quoted in M. Gilbert, *First World War*, HarperCollins, London, 1995, p.140.

[5] Hankey quoted in Evans, *From Legend to Learning: Gallipoli and the military revolution of WorldWar I*, Land Warfare Studies Centre, Canberra, 2000, p.10.

[6] Major General E. Sixsmith, *British Generalship in the Twentieth Century*, Arms and Armour Press, London, 1970, p.148.

[7] D. Winter, *25 April 1915: the inevitable tragedy*, UQP Press, St Lucia, 1994, p.76.

[8] Morshead diary, 9, 12 & 16 April 1915.

[9] Toft, 'Playing a Man's Game', *The Queensland Digger*, 1 July 1937, p.20.

[10] Guppy diary, 19 April 1915.

[11] Toft, 'Playing a Man's Game', *The Queensland Digger*, 1 January 1936, p.17.

[12] William Fitzpatrick interview.

[13] Diary, Charles Rosenthal, 24 April 1915, Rosenthal diary 1914-15, Mitchell Library, ML MSS2739/1.
[14] Bradnock interview.
[15] Barwick diary, 24 April 1915.
[16] Ibid.
[17] J. Robertson, *Anzac and Empire: the tragedy and glory of Gallipoli*, Hamlyn, Port Melbourne, 1990, p.68.
[18] Charles Kelly interview.
[19] Quoted in P. Lindsay, *The Spirit of Gallipoli: the birth of the Anzac legend*, Hardie Grant Books, Prahan, Vic., 2006, p.63.
[20] Bradnock interview.
[21] Colmer interview.
[22] Winter, *Making the Legend*, p.39.
[23] Toft. 'Playing a Man's Game,' *The Queensland Digger*, 1 January 1936, p.17.
[24] Cunliffe interview.
[25] Ernest Guest interview.
[26] Diary Colonel J.J.T. Hobbs, 25 April 1915, Hobbs papers, J.S. Battye Library of Western Australia History, MN 1460, item 5523A.
[27] Hamilton to Birdwood, 25 April 1915, Hamilton papers, King's College, London, 7/1/16.

[28] Toft, 'Playing a Man's Game', *The Queensland Digger*, 1 January 1936, p.17.
[29] Bean, *The Story of Anzac*, vol. I, pp.284-5.
[30] Cunliffe interview.
[31] Toft, 'Playing a Man's Game', *The Queensland Digger*, 1 February 1936, p.11.
[32] Bean, *Anzac to Amiens*, p.119.
[33] R. Perry, *Monash: the outsider who won a war*, Random House, Milsons Point, NSW, 2004, p.185.
[34] E.F. Hanman, *Twelve Months with the ANZACS*, R.G. Gillies & Co., Brisbane, 1918 (1916), p.147.
[35] Bradnock interview.
[36] J.A. Kidd, 'Gallipoli Recollections,' unpublished manuscript, John A. Kidd papers, AWM 3DRL 3554.
[37] Toft, 'Playing a Man's Game', *The Queensland Digger*, 2 March 1936, p.10.
[38] Fraser interview.
[39] Hanman, *Twelve Months with the ANZACS*, p.147.
[40] Ellis Silas, 'Crusading at ANZAC: Anno Domini 1915,' *The British-Australasian*, London, 1916, np.
[41] Morshead diary, 8 May 1915.

[42] Field service book, Colonel Talbot Hobbs early May 1915, papers of Lt Gen Sir JJT Hobbs, AWM 3DRL2600 419/48/4, item 1.
[43] Cunliffe interview.
[44] Diary, Lieutenant Burford Sampson, 9—10 May 1915, Chalk Collection; and Bean, *The Story of Anzac*, vol. II, pp.100—101.
[45] Eugene Fathers interview.
[46] Bradnock interview.
[47] Kyle, *An ANZAC's Story*, p.156.
[48] Guppy diary, 19 May 1915.
[49] Diary, William Donald Howard, 19 May 1915, Chalk Collection.
[50] Winter, *Making the Legend*, p.56.
[51] Charles Devers interview.
[52] See Bean, *The Story of Anzac*, vol. II, chapter XVIII.
[53] Devers interview.
[54] Bean, *Anzac to Amiens*, p.148.
[55] Doggett interview.
[56] Guppy diary, 7 & 8 August 1915.
[57] Fitzpatrick interview.
[58] This is the battle so poignantly recreated in Peter Weir's 1981 film *Gallipoli*. For a more recent account, see Peter Burness, *The Nek: the tragic charge of the Light Horse at Gallipoli*,

	Kangaroo Press, Kenthurst, NSW, 1996.
[59]	Bean, *The Story of Anzac*, vol. II, p.613.
[60]	Gammage, *The Broken Years*, p.75.
[61]	S. Welborn, *Lords of Death: a people, a place a legend*, Fremantle Arts Centre Press, Fremantle, WA, 1982, pp.91—93; and J. Smyth, *Leadership in Battle 1914-1918*, David & Charles, London, 1975, p.100.
[62]	Gammage, *The Broken Years*, p.76.
[63]	Murdoch report to the Australian Prime Minister, Hamilton papers.
[64]	Winter, *Making the Legend*, p.75.
[65]	P.A. Pedersen, *Monash as Military Commander*, Melbourne University Press, Carlton, 1985, pp.115-16.
[66]	Bean's diary 21 August 1915, quoted in Pedersen, *Monash as Military Commander*, p.117.
[67]	Guppy diary, 21 August 1915.
[68]	Toft, 'Playing a Man's Game', *The Queensland Digger*, 1 October 1936, p.19.
[69]	Pedersen, *Monash as Military Commander*, pp.118—19.
[70]	Monash's diary, 27 August 1915, quoted in Pedersen, *Monash as Military Commander*, p.119.

[71] Diary of Private A.A. Fletcher, 29 November 1915, Chalk Collection.
[72] Alec Campbell interview.
[73] Letter, Pte A.L. Smith, 30 December 1915, quoted in Gammage, *The Broken Years*, p.123.
[74] Winter, *Making the Legend*, p.76.
[75] Guppy diary, 15 December 1915.
[76] Gammage, *The Broken Years*, p.127.
[77] Toft, 'Playing a Man's Game', *The Queensland Digger*, 1 January 1937, p.15.
[78] Keith Tamblyn interview.
[79] Guppy diary, 25 & 26 December 1915.
[80] Toft, 'Playing a Man's Game', *The Queensland Digger*, 1 February 1937, p.8; and Bean, *Anzac to Amiens*, p.185.
[81] Quoted from '2nd Division AIF, 90th Anniversary,' *The Advocate*, 26 July 2005.
[82] Edward Pinnell interview.
[83] Len Pooley interview.
[84] Pedersen, *Monash as Military Commander*, pp.128—9.
[85] Letter, Percy Mansfield to his family, 1 & 9 February 1916, AWM PR00598.
[86] Letter, Will Peach to his mother, 2 February 1916, AWM PR00597.
[87] Fraser interview.
[88] Henry interview.

[89] Ibid.
[90] Kyle, *An ANZAC's Story*, p.200.
[91] Doggett interview.
[92] Pedersen, *Monash as Military Commander*, p.133; and Toft, 'Playing a Man's Game', *The Queensland Digger*, 1 March 1937, p.14.
[93] Grey, *A Military History of Australia*, p.101.
[94] Frank Lawrie interview.
[95] Pedersen, *Monash as Military Commander*, p.135.
[96] Kyle, *An ANZACs Story*, pp.198—99.
[97] Toft, 'Playing a Man's Game', *The Queensland Digger*, 1 March 1937, p.14.
[98] Henry interview.
[99] Ibid.
[100] Letter, Ernie Chalk to his mother, 23 April 1916, quoted in Chalk, 'ANZAC Day 1916', *This Australia*, Autumn 1986, p.6.
[101] Tom Carroll, Ernie Chalk and Bill Bradnock interviews, quoted in Chalk, 'ANZAC Day 1916,' in *This Australia*, Autumn 1986, pp.8—9.
[102] Henry interview.
[103] Letter, Charles Devers to Chrissie, 4 April 1916, Chalk Collection.

[104]   William Barry, untitled POW narrative, papers of William Charles Barry, AWM PR00814.
[105]   Tamblyn interview.
[106]   Toft, 'Playing a Man's Game', *The Queensland Digger*, 1 April 1937, p.42.
[107]   Barry, untitled POW narrative.

Chapter Three

[1]   Etchell interview.
[2]   C.E.W. Bean, *The AIF in France, 1916*, vol. III, UQP, St Lucia, 1982 (1929), pp.136—7.
[3]   Quoted in Pedersen, *Monash as Military Commander*, p.217.
[4]   Quoted in Kyle, *An ANZAC's Story*, p.217.
[5]   Pedersen, *Monash as Military Commander*, p.139.
[6]   Henry interview.
[7]   Roy Easton to 'Dad and children,' 25 June 1916, papers of Roy Easton, AWM 2DRL173.
[8]   Etchell interview.
[9]   Clarence James interview.
[10]   Toft, 'Playing a Man's Game', *The Queensland Digger*, 1 May 1937, p.14.
[11]   N. Meagher, *With the Fortieth*, R.J. Meagher, Hobart, 1918, p.27.

[12] Toft, 'Playing a Man's Game', *The Queensland Digger*, 1 May 1937, p.14.
[13] Bean, *The AIF in France*, vol. III, p.301.
[14] Ibid., pp.301—2.
[15] Ibid., pp.303-4.
[16] Etchell interview.
[17] T. Chataway, 'Death Rides Abroad,' unpublished manuscript, Chalk Collection.
[18] Toft, 'Playing a Man's Game', *The Queensland Digger*, 1 May 1937, p.14.
[19] For a worthwhile, if somewhat dated, account of the first day's objectives and battles, see M. Middlebrook, *The First Day of the Somme: 1 July 1916*, Allen Lane, London, 1971.
[20] White to Bean, nd, quoted in Winter, *Making the Legend*, p.89.
[21] Diary, C.E.W. Bean, 31 July 1916, quoted in Winter, *Making the Legend*, p.101.
[22] Bradnock, interview.
[23] Letter, John Doggett to Edith, 24 & 26 July 1916, papers of John Doggett, Chalk Collection.
[24] Letter, Len Wadsley to his family, 30 July 1916, papers of Lieutenant Len Wadsley, Chalk Collection.

[25]   Toft, 'Playing a Man's Game', *The Queensland Digger*, 1 May 1937, p.14.
[26]   Hamilton Warrell, 'War Memoirs', unpublished manuscript, Chalk Collection.
[27]   Doggett interview.
[28]   Massey interview.
[29]   Etchell interview.
[30]   Bean, *The AIF in France*, vol. III, pp.708-9.
[31]   T. Chataway, 'Lewis Gun Tactics,' unpublished manuscript, Chalk Collection.
[32]   Lawrie interview.
[33]   James interview.
[34]   Toft, 'Playing a Man's Game', *The Queensland Digger*, 1 May 1937, p.14.
[35]   Bean, *The AIF in France*, vol. III, p.720.
[36]   Chataway, 'Lewis Gun Tactics'.
[37]   Fitzpatrick interview.
[38]   Letter, Hubert Brettingham-Moore to his mother, 16 August 1916, papers of Captain Hubert M. Brettingham-Moore, Chalk Collection.
[39]   R. Prior and T. Wilson, *The Somme*, Yale University Press, New Haven, CT, 2005, p.180.
[40]   Doggett interview.
[41]   Chataway, 'Lewis Gun Tactics'.

[42] Quoted in Williamson, 'Scottish Anzac'.
[43] Tamblyn interview.
[44] Toft, 'Playing a Man's Game', *The Queensland Digger*, 1 June 1937, p.14.
[45] Chataway, 'Lewis Gun Tactics'.
[46] Lawrie interview.
[47] Massey interview.
[48] Frederick Febey interview.
[49] Etchell interview.
[50] Bean, *The AIF in France*, vol. III, p.728.
[51] Bean, *Anzac to Amiens*, p.261.
[52] Bean, *The AIF in France*, vol. III, pp.769—70.
[53] Toft, 'Playing a Man's Game', *The Queensland Digger*, 1 June 1937, p.15; and G. Franki and C. Slatyer, *Mad Harry: Harry Murray VC, CMG, DSO and bar, DCM, CdeG, Australia's most decorated soldier*, Kangaroo Press, East Roseville, NSW, 2003, p.63.
[54] Toft, 'Playing a Man's Game', *The Queensland Digger*, 1 June 1937, p.15 & 1 July 1937, p.20.
[55] Toft, 'Playing a Man's Game', *The Queensland Digger*, 1 July 1937, p.20.
[56] T.A. White, *The Fighting Thirteenth: the history of the 13th Battalion AIF*, Tyrells Ltd. for the 13th Battalion, Sydney, 1924, p.72.

[57] Franki and Slatyer, *Mad Harry*, p.64.
[58] White, *The Fighting Thirteenth*, p.75.
[59] Bean, *Anzac to Amiens*, p.264.
[60] Toft, 'Playing a Man's Game', *The Queensland Digger*, 2 August 1937, p.18.
[61] Pinnell interview.
[62] Toft, 'Playing a Man's Game', *The Queensland Digger*, 2 August 1937, p.18.
[63] Toft, 'Playing a Man's Game', *The Queensland Digger*, 1 September 1937, p.22.
[64] D. Kent, *From Trench and Troopship: the experience of the Australian Imperial Force 1914-1919*, Hale & Iremonger, Alexandria, NSW, 1999, pp.127-8.
[65] Toft, 'Playing a Man's Game', *The Queensland Digger*, 1 October 1937, p.22.
[66] Ibid., pp.22-3.
[67] Bradnock interview.
[68] Doggett interview.
[69] Cunliffe interview.
[70] J.E. Hatwell, *No Ordinary Determination: Percy Black and Harry Murray of the First AIF*, Fremantle Arts Centre Press, Fremantle, 2005, p.135.
[71] Toft, 'Playing a Man's Game', *The Queensland Digger*, 1 October 1937, p.23.

[72]   Febey interview.

Chapter Four

[1]   Bean, *The AIF in France, 1917*, vol. IV, UQP, St Lucia, 1982 (1933), p.25.
[2]   Toft, 'Playing a Man's Game', *The Queensland Digger*, 1 December 1937, p.28.
[3]   Lewis Sharp interview.
[4]   Horatio Ganson, interview.
[5]   Gammage, *The Broken Years*, p.179.
[6]   Guppy diary, 18 & 24 January 1917.
[7]   Pinnell, interview.
[8]   W.H. Downing, *To The Last Ridge*, Duffy & Snellgrove, Sydney, 1998 (1920), p.33; and Gammage, *The Broken Years*, p.205.
[9]   Ganson interview.
[10]   Bean, *The AIF in France*, vol. IV, pp.25—6.
[11]   Ibid., p.28.
[12]   Fraser, 'Memoirs', unpublished manuscript, Chalk Collection.
[13]   Toft, 'Playing a Man's Game', *The Queensland Digger*, 10 January 1938, p.28.
[14]   Bean, *The AIF in France*, vol. IV, p.29.

[15] Toft, 'Playing a Man's Game', *The Queensland Digger*, 10 January 1938, p.28.
[16] Bean, *The AIF in France*, vol. IV, p.29.
[17] Quoted in Bean, ibid., p.31.
[18] Toft, 'Playing a Man's Game', *The Queensland Digger*, 10 January 1938, p.28.
[19] Ibid.
[20] Bean, *The AIF in France*, vol. IV, p.32.
[21] Hatwell, *No Ordinary Determination*, p.141.
[22] Bean, *The AIF in France*, vol. IV, p.32.
[23] Quoted in Hatwell, *No Ordinary Determination*, p.142.
[24] Bean, *The AIF in France*, vol. IV, p.33.
[25] Ibid., p.34.
[26] Ibid., pp.35—6.
[27] Groutsch interview.
[28] Bean, *The AIF in France*, vol. IV, p.36.
[29] Hatwell, *No Ordinary Determination*, p.146.
[30] Jack King interview.
[31] Quoted in Hatwell, *No Ordinary Determination*, pp.144—5.
[32] Fraser interview.
[33] Hatwell, *No Ordinary Determination*, pp.143—7.
[34] Colmer interview.

[35] Sharp interview.
[36] Quoted in Hatwell, *No Ordinary Determination*, p.148.
[37] Ibid., p.150.
[38] Quoted in Bean, *The AIF in France*, vol. IV, pp.37—8.
[39] Hatwell, *No Ordinary Determination*, p.148.

Chapter Five

[1] Letter, William Shirtley to his mother, 6 January 1917, Lieutenant William Shirtley papers, AWM 2DRL792.
[2] Toft, 'Playing a Man's Game', *The Queensland Digger*, 1 February 1938, p.10; and 1 March 1938, pp.8-9.
[3] C. Falls, *Military Operations France and Belgium 1917*, vol.1, Macmillan, London, 1940, p.358.
[4] AIF unit war diaries, General Staff Headquarters, 4th Australian Division, 'Report on attack against Hindenburg Line by 4th Australian Division,' 11 April 1917, AWM 4, item 1/48/13, Part 2.
[5] For a good outline of planning and the British attack at Arras, see Lawrence James, *Imperial Warrior: the life and times of Field-Marshal Viscount Allenby*

1861-1936, Weidenfeld & Nicolson, London, 1993, Chapter 9.

[6] For reasons behind the mutiny and the outcome, albeit in one French army division, see L.V. Smith, *Between Mutiny and Obedience: the case of the French Fifth Infantry Division during World War One*, Princeton University Press, Princeton, NJ, 1994.

[7] R. Neillands, *The Great War Generals on the Western Front 1914-1918*, Robinson Publishing Ltd, London, 1999, p.356.

[8] I.L. Polanski, *We were the 46th: the history of the 46th Battalion in the Great War of 1914-18*, Puttees and Puggarees, Townsville, 1999, p.38.

[9] Falls, *Military Operations France and Belgium 1917*, vol.1, p.361.

[10] C. Johnson and A. Barnes (eds.) *Jacka's Mob: a narrative of the Great War by Edgar John Rule*, Military Melbourne, Prahran, 1999, p.74.

[11] Polanski, *We Were the 46th*, p.38.

[12] Comments by Brigadier General R.L. Leane on First Bullecourt, 27 July 1937, Bean papers, AWM 38, 3DRL 7953/30, Part 2.

[13] White, *The Fighting Thirteenth*, p.93.

[14] N. Wanliss, *The History of the Fourteenth Battalion A.I.F: being the vicissitudes of an Australian Unit during the Great War*, The Arrow Printery, Melbourne, 1929, p.193.
[15] Hatwell, *No Ordinary Determination*, p.160.
[16] Bean, *ANZAC to Amiens*, p.330.
[17] Ganson, interview; and Polanski, *We Were The 46th*, p.43.
[18] Wanliss, *The History of the Fourteenth Battalion A.I.F.*, p.194.
[19] Polanski, *We Were The 46th*, p.39.
[20] Hatwell, *No Ordinary Determination*, pp.161-2.
[21] C. Longmore, *The Old Sixteenth: being a record of the 16th Battalion, A.I.F., during the Great War 1914—1918*, History Committee of the 16th Battalion Association, Perth, 1929, p.135.
[22] Fraser, interview.
[23] J. Durrant, 'The Lessons of 11 April 1917', papers of Major General J.M. Durrant, AWM PR88/009.
[24] Fraser, 'Memoirs', p.21.
[25] Albert Marshall, interview.
[26] D. Kelly, *Just Soldiers: stories of ordinary Australians doing extraordinary things in*

time of war, ANZAC Day Commemoration Committee (Queensland) Publications, Aspley, 2004, p.13.
[27] Longmore, *The Old Sixteenth*, p.135.
[28] Polanski, *We Were The 46th*, p.40.
[29] Falls, *Military Operations France and Belgium 1917*, vol.1, p.367.
[30] Comments by Brigadier General R.L. Leane on First Bullecourt, 27 July 1937.
[31] Bean, *The A.I.F. in France*, vol. IV, p.317.
[32] Diary number 183, 11 April 1917, Bean papers, AWM 38, 3DRL606, item 183[3].
[33] Bean, *The A.I.F. in France*, vol. IV, p.317.
[34] Durrant, 11 April 1917.
[35] P. Pedersen, *The ANZACS: Gallipoli to the Western Front*, Viking, Camberwell, Vic., 2007, p.204.
[36] Durrant, 11 April 1917.
[37] Massey, interview.
[38] Fraser, 'Memoirs'.
[39] Bean, *The A.I.F. in France Vol IV 1917*, p.333.
[40] Hatwell, *No Ordinary Determination*, p.170.
[41] James, interview.
[42] Fraser, interview.
[43] Polanski, *We Were The 46th*, p.40.

[44] 46th Infantry Battalion War Diary, 11 April 1917, AWM 4, item 23/63/15.
[45] Guppy diary, 11 April 1917.
[46] 46th Infantry Battalion War Diary, 11 April 1917, AWM 4, item 23/63/15.
[47] Polanski, *We Were The 46th*, p.42.
[48] Bean, *ANZAC to Amiens*, p.334.
[49] Durrant, 11 April 1917.
[50] J. Walker, *The Blood Tub: General Gough and the Battle of Bullecourt 1917*, Spellmount, Staplehurst, 2000, p.107.
[51] Toft, 'Playing a Man's Game', *The Queensland Digger*, 10 May 1938, p.21.
[52] AIF unit war diaries, General Staff Headquarters, 4th Australian Division, Major General Walker, 'Report on Attack against Hindenburg Line by 4th Australian Division,' 11 April 1917, AWM 4, item 1/48/13 Part 2.
[53] Chataway, 'Death Rides Abroad'.
[54] Comments by Brigadier General R.L. Leane on First Bullecourt, 27 July 1937.
[55] Walker, *The Blood Tub*, p.105.
[56] Falls, *Military Operations France and Belgium 1917*, vol. I, p.369.
[57] Quoted in J. Williams, *Anzacs, The Media and The Great War*, UNSW Press, Sydney, 1999, pp.165-6.

[58] Bean, *The A.I.F. in France*, vol. IV, 1917, p.344.
[59] Toft, 'Playing a Man's Game', *The Queensland Digger*, 1 June 1938, p.20.
[60] *The Times*, 14 May 1917, quoted in Williams, *Anzacs, The Media and The Great War*, p.179.

Chapter Six

[1] A.G. Butler, *The Official History of the Australian Army Medical Services in the War of 1914-1918*, vol. II, *The Western Front*, Australian War Memorial, Canberra, 1930, p.135.
[2] Quoted in Winter, *Making the Legend*, pp.168-9.
[3] White, *The Fighting Thirteenth*, p.99.
[4] Etchell interview.
[5] A.J. Whittington interview.
[6] Corporal Lancelot Davies, 'A Narrative of POW Experiences' (untitled), AWM PR00140.
[7] Walker, *The Blood Tub*, p.104.
[8] Ganson interview.
[9] Fraser interview.
[10] George Bean to W.C. Groves, 26 September 1930, papers of Sergeant. W.C. Groves, AWM 2DRL268.

[11] Ernest Chalk, 'Experiences as a Prisoner-of-War in Germany,' unpublished manuscript, Chalk Collection.
[12] Marshall interview.
[13] 2nd Lieutenant A.V. Watkinson, Statement by Repatriated Prisoner of War, 4 December 1918, AWM 30, item B13.18.
[14] Fraser, 'Memoirs'.
[15] Fraser interview.
[16] Pooley interview.
[17] Ganson interview.
[18] William Groves, 'Things I Remember: a prisoner of war looks back,' *Reveille*, 29 February 1932, p.24.
[19] CSM C. Emerson, Statement by Repatriated Prisoner of War, 31 December 1918, AWM 30, item B13.18.
[20] Guppy diary, 11 April 1917.
[21] White, *The Fighting Thirteenth*, p.100.
[22] Chalk, 'Experiences as a Prisoner-of-War in Germany'.
[23] Thomas Taylor, 'Peregrinations of an Australian Prisoner-of-War,' unpublished manuscript, Chalk Collection.
[24] Horace Rumble interview.

[25] Diary Campbell Nelson Stewart, 11-12 April 1917, Chalk Collection.
[26] Jim Wheeler interview.
[27] Claude Benson, 'Particulars of My Doings While a Prisoner-of-War in Germany,' unpublished manuscript, Mitchell Library, MSS885.
[28] Claude Benson, Statement by Escaped Prisoner of War, Mitchell Library, MSS855.
[29] Davies, 'A Narrative of POW Experiences'.
[30] Ganson interview.
[31] Marshall interview.
[32] Diary, Lieutenant Garnet Veness, 12 April 1917, AWM PRO1059.
[33] Reginald Sanders, 'Narrative,' unpublished manuscript, papers of Captain Reginald Edwin Sanders, AWM 2DRL417.
[34] Ganson interview.
[35] Whittington interview.
[36] Guppy diary, 11-15 April 1917.
[37] Harold Horner, 'An Australian Prisoner of War in the Hands of the Hun,' unpublished manuscript, Chalk Collection.
[38] Guppy diary, 11-15 April 1917.

Chapter Seven

[1] R. Jackson, *The Prisoners, 1914-18*, Routledge, London, 1989, p.4.
[2] Adam-Smith, *Prisoners of War*, p.6.
[3] C. Carr-Gregg, 'The Impact of War on Society as Reflected in the Status and Treatment of Prisoners of War,' PhD thesis, UNSW, 1977, pp.377-8.
[4] Jackson, *The Prisoners*, pp.5-6.
[5] Ibid., p.6.
[6] Ibid.
[7] Ganson interview.

Chapter Eight

[1] R. Carson, J. Butcher and S. Mineka, *Abnormal Psychology and Modern Life* (eleventh edn.), Allyn and Bacon, Boston, 2000, pp.145-6.
[2] Horner, 'An Australian Prisoner of War in the Hands of the Hun'.
[3] Davies, 'A Narrative of POW Experiences'.
[4] Chalk, 'Experiences as a Prisoner-of-War in Germany'.
[5] Taylor, 'Peregrinations of an Australian Prisoner-of-War'.

[6] Chalk, 'Experiences as a Prisoner-of-War in Germany'.
[7] Stewart diary, 17-18 April 1917.
[8] Quoted in Adam-Smith, *Prisoners of War*, pp.48-9.
[9] Robert Ayres, 'POW Narrative,' unpublished manuscript, Chalk Collection.
[10] Groves, 'Captivity: a prisoner-of-war looks back', p.28.
[11] Davies, 'A Narrative of POW Experiences'.
[12] Guppy diary, 16 April 1917.
[13] Davies, 'A Narrative of POW Experiences'.
[14] Benson, Statement by Escaped Prisoner of War.
[15] Groves, 'Captivity: a prisoner-of-war looks back', p.17.
[16] Horner, 'An Australian Prisoner of War in the Hands of the Hun.'
[17] Ibid.
[18] Taylor, 'Peregrinations of an Australian Prisoner-of-War'.
[19] Ibid.
[20] Davies, 'A Narrative of POW Experiences'.
[21] Ganson interview.
[22] Taylor, 'Peregrinations of an Australian Prisoner-of-War'.

[23] Benson, Statement by Escaped Prisoner-of-War.
[24] Adam-Smith, *Prisoners of War*, p.49.
[25] Wheeler interview.
[26] Ganson interview.
[27] Horner, 'An Australian Prisoner of War in the Hands of the Hun'.
[28] Private F.W.R. Longwill, A Company, 15th Battalion, Statement by Repatriated Prisoner of War, 22 January 1919, AWM 30, item B13.18.
[29] Hallihan, 'In the Hands of the Enemy'.
[30] Stewart, diary, 22-23 &28 April 1917.
[31] Pooley interview.
[32] Davies, 'A Narrative of POW Experiences'.
[33] Robert Ayres, 'Account of happenings whilst a prisoner,' unpublished manuscript, AWM PR89/136.
[34] Pooley interview.
[35] Davies, 'A Narrative of POW Experiences'.
[36] Horner, 'An Australian Prisoner of War in the Hands of the Hun'.
[37] Ibid.
[38] Ibid.
[39] Stewart diary, June-August 1917.
[40] Taylor, 'Peregrinations of an Australian Prisoner-of-War'.

[41] Charles George Neander, diary, 25 November 1917, AWM PRO1602.
[42] Davies, 'A Narrative of POW Experiences'.
[43] Tamblyn interview.
[44] Horner, 'An Australian Prisoner of War in the Hands of the Hun'.
[45] Davies, 'A Narrative of POW Experiences'.
[46] Ibid.
[47] Tamblyn interview.
[48] Stewart diary, 11 August 1917.
[49] Benson, Statement by Escaped Prisoner-of-War.
[50] Guppy diary.
[51] Adam-Smith, *Prisoners of War*, pp.51—2.
[52] Guppy diary.
[53] Taylor, 'Peregrinations of an Australian Prisoner-of-War'.
[54] Ibid.

Chapter Nine

[1] Barry, untitled POW narrative.
[2] Barry, notebook, nd, papers of William Charles Barry, AWM PRO0814.
[3] Barry, untitled POW narrative.

[4] Hugh Anthony, 'Memoirs', unpublished manuscript, papers of Captain Hugh Anthony, AWM 1DRL/0046.
[5] Sapper Leslie Barry, 'Memoirs of My Experiences in Germany,' unpublished manuscript, Mitchell Library, ML MSS 695.
[6] Fraser, 'Memoirs'; and Fraser interview.
[7] From '3797', 48th Battalion, AIF, to William Groves, 3 October 1930, papers of Sergeant W.C. Groves.
[8] Second Lieutenant A.V. Watkinson, Statement by Repatriated Prisoner of War.
[9] G.W.D. Bell, 'Thirteen Months Captivity in Hunland', unpublished manuscript, ML MSS893.
[10] Rumble interview.
[11] Longwill, Statement by Repatriated Prisoner of War.
[12] Edmund Sadler, 'Gentle Courage,' unpublished manuscript, AWM PR87/182.
[13] Wheeler interview.
[14] D. Winter, *Death's Men: soldiers of the Great War*, Penguin, Ringwood, Vic., 1979, p.117.
[15] R. Christensen (ed), *To All My Dear People: the diary and letters of Private*

Hubert P Demasson 1916/1917, Fremantle Arts Centre Press, Fremantle, WA, 1988, pp.151-4.
[16] Rumble interview.
[17] Adam-Smith, *Prisoners of War*, pp.52-4.
[18] *The North-Western Advocate and Emu Bay Times*, 12 June 1917.
[19] Chalk, 'Experiences as a Prisoner-of-War in Germany'.
[20] Stewart diary, August 1917.
[21] Tamblyn interview.
[22] Keith Tamblyn, 'Memoirs', unpublished manuscript, Chalk Collection.
[23] Pooley interview.
[24] Taylor, 'Peregrinations of an Australian Prisoner-of-War', pp.9-14.

Chapter Ten

[1] Jackson, *The Prisoners 1914-18*, pp.62-3.
[2] Dennis et al (eds.), *The Oxford Companion to Australian Military History*, pp.73-4.
[3] Captain G.D.J. McMurtrie, 'Narrative,' Imperial War Museum, London, quoted in Jackson, *The Prisoners 1914-18*, pp.64-6.
[4] Stewart diary, 31 August, 1 & 3 September 1917.

[5] Quoted in J. King, *The Western Front Diaries*, Simon & Schuster, Pymble, NSW, 2008, p.396.
[6] Guppy diary.
[7] Davies, 'A Narrative of POW Experiences'.
[8] Wheeler interview.
[9] Whittington interview.
[10] Ganson interview.
[11] Rumble interview.
[12] Fraser interview.
[13] Horner, 'An Australian Prisoner of War in the Hands of the Hun'.
[14] Taylor, 'Peregrinations of an Australian Prisoner-of-War'.
[15] Davies, 'A Narrative of POW Experiences'.
[16] Barry, untitled POW narrative.
[17] Ibid.
[18] Ibid.
[19] Wheeler interview.
[20] Ibid.
[21] Horner, 'An Australian Prisoner of War in the Hands of the Hun'.
[22] Fraser, 'Memoirs'.

Chapter Eleven

[1] Jackson, *The Prisoners 1914-1918*, pp.97—8.
[2] Fred Allen to 'Uncle Tom,' 20 September 1918, papers of Private Fred J. Allen, AWM 1DRL0028.
[3] Adam-Smith, *Prisoners of War*, p.52.
[4] Davies, 'A Narrative of POW Experiences'.
[5] G. Harding, *Escape Fever*, John Hamilton, London, 1932, p.197.
[6] Quoted in Adam-Smith, *Prisoners of War*, pp.40—5.
[7] Quoted from the papers of Lieutenant Colonel J.E. Mott, AWM 2DRL12.
[8] Marshall interview.
[9] For a worthwhile account written by one of the British POWs, see H.G. Durnford, *The Tunnellers of Holzminden*, Penguin, Middlesex, 1940.
[10] Marshall interview.
[11] Jackson, *The Prisoners 1914-18*, pp.95—6.
[12] Veness diary, 9 July – 23 August 1917.
[13] Williamson, 'Scottish Anzac'.
[14] Horner, 'An Australian Prisoner of War in the Hands of the Hun'.
[15] Wheeler interview.

[16] Benson, Statement by Escaped Prisoner-of-War.
[17] Whittington interview.
[18] Fraser, 'Memoirs'.
[19] Taylor, 'Peregrinations of an Australian Prisoner-of-War'.
[20] Whittington interview.
[21] Jackson, *The Prisoners 1914-1918*, pp.93—4.
[22] Second Lieutenant A.V. Wilkinson, Statement by Repatriated Prisoner of War, 4 December 1918, AWM 30, item B13.18.
[23] Wheeler interview.
[24] Tamblyn interview.
[25] Fraser, 'Memoirs'.
[26] Horner, 'An Australian Prisoner of War in the Hands of the Hun'.
[27] Diary, Lance Corporal Arnold Mason, 10 October 1917, AWM PRO1877.
[28] Captain Joseph Honeysett, 'Aussies in Exile', unpublished manuscript, AWM 3DRL4043.
[29] Veness diary, 2 November 1917.
[30] J.R. Ackerley, *Escapers All*, Bodley Head, London, 1932, p.9.
[31] Pooley interview.
[32] Henry interview.
[33] Tamblyn, 'Memoirs'.

[34]   Tamblyn interview.

Chapter Twelve

[1]   Barry, untitled POW narrative.
[2]   Mott, Statement by Repatriated Prisoner of War.
[3]   R. Speed III, *Prisoners, Diplomats and the Great War: a study in the diplomacy of captivity*, Greenwood Press. New York, 1990, pp.75-6.
[4]   D.J. McCarthy, *The Prisoner of War in Germany*, Moffat, Yard & Co., New York, 1918, pp.63-5.
[5]   Paybook, Private A Joseph, AWM PR90/132.
[6]   Adam-Smith, *Prisoners of War*, p.46.
[7]   Harry Still, 'Some experiences as a member of the Australian Imperial Forces 3 July 1915 to 1 February 1920', unpublished manuscript, AWM PR00755.
[8]   Wesley Choate, 'A Bold Bid for Blighty', unpublished manuscript, Mitchell Library, ML MSS1504.
[9]   Henry interview.
[10]   Raymond Embrey, 'This Is My Story,' unpublished manuscript, AWM PR02022.
[11]   Hallihan, 'In the Hands of the Enemy'.

[12] Warrell, 'War Memoirs'.
[13] Barry, untitled POW narrative.
[14] Marshall interview.
[15] Quoted in Jackson, *The Prisoners 1914-1918*, pp.51-2.
[16] Sanders reply to Graves, radio talk 'Two Years in Captivity'.
[17] Quoted in Jackson, *The Prisoners 1914-1918*, p.78.
[18] Veness diary, 17 April – 29 April 1917.
[19] Captain David Dunworth, Statement by Repatriated Prisoner of War, AWM 30, item B13.18.
[20] Veness diary, 22 June – 22 July 1917.
[21] Letter, Max Gore to his mother, 31 August 1918, diary and letters of Captain Max Gore, Chalk Collection.
[22] Max Gore, 'The Long Dim Tunnel,' unpublished manuscript, Chalk collection.
[23] Durnford, *The Tunnellers of Holzminden*, p.49.
[24] Marshall interview.
[25] Henry interview.
[26] Diary, Private Frank Sturrock, 1 April 1918, AWM PR00122.
[27] Tamblyn interview.
[28] Gore, 'The Long Dim Tunnel'.
[29] Sturrock diary, 26 December 1917.

[30] Quoted in S. Probert and J. Probert, *Prisoner of Two Wars: an Australian soldier's story*, Wakefield Press, Kent Town, SA, 2001, p.71.
[31] Bell, 'Thirteen Months Captivity in Hunland'.
[32] Guppy diary, May 1917.
[33] Chalk, 'Experiences as a Prisoner-of-War in Germany'.
[34] Pooley interview.
[35] Davies, 'A Narrative of POW Experiences'.
[36] Groves, 'Captivity: a prisoner-of-war looks back', p.32.
[37] Ganson interview.
[38] Taylor, 'Peregrinations of an Australian Prisoner-of-War'.
[39] Howard diary, August 1917.
[40] Honeysett, 'Aussies in Exile'.
[41] Benson, Statement by Escaped Prisoner of War.
[42] Horner, 'An Australian Prisoner of War in the Hands of the Hun'.
[43] Fraser, 'Memoirs'.
[44] Ibid.
[45] Rumble interview.
[46] Ibid.
[47] Horner, 'An Australian Prisoner of War in the Hands of the Hun'.

[48] Davies, 'A Narrative of POW Experiences'.
[49] Wheeler interview.
[50] Davies, 'A Narrative of POW Experiences'.
[51] Quoted in King, *The Western Front Diaries*, p.396.
[52] Fraser, 'Memoirs'.
[53] Women were sent to the mines to assist with the POWs' food rations, and anything else that might be required—sometimes even manual labour. See Jackson, *The Prisoners 1914-1918*, p.49.
[54] Henry interview.
[55] Ganson interview.
[56] Ibid.
[57] Chalk, 'Experiences as a Prisoner-of-War in Germany'.
[58] Horner, 'An Australian Prisoner of War in the Hands of the Hun'.
[59] Fraser interview.
[60] Guppy diary, May 1917.
[61] Pooley interview.
[62] Henry interview.
[63] Quoted in Jackson, *The Prisoners 1914-1918*, p.42.
[64] Fraser, 'Memoirs'.

[65]	Whittington interview and Rumble interview.
[66]	Fraser interview.
[67]	Fraser, 'Memoirs'.
[68]	Ganson, interview.
[69]	Horner, 'An Australian Prisoner of War in the Hands of the Hun'.
[70]	Rumble interview.
[71]	Paul Vincent, *The Politics of Hunger: the Allied blockade of Germany 1915-1919*, Ohio University Press, Athens, OH, 1985, pp.162—3.
[72]	Fraser interview.
[73]	N. Hanson, *The Unknown Soldier: the story of the missing of the Great War*, Doubleday, London, 2005, p.205. For an excellent overview of the German spring offensive, see G. De Groot, *The First World War*, Palgrave, Houndmills, Hampshire, 2001, pp.112—126. For a more comprehensive analysis see T. Travers, *The Killing Ground: the British Army, the Western Front and the emergence of modern warfare 1900-1918*, Routledge, London, 1992, Chapter 9.
[74]	Warrell, 'War Memoirs'.
[75]	Fraser, 'Memoirs'.
[76]	Horner, 'An Australian Prisoner of War in the Hands of the Hun'.

[77]	Howard diary, March 1918.
[78]	Horner, 'An Australian Prisoner of War in the Hands of the Hun'.
[79]	For an account of Horner's attempted escape, see Chapter 11.
[80]	Fraser, 'Memoirs'.
[81]	Tamblyn interview and Tamblyn, 'Memoirs'.
[82]	Second Lieutenant W.S. Missingham, Statement by Repatriated Prisoner of War, nd, AWM 30, item B13.18.
[83]	Howard diary, September-November 1918.
[84]	Horner, 'An Australian Prisoner of War in the Hands of the Hun'.

Chapter Thirteen

[1]	Tamblyn, 'Memoirs'.
[2]	Corporal Albert Speight, Durham Light Infantry, Memoirs, Imperial War Museum, London, quoted in Jackson, *The Prisoners 1914-1918*, pp.120—1.
[3]	Tamblyn, 'Memoirs'.
[4]	Embrey, 'This Is My Story'.
[5]	Pooley interview.
[6]	Sanders, 14th Battalion, reply to Graves radio talk 'Two Years in Captivity'.

[7] Second Lieutenant John Ingram, Statement by Repatriated Prisoner of War.
[8] Fraser, 'Memoirs'.
[9] Horner, 'An Australian Prisoner of War in the Hands of the Hun'.
[10] Howard diary, November-December 1918.
[11] Tamblyn interview.
[12] Henry interview.
[13] Rumble interview.
[14] Etchell interview.
[15] Sadler, 'Gentle Courage'.
[16] Ganson interview.
[17] Ibid.
[18] Fraser, 'Memoirs'.
[19] Ibid.
[20] Horner, 'An Australian Prisoner of War in the Hands of the Hun'.
[21] There are no records of how many and which ex-Australian POWs took up the offer.
[22] Fraser, 'Memoirs'.
[23] Pinnell interview.
[24] C. Lloyd and J. Rees, *The Last Shilling: a history of repatriation in Australia*, Melbourne University Press, Carlton, 1994, p.132.
[25] Hallihan, 'In the Hands of the Enemy'.

[26] D. Coombes, *The Lionheart: a life of Lieutenant-General Sir Talbot Hobbs*, Australian Military History Publications, Loftus, NSW, 2007, p.306.

[27] See A.L. Vischer (trans. A.L. Vischer), *Barbed Wire Disease: a psychological study of the prisoner of war*, John Bales Sons, & Danielsson, London, 1919, pp.24-52. For some analysis of Vischer's work see J. Vance (ed.), *Encyclopaedia of Prisoners of War and Internment*, ABC-CLIO, Santa Barbara, 2000, p.20.

[28] Carson, Butcher and Mineka, *Abnormal Psychology and Modern Life*, pp.145-6.

[29] Etchell interview.

[30] S. Macintyre, *The Succeeding Age 1901-1942*, vol.4, *The Oxford History of Australia*, Oxford University Press, South Melbourne, 1993 (1986), p.208.

[31] D. Coombes, *Morshead: hero of Tobruk and El Alamein*, Oxford University Press, South Melbourne, 2001, p.71.

[32] Rumble interview.

[33] C. Whimey, 'Random Jottings on Ernest Tasman Chalk,' unpublished manuscript, Chalk Collection.

[34] Ganson interview.

[35] Sadler, 'Gentle Courage'.

[36] Horner, 'An Australian Prisoner of War in the Hands of the Hun'.
[37] Taylor, 'Pergrinations of an Australian Prisoner-of-War'.
[38] Marshall interview.

Postscript

[1] Quoted from the papers of Private P.J. Hogan, 15th Battalion, AWM PR 85/69.

Bibliography

Primary Sources

Australian War Memorial, Canberra

AWM 4, item 1/29/15, Parts 1 & 2, AIF Unit War Diaries, General Staff, Headquarters 1st ANZAC Corps.

AWM 4, item 1/30/15, Part 1, AIF Unit War Diaries, Intelligence Headquarters, 1st ANZAC Corps.

AWM 4, item 1/48/13, Part 2, AIF Unit War Diaries, General Staff, Headquarters, 4th Australian Division.

AWM 4, item 22/33/17, AIF Unit War Diaries, 16th Infantry Battalion, 4th Australian Infantry Brigade.

AWM 30, Statements by Repatriated Prisoners of War.

AWM 38, Official History, 1914—18 War: Records of C.E.W. Bean, Official Historian. Documents used in preparing the Official History, including diaries, notebooks and correspondence.

AWM 1DRL0028, Papers of Private Fred J. Allen.

AWM 1DRL0046, Papers of Captain Hugh Anthony.

AWM 1DRL411, Papers of Captain A.E. Leane.

AWM 2DRL0417, Papers of Captain R.E. Sanders.

AWM 2DRL12, Papers of Lieutenant Colonel J.E. Mott.

AWM 2DRL173, Papers of Roy Easton.

AWM 2DRL268, Papers of Sergeant W.C. Groves.

AWM 2DRL417, Papers of Captain Reginald Edwin Sanders.

AWM 2DRL792, Papers of William Shirtley.

AWM 3DRL465, Frank Hallihan, 'In the Hands of the Enemy', unpublished manuscript.

AWM 3DRL2600, Papers of Lieutenant General Sir J.J.T. Hobbs.

AWM 3DRL3554, Papers of John A. Kidd.

AWM 3DRL4043, Captain Joseph Honeysett, 'Aussies in Exile', unpublished manuscript.

AWM PR85/69, Papers of Private P.J. Hogan.

AWM PR87/82, Edmund Sadler, 'Gentle Courage', unpublished manuscript.

AWM PR88/009, Papers of Major General J.M. Durrant.

AWM PR89/136, Raymond Ayres, 'Account of happenings whilst a prisoner', unpublished manuscript.

AWM PR90/132, Pay-book of Private A. Joseph.

AWM PR00122 Diary of Private Frank Sturrock.

AWM PR00140, Lancelot Davies, A Narrative of POW Experiences (untitled), 11 April 1917-December 1917, unpublished manuscript.

AWM PR00597, Papers of Will Peach.

AWM PR00598, Papers of Percy Mansfield.

AWM PR00755, Corporal Harry Still, 'Some Experiences as a Member of the Australian Imperial Forces 3 July 1915 to 1 February 1920', unpublished manuscript.

AWM PR00814, Papers of William Charles Barry.

AWM PR00884, Papers of Brigadier General C.H. Brand.

AWM PR01020, Papers of Private C.G. Etherton.

AWM PR01059, Diary of Lieutenant Garnet Veness.

AWM PRO1602, Diary of Charles George Neander.

AWM PRO1877, Diary of Lance Corporal Arnold Mason.

AWM PRO2022, Raymond Embrey, 'This is My Story', unpublished manuscript.

J.S. Battye Library of Western Australia

MN 1460 Papers of Lieutenant General Sir John Joseph Talbot Hobbs.

Liddell Hart Centre for Military Archives, King's College, London

Papers of General Sir Ian Hamilton

Mitchell Library, Sydney

ML MSS695, L., Barry, 'Memoirs of My Experiences in Germany', unpublished manuscript.

ML MSS885, C. Benson, 'Particulars of My Doings While a Prisoner-of-War in Germany', unpublished manuscript & Statement by Escaped Prisoner of War, 10 October 1918, Corporal C.C. Benson.

ML MSS893, G.W.D. Bell, 'Thirteen Months Captivity in Hunland', unpublished manuscript.

ML MSS1504, W. Choat, 'A Bold Bid for Blighty', unpublished manuscript.

ML MSS2739, Papers of Major General Sir Charles Rosenthal.

ML MSS3013, Papers of R.A. Goldrick.

Mortlock Library of South Australia

PRG500, series 6 & 7, Diary of C.W. Avery

D7145 (L), Diary of R.L. Osborne.

The University of Tasmania

The Chalk Collection

Letters, diaries, unpublished manuscripts etc

papers of Lieutenant Fred Appleton.
Papers of Captain Hubert M. Brettingham-Moore.
Papers of Charles Devers.
Papers of John Doggett.
Diary of Private A.A. Fletcher.
Diary and letters of Captain Max Gore.
Diary of CQMS A.L. Guppy.

Diary of William Donald Howard.
Diary of Lieutenant Burford Sampson.
Diary of Campbell Nelson Stewart.
Papers of Lieutenant Len Wadsley.
Ayres, Robert, 'POW Narrative', unpublished manuscript.
Chalk, Ernest, 'Experiences as a Prisoner-of-War in Germany', unpublished manuscript.
Chataway, T., 'Death Rides Abroad', unpublished manuscript.
Chataway, T., 'Lewis Gun Tactics', unpublished manuscript.
Fraser, D., 'Memoirs', unpublished manuscript.
Gore, M., 'The Long Dim Tunnel', unpublished manuscript.
Horner, H., 'Reason or Revolution', unpublished manuscript.
Horner, H., 'An Australian Prisoner of War in the Hands of the Hun', unpublished manuscript.
Silas, 'Crusading at ANZAC: *Anno Domini 1915*', *The British-Australasian,* London, 1916, np.
Tamblyn, K., 'Memoirs', unpublished manuscript.

Taylor, Thomas, 'Peregrinations of an Australian Prisoner-of-War', unpublished manuscript.

Warrell, Hamilton, 'War Memoirs', unpublished manuscript.

Whimey, C., 'Random Jottings on Ernest Tasman Chalk', unpublished manuscript.

Interviews

All the men were interviewed by the late David Chalk and have been quoted in the text.

Percy Bland, np or nd.

William Bradnock, 15th Battalion, Beachmere, Qld, 10 & 16 July and 7 September 1985.

Alec Campbell, 15th Battalion, 4 January 1986.

Reginald Colmer, 13th Battalion, np or nd.

John Cunliffe, 13th Battalion, Sydney, NSW, 12 December 1987.

Charles Devers, 15th Battalion, Brisbane & Samford, Qld, 14 July & 19 December 1987.

John Doggett, 15th Battalion, Hobart, Tas, 30 & 31 December 1985 and 3 January 1987.

Ernest Etchell, 15th Battalion, Melbourne, Vic, 26 February & 18 December 1985.

Eugene Fathers, 16th Battalion, Perth, WA, 30 March 1988.

Frederick Febey, np or nd.

William Fitzpatrick, np or nd.

Donald Fraser, 13th Battalion, np 13 & 14 December 1985.

Horatio Ganson, 16th Battalion, Perth WA, 22, 23 & 26 March 1986 & 27, 28 March 1988.

Ernest Guest, np or nd.

Victor Groutsch, 13th Battalion, np or nd.

Clarence James, np or nd.

Robert Henry, 31st Battalion, Drouen, 8 February 1990.

Charles Kelly, np or nd.

John 'Jack' King, 13th Battalion, np or nd.

Aaron 'Frank' Lawrie, 16th Battalion, Perth, WA, 27 March 1986 & 2 April 1988.

Frank McGinty, 13th Battalion, np or nd.

Albert Marshall, Ulverstone, Tas, 23 & 27 December 1985.

Frank Massey, 13th Battalion, np or nd.
John Norris, Perth, WA, nd.

Edward Pinnell, 16th Battalion, Perth, WA, 31 March 1988.

Len Pooley, 16th Battalion, Perth, WA, 31 March & 4 April 1988.

Horace Rumble, Perth, WA, 29 March 1986.

Lewis Sharp, 13th Battalion, Brisbane, Qld, or nd.

Edmund Spencer, np or nd

Keith Tamblyn, 50th Battalion, Renmark, SA, 30 September 1989.

Jim Wheeler, np, 15 September, 20 October, 3 November 1985 & 22 March 1986.

Richard 'Dick' Whittington, np, 24 & 31 March 1986.

Published Material

Anonymous, 'Brief Summary of the 15th Battalion AIF, 1914-1918', 15th Battalion AIF, Newsletter, 30 June 1964.

The British-Australasian, 1916.

Toft, P., 'Playing a Man's Game', *The Queensland Digger*, bound copies.

Official Histories

Bean, C.E.W., *The Story of Anzac: from the outbreak of war to the end of the first phase of the Gallipoli campaign,* vol. I, 4 May 1915, UQP, St Lucia, 1981 (1921).

Bean, C.E.W., *The Story of Anzac: from 4 May 1915 to the evacuation of the Gallipoli Peninsula,* vol. II,

UQP, St Lucia, 1981 (1924).

Bean, C.E.W., *The A.I.F. in France 1916,* vol. III, UQP, St Lucia, 1982 (1929).

Bean, C.E.W., *The A.I.F. in France 1917,* vol. IV, UQP, St Lucia, 1982 (1933).

Butler, A.G., *The Australian Medical Services in the War of 1914-1018,* vol. II: *The Western Front,*

Australian War Memorial, Canberra, 1930.

Falls, C., *Military Operations France and Belgium 1917,* vol. I, Macmillan, London, 1940.

Scott, E., *The Official History of Australia in the War of 1914—1918,* vol. XI, *Australia During the War,*

Angus & Robertson, Sydney, 1936.

Books & Journal Articles

Ackerley, J.R., *Escapers All,* Bodley Head, London, 1932.

Adam-Smith, P., *The Anzacs,* Penguin, Ringwood, Vic., 1991 (1978).

Adam-Smith, P., *Prisoners of War: From Gallipoli to Korea*, Viking, Ringwood, Vic., 1992.

Andrews, E.M., *The Anzac Illusion: Anglo-Australian relations during World War I*, Cambridge University Press, Oakleigh, Vic., 1993.

Barrett, J., *Falling In: Australians and 'Boy Conscription' 1911-1915*, Hale & Iremonger, Sydney, 1979.

Bean, C.E.W., *What to Know in Egypt: a guide for Australasian soldiers*, Societe Orientale de Publicite, Cairo, 1915.

Bean, C.E.W., *Anzac to Amiens*, Penguin, Ringwood, Vic., 1993 (1946).

Bennett, R., *Australian Society and Government*, MM & B Book Co., Sydney, 1992.

Brugger, S., *Australians and Egypt 1914-1919*, Melbourne University Press, Carlton, 1980.

Burness, P, *The Nek: the tragic charge of the Light Horse at Gallipoli*, Kangaroo Press, Kenthurst, NSW, 1996.

Carson, R., Butcher, J. & Mineka, S., *Abnormal Psychology and Modern Life, Eleventh Edition*, Allyn and Bacon, Boston, 2000.

Christensen, R. (ed), *To All My Dear People: the diary and letters of Private Hubert*

P. Demasson 1916-1917, Fremantle Arts Centre Press, Fremantle, WA, 1988.

Coombes, D., *Morshead: hero of Tobruk and El Alamein*, Oxford University Press, South Melbourne, 2001.

Coombes, D., *The Lionheart: a life of Lieutenant-General Sir Talbot Hobbs*, Australian Military History Publications, Loftus, NSW, 2007.

De Groot, G., *The First World War*, Palgrave, Houndmills, Hampshire, 2001.

Dennis, et al., *The Oxford Companion to Australian Military History*, Oxford University Press, South Melbourne, 1995.

Devine, W., *The Story of a Battalion*, Melville & Mullen, Melbourne, 1919.

Downing, W.H., *To the Last Ridge*, Duffy & Snellgrove, Sydney, 1998 (1920).

Durnford, H.G., *The Tunnellers of Holzminden*, Penguin, Middlesex, 1940.

Ebury, S., *Weary: the life of Sir Edward Dunlop*, Viking, Ringwood, Vic., 1994.

Evans, M., *From Legend to Learning: Gallipoli and the military revolution of World War I*, Land Warfare Studies Centre, Canberra, 2000.

Franki, G. and Slatyer C., *Mad Harry: Harry Murray VC, CMG, DSO and bar, DCM,*

CdeG, Australia's most decorated soldier, Kangaroo Press, East Roseville, NSW, 2003.

Fuller, J.G., *Troop Morale and Popular Culture in the British and Dominion Armies 1914-1918*, Clarendon Press, Oxford, 1990.

Gammage, B., *The Broken Years: Australian soldiers in the Great War*, Penguin, Ringwood, Vic., 1987 (1974).

Gilbert, M., *First World War*, HarperCollins, London, 1995.

Grey, J., *A Military History of Australia*, Cambridge University Press, Oakleigh, Vic, 1990.

Grey, J., *The Australian Army*, vol.1, *The Australian Centenary History of Defence*, Oxford University Press, South Melbourne, 2001.

Guinn, P., *British Strategy and Politics 1914 to 1918*, Clarendon Press, Oxford, 1965.

Hanman, E.F., *Twelve Months with the ANZACS*, R.G. Gillies & Co., Brisbane, 1918 (1916).

Harding, G., *Escape Fever*, John Hamilton, London, 1932.

Hanson, N., *The Unknown Soldier: the story of the missing of the Great War*, Doubleday, London, 2005.

Hatwell, J.E., *No Ordinary Determination: Percy Black and Harry Murray of the First AIF*, Fremantle Arts Centre Press, Fremantle, 2005.

Horner, D., *The Gunners: a history of Australian artillery*, Allen & Unwin, St Leonards, NSW, 1995.

Jackson, R., *The Prisoners, 1914-18*, Routledge, London, 1989.

James, L., *Imperial Warrior: the life and times of Field-Marshal Viscount Allenby 1861-1936*, Weidenfeld & Nicolson, London, 1993.

Johnson, C. & Barnes, A. (eds.), *Jacka's Mob: a narrative of the Great War by Edgar John Rule*, Military Melbourne, Prahran, 1999.

Kelly, D., *Just Soldiers: stories of ordinary Australians doing extraordinary things in time of war*, ANZAC Day Commemoration Committee (Queensland) Publications, Aspley, 2004.

Kent, D., *From Trench and Troopship: the experience of the Australian Imperial Force 1914-1919*, Hale & Iremonger, Alexandria, NSW, 1999.

King, J., *The Western Front Diaries*, Simon & Schuster, Pymble, NSW, 2008.

Kyle, R., *An Anzac's Story*, Penguin, Camberwell, Vic., 2003.

Laffin, J., *Digger: the legend of the Australian soldier*, Sun Books, South Melbourne, 1990 (1959).

Lindsay, P., *The Spirit of Gallipoli: the birth of the Anzac legend*, Hardie Grant Books, Prahan, Vic., 2006.

Lloyd, C. and Rees, J., *The Last Shilling: a history of repatriation in Australia*, Melbourne University Press, Carlton, 1994.

Longmore, C., *The Old Sixteenth: being a record of the 16th Battalion, A.I.F., during the Great War 1914—1918*, History Committee of the 16th Battalion Association, Perth, 1929.

McCarthy, D.J., *The Prisoner of War in Germany*, Moffat, Yard & Co., New York, 1918.

McMullin, R., *Pompey Elliott*, Scribe Publications, Carlton, Vic., 2002.

McQuilton, J., 'A Shire at War: Yackandandah, 1914-18,' *Journal of the Australian War Memorial*, no.11, 1987, pp.3-13.

Macintyre, S., *The Succeeding Age 1901-1942*, vol.4, *The Oxford History of Australia*, Oxford University Press, South Melbourne, 1993 (1986).

Meagher, N., *With the Fortieth*, R.J. Meagher, Hobart, 1918.

Meaney, N., *A History of Australian Defence and Foreign Policy 1901-23*, vol.1, *The Search for Security in the Pacific, 1901-14*, Sydney University Press, 1976.

Middlebrook, M., *The First Day of the Somme 1 July 1916*, Allen Lane, London, 1971.

Mitchell, G.D., *Backs to the Wall*, Angus & Robertson, Sydney, 1937.

Mordike, J., *An Army for a Nation: a history of Australian military developments 1880-1914*, Army Department, Canberra and Allen & Unwin, North Sydney, 1992.

Morrow, John H. Jr., *The Great War an Imperial History*, Routledge, London, 2004.

Neillands, R., *The Great War Generals on the Western Front 1914-1918*, Robinson Publishing Ltd, London, 1999.

Paul Vincent, C., *The Politics of Hunger: the Allied blockade of Germany 1915-1919*, Ohio University Press, Athens OH, 1985.

Pedersen, P.A., *Monash as Military Commander*, Melbourne University Press, Carlton, 1985.

Pedersen, P., *The ANZACS: Gallipoli to the Western Front*, Viking, Camberwell, Vic., 2007.

Perry, F.W., *The Commonwealth Armies: manpower and organisation in two world wars*, St Martins Press, New York, NY, 1988.

Perry, R., *Monash: the outsider who won a war*, Random House, Milsons Point, NSW, 2004.

Polanski, I.L., *We Were The 46th: the history of the 46th Battalion in the Great War of 1914-18*, Puttees and Puggarees, Townsville, 1999.

Prior, R. and Wilson, T., *The Somme*, Yale University Press, New Haven, CT, 2005.

Probert, S. and Probert, J., *Prisoner of Two Wars: an Australian soldier's story*, Wakefield Press, Kent Town, SA, 2001.

Ramsay, R. (ed.), *Hell, Hope and Heroes: life in the field ambulance in World War I*, Rosenberg Publishing, Dural, NSW, 2005.

Robbins, S., *British Generalship on the Western Front 1914-18: defeat into victory*, Frank Cass, London, 2005.

Robertson, J., *Anzac and Empire: the tragedy and glory of Gallipoli*, Hamlyn, Port Melbourne, 1990.

Robson, L.L., 'The Origin and Character of the First AIF, 1914-18: some statistical evidence,' *Historical Studies*, vol.15, no.61, October 1973, pp.737-49.

Robson, L.L., *Australia and the Great War 1914-1918*, McMillan, South Melbourne, 1969.

Ross, J., *The Myth of the Digger: the Australian soldier in two world wars*, Hale & Iremonger, Sydney, 1985.

Rule, E.J., *Jacka's Mob*, Angus & Robertson, Sydney, 1933.

Samuels, M., *Doctrine and Dogma: German and British infantry tactics in the First World War*, Greenwood Press, Westport CT, 1992.

Seal, G., *Inventing Anzac: the digger and national mythology*, UQP, St Lucia, 2004.

Sheffield, G., *Forgotten Victory The First World War: myths and realities*, Headline, London, 2001.

Sheffield, G. and Bourne, J. (eds.), *Douglas Haig War Diaries and Letters 1914-1918*, Weidenfeld & Nicolson, London, 2005.

Sixsmith, E. (Major General), *British Generalship in the Twentieth Century*, Arms and Armour Press, London, 1970.

Smith, L.V., *Between Mutiny and Obedience: the case of the French Fifth Infantry Division during World War One*, Princeton University Press, Princeton, NJ, 1994.

Smyth, J., *Leadership in Battle 1914-1918*, David & Charles, London, 1975.

Speed III, R., *Prisoners, Diplomats and the Great War: a study in the diplomacy of captivity*, Greenwood Press, New York, 1990.

Stevenson, D., *1914-1918: the history of the First World War*, Penguin, London, 2005.

Taylor, F.W. and Cusack, T.A., *Nulli Secundus: a history of the 2nd Battalion AIF 1914-1919*, New Century Press, Sydney, 1942.

Travers, T., *The Killing Ground: the British Army, the Western Front and the emergence of modern warfare 1900-1918*, Routledge, London, 1992.

Vance, J. (ed.), *Encyclopaedia of Prisoners of War and Internment*, ABC-CLIO, Santa Barbara, 2000.

Vischer, A.L. (trans. A.L. Vischer) *Barbed Wire Disease: a psychological study of the prisoner of war*, John Bales, Sons & Danielsson, London, 1919.

Walker, J., *The Blood Tub: General Gough and the Battle of Bullecourt 1917*, Spellmount, Staplehurst, 2000.

Wanliss, N., *The History of the Fourteenth Battalion, A.I.F.: being the vicissitudes of an Australian Unit during the Great War*, The Arrow Printery, Melbourne, 1929.

Welborn, S., *Lords of Death: a people, a place a legend*, Fremantle Arts Centre Press, Fremantle, WA, 1982.

White, T.A., *Diggers Abroad*, Angus & Robertson, Sydney, 1920.

White, T.A., *The Fighting Thirteenth: the history of the 13th Battalion AIF*, Tyrells Ltd. for the 13th Battalion, Sydney, 1924.

White, R., 'Motives for Joining Up: self-sacrifice, self-interest and social class, 1914-1918', *Journal of the Australian War Memorial*, no.9, 1986, pp.3—15.

Williams, J., *ANZACS, the Media and the Great War*, UNSW Press, Sydney, 1999.

Winter, D., *Death's Men: soldiers of the Great War*, Penguin, Ringwood, Vic., 1979.

Winter, D., *Making the Legend: the war writings of C.E.W. Bean*, UQP, St Lucia, 1992.

Winter, D., *25 April 1915: the inevitable tragedy*, UQP Press, St Lucia, 1994.

Other unpublished manuscripts and theses

Carr-Gregg, C., 'The Impact of War on Society as Reflected in the Status and Treatment of Prisoners of War', PhD thesis, UNSW, 1977.

Coombes, D., 'The Greatest Rat: a biography of Lt-Gen Sir Leslie Morshead', PhD thesis, The University of Sydney, 1998.

Williamson, J.L., 'Scottish Anzac: the story of Jock Williamson MM of the "Old 16th" Battalion Australian Imperial Forces 1914-18', unpublished manuscript.

Newspapers & Periodicals

The Advocate, Burnie, Tas.
The North-Western Advocate and Emu Times, Burnie, Tas.
This Australia. .
Reveille.
The Sydney Morning Herald.

Back Cover Material

The experiences of Australian prisoners of war (POWs) or Kriegsgefangeners held captive in Germany has been largely forgotten or ignored – overshadowed by the horrid stories of Australians imprisoned by the Japanese during World War Two. Yet, as David Coombes makes known, the stork's arc interesting and significant – not only providing an account of what those young Australian soldiers experienced, and the spirit they showed in responding to captivity – hut also for the insight ii provides into tier many in the last eighteen months of the war.

Coombes draws upon previous inaccessible records – including the interviews conducted many years before by Chalk – as well as private papers and unpublished manuscripts. He paints a vivid picture of young soldiers who survived the trauma of battle, only to find themselves facing an unknown fate at the hands of an often vindictive and cruel enemy These 'comrades in distress', many wounded and traumatised by trench warfare, quickly discovered the bond of brotherhood, often the key to survival in a harsh environment with little food, poor medical treatment, back-breaking work and the anguish of confinement.

What emerges in the pages of this amazingly detailed account is the typical Australian sense of humour and the sheer will to live that marked these men. Ahove all, it was their determination to be free and to return once more to their families that ensured their survival; often against overwhelming odds.

Australian POWs is a fitting Tribute to the World War One soldiers and POWs, David Coombes highlights the ordeals these men went through, their stoicism in enduring their mistreatment, and the fearlessness of a few in launching ingenious attempts to escape. He proves beyond doubt that their stories are by no means less compelling than those of their World War 11 brothers.

Index

A

Adam-Smith, Patsy, *418*
Alexandria, *30, 134, 166, 564*
Allen, Private Fred, *629, 632*
Allied blockade of the Atlantic, *540*
American Civil War status and treatment of captured soldiers, *422*
Andrews, Eric, *5*
Anthony, Hugh, *541, 545*
Antill, Colonel J.M., *119*
Anzac Cove, *66, 108*
   landing site, *72*
Anzac Day 1916, *159, 161*
Arras, *323, 325, 329*
Australia Citizen Military Force (CMF), *8*
   conscription, *8*
   enlistment, *5*
   loyalty to Empire, *5*
   mobilisation, *8*
   recruitment,
     see First AIF (Australian Imperial Force),
   support for World War I, *5, 8*
Australian Defence Bill, *5*
Australian Imperial Force (AIF),
   1st AIF, *11*
   Battalions,
     7th Battalion, *139*
     9th Battalion, *114*
     13th Battalion, *30, 33, 72, 75, 78, 122, 189, 193, 212, 219, 225, 233, 234, 243, 245, 275, 290, 302, 307, 320, 332, 334, 340, 349*
     14th Battalion, *30, 33, 78, 89, 100, 114, 122, 134, 153, 189, 193, 219, 230, 285, 294, 302, 307, 332, 334, 337, 564*

15th Battalion, *30, 33, 72, 89, 97, 103, 108, 122, 137, 153, 206, 212, 219, 225, 230, 233, 243, 281, 285, 332, 334, 337, 388, 402*
16th Battalion, *30, 33, 40, 89, 97, 112, 193, 214, 243, 245, 253, 277, 332, 334, 337, 555, 564, 632*
45th Battalion, *309, 332, 337*
46th Battalion, *309, 332, 334, 340, 349, 351*
47th Battalion, *153, 223, 332, 337, 349*
48th Battalion, *219, 332, 334, 340, 349, 351, 357, 647*
49th Battalion (13th Brigade), *108*
50th Battalion, *234*
57th Battalion, *309*
Brigades,
  2nd Australian Infantry Brigade, *139*
  3rd Australian Infantry Brigade, *60, 63*
  4th Australian Infantry Brigade, *30, 44, 60, 78, 103, 137, 208, 240, 243, 253, 255, 260, 290, 320, 332, 334, 337, 340, 349, 351*
  12th Brigade, *153, 212, 334, 337, 340, 349*
  13th Brigade, *153, 283*
casualties, *202, 237, 240, 307, 351, 360*
companies, *30*
conditions on ships, *33, 36*
confidence in higher command, *245, 253*
'digger tradition', *11*
Divisions,
  1st Australian Division, *164, 202, 243, 253, 294, 320*
  2nd Australian Division, *164, 202, 243, 253, 281, 320, 357*
  3rd Australian Division, *193*

4th Australian Division, *153, 164, 202, 208, 223, 240, 243, 253, 281, 297, 320, 323*
billets in France, *189*
camels, *153*
convoy to Turkey, *40, 44*
enemy shelling, *219*
Gallipoli, see Gallipoli gambling, *156, 159*
leave, *260, 268*
military honours, *313*
manoeuvres in Egypt, *137, 153*
reputation, *134*
sport, *320*
Tel-el-Kebir, *134, 164*
training in trench warfare, *166, 169, 189*
trench-foot, *277*
Western Front, *177, 181, 183, 189, 193, 197, 200, 202, 206, 208, 212, 214, 219, 223, 225, 230, 233, 234, 237, 240, 243, 245, 253, 255, 260, 268*

5th Australian Division, *200, 268, 297, 320, 360*
leaving Australia, *30*
letters home, *189, 490*
machine gun sections, *177, 181*
reasons for volunteering, *14, 16, 19, 134*
recruitment, *14, 16, 30, 40, 134*
reinforcements, *275, 277*
shell shock, *212*
training, *22, 25, 30, 40, 44, 134, 166, 169, 189, 193*
Australian Light Horse, *36*
3rd Brigade, *119*
Australian Red Cross, *597, 600, 606*
  Voluntary Aid Detachments (VAD), *597*
Avery, Private C.W., *40*
Ayres, Robert, *444, 479*
amphibious assault, *44, 54, 60*

Anzac Cove, *66, 72, 108*
Cape Helles, *63, 108*
casualties, *66, 134*
Chunuk Bair, *66, 108, 119*
conditions, *103*
Courtney's Post, *89, 91*
deaths, *134*
dysentery, *97*
evacuation, *127, 134*

B

Barry, Sapper Leslie, *545, 547, 638, 640, 643*
Barry, William, *164, 169, 535, 540, 541, 615, 617*
Barwick, Archibald, *25, 66*
Bean, C.E.W., *14, 122, 189, 193, 202, 233, 234, 237, 253, 285, 290, 294, 297, 369*
  'A Guide for Australasian Soldiers, What to Know in Egypt', *36*
Bean, George, *377*
Beersheba, *153*
Bell, Lance Corporal G.W.D., *555*
Benn, Lance-Corporal, *451, 517, 520*
Benson, Corporal Claude, *396, 441, 451, 468, 470, 517, 520, 522, 525, 564, 567, 569, 574, 632*
Berrima, *33*
Bey, Major Mahmut, *66*
Biddle, Captain F.L., *189*
Birdwood, General Sir William, *66, 127, 206, 271, 320, 332, 334, 349, 354*
Black, Major Percy, *134, 337*
Boer War, *5, 422*
Bouchain, *507*
  POW strike, *507, 510*
Bradley, Corporal, *476*
Bradnock, Bill, *16, 63, 72, 89, 97, 161, 206, 260*
Brand, Brigadier General Charles, *193, 200, 240, 243, 283, 290, 332, 334, 351*
Brebries, *468*
Brennan, John, *555, 564*
Brettingham-Moore, Captain Hubert, *219*
Bridges, Brigadier General William, *8, 11*

Brierley, Lieutenant A.N., *122, 127*
British Brigade (163rd British Brigade), *122*
British Expeditionary Force (BEF), *177, 200*
British Manual of Military Law, *430*
British Red Cross, *600*
Brownell, Gunner Ray, *40*
Buchanan, Don, *108*
Bullecourt First Battle of, see First Battle of Bullecourt,
  map, *325*
  second attack, *357, 360*
  trench lines, *329*
Butler, A.G., *369*

C

Cairo, *36, 40, 139, 153*
  Battle of Wazzir, *36*
  desert training, *156*
  Mena camp, *36*
  review of ANZAC troops, *40*
Cannan, Lieutenant Colonel J.H., *30, 97*
Carden, Admiral, *54*
Carroll, Tom, *161*
Carter, Major H.R., *30*
Ceramic, *33*
Chalk, David,
Chalk, Ernest, *134, 137, 159, 377, 382, 396, 435, 438, 441, 574, 578, 580*
Chalk, George, *134, 574*
Chalk, Richard 'Dick', *574*
  mementos, *585*
Chataway, Lieutenant Tom, *193, 212, 225, 230, 351*
Choate, Wesley, *638, 640, 643*
Chomley, Miss E., *597*
Churchill, Winston, *54, 418*
Claremont Camp (Tasmania), *30*
Colmer, Reginald, *19, 72*
Constantinople, *54*
Courcelette, *223*
Cox, Major General Vaughan, *153, 245*
Cranzke, Ernie, *307*
Cunliffe, John, *16, 36, 75, 81, 89, 94, 260, 268*

D

damage to personal items, *569*
Dardanelles campaign, see Gallipoli,
Dardanelles Committee, *119*
Davies, Corporal Lancelot, *375, 396, 399, 402, 435, 444, 451, 463, 466, 479, 483, 496, 501, 507, 510, 607, 612, 632*
de Robeck, Admiral John, *54*
Deakin, Alfred, *5*
Demasson, Private Hubert, *564*
Denain, *501, 510, 564, 580, 585*
Denham, Lieutenant Colonel H.K., *340*
Devers, Charles, *103, 108, 164*
'digger tradition', *11*
Doggett, Corporal John, *16, 108, 153, 206, 208, 223, 225, 260*
Domeney, Lieutenant W., *285*
Dortmund, *545*
Douai, *432, 435, 454, 468, 470, 496, 564*
Downing, Walter, *277*
Dulmen POW Camp, *547*
Dunant, Henri, *422, 594*
Dunkirk Hospital, *564*
Duntroon, *11*
Dunworth, Captain David, *219, 283*
Durrant, Lieutenant Colonel J., *290, 294, 300, 307, 309, 313, 349*

E

Eastern Front, *54*
Easton, Roy, *189, 193*
Ecourt St Quentin, *451*
Egypt, *30, 36, 94, 97, 134, 142*
Embrey, Private Raymond, *183, 230*
Emerson, Sergeant-Major, *388, 451*
escapes by POWs, *626, 629, 632, 638, 640, 643, 646, 647*
    kits, *626*
Etaples camp, *183, 253*
Etchell, Ernest, *30, 177, 181, 189, 212, 233, 371, 375*

F

Falls, Captain Cyril, *354, 357*
Farr, Sergeant, *253, 255*
Fathers, Eugene, *97*
Febey, Frederick, *233*
Feist, Sergeant-Major G.S., *44*
First Battle of Bullecourt, *320, 323, 325, 329, 332, 334, 337, 340, 349, 351, 354, 357, 360, 643*
    captured British tank, *354*
    11 April 1917, *349*
    stranded survivors, *369, 371, 375*
Fisher, Andrew, *5*
Fitzpatrick, William, *114, 219*
Fletcher, Private A.A., *127*
Fort Macdonald, *412, 430, 441, 444, 451, 488, 632*
    conditions, *454, 457, 460, 463, 466, 468*
Franco-Prussian War, *422*
Fraser, Donald, *22, 25, 89, 153, 283, 302, 349, 377, 382, 451, 460, 547, 550, 612, 623*
Freiburg POW camp, *550*
Friedrichsfeld POW Camp, *564, 612*
Fromelles, *200, 202, 535, 629, 638*

G

Gallipoli, *11, 25, 54, 60, 63, 66, 72, 75, 78, 81, 89, 91, 94, 97, 100, 103, 108, 112, 114, 116, 119, 122, 127, 134, 137, 139, 142, 153, 156, 159, 161, 164, 166, 169*
Gaba Tepe, *60, 78*
    Hill, *122, 127, 134*
    Hill 971, *108, 112, 114*
    landings, *60, 63, 66, 72, 75, 78, 81*
    Lone Pine battle, *72, 108*
    Mal Tepe, *63*
    Monash Valley, *81, 89*
    Nek, The, *119*
    Quinn's Post, *81, 89, 97*
    reinforcements, *103*
    Sari Bair, *108, 112*

shellfire, *94*
snipers, *89, 91*
Steele's Post, *78*
Suvla landing, *108*
trenches, *97, 119*
tunnelling, *103*
Turkish attack May 1915, *100*
weather, *127*
Gammage, Bill, *5, 14, 33, 119, 277*
Ganson, Horatio, *275, 277, 281, 377, 384, 402, 405, 430, 466, 468, 474, 612*
Gardiner, Captain G.G., *349*
Geneva Convention, *422, 594*
Giles, John 'Bertie', Glasgow, Brigadier General Thomas, *283*
Godley, Major General Alexander, *8, 11*
Goldrick, R.A., *19*
Gough, General Sir Hubert, *223, 233, 234, 237, 313, 323, 329, 332, 334, 354, 357, 360*
Grant, Douglas, *606*

Grey, J., *44, 153*
Groutsch, Victor, *19, 22, 300*
Groves, William, *441, 444, 451*
Guest, Ernest, *78*
Gun Ridge, *72*
Guppy, Sergeant A.L., *30, 33, 36, 40, 44, 60, 100, 108, 112, 122, 127, 277, 351, 388, 405, 407, 412, 451, 512, 515, 517, 525, 607*
Gutersloh, *550*

H
Hague Conventions, *430, 527, 594, 643*
   escaping prisoners, *626*
   punishment, *643, 646*
   rights of captured soldiers, *422*
Haig, General Sir Douglas, *177, 200, 320, 323, 325, 360*
Hallihan, Frank, *474, 476*
Hamilton, General Sir Ian, *40, 54, 60, 78, 114, 122*
Hamilton, Lieutenant, *100*
Hanby, Gordon, *89*

Hankey, Sir Morris, *54*
Hanman, Eric, *89, 91*
Hansen, Captain S., *307*
Hardress-Lloyd, Lieutenant Colonel J., *329, 354*
Harrington, Lieutenant George, *183*
Harvey, Lieutenant A.T., *193*
Havers, Sergeant George, *253*
Henry, Private Robert, *33, 153, 159, 164, 189*
Hindenburg Line, *320, 323, 329, 332, 349*
Hinman, Lieutenant A.G., *97*
Hird, Bob, *302*
HMAT Hororata, *40*
HMS Orion, *89*
Hobbs, Lieutenant General Sir Talbot, *78, 94*
Hoggart, Captain, *89*
Holmes, Major General William, *281, 285, 290, 323, 329, 332, 349*
Honeysett, Captain Joseph,
Horner, Harold, *407, 410, 412, 432, 435, 454, 474, 483, 485, 488, 501, 612, 623*
Howard, William, *100*
Hughes, Brigadier General, *119*

I

Indian Brigade (29th Indian Brigade), *108*
International Committee of the Red Cross, *422, 594, 597, 600, 603, 606, 607, 612, 615, 617, 623*
   role, *430, 594*
International Prisoners of War Agency, *594*

J

Jacka, Albert, *134, 219*
Jackson, Robert, *418*
James, Clarence, *189, 219, 349*
Jamieson, George, *108, 214*
   continuous service medallion, *114*
   memorabilia, *116*
   Military Cross, *127, 214*
Japan, *5*

Job, Corporal Percy, *632*
Joffre, Marshal Joseph, *200*
Julin, Lieutenant J., *369*

K
Karlsruhe POW Camp, *405, 555*
Kell, Lieutenant R.H., *290*
Kelly, Charles, *66*
Kemal, Mustafa, *89*
Kidd, Sergeant John, *89*
King, Jack, *300*
Kitchener, Field Marshal Lord, *5, 54*
Kriegsbrauch, *430*
Kyle, Roy, *25, 36, 153*

L
Langensalza Lazarette, *564*
Lane, Lieutenant Frank, *30*
Laseron, Sergeant C.F., *33*
Lawrie, Frank, *153, 214, 230, 234, 237*
Le Quesnoy, *407, 412, 438, 474, 512, 525, 574*

Leane, Lieutenant Colonel Ray, *212, 340, 349, 351*
Legge, Major General J.G., *202*
Lemnos Island, *40, 60, 66*
Longwill, F.W., *474, 564*
Lubeck, *585*
Luther, Dr, *63*

M
McGinty, Frank, *19*
McMurtrie, Captain G., *600*
McPherson, Lieutenant W., *283*
McQuilton, John, *14*
McSharry, Major Terence, *212, 230, 243, 283*
Maidos, *63*
Malta, *100*
Mansfield, Lance Corporal Percy, *139*
Marquion, *466, 476, 479, 632*
Marseilles, *166*
Marshall, Lieutenant Albert, *337, 382, 402, 647*
mascots, *189*

Massey, Frank, *212, 233, 349*

Meagher, Lieutenant Norman, *193*

Mediterranean Expeditionary Force (MEF), *40, 54*

Menier, Armedie, *525*

Military Cross, *127, 214, 219*

Minden POW Camp, *574, 578*

Monash, General John, *30, 36, 60, 78, 89, 108, 122, 134, 137, 189, 193, 240*

Montaigu, *522*

Moore, Lieutenant Rex, *253, 255*

Moran, Captain Frank, *89*

Morshead, Captain Leslie, *60*

Mouquet Farm, battle for, *223, 225, 230, 233, 234, 237, 240, 243, 245, 268, 541*

Mudros Island, *40, 60, 63, 134*

Mulholland, Captain, *183*

Mundell, Major W., *283, 285*

Munro, General Charles, *122*

Munster, *629*

Munster Lazarette, *545, 547, 555, 564*

Murdoch, Keith, *119*

Murdoch, Lieutenant W., *285*

Murray, Captain Harry, *134, 234, 245, 253, 268, 290, 294, 297, 300, 302, 307, 309, 340, 349, 382*

   letter of congratulations to, *245*

   Victoria Cross, *309, 313*

N

Neander, Charles, *496*

Neillands, Robin, *329*

Neuenkirchen POW Camp, *626*

New Zealand Expeditionary Force, *8, 33*

Newton, George, *230*

Nivelle, General Robert, *320*

Noreuil, *332*

North-Western Advocate and Emu Bay Times, *134*

O

O'Donnell, Rev Father, *134*
O'Neil, Lieutenant, *183*
O'Shea, 'Red', *547, 550*

P

Peach, Will, *139, 142*
Phalempin, *483, 501*
Picardy, *200*
Pinnell, Edward, *134, 253, 277*
Pooley, Len, *134, 137, 382, 384, 476, 479, 585*
POWs,
　allowances and pay, *617*
　captivity, *432, 435, 438, 441, 444, 451, 454, 457, 460, 463, 466, 468, 470, 474, 476, 479, 483, 485, 488, 490, 496, 501, 507, 510, 512, 515, 517, 520, 522, 525, 527*
　escape, *485, 517, 525, 574, 626, 629, 632, 638, 640, 643, 646, 647*
　exchanges, *564, 567*
　food, *422, 430, 432, 435, 441, 444, 451, 454, 457, 468, 470, 476, 479, 485, 490, 496, 501, 512, 515, 517, 540, 545, 578, 580*
　friendly fire, *496*
　funerals, *545, 564, 580*
　German, *307*
　German doctors, *540*
　German treatment of, *382, 384, 388, 396, 399, 402, 405, 407, 430, 476*
　hospitals, *535, 540, 541, 545, 547, 550, 555, 564, 567, 569, 574, 578, 580, 585, 588*
　illness, *522*
　information to families,
　letters from home, *612*
　lists of, *597*
　numbers in World War I, *202*
　psychological trauma, *432*
　punishment for escapes, *643, 646*

Red Cross and, *594, 597, 600, 603, 606, 607, 612, 615, 617, 623*
Russian, *496*
sleeping arrangements, *479, 496*
status and treatment, *418, 422, 430*
work, *466, 468, 483, 485, 488, 490, 507, 510, 512, 515*
wounded, *535, 540, 541, 545, 547, 550, 555, 564, 567, 569, 574, 578, 580, 585, 588*
Pozières, *200, 202, 223, 225, 240, 268*
prisoners of respite, *457, 470*
'Quarantine Theory', *422*

Q
Queen Elizabeth, *54, 75, 78*

R
Rabett, Lieutenant Colonel R.L.R., *349*
Raismes, *501*
Ranford, Private, *100*
Red Cross parcels, *412, 550, 564, 580, 588, 597, 600, 603, 606, 607, 612, 615, 617, 623, 638*
  dead men's parcels, *617*
  procedure, *600, 603*
Regulations Respecting the Laws and Customs of War, *422*
Riencourt, *332, 334, 349, 351, 384, 388*
Robertson, Brigadier General J.C., *332*
Robertson, Corporal M., *313*
Robson, Lloyd, *14*
Ross, Lieutenant Colonel A.M., *234*
Royal Navy, *5, 54, 63*
Rumble, Horace, *396, 555, 564, 612*
Russian army, *5, 54*

S
Sadler, Edmund, *564*
Sadler, Sergeant, *100*
Sampson, Lieutenant Burford, *97*
Sanders, Lieutenant Reginald, *405*

Schultz, Professor, *540, 541*
Seal, Graham, *11*
Seang Choon, *60*
Septz, Dr, *540*
Sharp, Lewis, *275, 307*
Shirtley, Lieutenant William, *320*
Silas, Signaller Ellis, *91, 94*
Sloss, Private T., *564*
Smith, Private A.L., *127*
Smyth, Major General Neville, *281*
snipers, *89, 91*
Snowdon, 'Eccles', *225*
Solferino, Battle of, *422*
Soltau POW Camp, *550*
Somme, the, *177, 193, 200, 223, 271, 600*
Stephens, Private A.A., *193*
Stewart, Campbell, *396, 441, 476, 488, 515, 580, 606*
Strohen POW Camp, *626, 646, 647*
Suez Canal, *36, 54, 153, 161, 164*
Sydney Morning Herald, *5*

T
Tamblyn, Keith, *134, 166, 225, 496, 501, 510, 512, 580, 585*
Tasmania recruitment campaign, *134*
Taylor, Private Thomas, *396, 438, 441, 457, 468, 490, 496, 525, 527, 585*
Thiepval, *202, 208*
Thomas, Leo, *108*
Thompson, Sergeant 'Scotty', *297*
Times, The, *360*
Toft, Percy, *25, 33, 36, 40, 60, 66, 75, 78, 81, 89, 91, 122, 134, 153, 156, 193, 200, 208, 219, 225, 230, 240, 243, 253, 255, 260, 268, 271, 283, 285, 289, 290, 320, 351, 357*
Tournai, *527*
Turkey, *30, 54*
Turner, Tom, *230*
two-up, *181*

U
Ulysses, *33, 36*

V
Valenciennes, *555*

Veness, Lieutenant Garnet, *402, 405*
Verdun, *200*
Victoria Cross, *134, 219, 309, 313*
von Falkenhausen, Freiherr, *351*
von Hindenburg, Field Marshal Paul, *540, 541*

W

Wadsley, Lieutenant Len, *206*
Waine, Major V.J., *351*
Waite, Lieutenant Colonel W., *290, 300*
Walker, General, *351*
Walker, Jonathon, *351*
Wanliss, Captain H.B., *193*
War Council, *54*
Warrell, Hamilton, *208*
Watkinson, Lieutenant A.V., *382, 550*
Watson, Major, *354*
Wells, Captain D.P., *388, 396*
Western Front, *30, 54, 164, 177, 181, 183, 189, 193, 197, 200, 202, 206, 208, 212, 214, 219, 223, 225, 230, 233, 234, 237, 240, 243, 245, 253, 255, 260, 268*
   area of operations 1916-1918, *197*
   first impressions, *189*
   raids, *193, 253, 255*
   strategy, *271, 320*
   trench warfare, *166, 169, 193, 208, 212, 214, 219, 223, 271, 275, 277, 281, 283, 285, 289, 290, 294, 297, 300, 302, 307, 309, 313*
   weather, *271, 275, 277, 320*
Wheeler, Corporal Jim, *349, 396, 470, 474, 564, 612, 617*
White, Major Cyril Brudenell, *8, 36, 40, 134, 137, 202, 332*
White, Richard, *14*
White, T.A., *225, 243*
Whitsitt, J.T.H., *134*
Whittington, A.J., *375, 405, 412, 612*
Williamson, Jock, *40, 108*
Winn, Captain, *294*
Withers, Corporal Roy, *294, 300, 307, 313*

Wulfrath stone quarries,

Y
Ypres, *320*

www.ingramcontent.com/pod-product-compliance
Lightning Source LLC
Chambersburg PA
CBHW011711290426
44111CB00020B/2930